GROWTH, INEQUALITY, AND POVERTY

UNU WORLD INSTITUTE FOR DEVELOPMENT ECONOMICS RESEARCH (UNU/WIDER)

was established by the United Nations University as its first research and training centre and started work in Helsinki, Finland, in 1985. The purpose of the Institute is to undertake applied research and policy analysis on structural changes affecting the developing and transitional economies, to provide a forum for the advocacy of policies leading to robust, equitable, and environmentally sustainable growth, and to promote capacity strengthening and training in the field of economic and social policy-making. Its work is carried out by staff researchers and visiting scholars in Helsinki and through networks of collaborating scholars and institutions around the world.

UNU World Institute for Development Economics Research (UNU/WIDER)
Katajanokanlaituri 6B, FIN-00160 Helsinki, Finland

Growth, Inequality, and Poverty

Prospects for Pro-Poor Economic Development

Edited by

ANTHONY SHORROCKS AND
ROLPH VAN DER HOEVEN

A study prepared by the World Institute for Development Economics Research of the United Nations University (UNU/WIDER)

OXFORD
UNIVERSITY PRESS

Great Clarendon Street, Oxford OX2 6DP

Oxford University Press is a department of the University of Oxford.
It furthers the University's objective of excellence in research, scholarship,
and education by publishing worldwide in

Oxford New York

Auckland Bangkok Buenos Aires Cape Town Chennai
Dar es Salaam Delhi Hong Kong Istanbul Karachi Kolkata
Kuala Lumpur Madrid Melbourne Mexico City Mumbai Nairobi
São Paulo Shanghai Taipei Tokyo Toronto

Oxford is a registered trade mark of Oxford University Press
in the UK and in certain other countries

Published in the United States
by Oxford University Press Inc., New York

World Institute for Development Economics Research of the United Nations University
(UNU/WIDER), Katajanokanlaituri 6B, 00160 Helsinki, Finland

First published 2004

British Library Cataloguing in Publication Data

Data available

Library of Congress Cataloging in Publication Data

ISBN 0–19–926865–7(hbk.)

1 3 5 7 9 10 8 6 4 2

Typeset by Newgen Imaging Systems (P) Ltd., Chennai, India
Printed in Great Britain
on acid-free paper by
Biddles Ltd., King's Lynn, Norfolk

Contents

List of Figures

List of Tables

List of Acronyms and Abbreviations

BNPP	Bank Netherlands Partnership Program
CAISTAB	Caisse de Stabilization
CFA	Communauté financière d'Afrique
CGE	Computable general equilibrium
DAC	Development Assistance Committee
DDSS	Direction de la Démographie et Statistique Social
DFID	Department for International Development
DNG	distribution-neutral growth
DSM	Direction des Statistique des Ménages
EA	enumeration area
ECV	Encuesta de Condiciones de Vida. Sample survey based on the Living Standards Measurement Surveys approach developed by the World Bank
EDG	equal distribution growth
ENV	Enquête de Niveau de Vie (INS survey)
EP	Enquête Prioritaire (INS survey)
EPM	The Enquête Permanente Auprès des Ménages
FGT	Foster, Greer, and Thorbecke
FGT1	headcount and poverty gap measure: Foster, Greer, and Thorbecke index 1984
FGT2	squared poverty gap measure: Foster, Greer, and Thorbecke index 1984.
GATT	General Agreement on Tariffs and Trade
GDP	Gross domestic product
GIS	geographic information systems
Globkom	Swedish Parliamentary Commission on Global Development
GLSS	Ghana Living Standards Survey
GMM	generalized method of moments
HIPC	Heavily Indebted Poor Countries
IBGE	Instituto Brasileiro de Geografia e Estatística
IFI	international financial institution
IES	income and expenditure survey
ILO	International Labour Organization
INEC	Instituto Nacional de Estadistica y Census (National Statistical Institute of Ecuador)
INS	Institut National de la Statistique of Côte d'Ivoire
INSTAT	Institut National de la Statistique of Madagascar
LDCs	least developed countries

LSMS	Living Standards Measurement Study of the World Bank
MDG	Millennium Development Goal
MTEF	Medium-term expenditure framework
NAS	national accounts
NGO	non-governmental organization
OECD	Organisation for Economic Co-operation and Development
OHS	October Household Survey
OLS	ordinary least squares
OPM	ordered probit model
PBG	poverty bias of growth
PCE	private consumption expenditure
PNAD	Pesquisa nacional por amostra de domicílios
POVCAL	Program for Calculating Poverty Measures from Grouped Data
PPP	purchasing power parity
PWT	Penn World Tables
SEWA	Self-Employed Women's Association
SOAS	School of Oriental and African Studies
UNDP	United Nations Development Programme
WDR	World Development Report

List of Contributors

Sanghamitra Bandyopadhyay is a tutorial fellow in the Department of Economics and post-doctoral fellow at the Suntory Toyota International Centre for Economics and Related Disciplines, at the London School of Economics. She recently completed her Ph.D. studies on unequal economic growth across Indian states.

Arne Bigsten is a professor of development economics at Göteborg University. He has published extensively on income distribution and poverty, industrial development, trade, aid, and economic policy in less developed countries, particularly in Africa.

Hűlya Dağdeviren is a senior lecturer at the Business School of the University of Hertfordshire, UK. Her research interests include deregulation policies, capital accumulation and growth, income distribution, growth and poverty, and heavy indebtedness in the developing world.

Gabriel Demombynes is a Ph.D. candidate in economics at the University of California, Berkeley. He has worked at the World Bank on research related to the geography of poverty and inequality.

David Dollar is an economist at the Research Department of the World Bank.

Chris Elbers teaches international and development economics at the Vrije Universiteit of Amsterdam. His research includes environmental and development economics with emphasis on the analysis of poverty.

Francisco Ferreira is a senior economist at the Research Department of the World Bank and a regular visiting professor at the Pontificia Universidade Catolica at Rio de Janeiro. He has published widely on the economics of income distributions.

Michael Grimm is a research associate at the European Centre for Research in Development Economics (DIAL) in Paris. His research is concerned with the evaluation of distributional consequences of macroeconomic shocks and policies in sub-Saharan Africa.

Erich Gundlach heads a research group at the Kiel Institute of World Economics and lectures at the University of the Federal Armed Forces in Hamburg. He has published on topics related to globalization, the empirics of growth, and the economics of education.

Rasmus Heltberg is an economist at the World Bank, having previously taught development economics at the University of Copenhagen. His research has focused on poverty and inequality, rural development, property rights, and natural resource management.

Ravi Kanbur is the T. H. Lee Professor of World Affairs and Professor of Economics at Cornell University, having previously taught at the Universities of Oxford, Cambridge, Essex, Princeton, and Warwick. He has also served on the staff of the World Bank, including as the Chief Economist for Africa.

Aart Kraay is a senior economist in the Development Research Group at the World Bank. His research interests include international capital movements, growth and inequality, governance, and China's economy. He has taught courses in macroeconomics, international economics, and growth at Georgetown University and the Sloan School of Management at MIT.

Jean Lanjouw is a senior fellow in economic studies and governance studies at the Brookings Institution and a senior fellow at the Center for Global Development, Washington DC. She is an associate professor of economics in the Department of Agricultural and Resource Economics, University of California at Berkeley, and a research fellow of the National Bureau of Economic Research.

Peter Lanjouw is a lead economist in the Development Economics Research Group of the World Bank, and fellow at the Amsterdam Institute of International Development. He has taught at the Free University of Amsterdam and at the University of Namur. His research has focused on poverty and inequality measurement, as well as on rural development issues.

Phillippe George Leite is a fellow at the Department of Economics at the Pontifícia Universidade Católica do Rio de Janeiro. His research has focused on various aspects of poverty and inequality measurement.

Jörgen Levin is a lecturer at the Department of Economics, Örebro University, Sweden. He has worked on various issues related to structural adjustment in Kenya and Tanzania. Currently he is working on a project analysing poverty reduction strategies and domestic resource mobilization in Kenya, Uganda, and Tanzania.

Johan Mistiaen is with the Development Research Group of the World Bank. His current research focuses on poverty measurement issues, the geography of poverty, targeting, and policy impacts. Recently he has been working extensively on Madagascar and East Africa.

Felix Naschold is a Ph.D. student at the Department of Applied Economics and Management at Cornell University, having previously worked at the Overseas Development Institute in London and at the Ministry of Finance and Economic Development in Fiji. Key research areas include the dynamics of poverty and inequality.

José Navarro de Pablo is an economist at Group Public Policy International of UBS in Zurich, Switzerland. He has worked on topics such as globalization and wealth distribution, Japan's and China's economies, Japanese financial reform, and economic and financial integration in Asia Pacific.

Berk Özler is an economist in the Development Research Group Poverty Cluster at the World Bank. His research interests include poverty mapping and the economics of education. Current research focuses on the relationship between local welfare and various social outcome indicators, such as individual health, crime, and targeting efficiency.

Martin Ravallion is Senior Adviser at the Research Department of the World Bank. His main research interests concern poverty and the policies for fighting it. He has written extensively on this topic and advised numerous governments.

Anthony Shorrocks is Director of WIDER, having previously held permanent positions at the London School of Economics and the University of Essex. He has published extensively on topics related to income and wealth distribution, inequality, and poverty, and has been working recently on various issues concerned with the social problems facing Russia in the post reform era.

Rolph van der Hoeven is Manager of the Technical Secretariat of the World Commission on the Social Dimension of Globalization, established by the International Labour Organization in Geneva. Previous positions include chief of the ILO's Macroeconomic Policy Unit and economic advisor to UNICEF. He is widely published on employment, poverty, inequality, and economic reform issues.

John Weeks is a professor of development economics at the School of Oriental and African Studies, and Director of the Centre for Development Policy and Research. His current research is on poverty issues, especially in the context of Poverty Reduction Strategy Papers.

Natascha Weisert is a student of international economics and international relations at the Graduate Institute of International Studies, Geneva. She is currently conducting research on the Argentine crisis for her master's thesis.

Acknowledgements

This volume has its origins in an international conference on growth and poverty which took place in Helsinki in May 2001, and was attended by 150 persons from all around the globe. We would like to thank the paper presenters and other conference participants for their valuable contributions to the scholarly discussions, and the staff of UNU/WIDER in Helsinki for their smooth running of the backstage arrangements. All helped to make the conference a great success.

We are grateful to the many people who were involved in the preparation of this volume. Tony Addison and Cecilia Ugaz assisted in the selection of papers. Numerous peer reviewers wrote anonymous reports on the draft chapters, offering incisive and useful comments on the substance and quality of each of the studies. We also thank the chapter authors whose careful attention to the points raised by the reviewers and editors significantly improved the quality of the published material. Adam Swallow liaised with Oxford University Press and ensured the efficient processing of the manuscript.

Special thanks are due to Anne Ruohonen, who handled most of the formatting and checking of the chapters, and to Lorraine Telfer-Taivainen, who not only had primary administrative responsibility for the original WIDER conference but also dealt with the final preparation of the manuscript.

Helsinki and Geneva
September 2003

Anthony Shorrocks
Rolph van der Hoeven

Introduction

ANTHONY SHORROCKS AND ROLPH VAN DER HOEVEN

INTRODUCTION

The relationship between growth, inequality, and poverty lies at the heart of development economics. It has been, and remains, one of the most controversial topics. Indeed, very few of the other core areas in development economics can compare with the shifts, reversals, and reaffirmations of views that have characterized the analysis of the interaction between growth, poverty, and inequality. Evidence that inequality and poverty rose in the 1980s and 1990s in many countries, including some of the OECD countries, rekindled the ongoing controversies, which have not so much evolved as fluctuated over the past 50 years.

From the 1950s to the early 1970s, the debate emphasized the likely trade-offs between growth and income inequality. This derived in part from Kuznets' famous 'inverted U-hypothesis', which posited that inequality rises during the initial phases of development and then declines after some crucial level is reached (Kuznets 1955). The idea of a trade-off between growth and inequality is supported by certain theories of growth. Kanbur (1998), for example, points out the obvious correspondence between Kuznets' empirical results and Lewis' labour surplus model (Lewis 1954). The latter predicts that in an economy with an 'unlimited supply of labour' the profit share rises relative to the wage share until the labour surplus is exhausted. Similarly, Kaldor's growth model, in which capitalists have a higher marginal propensity to save than workers, implies that redistribution in favour of profits raises the growth rate (Kaldor 1967). However, this model applies more to developed countries—where the functional distribution of income largely consists of wages and profits—rather than to developing countries.

The mood shifted in the 1970s when attempts were made to identify redistributive mechanisms which aid poverty reduction without hampering growth. Studies also began, for the first time, to emphasize non-income measures of poverty in the related 'basic needs' literature. This change of focus was relatively short-lived, and went into reverse with the rise of neoliberalism and the so-called 'Washington Consensus' in the early 1980s. Bolstered in part by the successful experience in East Asia, growth itself would be the main vehicle for poverty reduction, achieved through trickle-down mechanisms not always clearly specified.

We thank Tony Addison and John Weeks for helpful suggestions.

The 1990s saw a number of challenges to both the neoliberal analysis and the earlier view of a trade-off between growth and equity. An expanding volume of empirical evidence showed no consistent relationship between growth, inequality, and poverty across countries and over time. At the same time, studies suggested that in many developing countries in Africa, in transitional economies, and in Latin America, stabilization and adjustment policies had an adverse impact on poverty and inequality or, at best, did little to improve the conditions of the poor. Furthermore, a consensus emerged that the 'high performing' Asian countries, prior to the financial crisis of the late 1990s, combined rapid growth of per capita income with relatively low and stable inequality.

The recent literature that challenges the trade-off and trickle-down approaches has its roots in the pro-distribution arguments of the 1970s which constructed a model of 'distribution with growth' in which social groups are distinguished by asset ownership or mode of access to assets. Growth and distribution were related through income linkages between social groups via connections between the labour and commodity markets. Simulation experiments with this model indicated that if aggregate productivity increased then redistribution would lead to substantial improvements in the incomes of not only the poor, but other social groups as well.

More recent contributions have built on these ideas of how inequality and poverty reduce the capacity for growth, and vice versa. They also argue that lower initial inequality raises the likelihood that growth will reduce poverty. However, it has also been noted that income inequality is relatively stable within countries, providing some support for the pessimistic conclusion that poverty will tend to persist as countries grow.

In recognition of the importance of these issues, UNU/WIDER organized a conference on growth and poverty in May 2001.[1] Its purpose was to review current thinking on the topic, to seek and encourage fresh research, and to bring researchers from different backgrounds together to discuss whether the relation between growth, poverty and inequality can be put into a sharper perspective for policy-making. About fifty papers were presented at the conference. This volume contains a selection of those papers together with other material linked to activities at UNU/WIDER.[2]

The volume starts with an essay by Kanbur which captures well the tone of the debate on poverty at the beginning of the twenty-first century. It reviews why, with so much new research and improved data, there is profound disagreement on crucial issues of growth, poverty, and inequality within academic circles, and among organizations and various groups active in the development field. Before spelling out the different perceptions towards growth, poverty, and inequality, Kanbur points out that there is now harmony on a variety of issues which were contentious a couple of decades ago. The fierce debates on growth and poverty have unfortunately tended to obliterate these areas of agreement. One consensus to have emerged is the view that improved education

[1] This meeting was the first of a series of large-scale conferences at UNU/WIDER on poverty related issues, and focused on income poverty. Future meetings will give more prominence to the non-income aspects of poverty and well-being.

[2] Three of the papers have recently appeared in academic journals. The remaining papers were refereed, rewritten, and edited for this volume.

and health should be regarded on a par with improved income when assessing poverty alleviation and the social progress outcomes of economic policy.[3] A second point of agreement is that transnational 'goods' or 'bads' such as environmental spillovers, unstable financial markets, or research into tropical agriculture and diseases, have enormous spillover effects, and that public intervention is needed in these areas.

The old 'market versus the state' debate provides a third example of converging views, with a clear acceptance that both markets and states are important. Development practitioners, including NGOs, have demonstrated very practical approaches, and divisions are far less than they were at the end of the Cold War. Another related area of agreement is growing recognition of the importance of institutions in regulating markets, constraining governments, and determining the interaction between households in the market place. These areas of recent agreement are very broad, of course, and disputes may well resurface if and when policies are actually implemented. Nevertheless, it is important to note that some degree of consensus has been reached in a number of areas.

THE NATURE OF DISAGREEMENTS ON POVERTY AND GROWTH

Kanbur argues that much of the disagreement can be traced to differences in perspectives towards three key features of the framework of the debate, namely, aggregation, time horizon, and market structure.

As regards *aggregation*, progress in poverty reduction is often measured as the decline in the percentage of the population below a certain income poverty line, and much is made of the fact that according to this definition poverty has gone down in many countries. But such analysis needs to be qualified. First, the value of public services and access to market opportunities is rarely taken into account; often these services have deteriorated making people feel worse off. Second, a national poverty figure is composed from different groups (regional, urban-rural, gender) whose poverty experiences frequently move in opposite directions. Third, those working with the poor often think in terms of absolute numbers rather than percentages. While the percentage of the population in poverty may have gone down, absolute numbers may have remained stable or even increased, especially in countries with fast rates of population growth.

A second aspect concerns the length of the *time horizon*. For example, in discussing the consequences of trade reform, most commentators will have in mind a medium time frame. This is driven by the equilibrium theory on which many assumptions are based. Markets and factors of production need time to adjust to structural changes in the economy. Activists, however, are usually concerned with short-term aspects, not least because 'short-run survival trumps medium-term benefits'.[4] Yet, other groups

[3] Education and health are seen as both desirable outputs as well as a necessary inputs. However, opinions remain divided on the relative importance of aspects of poverty which deal with processes of change such as empowerment, and the attention these should be given in policy formulation and budgetary allocations.

[4] There is more agreement on this issue now, especially with regard to the 'safety nets' which are intended to compensate for short-term negative effects. But those concerned with negative effects argue that safety

have a much longer time horizon in mind, arguing, for example, that economic growth cannot be sustained given the environmental capacity of the earth. To achieve global poverty reduction such groups call for explicit redistribution from North to South as a substitute for substantial economic growth.

A third area of disagreement lies in the *assumptions of market structure*. Proponents of the optimistic view of events often assume a competitive market structure, with a large number of agents interacting without market power. Others, however, point to distorted market structures governed by big institutions and corporations (e.g. in the trade of many tropical products), the power of money lenders in villages, and the attitudes of large countries in trade negotiations, to give some examples. Kanbur argues that the perception of certain market structures determines the way in which the poor perceive the benefits and costs of policies such as trade liberalization, capital mobility, and privatization. He argues strongly for a more detailed analysis of the distributional consequences of economic policies in the context of non-competitive market structures.

In his final section Kanbur introduces what he calls the 'red herring' debate on growth. He cites empirical studies which demonstrate that growth is strongly correlated across countries and over time with reductions in national-level measures of income poverty. Such observations lie at the heart of the 'growth is good for the poor' position. He further argues that the group of analysts who have difficulty with this position never claimed that a zero growth rate is good for the poor, or that growth is always bad for the poor. What is at issue are the policies used to stimulate growth, and the fact that the 'growth is good for the poor' stance often implies policy packages prescribed by the international financial institutions and northern finance ministers. According to Kanbur, the real debate should focus on the alternative policy packages and their consequences for redistribution and poverty. Confusion on this issue is exacerbated by the common practice of using growth to mean both an increase in per capita income and as shorthand for 'growth-oriented policies'.

DIFFERENT VIEWS OF GROWTH, INEQUALITY, AND POVERTY

The next six contributions in this volume (Chapters 2–7) deal with various aspects of the growth and poverty debate outlined by Kanbur. The first is the paper by Dollar and Kraay entitled 'Growth is Good for the Poor'. This study, which has provoked wide debate, observes that the average incomes of the poorest fifth of society rise proportionately with average incomes, a direct consequence of the fact that the share of income accruing to the bottom quintile does not vary systematically with average income. Dollar and Kraay document this empirical regularity in a large sample of ninety-two countries spanning the past four decades, and show that it holds across regions, time periods, income levels, and growth rates.

This finding is not entirely unexpected. In fact, in any long-run equilibrium the income share of the poorest quintile must be constant. The share cannot grow forever

nets often cannot be put in place fast enough and cannot compensate for major structural imbalances which cause severe poverty.

at a positive rate, since the income share of the bottom quintile cannot, by definition, exceed 20 per cent. Nor can the share contract continuously without risking the likelihood that most or all members of the bottom quintile will be unable to sustain life. Distributional neutral growth, therefore, may be regarded as the norm. However, this observation does not imply that the income share of the poorest quintile cannot rise or fall in the short or medium term, or in response to particular circumstances or policies.

Dollar and Kraay go on to show that several determinants of growth—such as good rule of law, openness to international trade, and developed financial markets—have little systematic effect on the share of income of the bottom quintile. The authors, therefore, conclude that these factors benefit the poorest fifth of society as much as everyone else. The evidence also offers weak support for the view that stabilization from high inflation, as well as reductions in the overall size of government, not only raises growth but also increases the income share of the poorest quintile.

Finally, the authors examine several factors commonly thought to disproportionately benefit the poorest in society, such as public expenditure on health and education, labour productivity in agriculture, and formal democratic institutions. They find little evidence of their effects. According to the authors, the absence of robust findings indicates that relatively little is known about the broad forces that account for the cross-country and intertemporal variation in the share of income accruing to the poorest quintile. Based on these findings the authors argue that the growth enhancing policies of a good rule of law, fiscal discipline, and openness to trade should be at the centre of successful poverty reduction strategies.

The next chapter by Ravallion agrees that the poor in developing countries usually share in the gains from rising aggregate affluence and in the losses from aggregate contraction. He observes, however, that there are large differences between countries in how much poor people share in growth, and that there are diverse impacts amongst the poor in a given country. He argues, furthermore, that cross-country correlations are clouded in data problems and hide welfare impacts, and can therefore be deceptive for development policy.

Looking beyond the averages in the relation between poverty rates and growth, Ravallion emphasizes the importance of initial conditions. Ignoring extreme values, he finds that 95 per cent confidence interval estimates of the growth elasticity imply that a 1 per cent rate of growth in average household income will result in anything from a modest 0.6 per cent drop in the poverty rate to a more dramatic 3.5 per cent decline. Hence, the variance of the growth elasticity of poverty is extremely important.

Ravallion goes on to note that inequality increased in half of the cases with spells of positive income growth, which leads him to present a two-by-two classification of rising and falling household income and of rising and falling inequality. Amongst countries with rising average income and rising inequality, the median rate of decline in the proportion of the population living below the $1-a-day poverty line was 1.3 per cent per year. In contrast, in countries with rising average income and falling inequality, the median rate of poverty reduction was seven times higher (about 10 per cent). In countries with falling average income and rising inequality poverty rates rose by a dramatic 14 per cent, while in countries with falling average income and falling inequality, poverty rates rose by less than 2 per cent.

Ravallion argues further that, even when inequality is not rising, a high level of initial inequality can stifle prospects for pro-poor growth, as high initial inequality lowers considerably the growth elasticity of poverty. He goes on to point out that when negligible correlations are found between changes in inequality and indicators of policy reform, as in Dollar and Kraay, this does not imply as a matter of course that the outcomes of such reforms for the poor depend solely on the growth effects. Averaging across the diversity of initial conditions can hide systematic effects; in one group of countries initial conditions may ensure that the rich benefit, keeping inequality high, while in another group of countries initial conditions can lead the poor to benefit. In these circumstances, reform policies entail a sizeable redistribution between the poor and the rich, but in opposite directions for the two groups of countries. Across all countries one could then well find zero correlation between growth and changes in inequality, or discover that the average impact of policy reform on inequality is not significantly different from zero. Yet, these results mask the fact that non-random distributional change is going on below the surface. An example is trade liberalization, which has been shown to decrease inequality in some countries and increase inequality in others.

The next contribution is by Heltberg which elaborates the elasticity of poverty as discussed by Ravallion. Heltberg first reiterates that the magnitude of the elasticity of poverty with respect to distribution-neutral changes in mean income depends on the location of the poverty line and, hence, should not be treated as a constant across countries or time. It tends to increase monotonically with mean income, holding the poverty line constant and depends strongly (and negatively) on the degree of inequality. As a consequence, an unequal income distribution is a serious impediment to effective poverty alleviation. Heltberg infers from these observations that the 'growth versus redistribution' dichotomy is misleading. Furthermore, he cautions against simplistically decomposing poverty changes into growth and distribution components, because the growth effect is itself a function of the degree of inequality. The manner in which growth and inequality interact to shape poverty is not additive. Heltberg admits that redistribution often has limited potential given existing structures, and that growth therefore remains a necessary condition for poverty alleviation. Yet, the level of inequality, and changes therein, still matter. This is because (i) for any given level of average income, the level of inequality affects the degree of poverty; (ii) inequality strongly affects the growth elasticity of poverty, with lower inequality contributing to an acceleration of poverty reduction for a given rate of growth; and (iii) if recent cross-country regression studies are to be believed, initial inequality, especially asset inequality, is harmful for growth. For these reasons, Heltberg argues that inequality remains important, and that there is a continuing need to search for effective policies for reducing inequalities, or at least for preventing them from rising.

While Ravallion emphasizes the importance of initial conditions, and is therefore cautious against findings that 'no correlation means no impact (on poverty)', Gundlach, Pablo, and Weisert in Chapter 5 take issue with the finding by Dollar and Kraay that higher primary educational attainment of the workforce is not correlated with increases in the income of the poor. They use a broader measure of human capital which accounts for international differences in the quality of education, and derive significant correlations suggesting that an increase in quality-adjusted education raises the relative income of the poor as well as average incomes. Thus, education is not distribution-neutral. It seems to improve the income distribution, allowing the poor to benefit disproportionately from growth. As a consequence, they support a focus of economic policies on education in order to reduce poverty and to speed up development.

THE ARGUMENTS FOR INCREASED REDISTRIBUTION

In Chapter 6, Naschold observes that changes in consumption, income distribution, and levels of poverty are intrinsically linked. He uses three methods to assess the relationship between these variables across countries, concentrating in particular on the differences between countries at different stages of development. An important finding is that consumption elasticities of growth vary significantly between the least developed countries (LDCs) and other developing countries, a result strongly supported by all methodologies. In addition, he finds that the distribution of income matters for poverty reduction, particularly so in LDCs. Simulations of poverty trends suggest that for poverty reduction in this group of countries, changes in distribution can be as important as changes in the level of consumption. In order to make substantial progress towards halving poverty by 2015, Naschold argues that LDCs will have to improve the distribution of income (or at least prevent it from getting worse) as well as achieving higher rates of economic growth. While distribution issues are clearly important for poverty reduction, he concludes that we need to know more about what drives changes in inequality if we are to identify ways in which policy can support efficient improvements in the distribution of national income.

The next contribution by Dağdeviren, van der Hoeven, and Weeks, begins with an overview of past and present literature on inequality and poverty in general, and on methods and incidence of redistribution in particular, emphasizing the growing consensus that countries with relatively egalitarian distribution of assets and incomes tend to grow faster. They argue that reducing inequality cuts both ways. A pro-poor growth path not only directly benefits the poor in the short run, but also creates in each subsequent period the lower inequality initial conditions which enhance future growth prospects. The authors go on to show empirically that economic growth has tended to be no better than distribution-neutral (echoing the points made by Dollar and Kraay and Ravallion in the earlier chapters). This leads them to explore in more detail the relationships between growth, inequality, and poverty, and to carry out three simulation exercises based on: (i) a 1 per cent distribution-neutral increase in per capita GDP; (ii) a 1 per cent increase in per capita GDP distributed equally across income percentiles; and (ii) a 1 per cent redistribution of income from the richest 20 per cent to the poorest 20 per cent. Countries are then classified according to which of those three simulations yields the greatest reduction in poverty.

For the overwhelming majority of middle-income countries, the simulation exercises demonstrate that poverty reduction is most effectively achieved by a redistribution of current income. Redistribution with growth is the second best option, while distribution-neutral growth is a poor third. In contrast, low-income countries require a growth strategy. Nevertheless, for most of these countries redistribution with growth is more effective than the (distribution-neutral) status quo growth.

The authors conclude by discussing several policies that make growth more equitable. They point out that objections against redistribution in developing countries, based on the argument that redistribution is costly and requires a minimum set of administrative capacities, should be set against the fact that status quo economic policy making is also costly and requires a minimum set of administrative capacities. Hence, under both scenarios, one often needs to operate in a second best environment. Policies for redistribution should therefore also be pursued.

POVERTY REDUCTION AND MICROECONOMIC ANALYSIS

The previous contributions emphasized that poverty can be reduced at a faster rate when pro-poor growth strategies are applied and when special redistribution policies are undertaken. However, as Ravallion and Dagdeviren *et al.* argue, there are no blanket policy proposals—the scope and nature of pro-poor growth strategies and of redistribution policies depend on the initial situation and on specific country circumstances. This, in turn, calls for improved microeconomic studies which can inform poverty analysis and contribute to the design of pro-poor policies. The next four chapters illustrate a variety of new approaches to distributional analysis.

Demombynes *et al.* use a new methodology in Chapter 8 to produce disaggregated estimates of poverty for three developing countries: Ecuador, Madagascar, and South Africa. The countries are very dissimilar—with different geographies, stages of development, quality and types of data, and so on. Nevertheless, the authors demonstrate that the methodology works well in all three countries and produces valuable information about the spatial distribution of poverty within these countries, information that was previously not available. Their methodology is based on a statistical procedure which combines household survey data with population census data, by imputing into the latter a measure of economic welfare from the former. Like the usual sample-based estimates, the poverty rates produced are also estimates and are subject to statistical error. They demonstrate that the poverty estimates produced from census data match well the estimates calculated directly from the country's surveys. The precision of the poverty estimates produced with this methodology depends on the degree of disaggregation. In all three countries the constructed poverty estimators allow a level of disaggregation far below that which can be achieved with surveys. They then illustrate how the poverty estimates produced with this method can be represented by maps, thereby conveying an enormous amount of information about the spread and relative magnitude of poverty across localities (as well as the precision of estimates) in a way which is quickly and intuitively absorbed, particularly by a non-technical audience. Such detailed geographical profiles of poverty can inform a wide variety of debates and deliberations amongst policy-makers as well as civil society.

In Chapter 9, Bandyopadhyay describes the dynamics of growth and the convergence of real per capita incomes across Indian states over the period 1965–97, and then attempts to analyse some of the factors underpinning such income dynamics. A number of specific issues are addressed: the trend towards equality in the cross-sectional income distribution across Indian states; the possibilities for interregional mobility; and the persistence of differential growth performance.

Unlike standard practice, Bandyopadhyay examines interstate income inequalities in terms of the behaviour of the entire cross-sectional distribution. This approach essentially posits a law of motion of the cross section income distribution which allows researchers to study not just the likelihood, but also the potential causes, of poorer economies becoming richer than those currently rich, and of the rich regressing to become relatively poor. Over the period 1965–97, Bandyopadhyay finds a strong tendency towards polarization resulting from the formation of two income 'convergence clubs'; one at 50 per cent of the national average, the other at 125 per cent of the national average. Although cohesive tendencies were observed in the late 1960s, these weakened considerably with the reform policies of the following decades, with increasingly polarizing consequences. Unequal investment in infrastructure contributed significantly to the observed polarization, particularly with respect to the lower income club. Indicators of macroeconomic stability—principally capital expenditure and fiscal deficits—also help explain the lack of convergence and the trend towards polarization among Indian states.

The tenth contribution in the volume, by Grimm, analyses Ivorian income distribution data over the period 1992–98, and examines the link with the profound economic and sociodemographic changes which occurred in the 1990s, including the devaluation of the CFA franc in 1994 and the accompanying structural adjustment programmes. Microsimulations show that both the negative income growth in Abidjan and the positive income growth in rural Côte d'Ivoire were related to rising inequality. However, the devaluation of the CFA franc, and the structural adjustment programme (including the recovery of international aid), coupled with the price boom in the coffee/cocoa sector, caused a significant redistribution between rural and urban areas. Within-region inequality increased and between-region inequality decreased, leading to a rise in the proportion of the urban population among the poor.

Grimm's findings comply with most of the short and medium-term predictions of computable general equilibrium (CGE) models applied to the Ivorian case. However, recent movements in world prices of export crops show that a large part of the Ivorian population remains vulnerable to external shocks. Furthermore, the political instability evident since December 1999, and the subsequent freeze of international aid, discouraged and hindered private investment. In 2000 and 2001, Côte d'Ivoire experienced negative GDP growth, suggesting that the Ivorian economy today faces a crisis comparable to that of the early 1990s.

In Chapter 11, Ferreira and Leite ask whether more education really means less poverty, and undertake to answer this question by means of a microsimulation for the Brazilian state of Ceará. They conclude that a rise in the average endowment of education resulting from a broad-based expansion of enrolment coupled with a reduction in dropout rates would very likely make a substantial contribution to poverty reduction. Just how substantial depends on the way in which the structure of returns to education develops over time. Increased enrolment and a reduction in dropout rates would not, however, have the same impact on inequality. While the simulated educational expansion would be moderately equalizing if returns flattened in the future, it would be neutral if returns did not change; and inequality would actually rise if returns increased at the same time as the expansion took place.

Their second conclusion is that a combination of policies which succeed in expanding education in a more targeted way would help make educational expansions more progressive. At best, an increase in mean schooling leads to a small reduction in inequality. A more targeted effort, focussing on reducing illiteracy and keeping in school those most likely to leave, can play an important role in reducing income inequality. So a targeted exercise should not be a substitute for, but rather a complement to, a broader expansion of educational opportunities. Ferreira and Leite stress that all results depend heavily on what happens to returns to education, which are determined by the interaction between the relative supply of and demand for different skills. Given that gains in labour earnings to the poor are very sensitive to changes in demand for unskilled labour, stagnation of demand for unskilled labour is of particular concern, but could not be modelled in the paper.

Household dynamics play a crucial role in the analysis. As women acquire education and enter the labour force, their fertility behaviour also changes, reducing the number of children in the family. In income terms, each of these tendencies is positive for the families to which they belong. The model attaches great importance to such gender-sensitive effects on the overall welfare of poor families. But a large supply of female labour may generate downward wage pressure or enhance job competition. The extent to which Ceará will be able to capitalize on a more educated labour force depends, in large measure, on how effectively it can produce an overall growth strategy generating sufficient labour demand.

These four chapters, all stress the importance of looking in more detail at the microeconomic aspects of poverty analysis, applying simulation techniques and other methods to household data. However, it is also recognized that the outcomes of microsimulation exercises are often very sensitive to macroeconomic and growth variables. Hence the need, as expressed in the papers of Kanbur, Ravallion, and Dağdeviren *et al.* to pay attention to the distributional effects of macroeconomic and growth policies, and not to take the distributional outcome of such policies for granted.

POLICIES FOR POVERTY ALLEVIATION AND GROWTH

The final chapter by Bigsten and Levin reviews recent theoretical and policy research dealing with the relationship between economic growth, income distribution, and poverty. They do not find any systematic pattern of change in income distribution during recent decades, nor any systematic link from fast growth to increasing inequality. In contrast to previous studies, they claim that the level of initial income inequality is not a robust explanatory factor of growth, but admit that some recent empirical studies have found a negative impact of asset inequality on growth. Possible channels for this are credit rationing, reduced possibilities for participation in the political process, and social conflicts. Among the strategic elements that have contributed to reduced poverty, Bigsten and Levin emphasize agricultural and rural development; investment in physical infrastructure and human capital; efficient institutions that provide the right set of incentives to farmers and entrepreneurs; and effective social policies to promote health, education and social capital, as well as safety nets to protect the poor. They conclude that growth can be substantial if the policy and institutional environment is right.

CONCLUSION

The range of views covered in this volume makes a consensus of opinion unlikely. However, some general inferences can be drawn—the first being the difficulty of drawing general conclusions. Many of the chapters show that sweeping statements such as 'growth is good for the poor', 'education is good for the poor', or 'redistribution reduces poverty more than growth' can be supported by cross-country regressions. But since these observations have little or no policy implications, they tend to blur the debate on growth and poverty rather than illuminate it.

What the chapters in this volume show, each in their own context, is that initial conditions matter, specific country structures matter, and time horizons matter. Ravallion shows that initial conditions affect the speed with which growth can reduce poverty. Initial conditions and the structure of the economy also affect whether policies have a pro-poor or an anti-poor outcome—trade liberalization was mentioned as a case in point. Improved education is an end in itself, and can also contribute to reducing poverty; but its effect on inequality depends on supply and demand factors, which differ significantly across countries. Likewise, in some countries a redistribution of 1 per cent of income from the rich to the poor would reduce poverty more than a 1 per cent increase in total national income, but in other countries this is not the case. The later chapters in this volume support this attention to detail by illustrating how improved poverty analysis can better inform the debates on poverty.

Since the appropriate poverty reduction strategy is so country and context-specific, it seems clear that national creative solutions need to be encouraged. However, an emphasis on national policies also implies national ownership of such policies. While the term 'ownership' has recently acquired some negative connotations,[5] we use it here to refer to the benefits of ownership of policy analysis and an informed policy debate. Such a debate might hopefully lead to a more pro-poor set of development policies if consensus between different interest groups at the national level can be reached. It

[5] In negotiations with developing countries, international financial institutions have often insisted that countries 'own' their economic and fiscal policies, although these may well have been drawn up by the IFIs themselves.

might also lead to a sharpening of the issues and the various policy options without reaching consensus. In both cases, issues of poverty and inequality will have been put at the centre of public concern.

It is the task of UNU/WIDER and other UN research institutes to assist in such a debate and this is what we have attempted to do with this book.

REFERENCES

Kaldor, N. (1967). *Strategic Factors in Economic Development*. New York State School of Industrial and Labour Relations, Cornell University, Ithaca.

Kanbur, R. (1998). 'Income Distribution and Growth'. *World Bank Working Papers* 98–13, World Bank, Washington.

Kuznets, S. (1955). 'Economic Growth and Income Inequality'. *American Economic Review*, 45, 1–28.

Lewis, W. A. (1954). 'Economic Development with Unlimited Supplies of Labour'. *Manchester School of Economics and Social Studies*, 22, 139–81.

1

Economic Policy, Distribution, and Poverty: The Nature of Disagreements

RAVI KANBUR

1.1. INTRODUCTION

The end of history lasted for such a short time. If the early 1990s raised hopes of a broad-based consensus on economic policy for growth, equity, and poverty reduction, the late 1990s dashed them. The East Asian crisis and the Seattle debacle saw to that. In the year 2000, the governors of the World Bank, whose mission it is to eradicate poverty, could meet only under police protection, besieged by those who believe instead that the institution and the policies it espouses cause poverty. The street demonstrations in Prague, Seattle, and Washington DC, are one end of a spectrum of disagreement, which includes vigorous debate in the pages of the leading newspapers, passionate involvement of faith-based organizations, and the genteel cut and thrust of academic discourse.

The last 2 years have seen my involvement in an extensive process of consultation on poverty reduction strategies.[1] The consultation reached out to most interested constituencies in the academic, policy-making, and advocacy communities. It covered the international financial institutions (IFIs) and the myriad UN specialized agencies, government ministries in the North and the South, northern aid agencies, academic analysts in rich and poor countries, northern and southern advocacy non-governmental

Reprinted from *World Development* Vol. 29, Ravi Kanbur 'Economic Policy Distribution and Poverty: The Nature of Disagreements', pages 1083–94 (2001) with permission from Elsevier Science. This chapter is based on an invited presentation to the Swedish Parliamentary Commission on Global Development (Globkom) on 22 September 2000. I am grateful to Mia Horn-af-Rantzien, Secretary of the Commission, for her encouragement to produce a written version of the presentation. These ideas have also been presented at meetings organized by the Canadian Ministry of Finance in Ottawa, the World Food Day Symposium at Cornell University, the PREM network of the World Bank, and the Faculty of Social Studies seminar at the University of Warwick. I am grateful to the participants in these meetings for their constructive comments. The observations in this chapter are based on my operational experiences over the last few years. For more formal academic assessment of the literature on distribution, poverty, and development see Kanbur (1998, 2000). For an assessment of the implications for development assistance, see Kanbur, Sandler, and Morrison (1999), and for World Bank specific commentary see Kanbur and Vines (2000).

[1] Most of this consultation was under the auspices of the World Bank's World Development Report on Poverty, of which I was Director until I resigned in May 2000.

organizations (NGOs), and NGOs with ground-level operations working with the poor. It involved a global electronic consultation, as well as conventional written contributions, and scores of meetings. A particularly valuable exercise was the systematic attempt to elicit directly the 'voices of the poor' through participatory assessments.

This chapter presents an analysis of the broad themes of disagreement in these consultations and more generally among those concerned with poverty reduction. It has to be noted, first of all, that there are swathes of agreement in areas where there would not have been consensus two decades ago. Any discussion of disagreements has to start with an acknowledgement of these areas of agreement. But, clearly, there are deep divisions on economic policy, distribution, and poverty. These divisions spilled out in the consultations, mostly politely, but sometimes in vehement discourse, written and oral, harbingers of the street battles to come.

The chapter tries to answer an obvious question: How can people with seemingly the same ends disagree so much about means, and how can seemingly the same objective reality be interpreted so differently? The simple answer, which the protagonists themselves often provide, is of course to question the motives or the analytical capacity of those one disagrees with. The suggestion that 'the others' are either not truly interested in attacking poverty (quite the opposite, in fact), or that they make elementary errors of fact or interpretation, is never very far below the surface.

It is argued here, however, that at least some of the disagreement can be understood in terms of differences in perspective and framework. Understanding disagreements in these terms—rather than in terms of motives or intelligence—is more conducive to encouraging dialogue rather than confrontation. The object of this chapter is to provide an account of some of the underlying reasons for deep disagreements on economic policy, distribution, and poverty, and to couch these in an analytical rather than a rhetorical frame. But before doing this, we need to say a little more about disagreements over what and disagreements between whom.

1.2. DISAGREEMENTS OVER WHAT AND BETWEEN WHOM?

Disagreements over what? The next section will review some broad areas of consensus on poverty reduction strategies. But the focus of this chapter is on disagreements, and these have begun to coalesce around a seemingly irreduceable core of economic policy instruments. There are major disagreements on the pace and sequencing of fiscal adjustment, monetary and interest rate policy, exchange rate regimes, trade and openness, internal and external financial liberalization including deregulation of capital flows, the scale and methods of large-scale privatization of state-owned enterprises, etc. Perhaps trade and openness is the archetypal, emblematic area around which there are deep divisions, and where certainly the rhetoric is fiercest.

Disagreements between whom? Any attempt at categorization and classification risks doing violence to a complex and richly textured reality. But the following grouping would be recognizable to many, and captures broad elements of policy disagreements. One group, call them Group A, could be labeled 'finance ministry'. In this group would obviously be some who worked in finance ministries in the North, and in the South. It would also include many economic analysts, economic policy managers and operational managers in the IFIs and the regional multilateral banks. A key constituent would be the financial press, particularly in the North but also in the South. Finally, one would include many, though not all, academic economists trained in the Anglo-Saxon tradition. Another group, call them Group B, could be labelled 'civil society'. This group would obviously include analysts and advocates in the full range of advocacy and operational NGOs. There would also be people who worked in some of the UN specialized agencies, in aid ministries in the North and social sector ministries in the South. Among academics, non-economists would tend to fall into this group.

To repeat, any such classification is bound to be too simple a reflection of reality. Although the terminology of 'Group A' and 'Group B' is easier to deploy, A and B are better thought of as tendencies rather than as defined and specific individuals. There are clearly people who work in the IFIs who are not 'finance ministry types', just as there are academic economists trained in the Anglo-Saxon tradition who would, for example, caution strongly on capital account liberalization. The UN specialized agencies and northern aid agencies are often a battle ground between finance ministry and civil society tendencies. As the next section makes clear, some NGO positions on specific policies would be approved of in finance ministries, and vice versa.

This being said, however, the proposed classification offers a sharp enough, and recognizable enough, characterization of divisions to help us understand the nature of disagreements. Group A types are those who tend to believe that the cause of poverty reduction is best served by more rapid adjustment to fiscal imbalances, rapid adjustment to lower inflation and external deficits and the use of high interest rates to achieve these ends, internal and external financial sector liberalization, deregulation of capital controls, deep and rapid privatization of state-owned enterprises and, perhaps the strongest unifying factor in this group—rapid and major opening up of an economy to trade and foreign direct investment. On each of these issues, Group B types tend to lean the other way.

The real question we face is why? Why is it that these two groups disagree so much across key areas of economic policy? The basic contention of this chapter is that much of the reason lies in differences in perspective and framework on three key features characterizing assessments of economic policy, distribution, and poverty: aggregation, time horizon, and market structure. First, Group A tends to view the consequences of economic policy in much more aggregative terms than does Group B. Second, Group B's major concerns are with consequences over a time horizon which is both much shorter and much longer than the 'medium-term' horizon which Group A typically adopts. Third, Group A instinctively approaches the distributional consequences of economic policy through a competitive market structure, while Group B instinctively thinks of a world in which market structure is characterized by pockets of market power, and economic policy feeds through this non-competitive structure to the consequences for the poor.

The elaboration of Aggregation, Time Horizon, and Market Structure, as providing a framework for understanding deep disagreements on economic policy, distribution, and poverty, is the core task of this chapter. But before elaborating on disagreement, let us consider areas of agreement.

1.3. SOME AREAS OF AGREEMENT

The consultations revealed wide areas of agreement—some old, some new, and some surprising. There is no question that there is now a broad agreement that education and health outcomes are on par with income in assessing poverty and the consequences of economic policy. This is now so commonplace that it is easy to forget it was not always the case, that 25 years ago great intellectual and policy battles were fought in the World Bank on broadening the conception of development and poverty reduction. Perhaps today's new proposals on conceptualizing poverty—for example, that empowerment and participation should in their turn be treated on par with education and health and income—will equally become tomorrow's foundations.

Another area in which the consultations revealed considerable agreement, at least at a certain level of generality, was on the role of international public goods in determining the well-being of the poor. Whether couched in terms of cross-border spillovers of environmental externalities or financial instability, or in terms of the central role of basic research into tropical agriculture and tropical diseases, the recognition was clearly abroad that public intervention is needed in these areas. The emerging importance of this issue was instinctively grasped by most. It may well be that this happy state of affairs is due precisely to the fact that this is a relatively new issue in the policy arena, that once we get into the details, divisions will grow. Thus, for example, while there was overall broad support for the idea of a vaccine purchase fund to bridge the gap between the costs of basic research and the purchasing power of the poorest countries, there was already some dissent on such funds being unwarranted subsidies to corporations, who should, instead, be directed to supply drugs they already have at prices the poorest can afford.

A third area where there is a surprising amount of agreement, or more accurately not as much disagreement as there was 20 or even 10 years ago, is on the old 'markets versus state' debate. There has definitely been some coming together on this. Particularly interesting were the positions of NGOs with actual ground-level operations working directly with poor. In the consultations, these organizations tended to be very pragmatic. The question for them was always what worked to improve the standard of living of the people they were helping, not about ideologies favouring state over market or the other way round.

Consider, for example, the work and philosophy of SEWA, the Self Employed Women's Association, which operates in Gujarat State in India.[2] SEWA grew out of the long history of organizing textile workers in Ahmedabad, but applied and modified those lessons to organizing women in the informal sector. Starting from an urban base, it has now also expanded to organizing in rural areas (www.sewa.org). SEWA's

[2] In July 1999 I was involved in an immersion exercise organized by SEWA and the German Institute for North–South Dialogue. Officials from aid agencies and parliaments were taken by SEWA to experience for a few days the lives of the women SEWA works for and with.

ground-level campaigns, and their national advocacy work, reflects a pragmatism which eschews ideological positions on 'state versus market'. They have supported certain types of trade liberalization because they increase the demand for the output and labour of their members. But they have opposed other types of trade liberalization when they hurt, for example, the employment and incomes of the husbands and brothers and fathers of their members. They are strong supporters of deregulating the control of the Gujarat State Forestry Commission on the livelihoods of their members. But they oppose deregulation of the pharmaceutical industry because of the devastating impact of these on basic drug prices, and they support increased regulation in Export Processing Zones to ensure that labour standards are met. Is SEWA pro-state or pro-market? It is difficult to say. What is clear is that SEWA is pro-poor. One of their best-known pamphlets is in fact entitled 'Liberalizing for the Poor'.

The more one moves away from ground-level operations, the more one moves to advocacy groups of any shade, pragmatism gives way to more defined a priori positions on state and market. But even here, the divides are not as great as they were at the height of the Cold War, or at the zenith of post Cold War triumphalism that heralded the 'end of history'. At the turn of the century the real questions are to do with the right balance of market and state, and how things actually work on the ground.

Alongside this lessened divide on markets versus state, there is broad agreement on the central importance of institutions in regulating markets, in regulating government, in determining the interaction between households in the market place, and thus in determining the outcomes for the poor. One of the striking findings from the Voices of the Poor exercise was how important institutions such as the police and the courts were to the reality of poor people's lives. At the macro level, the role of institutions in determining the investment climate was also agreed upon in the consultations. Of course, once again, this was at a certain level of generality. When detailed discussions started, and especially when they impinged on economic policies, divisions tended to appear.

So there is broad consensus in some areas and at a certain level of discourse, to set against the divisions that are the focus of this chapter. But these very agreements throw into sharp relief the disagreements that remain. It is almost as if the battle is more intense because it is now focused more sharply on fewer and fewer remaining issues. Let us turn now to the nature of these disagreements.

1.4. THE NATURE OF DISAGREEMENTS I: AGGREGATION

In the current discourse on economic policy, distribution and poverty, there is a strong sense of people talking past each other, each side equally convinced that it has the truth, even when confronted with seemingly the same objective reality. How can that be? One key factor is that different people instinctively operate at different levels of aggregation when they talk about outcomes, or about the consequences of different economic policy interventions. This goes beyond the simple point about GDP versus poverty or other distribution indicators, which is the usual way in which this divide is portrayed. Many in Group A now work with poverty measures which calculate, for example, the fraction of people in a country who fall below a critical level of income or expenditure—the most commonly used threshold is the famous $1 per person per day poverty line. Even with something like this measure, the two groups have very different perspectives on poverty outcomes. Some of the differences are obvious, others less so.

The following personal experience illustrates the reaction that many analysts in Group A get when they present their formal poverty analysis to broader audiences. After doing detailed academic work on the Ghana Living Standards Survey (GLSS) in the 1980s and early 1990s, in 1992 I found myself as the head of the World Bank's Field Office in Ghana. Work on GLSS data by a range of analysts showed that the incidence of poverty in Ghana, defined as above but with a local poverty line, fell during 1987–91. The exact magnitude varied depending on the detailed calculations, but there was a three or four percentage point decline over these 4 years. This was pitifully small, but it was actually very good by African standards.

The analysis presented, in common with the best practice in this area, had made all the necessary adjustments and corrections to overcome the shortcomings of these sorts of data. For example, considerable effort was put into, correcting for regional price variations, making imputations for dwellings, correcting for household size, etc. in arriving at the poverty measure. But when the analysis was presented in Ghana, very few people believed it. From academics in the universities, through foreign and local NGOs, to the trade unions and the rotary clubs—there was an astonishing degree of disbelief. This is not an uncommon reaction, at least in Africa, to such analysis which shows poverty decreasing. The natural reactions of Group A analysts to this disbelief usually go through the whole gamut—that people do not really understand the detailed statistical analysis, that those who criticize represent special interest groups, that some people will never admit that they are better off, etc.[3] But before dismissing disbelief in this way, it is as well to consider that there might be legitimate reasons for this response, understandable even within the standard framework of household survey-based analysis.

There are at least three reasons why the claim that poverty had gone down in Ghana, for example, could be questioned. The first of these is well recognized by household survey analysts. The income–expenditure based measurement of well-being has improved a lot over the years—for example, production for home consumption is now routinely included, capturing of regional price variation is getting better, and imputing use value to dwellings is also becoming standard. But, one thing that these measures do not capture very well, or at all, is the value of public services. There are separate modules in these surveys with questions on education and health and infrastructure, and so on, but these are rarely, almost never, integrated into the income–expenditure measure of well-being because of conceptual and data difficulties. It is this income–expenditure measure that is used in calculating the headline poverty ratios.

So, it is quite possible for public services to worsen considerably, and yet, for this effect to not show up in the income–expenditure-based measures of poverty incidence. If the bus service that takes a woman from her village to her sister's village is cancelled, it will not show up in these measures. If the health post in the urban slum runs out

[3] I include myself among those who have had such reactions.

of drugs, it will not show up. If the primary school textbooks disappear, or if the teacher does not turn up to teach, it will not show up. But those with ground-level operations and personnel will pick these up. To them, as well as to the poor, the claim that poverty has gone down will ring hollow. None of this is to say that it is not useful to calculate nationally representative, household survey-based, income–expenditure poverty measures. It is simply to say that focusing on them solely misses out on disaggregated detail which others can help to fill in, and which influences the perceptions and assessments of these others.

The second reason for the disconnect one often finds between household survey based poverty measures used by Group A and the perceptions of Group B is that of regional or group disaggregation. Even accepting the income–expenditure-based measures to be an accurate representation of well-being, quite often a national decrease in the poverty incidence can be composed of large movements in opposite directions. For example, in Ghana, during 1987–91, the drop in national poverty was composed of a drop in rural areas and a rise in urban areas. In Mexico during 1990–94, the decrease in national poverty was composed of a drop in urban areas, but an increase in some rural regions. It is important to realize that we are not talking here about the odd household or two getting worse off. The poverty index for entire regions increased. While the decrease in the national poverty index, and the drops in those regions which are driving this decrease at the national level, are clearly to be welcomed, just focusing on the aggregate picture is liable to miss out the increasing poverty in Accra, the capital of Ghana, or in the Chiapas region of Mexico. For an NGO working with street children in Accra, or for a local official coping with increased poverty among indigenous peoples in Chiapas, it is cold comfort to be told, 'but national poverty has gone down'. A similar story can be told about gender-based disaggregation, and other groupings based on ethnicity and race.

It should be clear that in the above type of disconnect neither view is 'wrong'. Different parts of the same objective reality are being seen and magnified. It is both true that the national poverty incidence has declined, and that major groups have been made worse off. The problem is that instead of attempting to understand the other perspective each side hunkers down to defend its view in increasingly strident terms. Group A analysts just keep repeating that poverty has gone down, and do not make any concessions to the complex group specific patterns, while Group B analysts and advocates become increasingly irritated and alienated from a discourse which does not match the reality they know.

Consider now, a third and not frequently appreciated disconnect related to aggregation. The work horse poverty concept of Group A analysts is the incidence of poverty—the percentage of the total population below some poverty line, say one dollar per person per day. This is the concept they instinctively go for. For example, the leading international development target, broadly accepted by donor agencies, is to halve the incidence of poverty by 2015. But analysts and especially advocates and operational types in Group B instinctively think of the absolute numbers of poor as the criterion. The potential for disconnection should be clear. In Ghana, for example, while the incidence of poverty was falling at around one percentage point per year over

1987–91, the total population was growing at almost twice that rate, with the result that the absolute number of poor, even using the standard income–expenditure based measure, grew sizeably.

Think again of the local NGO with ground-level operations. If the number of people turning up at soup kitchens, the number of homeless indigents who have to be provided shelter, the number of street children, increases, then those who work in these organizations are, quite rightly from their perspective, going to argue that poverty has gone up. That the incidence of poverty has fallen is of little relevance to them, and to be told repeatedly and insistently that poverty has fallen is bound to lead to difficulties in communication and dialogue. One sees this also at the global level. The World Bank's figures show that over the 1990s the absolute numbers of the poor stayed roughly constant at around 1.2 billion. The incidence of poverty has fallen, since total world population is on the increase. Has global poverty fallen or stayed the same? One challenge often heard in the consultations was: 'How can you say economic growth helps the poor? Look, there has been all this growth in the 1990s, and yet the total number of poor has not changed at all!' Leaving to one side the growth issue, to which a whole section is devoted later in the chapter, it is easy to see how communication can be derailed by different groups meaning different things by the same word—poverty. In this case, a good start would be clarity and comprehension, but even that might not help because the issue of whether the criterion is the incidence of poverty or the absolute numbers of the poor is still left open.

Thus, instinctive adoption of different levels of aggregation in describing and evaluating the distributional and poverty consequences of economic policies explain at least some of the disconnection one observes. The above arguments and characterizations would all be present for each of the economic policies in dispute—for example, the impact of trade policy reform on distribution and poverty. Understanding these differences is the first step in more fruitful dialogue between those who primarily rely on national poverty incidence measures derived from household surveys to assess the evolution of poverty, and those who have a much more finely disaggregated view of the outcomes of economic policy. Unfortunately, at the moment the lack of mutual comprehension is leading to polarization, with Group A often retreating into the formal technical bunker, and simply repeating their findings without trying to understand what Group B is trying to say, and Group B dismissing Group A analysis as either out of touch with reality or, even worse, actively manipulated to get certain answers. Neither of these positions is healthy, and bridging the aggregation divide is essential if we are to move forward.

1.5. THE NATURE OF DISAGREEMENTS II: TIME HORIZON

Implicit or explicit differences in the time horizon over which the consequences of policy are assessed explain some of the deep disagreements on economic policy, distribution, and poverty.

The 'medium term' is the instinctive time horizon that Group A uses when thinking about the consequences of trade policy, for example. This is implicit in the equilibrium theory which underlies much of the reasoning behind the impact of policy on growth and distribution. It is also implicit in the way empirical analysts interpret their cross-country econometric relationships between growth, equity, or poverty on one side and measures of openness on the other. There is, of course, no simple way to link the short or medium or long term of economic theory and modelling to actual calendar time. But, by and large, when Group A talks about the consequences of policies for distribution and growth they have in mind a 5–10-year time horizon.

Group B has concerns that are both more short term and more long term. Those who work with the daily reality of poor people's lives, are extremely concerned, like the poor themselves, about short-term consequences of economic policy which can drive a family into starvation, to sell its assets at fire sale prices, or to pull its children out of school. For them it is no use to be told that over a 5–10-year horizon things will pick up again. In fact, it is not even good enough to be told that in the medium term things will be better than they would have been without the shock of this policy change because without the policy change things were in decline anyway. All this is true, but short-run survival trumps medium-run benefits every time, if the family is actually on the edge of survival. As Keynes might have said, in the short run they could all be dead.

Increasingly, Group A accepts the issue of short-term vulnerability and shocks as being an important one, not only because it affects well-being in the short term, but because behavioural responses to this vulnerability may themselves lead to inefficiencies which affect the prospects for growth and poverty reduction in the medium term. Moreover, the issue of safety nets is back on the table, after its banishment in the 1980s, the banishment itself being a reaction to their inefficiencies and misuse in the 1960s and 1970s. But safety nets are sometimes thought of by Group A as being an add-on, to address the negative short-term consequences of trade opening, for example. They tend to be cautious about them as a systematic part of an insurance and redistribution mechanism, and they certainly would not want to see trade opening to be halted or slowed down because these safety nets and compensation mechanisms, however temporary, were not in place. This last point is central, and an acid test. In the absence of safety nets, Group B would be cautious or downright hostile to trade openness. Group A would want to press ahead, often dismissing those who argue for caution as either not understanding that openness would actually lead to greater equity and poverty reduction, or as special interest groups with protection on their minds. Not facing up to the implicit difference in time horizon accounts for at least some of the vehement disagreements on this score.

There are also those who have what they see as a much longer time horizon than a decade. Environmental groups, including some with religious perspectives on stewardship of the earth's resources, fall into this category. For them, it is the 50 or the 100-year perspective that is important. They do not see how economic growth can be sustained given limits on the earth's carrying capacity, and they see both immediate and long-term negative consequences of resource depletion. An important corollary of this line of thinking is that implicit or explicit redistribution from rich countries to poor countries will have to substitute for economic growth as the foundation for global poverty reduction. Group A are essentially techno-optimists. They refer back to the gloomy scenarios painted by the Club of Rome in the 1970s and point out that none of these came to be true. While there are clearly some market distortions which lead to an inefficiently high level of resource depletion, and cross-border spillover effects which lead to their own coordination problems, their answer is to fix these distortions rather than forcibly hold down investment and growth. In any event, they do not see it as a politically feasible option over the 5–10-year horizon to ask the rich countries to undertake massive redistribution in favour of the poor countries, and they have a strong sense that technological change will come to the rescue over a 50 or 100-year horizon, as it always has in the past.

In the consultations, therefore, Group A was fending off both shorter-term and longer-term perspectives. But the real point is that oftentimes it was not clear that it was this difference in perspective, rather than the specifics of trade policy or privatization policy or whatever, which was driving the difference. Clarity is not resolution, but it is a start.

1.6. THE NATURE OF DISAGREEMENTS III: MARKET STRUCTURE AND POWER

Undoubtedly the most potent difference in framework and perspective centres on market structure and power. The implicit framework of Group A in thinking through the consequences of economic policy on distribution and poverty is that of a competitive market structure of a large number of small agents interacting without market power over each other. The instinctive picture that Group B has of market structure is one riddled with market power wielded by agents in the large and in the small. This is true whether they are talking about the power of big corporations in the market place or in negotiating with governments, or of the power of the local moneylender in determining usurious rates of interest in the village economy. They see the formulation and implementation of economic policy as being influenced by agents with market power, and they see policy feeding through to consequences through a market structure which is not competitive.

The immediate response of Group A to the suggestion that openness in trade, for example, might hurt the poor in poor countries is to (implicitly or explicitly) invoke the basic theorems of trade theory. Opening up an economy to trade will benefit the more abundant factor, because this factor will be relatively cheap and opening up will increase demand for this factor overall. Since unskilled labour is the factor abundant in poor countries, opening up will benefit unskilled labour and hence the poor. Leaving aside the fact that this is a theory of medium-term equilibrium, and thus subject to the disagreements discussed in the previous section, it is also a theory based on competitive product and factor markets. In particular, if local product and factor markets are segmented, because of poor infrastructure or because of the local monopoly power of middlemen and moneylenders, the simple theory will not go through quite so simply. But it is precisely such situations (as well as the disaggregated and the short-term consequences discussed earlier) that are highlighted repeatedly in discussions about the possible negative consequences of openness. The tendency among Group A is to dismiss these claims, and to revert again to stating the conclusion that openness is good for equity.

Another example is capital mobility. Leaving to one side the question of portfolio capital, where Group A has itself moved to a more cautious stance since the financial crises of the late 1990s, there is the issue of mobility of investment capital. A very strong belief in Group B is that increased mobility of investment capital makes workers in both receiving and sending countries worse off. Such a view is derided by Group A analysts as being incoherent—'How can you say that when capital leaves the US it hurts US workers, and when it gets to Mexico it hurts Mexican workers as well?!'

Of course, in a framework with perfectly competitive markets, it is indeed incoherent to suggest that increased capital mobility makes workers worse off everywhere. At most it will make workers in only one country worse off. Moreover, since with mobility capital will move to the highest return, this is more efficient so the gainers could more than afford to compensate the loser, if such a mechanism existed. But consider the following set-up. Capital and labour markets are not perfectly competitive. Rather, capital and labour bargain in each country over wages and employment. Now make capital mobile. It can be seen that this is akin to increasing the bargaining power of capital relative to labour, so that increasing capital mobility, whatever its effects on efficiency, could end up making workers in both countries worse off relative to capital. This is the implicit framework Group B used over and again in the consultations, with added emphasis on the political power of big multinational corporations to influence economic policy on such issues as capital controls or regulation of Foreign Direct Investment. The answer of Group A was to reply with the findings of the (implicit or explicit) competitive framework, and cycle of non-dialogue would go on from there.

The above are examples from trade and openness, but the same divide is present in discussions of the consequences of other economic policies such as privatization of state-owned enterprises. The implicit framework of those supporting rapid and large-scale privatization is one where state monopoly is replaced by a competitive structure of firms without monopoly power. The implicit framework of those more cautious in this regard is one of a state monopoly, which might be at least somewhat responsive to the needs of consumer through political pressure, being replaced by a private monopoly with no such restraints.

The point of the above discussion is to highlight differences in basic frameworks used instinctively in thinking through the distributional and poverty consequences of economic policies. Of course, many in Group A are aware of how non-competitive elements can affect their predictions (e.g. trade theory has made great strides in recent years in incorporating elements of monopolistic competition), but in policy discourse it seems as though Group A has, by and large, plumped for the competitive market structure framework. But thinking through the distributional consequences of economic policies when market structures are not competitive, in the small or in the large, will be needed before the framework of Group A can be made to speak to the concerns of Group B. For example, whether the capital–labour bargaining framework discussed above is valid is an empirical question that can be tested for different countries and industries. But until such models are worked out commensurately with the now standard competitive framework models, there can be no basis for comparison and assessment. Until that is done, it will be a standoff between two very different perspectives on market power.

1.7. A SEEMING DISAGREEMENT: THE 'GROWTH' RED HERRING

The word 'growth' was immediately divisive in the consultations, with Group A accusing Group B of being 'anti-growth', and Group B characterizing Group A as holding the view that 'growth is everything'. In fact, there is more agreement here than meets the eye, and the rhetoric of both groups stands in the way of seeing the degree of agreement that does exist.

Unfortunately, the word 'growth' is used in both in its technical sense of 'an increase in real national per capita income', and also to connote a particular policy package, disagreements over key elements of which has been the focus of this chapter. This package is 'growth-oriented policies' as seen by Group A and 'economic policies which hurt the poor' as seen by Group B. If used in the technical sense, one would probably find less disagreement on whether growth so defined could help poverty reduction. Or rather, the discussion could then focus on economic policies and on Aggregation, Time Horizon, and Market Structure as discussed in this chapter, which is where the true nature of disagreements is to be found.

Consider the claim by some that others are 'anti-growth', usually followed by empirical demonstrations that growth (increase in real per national per capita income) is strongly correlated across countries and over time with reductions in national-level measures of income poverty. There is no question that these correlations are very strong indeed. But that is not the point. In all of the consultations over the 2 years, not one person from Group B in Eastern Europe, for example, claimed that the disastrous increase in poverty and worsening of social indicators in Eastern Europe in the 1990s had nothing to do with the precipitous decline in real national per capita income during this period. Nobody made the claim that had the decline in per capita income been even greater, the poor would have somehow been better. The claim that they did make, however, was that the policy package that the transition economies were advised (or forced) to adopt was what led to the decline in per capita income and to the increase in poverty.

As another example, not one person from Group B in East Asia claimed that the tremendous improvement in poverty and social indicators in East Asia, over the 30 years prior to 1997, had nothing to do with the fact that per capita income in these countries multiplied several fold over this period. Nobody made the claim that the position of the poor would have been better had this growth been negative. But what they did claim was that the policy package put in place by these countries over these years differed in key elements from the policy package currently being recommended by the IFIs and some northern finance ministries. Finally, coming to 1997, not one person from

Group B in East Asia claimed that the sharp increases in poverty registered in East Asia during the crisis had nothing to do with the fact that per capita income collapsed. They did not make the claim that had the per capita income decline been greater, the poor would have been better off. What they did claim was that the policy package these countries were encouraged to adopt in the mid 1990s, especially rapid capital account and financial sector liberalizations, caused the crisis and the attendant decline in per capita income and the increase in poverty.

To characterize these positions of Group B as claims that growth does not help the poor, and to then refute them by showing the undoubted negative correlation between per capita income and poverty, not only misses the point—it does the debate a disservice as well. The real debate to be engaged is on the policy package and the consequences of different elements of it for distribution and poverty. Correlations between per capita income and poverty are beside the point because the real dispute is about the consequences of alternative policies.

Now, in fact, in written and oral contributions from Group B in the consultations, very often one would indeed find statements of the type 'growth is not the answer to poverty' or 'the IFIs are obsessed with growth as the answer to poverty'. But an effort must be made to understand what the true meaning of such statements is, from their context and from extended dialogue. Statements such as the ones above often captured intent much better if 'growth' were replaced by something like 'Washington Consensus policies' or 'the standard IFI package'. It might be argued that one should take the words for what they are, but one also finds very often that Group A uses 'growth' as shorthand for 'growth-oriented policies' by which they would mean a certain type of policy package, the contents of which we have been discussing. If Group A slips into this usage, it is understandable that in responding, Group B does the same. Thus, part of the problem is that the word 'growth' is used to mean both an increase in per capita income, and to refer to a policy package, and this is true of Group A and Group B.

None of the above is to minimize in any way the deep disagreements that do exist on Aggregation, Time Horizon, and Market Structure. Even with growth defined as increase in per capita income, Section 5 has already discussed how some in Group B argue that this is not the answer over a 50 or a 100-year time horizon. Moreover, Section 4 discussed how any given increase in per capita income could be associated with myriad disaggregated patterns of distributional and poverty change, even when national poverty falls. But the vehemence of the 'growth' debate, on both sides, is somewhat misplaced if by growth one means simply an increase in real national per capita income. The current growth debate, certainly as presented by some elements of Group A, misses the point, and derails dialogue on the real issues of poverty reduction strategies.

1.8. ON POLICY MESSAGING: NEGOTIATION VERSUS DIALOGUE

Faced with such deep divisions based on legitimate differences in perspective and framework, what should one do? The answer is clearly to develop dialogue based on an attempt at mutual understanding of the different frameworks, how they can lead to different interpretations and conclusions, what sort of evidence might help to resolve some of the differences, and to come out with measured and nuanced positions. Unfortunately, quite the opposite seems to be happening. Over the past few years, the divide has grown and a polarization has set in. For the IFIs, the siege of their biannual meetings is proving a traumatic experience. More generally, Seattle both symbolized and crystallized the vehemence of the disagreements. The stance everywhere is one of confrontation and negotiation, rather than understanding and dialogue.

My focus here is on Group A, especially when it presents policy messages that synthesize analytical work. Here again, a negotiating stance seems to be in play, especially among some parts of the IFIs and the G7 treasuries. Even when, intellectually and analytically, Group A accepts the complications, qualifications and nuances brought about by considerations of disaggregation, differences in time horizon, and non-competitive market structures, the tendency is for the policy messaging—for example, on trade and openness—to be sharp and hard, for fear that to do otherwise would be read as a sign of weakness by 'the other side'. Especially since Seattle, a 'line in the sand', 'this far, no further', mentality seems to have gripped elements of Group A—in the IFIs, in the G7 treasuries, in the financial press and some in academia. 'Give them an inch of nuance and they'll take a mile of protection' is the mindset. Paradoxically, the growing areas of agreement noted at the outset—for example on education and health, and on institutions—tend to lead to a sharper stance being taken on the remaining areas of dispute on core economic policies.

This is unfortunate. At least twice before, elements of Group A have taken such a hard stance, with a negotiating mindset, and both times have had to retreat after considerable conflict which negatively affected the prospects for future dialogue. The first example of this is capital account convertibility, on which the IFIs, with the broad support of G7 treasuries, took a bold stand in the early and mid-1990s, and dismissed those who were skeptical of the benefits and fearful of the consequences. Since the 1997 crisis the tune has changed, but the earlier intransigence did not help the dialogue when the need for a nuanced position was finally recognized.

The second example is debt relief for the poorest countries. Prior to 1995 the IFIs, again with broad backing from many G7 treasuries, stood very firm against debt relief. The policy messaging of the time was sharp and hard, for fear that any opening would be the 'thin end of the wedge' through which large-scale debt write-downs would break open the IFIs. In 1995, the policy messaging changed and indeed began to call for debt relief.[4] It is hard to believe that analysis and evidence suddenly revealed the truth in 1995. Rather, the G7 treasuries and the IFIs recognized political pressure from the growing global coalition for debt relief. But the negotiating stance adopted before 1995 sowed seeds of mutual suspicion that affect the dialogue on debt relief today, even under very different circumstances.

[4] As the World Bank's Chief Economist for Africa, in 1995/6 I was a member of the joint World Bank/IMF Task Force which put together the first proposal for debt relief to the Heavily Indebted Poor Countries (HIPC).

There is a second strand of argument in play on the simplicity or complexity of policy messages, this time directed at the IFIs and aid agencies by some elements of Group A, particularly some in the financial press and in the G7 treasuries. This is that these agencies should keep their policy messages simple, for fear that any complications and nuances will lead them into ever-more complicated activities. Keeping their messages simple, in this view, will save the aid agencies from themselves, or at least from their tendency to take on a broader and broader development agenda. This point is made in the context of economic policies, but also in fear that the agreement on the importance of institutions, for example, may lead aid agencies to intervene where they cannot and should not.

Some clear thinking is needed here. It is perfectly coherent to hold simultaneously the view that the consequences of economic policy for distribution and poverty are complex and nuanced, and that aid agencies and donors cannot and should not attempt too complex a set of interventions in developing countries. Indeed, there is an argument to be made for outside intervention to be highly cautious precisely because of the complexity of the situation on the ground. This is certainly true of institutional reform, but it is also true of economic policy. What is problematic, however, is to present a falsely simple view of the world in the policy messaging emerging from aid agency analysis, as a device to restrain complex and unproductive expansionism by aid agencies. The latter problem must be faced on its own terms, and must not be allowed to influence the synthesis of analysis.

If the world is complex, or if the evidence is uncertain, or if legitimate differences in perspective and framework explain differences in conclusions, analysis must take these on board. Moreover, the policy messaging that comes from such analysis must reflect the nature of those complexities. Inappropriate simplifying and hardening of policy messages, either as a way of constraining the operations of an aid agency, or as a negotiating device because of the fear that nuancing will be seen as a sign of weakness in policy debate, will only serve to polarize the debate further, and will not be conducive to broad-based dialogue.

1.9. CONCLUSION

When the institution whose self-stated mission it is to eradicate poverty can only hold its annual meetings under siege from those who believe its mission is to further the cause of the rich and powerful, there is clearly a gap to be bridged. Moreover, the gap is not just between the IFIs and their critics. There is a growing divide on key areas of economic policy, even as agreement broadens in other areas. Indeed, the conflict over economic policy gets more intense as the areas of disagreement shrink to what seem to be an irreduceable core.

This chapter has argued that underlying the seemingly intractable differences are key differences of perspective and framework on Aggregation, Time Horizon, and Market Structure. Simply recognizing and understanding the underlying nature of the disagreements in these terms would be one step in bridging the gap. But more is needed. More is needed from both sides, but my focus here is on Group A. For those at the more academic end of that spectrum, the message is that explicitly taking into account these complications is more likely to shift the intellectual frontier than falling back yet again on conventional analysis.[5] For those at the more operational and policy end of the spectrum, especially those in policy-making and policy-implementing institutions, the message is that recognizing and trying to understand legitimate alternative views on economic policy, being open and nuanced in messages rather than being closed and hard, is not only good analytics, it is good politics as well.

REFERENCES

Kanbur, R. (1998). 'Poverty Reduction Strategies: Five Perennial Questions'. In R. Culpeper and C. McAskie (eds), *Towards Autonomous Development In Africa*. The North-South Institute, Ottawa.

—— (2000). 'Income Distribution and Development'. In A. B. Atkinson and F. Bourguignon (eds), *Handbook of Income Distribution, Volume I*. North Holland, Amsterdam.

—— Sandler, T., and Morrison, K. (1999). *The Future of Development Assistance*. Overseas Development Council, Washington.

—— and Vines, D. (2000). 'The World Bank and Poverty Reduction: Past, Present and Future'. In C. Gilbert and D. Vines (eds), *The World Bank: Structure and Policies*. Cambridge University Press, Cambridge.

[5] An equally interesting set of further analytical issues is opened up when interactions between Aggregation, Time Horizon, and Market Structure are considered.

2

Growth is Good for the Poor

DAVID DOLLAR AND AART KRAAY

Globalization has dramatically increased inequality between and within nations ...

Jay Mazur

'Labor's New Internationalism', *Foreign Affairs* (Jan/Feb 2000)

We have to reaffirm unambiguously that open markets are the best engine we know of to lift living standards and build shared prosperity.

Bill Clinton

speech at the World Economic Forum (2000)

2.1. INTRODUCTION

The world economy grew well during the 1990s, despite the financial crisis in East Asia. However, there is intense debate over the extent to which the poor benefit from this growth. The two quotes above exemplify the extremes in this debate. At one end of the spectrum are those who argue that the potential benefits of economic growth for the poor are undermined or even offset entirely by sharp increases in inequality that accompany growth. At the other end of the spectrum is the argument that liberal economic policies such as monetary and fiscal stability and open markets raise incomes of the poor and everyone else in society proportionately.

In light of the heated popular debate over this issue, as well as its obvious policy relevance, it is surprising how little systematic cross-country empirical evidence is available on the extent to which the poorest in the society benefit from economic growth. In this chapter, we define the poor as those in the bottom fifth of the income distribution of a country, and empirically examine the relationship between growth in average incomes of the poor and growth in overall incomes, using a large sample of developed and developing countries spanning the last four decades. Since average incomes of the poor are proportional to the share of income accruing to the poorest

Reprinted from the *Journal of Economic Growth* (2002) Vol. 7, David Dollar and Aart Kraay 'Growth is Good for the Poor' pages 195–225, with kind permission from Kluwer Academic Publishers. The authors are grateful to Dennis Tao for excellent research assistance, and to two anonymous referees and the journal editor for helpful comments. This chapter and the accompanying data set are available at www.worldbank.org/research/growth. The opinions expressed here are the authors' and do not necessarily reflect those of the World Bank, its Executive Directors, or the countries they represent.

quintile times average income, this approach is equivalent to studying how a particular measure of income inequality—the first quintile share—varies with average incomes.

In a large sample of countries spanning the past four decades, we cannot reject the null hypothesis that the income share of the first quintile does not vary systematically with average incomes. In other words, we cannot reject the null hypothesis that incomes of the poor rise equiproportionately with average incomes. Figure 2.1 illustrates this basic point. In the top panel, we plot the logarithm of per capita incomes of the poor (on the vertical axis) against the logarithm of average per capita incomes (on the horizontal axis), pooling 418 country–year observations on these two variables. The sample consists of 137 countries with at least one observation on the share of income accruing to the bottom quintile, and the median number of observations per country is three. There is a strong, positive, linear relationship between the two variables, with a slope of 1.07 which does not differ significantly from 1. Since both variables are measured in logarithms, this indicates that on average incomes of the poor rise equiproportionately with average incomes. In the bottom panel we plot average annual growth in incomes of the poor (on the vertical axis) against average annual growth in average incomes (on the horizontal axis), pooling 285 country–year observations where we have at least two observations per country on incomes of the poor separated by at least 5 years. The sample consists of ninety-two countries and the median number of growth episodes per country is three. Again, there is a strong, positive, linear relationship between these two variables with a slope of 1.19. In the majority of the formal statistical tests that follow, we cannot reject the null hypothesis that the slope of this relationship is equal to one. These regressions indicate that within countries, incomes of the poor on average rise equiproportionately with average incomes. This is equivalent to the observation that there is no systematic relationship between average incomes and the share of income accruing to the poorest fifth of the income distribution. Below we examine this basic finding in more detail and find that it holds across regions, time periods, growth rates, and income levels, and is robust to controlling for possible reverse causation from incomes of the poor to average incomes.

Given the strong relationship between incomes of the poor and average incomes, we next ask whether policies and institutions that raise average incomes have systematic effects on the share of income accruing to the poorest quintile which might magnify or offset their effects on incomes of the poor. We focus attention on a set of policies and institutions whose importance for average incomes has been identified in the large cross-country empirical literature on economic growth. These include openness to international trade, macroeconomic stability, moderate size of government, financial development, and strong property rights and rule of law. We find little evidence that these policies and institutions have systematic effects on the share of income accruing to the poorest quintile. The only exceptions are that there is some weak evidence that smaller government size and stabilization from high inflation disproportionately benefit the poor by raising the share of income accruing to the bottom quintile. These findings indicate that growth-enhancing policies and institutions tend to benefit the poor—and everyone else in society—equiproportionately. We also show that the distributional

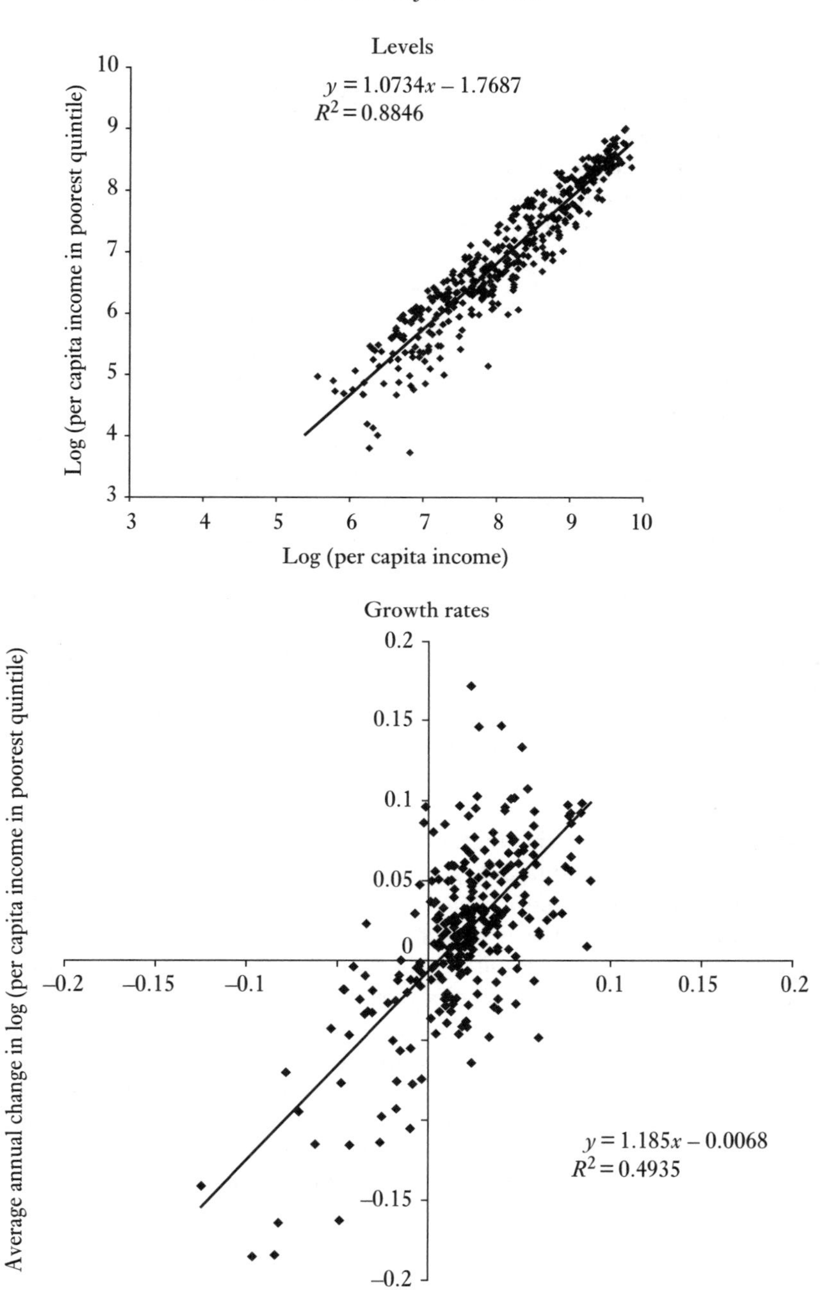

Figure 2.1. *Incomes of the poor and average incomes*

effects of such variables tend to be small relative to their effects on overall economic growth.

We next examine in more detail, the popular idea that greater economic integration across countries is associated with increases in inequality within countries. We first consider a range of measures of international openness, including trade volumes, tariffs, membership in the World Trade Organization, and the presence of capital controls, and ask whether any of these has systematic effects on the share of income accruing to the poorest in society. We find little evidence that they do so, and we find that this result holds even when we allow the effects of measures of openness to depend on the level of development and differences in factor endowments as predicted by the factor proportions theory of international trade. We, therefore, also cannot reject the null hypothesis that on average, greater economic integration benefits the poorest in society as much as everyone else.

In recent years there has been a great deal of emphasis in the development community on making growth even more 'pro-poor'. Given our evidence that neither growth nor growth-enhancing policies tend to be systematically associated with changes in the share of income accruing to the poorest fifth of societies, we interpret this emphasis on 'pro-poor' growth as a call for some other policy interventions that raise the share of income captured by the poorest in society. We empirically examine the importance of four such potential factors in determining the income share of the poorest: primary educational attainment, public spending on health and education, labour productivity in agriculture relative to the rest of the economy, and formal democratic institutions. While it is likely that these factors are important in bettering the lot of poor people in some countries and under some circumstances, we are unable to uncover any evidence that they systematically raise the share of income of the poorest in our large cross-country sample.

In short, we find little evidence that either average incomes, or a wide variety of policy and other variables, are significantly associated with the income share of the poorest quintile. We, therefore, cannot reject the null hypothesis that incomes of the poor, on average, rise equiproportionately with average incomes. This, of course, does not mean that growth is all that is required to improve the lot of the poorest in society, and that the distributional effects of policies should be ignored. As we discuss in greater detail below, existing cross-country data on income distribution that we use contains substantial measurement error. We, therefore, cannot rule out the possibility that our failure to uncover systematic effects of average incomes and policy on the income share of the poorest quintile is simply a consequence of this measurement error. We also cannot rule out the possibility that there are complex interactions between inequality and growth, not captured by our simple empirical models, that net out to small changes in the former that are uncorrelated with the latter.[1] What we can conclude, however,

[1] For example, economic growth might raise earnings inequality, but if earnings of the poor rise fast enough, credit constraints that limit educational opportunities for the poor become less binding, thus, offsetting the initial effects on inequality. See Galor and Zeira (1993) for an early reference on the links between credit constraints, inequality, and growth.

is that policies that raise average incomes are likely to be central to successful poverty reduction strategies, and that existing cross-country evidence—including our own—provides disappointingly little guidance as to what *mix* of growth-oriented policies might especially benefit the poorest in society.

Our work builds on and contributes to two strands of the literature on inequality and growth. Our basic finding that (changes in) income and (changes in) inequality are unrelated is consistent with the findings of several previous authors including Deininger and Squire (1996), Chen and Ravallion (1997), and Easterly (1999) who document this same regularity in smaller samples of countries. We build on this literature by considering a significantly larger sample of countries and by employing more elaborate econometric techniques that take into account the possibility that income levels are endogenous to inequality as suggested by the large theoretical and empirical literature on the effects of inequality on growth. Our results are also related to the small but growing literature on the determinants of the cross-country and intertemporal variation in measures of income inequality, including Gallup, Radelet, and Warner (1998), Li, Squire, and Zou (1998), Leamer *et al.* (1999), Spilimbergo, Londoño, and Székely (1999), Barro (2000), Lundberg and Squire (2000), and Foster and Székely (2001). Our work expands on this literature by considering a wider range of potential determinants of inequality using a consistent methodology in a large sample of countries, and can be viewed as a test of the robustness of these earlier results obtained in smaller and possibly less representative samples of countries. We discuss how our findings relate to these other papers throughout the discussion below. The rest of this paper proceeds as follows. Section 2 describes the data and empirical specification. Section 3 presents our main findings. Section 4 concludes.

2.2. EMPIRICAL STRATEGY

2.2.1. *Measuring Income and Income of the Poor*

We measure mean income as real per capita GDP at purchasing power parity in 1985 international dollars, based on an extended version of the Summers–Heston Penn World Tables Version 5.6.[2] In general, this need not be equal to the mean level of household income, due to a variety of reasons ranging from simple measurement error to retained corporate earnings. We, nevertheless, rely on per capita GDP for two

[2] We begin with the Summers and Heston (1991) Penn World Tables Version 5.6, which reports data on real per capita GDP adjusted for differences in purchasing power parity through 1992 for most of the 156 countries included in that data set. We use the growth rates of constant price local currency per capita GDP from the World Bank to extend these forward through 1997. For a further set of 29 mostly transition economies not included in the Penn World Tables we have data on constant price GDP in local currency units. For these countries we obtain an estimate of PPP exchange rate from the fitted values of a regression of PPP exchange rates on the logarithm of GDP per capita at PPP. We use these to obtain a benchmark PPP GDP figure for 1990, and then use growth rates of constant price local currency GDP to extend forward and backward from this benchmark. While these extrapolations are necessarily crude, they do not matter much for our results. As discussed, the statistical identification in the paper is based primarily on within-country changes in incomes and incomes of the poor, which are unaffected by adjustments to the levels of the data.

pragmatic reasons. First, for many of the country–year observations for which we have information on income distribution, we do not have corresponding information on mean income from the same source. Second, using per capita GDP helps us to compare our results with the large literature on income distribution and growth that typically follows the same practice. In the absence of evidence of a systematic correlation between the discrepancies between per capita GDP and household income on the one hand, and per capita GDP on the other, we treat these differences as classical measurement error, as discussed further below.[3]

We use two approaches to measuring the income of the poor, where we define the poor as the poorest 20 per cent of the population.[4] We are able to obtain information on the share of income accruing to the poorest quintile constructed from nationally representative household surveys for 796 country–year observations covering 137 countries. For these observations, we measure mean income in the poorest quintile directly, as the share of income earned by the poorest quintile times mean income, divided by 0.2. For a further 158 country–year observations we have information on the Gini coefficient but not the first quintile share. For these observations, we assume that the distribution of income is lognormal, and we obtain the share of income accruing to the poorest quintile as the 20th percentile of this distribution.[5]

Our data on income distribution are drawn from four different sources. Our primary source is the UNU/WIDER World Income Inequality Database, which is a substantial extension of the income distribution data set constructed by Deininger and Squire

[3] Ravallion (2001*a*) provides an extensive discussion of sources of discrepancies between national accounts and household survey measures of living standards and finds that, with the exception of the transition economies of Eastern Europe and the Former Soviet Union, growth rates of national accounts measures track growth rates of household survey measures fairly closely on average.

[4] At least three other measures of welfare of the poor have been used in this literature. First, one could define 'the poor' as those below a fixed poverty line such as the dollar-a-day poverty line used by the World Bank, and measure average incomes of those below the poverty line, as is done by Ali and Elbadawi (2001). The relationship between growth in average incomes and growth in this measure of average incomes of the poor is much more difficult to interpret. For example, if the distribution of income is very steep near the poverty line, distribution-neutral growth in average incomes will lift a large fraction of the population from just below to just above the poverty line with the result that average incomes of those below the poverty line fall. Not surprisingly in light of their different definition, these authors find an elasticity of incomes of the poor with respect to average incomes that is less than one. Second, Foster and Székely (2001) measure incomes of the poor using a 'generalized mean' which assigns greater weight to the poorest in society and is closely related to the Atkinson class of inequality measures. They find that the greater is the weight assigned to the incomes of the poor in the generalized mean, the lower is the elasticity of incomes of the poor to average incomes. However, Kraay and Ravallion (2001) show that this result is likely to be an artefact of the greater sensitivity to measurement error of the Atkinson class of inequality measures as the degree of inequality-aversion increases. Finally, a number of papers have examined how the fraction of the population below some prespecified poverty line varies with average income. See for example Ravallion (1997, 2001*b*) and Chen and Ravallion (1997). These papers generally find a strong negative relationship between growth and the change in the headcount.

[5] If the distribution of income is lognormal, that is, log per capita income $\sim N(\mu, \sigma)$, and the Gini coefficient on a scale from 0 to 100 is G, the standard deviation of this lognormal distribution is given by $\sigma = \sqrt{2} \cdot \Phi^{-1}((1+G/100)/2)$, where $\Phi(\cdot)$ denotes the cumulative normal distribution function (Aitchinson and Brown 1966). Using the properties of the mean of the truncated lognormal distribution (e.g. Johnston, Kotz, and Balakrishnan 1994) the 20th percentile of this distribution is given by $\Phi(\Phi^{-1}(0.2) - \sigma)$.

(1996). A total of 706 of our country–year observations are obtained from this source. In addition, we obtain ninety-seven observations originally included in the sample designated as 'high quality' by Deininger and Squire (1996) that do not appear in the UNU/WIDER data set. Our third data source is Chen and Ravallion (2000) who construct measures of income distribution and poverty from 265 household surveys in eighty-three developing countries. Since the Deininger–Squire and UNU/WIDER compilations directly report many of the observations from this and earlier Chen–Ravallion compilations, we obtain only an additional 118 recent observations from this source. Finally, we augment our data set with thirty-two observations primarily from developed countries not appearing in the above three sources, that are reported in Lundberg and Squire (2000). This results in an overall sample of 953 observations covering 137 countries over the period 1950–99. To our knowledge this is the largest data set used to study the relationship between inequality, incomes, and growth. Details of the geographical composition of the data set are shown in the first column of Table 2.1. Definitions and sources for all of the variables used in the paper are provided in a short data appendix, Table 2A.1

This data set forms a highly unbalanced and irregularly spaced panel of observations. While for a few countries continuous time series of annual observations on income distribution are available for long periods, for most countries only one or a handful

Table 2.1. *Sources for income distribution data*

	Number of observations		
	Total	Spaced sample	Changes
By source			
UNU-WIDER World Income Inequality Database	706	289	199
Deininger and Squire High Quality Sample	97	45	28
World Bank Poverty Monitoring Website	118	68	45
Lundberg and Squire (2000)	32	16	13
By region			
East Asia and Pacific	178	77	22
E. Europe and Central Asia	172	52	66
Latin America and Caribbean	160	88	95
Middle East/North Africa	41	31	24
South Asia	73	28	18
Sub-Saharan Africa	90	59	29
Other	239	83	31
Total	953	418	285

Notes: This table shows the four sources of data on income distribution on which we rely to construct estimates of mean incomes of the poor. Total refers to the total number of annual observations. Spaced sample refers to observations separated by at least 5 years from each other within countries. Changes refers to the source of the final year for each pair of observations for which it is possible to construct a 5-year change within countries in incomes of the poor.

Source: See text.

of observations are available, with a median number of observations per country of four. Since our interest is in growth over the medium-to-long run, and since we do not want the sample to be dominated by those countries where income distribution data happen to be more abundant, we filter the data as follows. For each country we begin with the first available observation, and then move forward in time until we encounter the next observation subject to the constraint that at least 5 years separate observations, until we have exhausted the available data for that country.[6] This results in an unbalanced and irregularly spaced panel of 418 country–year observations on mean income of the poor separated by at least 5 years within countries, and spanning 137 countries. The median number of observations per country in this reduced sample is three. In our econometric estimation (discussed in the following subsection) we restrict the sample further to the set of 285 observations covering ninety-two countries for which at least two spaced observations on mean income of the poor are available, so that we can consider within-country growth in mean incomes of the poor over periods of at least 5 years. The median length of these intervals is 6 years. When we consider the effects of additional control variables, the sample is slightly smaller and varies across specifications depending on data availability. The data sources and geographical composition of these different samples are shown in the second and third columns of Table 2.1.

As is well known there are substantial difficulties in comparing income distribution data across countries.[7] Countries differ in the coverage of the survey (national versus subnational), in the welfare measure (income versus consumption), the measure of income (gross versus net), and the unit of observation (individuals versus households). We are only able to very imperfectly adjust for these differences. We have restricted our sample to income distribution measures based on nationally representative surveys. For all surveys we have information on whether the welfare measure is income or consumption, and for the majority of these we also know whether the income measure is gross or net of taxes and transfers. While we do have information on whether the recipient unit is the individual or the household, for most of our observations we do not have information on whether the Lorenz curve refers to the fraction of individuals or the fraction of households.[8] As a result, this last piece of information is of little help in adjusting for methodological differences in measures of income distribution across countries. We, therefore, implement the following very crude adjustment for observable differences in survey type. We pool our sample of 418 observations separated by at least 5 years, and regress both the Gini coefficient and the first quintile share on a constant, a set of regional dummies, and dummy variables indicating whether the

[6] We prefer this method of filtering the data over the alternative of simply taking quinquennial or decadal averages since our method avoids the unnecessary introduction of noise into the timing of the distribution data and the other variables we consider. Since one of the most interesting of these, income growth, is very volatile, this mismatch in timing is potentially problematic.

[7] See Atkinson and Brandolini (1999) for a detailed discussion of these issues.

[8] This information is only available for the Chen–Ravallion data set which exclusively refers to individuals and for which the Lorenz curve is consistently constructed using the fraction of individuals on the horizontal axis.

Table 2.2. *Adjustments to Gini coefficients and income shares*

	Gini coefficient		**Income share of bottom quintile**	
	Coefficient	**Std. err.**	**Coefficient**	**Std. err.**
Constant	31.160	0.664 ***	0.072	0.002 ***
Gross income dummy	4.046	1.011 ***	−0.011	0.003 ***
Expenditure dummy	−1.397	1.412	0.002	0.003
East Asia and Pacific	4.673	1.088 ***	−0.001	0.003
E. Europe and Central Asia	−2.656	1.502 *	0.022	0.004 ***
Middle East/ North Africa	9.095	1.625 ***	−0.007	0.004
Latin America and Caribbean	15.550	1.015 ***	−0.023	0.003 ***
South Asia	3.519	1.502 **	0.009	0.004 **
Sub-Saharan Africa	16.186	1.772 ***	−0.018	0.005 ***

Notes: This table reports the results of a pooled OLS regression of the indicated inequality measures on the indicated variables. Standard errors are White-corrected for heteroskedasticity. *(**)(***) denote significance at the 10 (5) (1) per cent levels.

Source: See text.

welfare measure is gross income or whether it is consumption. We then subtract the estimated mean difference between these two alternatives and the omitted category to arrive at a set of distribution measures that notionally correspond to the distribution of income net of taxes and transfers.[9] The results of these adjustment regressions are reported in Table 2.2. As noted in the introduction however, it is clear that very substantial measurement error remains in this income distribution data, and so we cannot rule out the possibility that our failure to find significant determinants of the income share of the poorest quintile is due to this measurement error.

2.2.2. *Estimation*

In order to examine how incomes of the poor vary with overall incomes, we estimate variants of the following regression of the logarithm of per capita income of the poor (y^{P}) on the logarithm of average per capita income (y) and a set of additional control variables (X):

$$y_{ct}^{\mathrm{P}} = \alpha_0 + \alpha_1 \cdot y_{ct} + \alpha_2' X_{ct} + \mu_c + \varepsilon_{ct}, \tag{2.1}$$

[9] Our main results do not change substantially if we use three other possibilities: (1) ignoring differences in survey type, (2) including dummy variables for survey type as strictly exogenous right-hand-side variables in our regressions, or (3) adding country fixed effects to the adjustment regression so that the mean differences in survey type are estimated from the very limited within-country variation in survey type.

where c and t index countries and years, respectively, and $\mu_c + \varepsilon_{ct}$ is a composite error term including unobserved country effects. We have already seen the pooled version of eqn (2.1) with no control variables X_{ct} in the top panel of Fig. 2.1 above. Since incomes of the poor are equal to the first quintile share times average income divided by 0.2, it is clear that eqn (2.1) is identical to a regression of the log of the first quintile share on average income and a set of control variables:

$$\ln\left(\frac{Q1_{ct}}{0.2}\right) = \alpha_0 + (\alpha_1 - 1) \cdot y_{ct} + \alpha_2' X_{ct} + \mu_c + \varepsilon_{ct}. \quad (2.2)$$

Moreover, since empirically the log of the first quintile share is almost exactly a linear function of the Gini coefficient, eqn (2.1) is almost equivalent to a regression of a negative constant times the Gini coefficient on average income and a set of control variables.[10]

We are interested in two key parameters from eqn (2.1). The first is α_1, which measures the elasticity of income of the poor with respect to mean income. A value of $\alpha_1 = 1$ indicates that growth in mean income is translated one-for-one into growth in income of the poor. From eqn (2.2) this is equivalent to the observation that the share of income accruing to the poorest quintile does not vary systematically with average incomes ($\alpha_1 - 1 = 0$). Estimates of α_1 greater or less than one indicate that growth more than or less than proportionately benefits those in the poorest quintile. The second parameter of interest is α_2 which measures the impact of other determinants of income of the poor over and above their impact on mean income. Equivalently from eqn (2.2), α_2 measures the impact of these other variables on the share of income accruing to the poorest quintile, holding constant average incomes.

Simple ordinary least squares (OLS) estimation of eqn (2.1) using pooled country–year observations is likely to result in inconsistent parameter estimates for several reasons.[11] Measurement error in average incomes or the other control variables in eqn (2.1) will lead to biases that are difficult to sign except under very restrictive assumptions.[12] Since we consider only a fairly parsimonious set of right-hand-side variables in X, omitted determinants of the log quintile share that are correlated with either X or average incomes can also bias our results. Finally, there may be reverse causation from average incomes of the poor to average incomes, or equivalently from the log quintile share to average incomes, as suggested by the large empirical

[10] In our sample of spaced observations, a regression of the log first quintile share on the Gini coefficient delivers a slope of -23.3 with an R^2 of 0.80.

[11] It should also be clear that OLS standard errors will be inconsistent given the cross-observation correlations induced by the unobserved country-specific effect.

[12] While at first glance it may appear that measurement error in per capita income (which is also used to construct our measure of incomes of the poor) will bias the coefficient on per capita income towards one in eqn (2.1), this is not the case. From eqn (2.2) (which of course yields identical estimates of the parameters of interest as does eqn (2.1)) it is clear that we only have a problem to the extent that measurement error in the first quintile share is correlated with average incomes. Since our data on income distribution and average income are drawn from different sources, there is no a priori reason to expect such a correlation. When average income is taken from the same household survey, under plausible assumptions even measurement error in both variables will not lead to inconsistent coefficient estimates (Chen and Ravallion 1997).

literature which has examined the effects of income distribution on subsequent growth. This literature typically estimates growth regressions with a measure of initial income inequality as an explanatory variable, such as,

$$y_{ct} = \beta_0 + \rho \cdot y_{c,t-k} + \beta_1 \cdot \ln\left(\frac{Q1_{c,t-k}}{0.2}\right) + \beta_2' Z_{c,t-k} + \eta_c + v_{ct}. \qquad (2.3)$$

This literature has found mixed results using different sample and different econometric techniques. On the one hand, Alesina and Rodrik (1994), Persson and Tabellini (1994), Perotti (1996), Barro (2000), and Easterly (2001) find evidence of a negative effect of various measures of inequality on growth (i.e. $\beta_1 > 0$). On the other hand, Forbes (2000) and Li and Zou (1998) both find positive effects of income inequality on growth (i.e. $\beta_1 < 0$).[13] Whatever the true underlying relationship, it is clear that as long as β_1 is not equal to 0, OLS estimation of eqns (2.1) or (2.2) will yield inconsistent estimates of the parameters of interest. For example, high realizations of μ_c which result in higher incomes of the poor relative to mean income in eqn (2.1) will also raise (lower) mean incomes in eqn (2.3), depending on whether β_1 is greater than (less than) 0. This could induce an upwards (downwards) bias into estimates of the elasticity of incomes of the poor with respect to mean incomes in eqn (2.1).

A final issue in estimating eqn (2.1) is whether we want to identify the parameters of interest using the cross-country or the time-series variation in the data on incomes of the poor, mean incomes, and other variables. An immediate reaction to the presence of unobserved country-specific effects μ_c in eqn (2.1) is to estimate it in first differences.[14] The difficulty with this option is that it forces us to identify our effects of interest using the more limited time-series variation in incomes and income distribution.[15] This raises the possibility that the signal-to-noise ratio in the within-country variation in the data is too unfavourable to allow us to estimate our parameters of interest with any precision. In contrast, the advantage of estimating eqn (2.1) in levels is that we can exploit the large cross-country variation in incomes, income distribution, and policies to identify our effects of interest. The disadvantage of this approach is that the problem of omitted variables is more severe in the cross section, since in the differenced

[13] While we follow most of the empirical literature in specifying a linear relation between inequality and growth in eqn (2.3), it is worth noting that this need not be the case. Bannerjee and Duflo (1999) present some simple models and empirical evidence that changes in inequality in either direction lower growth. Galor and Moav (2001) develop a theoretical model in which inequality raises growth at low levels of development (where returns to physical capital are high, and so a reallocation of wealth to richer households with higher saving propensities raises growth), but lowers growth at higher levels of development (where returns to human capital are high, but a reallocation of wealth to richer households makes it more difficult for poor households to invest in education).

[14] Alternatively one could enter fixed effects, but this requires the much stronger assumption that the error terms are uncorrelated with the right-hand-side variables at all leads and lags.

[15] Li, Squire, and Zou (1998) document the much greater variability of income distribution across countries compared to within countries. In our sample of irregularly spaced observations, the standard deviation of the Gini coefficient pooling all observations in levels is 9.4. In contrast, the standard deviation of changes in the Gini coefficient is 4.7 (an average annual change of 0.67 times an average number of years over which the change is calculated of 7).

estimation we have at least managed to dispose of any time-invariant country-specific sources of heterogeneity.

Our solution to this dilemma is to implement a system estimator that combines information in both the levels and changes of the data.[16] In particular, we first difference eqn (2.1) to obtain growth in income of the poor in country c over the period from $t - k(c,t)$ to t as a function of growth in mean income over the same period, and changes in the X variables:

$$y^{\mathrm{P}}_{ct} - y^{\mathrm{P}}_{c,t-k(c,t)} = \alpha_1 \cdot \left(y_{ct} - y_{c,t-k(c,t)}\right) + \alpha_2'\left(X_{ct} - X_{c,t-k(c,t)}\right) + \left(\varepsilon_{ct} - \varepsilon_{c,t-k(c,t)}\right), \quad (2.4)$$

where $k(c,t)$ denotes the country- and year-specific length of the interval over which the growth rate is calculated. We then estimate eqns (2.1) and (2.4) as a system, imposing the restriction that the coefficients in the levels and differenced equation are equal. We address the three problems of measurement error, omitted variables, and endogeneity by using appropriate lags of right-hand-side variables as instruments. In particular, in eqn (2.1) we instrument for mean income using growth in mean income over the 5 years prior to time t. This preceding growth in mean income is by construction correlated with contemporaneous mean income, provided that ρ is not equal to zero in eqn (2.3). Given the vast body of evidence on conditional convergence, this assumption seems reasonable a priori, and we can test the strength of this correlation by examining the corresponding first-stage regressions. Differencing eqn (2.3) it is straightforward to see that past growth is also uncorrelated with the error term in eqn (2.1), provided that ε_{ct} is not correlated over time. In eqn (2.4) we instrument for growth in mean income using the level of mean income at the beginning of the period, and growth in the 5 years preceding $t - k(c,t)$. Both of these are by construction correlated with growth in mean income over the period from $t - k(c,t)$ to t. Moreover it is straightforward to verify that they are uncorrelated with the error term in eqn (2.4) using the same arguments as before.

In the version of eqn (2.1) without control variables, these instruments provide us with three moment conditions with which to identify two parameters, α_0 and α_1. We combine these moment conditions in a standard generalized method of moments (GMM) estimation procedure to obtain estimates of these parameters. In addition, we adjust the standard errors to allow for heteroskedasticity in the error terms as well as the first-order autocorrelation introduced into the error terms in eqn (2.4) by differencing. Since the model is overidentified we can test the validity of our assumptions that the instruments are uncorrelated with the error terms using tests of overidentifying restrictions.

When we introduce additional X variables into eqn (2.1) we also need to take a stand on whether to instrument for these as well. Difficulties with measurement error and omitted variables provide as compelling a reason to instrument for these variables as for income. It is also possible that at least some of the policy variables may respond

[16] This type of estimator has been proposed in a dynamic panel context by Arellano and Bover (1995) and evaluated by Blundell and Bond (1998).

endogenously to inequality.[17] Nevertheless, in what follows, we choose not to instrument for the X variables, for two reasons. First and pragmatically, using appropriate lags of these variables as instruments greatly reduces our sample size. Second, we take some comfort from the fact that tests of overidentifying restrictions pass in the specifications where we instrument for income only, providing indirect evidence that the X variables are not correlated with the error terms. In any case, we find qualitatively quite similar results in the smaller samples where we instrument, and so we only report selected instrumented results for brevity.

2.3. RESULTS

2.3.1. *Growth is Good for the Poor*

We start with our basic specification in which we regress the log of per capita income of the poor on the log of average per capita income, without other controls (eqn (2.1) with $\alpha_2 = 0$). The results of this basic specification are presented in detail in Table 2.3. The five columns in the top panel provide alternative estimates of eqn (2.1), in turn using information in the levels of the data, the differences of the data, and finally our preferred system estimator which combines the two. The first two columns show the results from estimating eqn (2.1) in levels, pooling all of the country–year observations, using OLS and single-equation two-stage least squares (2SLS), respectively. OLS gives a point estimate of the elasticity of income of the poor with respect to mean income of 1.07, which is (just) significantly greater than 1. As discussed in the previous section there are reasons to doubt the simple OLS results. When we instrument for mean income using growth in mean income over the five preceding years as an instrument, the estimated elasticity increases to 1.19. However, this elasticity is much less precisely estimated, and so we do not reject the null hypothesis that $\alpha_1 = 1$. In the first-stage regression for the levels equation, lagged growth is a highly significant predictor of the current level of income, which gives us some confidence in its validity as an instrument.

The third and fourth columns in the top panel of Table 2.3 show the results of OLS and 2SLS estimation of the differenced eqn (2.4). We obtain a point estimate of the elasticity of income of the poor with respect to mean income of 0.98 using OLS, and a slightly smaller elasticity of 0.91 when we instrument using lagged levels and growth rates of mean income. In both the OLS and 2SLS results we cannot reject the null hypothesis that the elasticity is equal to one. In the first-stage regression for the differenced equation (reported in the second column of the bottom panel), both lagged income and twice-lagged growth are highly significant predictors of growth. Moreover, the differenced equation is overidentified. When we test the validity of the overidentifying restrictions we do not reject the null of a well-specified model for the differenced equation alone at conventional significance levels.

In the last column of Table 2.3 we combine the information in the levels and differences in the system GMM estimator, using the same instruments as in the

[17] For example Easterly (2001) finds an effect of inequality on inflation and financial development, but not openness to international trade.

Table 2.3. *Basic specification*

	(1) Levels no inst	(2) Inst	(3) Differences no inst	(4) Inst	(5) System
Estimates of growth elasticity					
Intercept	−1.762	−2.720			−1.215
	(0.210) ***	(1.257) **			(0.629) *
Slope	1.072	1.187	0.983	0.913	1.008
	(0.025) ***	(0.150) ***	(0.076) ***	(0.106) ***	(0.076) ***
P-Ho: $\alpha_1 = 1$	0.004	0.213	0.823	0.412	0.916
P-OID				0.174	0.163
T-NOSC					−0.919
# Observations	269	269	269	269	269

	Dependent variable	
	ln (income)	Growth
First-stage regressions for system		
Intercept	8.238	
	(0.064) ***	
Lagged growth	0.956	
	(0.293) ***	
Lagged income		0.011
		(0.002) ***
Twice lagged growth		0.284
		(0.094) ***
p-Zero slopes	0.007	0.001

Notes: The top panel reports the results of estimating eqn (2.1) (columns 1 and 2), eqn (2.4) (columns 3 and 4), and the system estimator combining the two (column 5). OLS and IV refer to OLS and instrumental variables estimation of eqns (2.1) and (2.4). The bottom panel reports the corresponding first-stage regressions for IV estimation of eqns (2.1) and (2.4). The row labelled P-Ho: $\alpha_1 = 1$ reports the p-value associated with the test of the null hypothesis that $\alpha_1 = 1$. The row labelled P-OID reports the p-value associated with the test of overidentifying restrictions. The row labelled T-NOSC reports the t-statistic for the test of no second-order serial correlation in the differenced residuals. Standard errors are corrected for heteroskedasticity and for the first-order autocorrelation induced by first differencing using a standard Newey–West procedure. * (**) (***) denote significance at the 10 (5) (1) per cent levels.

Source: See text.

single-equation estimates reported earlier. The system estimator delivers a point estimate of the elasticity of 1.008, which is not significantly different from 1. Since the system estimator is based on minimizing a precision-weighted sum of the moment conditions from the levels and differenced data, the estimate of the slope is roughly an average of the slope of the levels and differenced equation, with somewhat more weight on the more-precisely estimated differenced estimate. Since our system estimator is overidentified, we can test and do not reject the null that the instruments are valid, in the sense of being uncorrelated with the corresponding error terms in eqns (2.1) and (2.4). Finally, the bottom panel of Table 2.3 reports the first-stage regressions underlying our estimator, and shows that our instruments have strong explanatory power for the potentially endogenous income and growth regressors.

We next consider a number of variants on this basic specification. First, we add regional dummies to the levels equation, and find that dummies for the East Asia and Pacific, Latin America, sub-Saharan Africa, and the Middle East and North Africa regions are negative and significant at the 10 per cent level or better (first column of Table 2.4). Since the omitted category consists of the rich countries of Western Europe plus Canada and the United States, these dummies reflect higher average levels of inequality in these regions relative to the rich countries. Including these regional dummies reduces the estimate of the elasticity of average incomes of the poor with respect to average incomes slightly to 0.91, but we still cannot reject the null hypothesis that the slope of this relationship is equal to one (the p-value for the test of this hypothesis is 0.313, and is shown in the fourth last row of Table 2.4). We keep the regional dummies in all subsequent regressions.

Next we add a time trend to the regression, in order to capture the possibility that there has been a secular increase or decrease over time in the share of income accruing to the poorest quintile (second column of Table 2.4). The coefficient on the time trend is statistically insignificant, indicating the absence of systematic evidence of a trend in the share of income of the bottom quintile. Moreover, in this specification we find a point estimate of $\alpha_1 = 1.00$, indicating that average incomes in the bottom quintile rise exactly proportionately with average incomes.

A closely related question is whether the elasticity of incomes of the poor with respect to average incomes has changed over time. In order to allow for the possibility that growth has become either more or less pro-poor in recent years, we augment the basic regression with interactions of income with dummies for the 1970s, 1980s, and 1990s. The omitted category is the 1960s, and so the estimated coefficients on the interaction terms capture differences in the relationship between average incomes and the share of the poorest quintile relative to this base period. We find that none of these interactions are significant, consistent with the view that the inequality–growth relationship has not changed significantly over time. We again cannot reject the null hypothesis that $\alpha_1 = 1$ ($p = 0.455$).

In the next two columns of Table 2.4 we examine whether the slope of the relationship between average incomes and incomes of the poorest quintile differs significantly by region or by income level. We first add interactions of each of the regional dummies with average income, in order to allow for the possibility that the effects of growth on the share of income accruing to the poorest quintile differ by region. We find that the coefficients on these interactions with average income all enter negatively, indicating that the elasticity of incomes of the poor with respect to average incomes is highest in the omitted category of the rich countries. In two regions (East Asia/Pacific and Latin America/Caribbean) we find significantly lower slopes than the omitted category of the rich countries. However, we cannot reject at the 5 per cent significance level the

Table 2.4. *Variants on the basic specification*

	Regional dummies		Regional dummies common trend		Regional dummies slopes differ by decade		Regional dummies slopes differ by region		Regional dummies slopes differ with income		Regional dummies slopes differ +/− growth	
	Coef	Std. err.	Coef	Std. err.	Coef	Std. err.	Coef	Std. err.	Coef	Std. err.	Coef	Std. err.
Constant	−0.114	0.876	−0.050	4.824	−0.465	0.698	−4.308	1.421 ***	−0.762	0.815	−1.254	0.647 *
ln(per capita GDP)	**0.905**	**0.094** ***	**1.003**	**0.139** ***	**0.941**	**0.079** ***	**1.355**	**0.153** ***	**0.988**	**0.196** ***	1.027	0.070 ***
EAP	−0.168	0.102 *	−0.079	0.143	−0.127	0.088	3.733	1.568 **	−0.103	0.064	−0.050	0.081
ECA	−0.023	0.147	0.085	0.202	0.003	0.131	2.965	3.944	0.050	0.115	0.132	0.109
LAC	−0.618	0.121 ***	−0.512	0.166 ***	−0.572	0.101 ***	8.244	3.083 ***	−0.542	0.095 ***	−0.490	0.095 ***
MENA	−0.275	0.140 **	−0.152	0.199	−0.246	0.118 **	2.213	2.380	−0.189	0.100 *	−0.127	0.109
SA	−0.079	0.208	0.128	0.311	0.000	0.166	2.615	1.616	0.055	0.135	0.185	0.154
SSA	−0.685	0.288 **	−0.369	0.355	−0.550	0.243 **	2.111	2.008	−0.422	0.170 **	−0.384	0.210 *
Time			0.000	0.003								
$y \times$ 1970s					−0.001	0.008						
$y \times$ 1980s					0.003	0.010						
$y \times$ 1990s					0.005	0.010						
$y \times$ EAP							−0.413	0.173 **				
$y \times$ ECA							−0.290	0.474				
$y \times$ LAC							−1.019	0.368 ***				
$y \times$ MENA							−0.243	0.285				
$y \times$ SA							−0.239	0.188				
$y \times$ SSA							−0.230	0.256				
$y \times y90$									−0.001	0.013		
$y \times$ (dummy negative growth)											0.009	0.008
P-Ho: $\alpha_1 = 1$	**0.313**		**0.983**		**0.455**		**0.020**		**0.949**		**0.694**	
P-OID	0.390		0.240		0.126		0.133		0.209		0.174	
T-NOSC	−0.948		−0.921		−0.938		−1.571		−0.932		−0.907	
# Observations	269		269		269		269		269		269	

Notes: The row labelled P-Ho: $\alpha_1 = 1$ reports the p-value associated with the test of the null hypothesis that $\alpha_1 = 1$. The row labelled P-OID reports the p-value associated with the test of overidentifying restrictions. The row labelled T-NOSC reports the t-statistic for the test of no second-order serial correlation in the differenced residuals. Standard errors are corrected for heteroskedasticity and for the first-order autocorrelation induced by first differencing using a standard Newey–West procedure. * (**) (***) denote significance at the 10 (5) (1) per cent levels.

Source: See text.

null hypotheses that all of the region-specific slopes are individually or jointly equal to one.[18]

Another hypothesis regarding the deviations from our general relationship is the Kuznets' hypothesis which suggests that inequality rises at low levels of development and only declines as countries pass a certain threshold level of income. In order to allow the relationship between income and the share of the bottom quintile to vary with the level of development, we interact average incomes in eqn (2.1) with real GDP per capita in 1990 for each country. When we do this, we find no evidence that the relationship is significantly different in rich and poor countries, contrary to the Kuznets' (1955) hypothesis that inequality increases with income at low levels of development.

In the last column of Table 2.4 we ask whether the relationship between growth in average incomes and incomes of the poor is different during periods of negative and positive growth. This allows for the possibility that the costs of economic crises are borne disproportionately by poor people. We add an interaction term of average incomes with a dummy variable which takes the value 1 when growth in average incomes is negative. These episodes certainly qualify as economic crises since they correspond to negative average annual growth over a period of at least 5 years. However, the interaction term is tiny and statistically indistinguishable from zero, indicating that there is no evidence that the share of income that goes to the poorest quintile systematically rises or falls during periods of negative growth. Of course, it could still be the case that the same proportional decline in income has a greater impact on the poor if social safety nets are weak, and so crises may well be harder on the poor. But this is not because their incomes tend to fall more than those of other segments of society. A good illustration of this general observation is the recent financial crisis in East Asia in 1997. In Indonesia, the income share of the poorest quintile actually *increased* slightly between 1996 and 1999, from 8.0 to 9.0 per cent, and in Thailand from 6.1 to 6.4 per cent between 1996 and 1998, while in Korea it remained essentially unchanged after the crisis relative to before.

2.3.2. *Growth Determinants and Incomes of the Poor*

The previous section has documented that average incomes in the bottom quintile tend to rise equiproportionately with average incomes. This finding suggests that a range of policies and institutions that are associated with higher growth will also benefit the poor proportionately. However, it is possible that growth from different sources has differential impact on the poor. In this section we take a number of the measures of policies and institutions that have been identified as pro-growth in the empirical growth

[18] The estimated coefficients imply an elasticity of incomes of the poor with respect to average incomes in Latin America of 0.33 which is very low. This somewhat surprising result appears not to be very robust and may be attributable to the unusually poor performance of our instruments in this particular subsample of countries. Uninstrumented results for this region alone produce a slope of 0.98 with a standard error of 0.06, which is more consistent with our priors. Moreover, Foster and Székely (2001) find an elasticity of average incomes of the bottom quintile with respect to average incomes statistically indistinguishable from one in a sample consisting primarily of Latin American countries.

literature, and examine whether there is any evidence that any of these variables has disproportionate effects on the poorest quintile. The five indicators that we focus on are inflation, which Fischer (1993) finds to be bad for growth; government consumption, which Easterly and Rebelo (1993) find to be bad for growth; exports and imports relative to GDP, which Frankel and Romer (1999) find to be good for growth; a measure of financial development, which Levine, Loayza, and Beck (2000) have shown to have important causal effects on growth; and a measure of the strength of property rights or rule of law. The particular measure is from Kaufmann, Kraay, and Zoido-Lobatón (1999).[19] The importance of property rights for growth has been established by, among others, Knack and Keefer (1995).

First, we take the basic regression from the first column of Table 2.4 and add these variables one at a time (shown in the first five columns of Table 2.5). Since mean income is included in each of these regressions, the effect of these variables that works through overall growth is already captured there. The coefficient on the growth determinant itself, therefore, captures any differential impact that this variable has on the income of the poor, or equivalently, on the share of income accruing to the poor. In the case of trade volumes, we find a small, negative, and statistically insignificant effect on the income share of the bottom quintile. The same is true for government consumption as a share of GDP, and inflation, where higher values of both are associated with lower income shares of the poorest quintile, although again insignificantly so. The point estimates of the coefficients on the measure of financial development and on rule of law indicate that both of these variables are associated with higher income shares in the poorest quintile, but again, each of these effects is statistically indistinguishable from zero. When we include all five measures together, the coefficients on each are similar to those in the simpler regressions. However, government consumption as a share of GDP now has an estimated effect on the income share of the poorest that is negative and significant at the 10 per cent level. In addition, inflation continues to have a negative effect, which just falls short of significance at the 10 per cent level.[20]

Finally, in the last column of Table 2.5, we report results which treat these measures of policy as endogenous to the income share of the poorest quintile, and use appropriate lags of these policy variables as instruments. As discussed above, this substantially reduces our sample size. However, we find results that are qualitatively not too different in this smaller sample. The main differences are that the negative effect of inflation becomes larger and more significant, while the effect of government consumption changes sign and becomes insignificant. Since we find throughout the rest of this

[19] This particular measure of institutional quality refers to the period 1997–98 and does not vary over time. We, therefore, can only identify the effects of this variable using the cross-country variation in our data using the levels equation.

[20] This particular result is primarily driven by a small number of very high inflation episodes in our sample. However, it is consistent with several existing findings: Agenor (1998) finds an adverse effect of inflation on the poverty rate, using a cross section of thirty-eight countries; Easterly and Fischer (2000) show that the poor are more likely to rate inflation as a top national concern, using survey data on 31,869 households in thirty-eight countries; and Datt and Ravallion (1999) find evidence that inflation is a significant determinant of poverty using data for Indian states.

Table 2.5. *Growth determinants and incomes of the poor*

	Trade volumes		Government consumption/GDP		log(1+inflation rate)		Financial development		Rule of law index		All growth variables		All growth variables, instrument	
	Coef	Std. err.	Coef	Std. err.	Coef	Std. err.	Coef	Std. err.	Coef	Std. err.	Coef	Std. err.	Coef	Std. err.
ln(per capita GDP)	**1.094**	**0.108** ***	**1.050**	**0.085** ***	**1.020**	**0.089** ***	**0.995**	**0.119** ***	**0.914**	**0.105** ***	**1.140**	**0.100** ***	**1.020**	**0.128** ***
(Exports+Imports)/ GDP	−0.039	0.088									0.023	0.056	−0.067	0.208
Government consumption/GDP			−0.571	0.419							−0.746	0.386 *	0.401	1.013
ln(1+inflation)					−0.136	0.103					−0.163	0.107	−0.216	0.077 ***
Commercial bank assets/Total bank assets							0.032	0.257			−0.209	0.172	0.264	0.282
Rule of law									0.084	0.069	−0.032	0.060	−0.011	0.071
P-Ho: $\alpha_1 = 1$	**0.386**		**0.555**		**0.825**		**0.968**		**0.412**		**0.164**		**0.876**	
P-OID	0.257		0.168		0.159		0.350		0.279		0.393		0.716	
T-NOSC	−0.751		−0.506		−0.261		−0.698		−0.945		−0.762		−0.563	
# Observations	223		237		253		232		268		189		137	

Notes: All regressions include regional dummies. The row labelled P-Ho: $\alpha_1 = 1$ reports the p-value associated with the test of the null hypothesis that $\alpha_1 = 1$. The row labelled P-OID reports the p-value associated with the test of overidentifying restrictions. The row labelled T-NOSC reports the t-statistic for the test of no second-order serial correlation in the differenced residuals. Standard errors are corrected for heteroskedasticity and for the first-order autocorrelation induced by first differencing using a standard Newey–West procedure. * (**) (***) denote significance at the 10 (5) (1) per cent levels.

Source: See text.

chapter that instrumented and uninstrumented results are generally quite similar, for reasons of space we report only the uninstrumented results below.

Our empirical specification only allows us to identify any differential effect of these macroeconomic and institutional variables on incomes of the poor relative to average incomes. What about the overall effect of these variables, which combines their effects on growth with their effects on income distribution? In order to answer this question we also require estimates of the effects of these variables on growth based on a regression like eqn (2.3). Since eqn (2.3) includes a measure of income inequality as one of the determinants of growth, we estimate it using the same panel of irregularly spaced data on average incomes and other variables that we have been using thus far.[21] Clearly, this limited data set is not ideal for estimating growth regressions, since our sample is very restricted by the relative scarcity of income distribution data. Nevertheless, it is useful to estimate this equation in our data set for consistency with the previous results, and also to verify that the main findings of the cross-country literature on economic growth are present in our sample.

We include in the vector of additional explanatory variables a measure of the stock of human capital (years of secondary schooling per worker) as well as the five growth determinants from Table 2.5. We also include the human capital measure in order to make our growth regression comparable to that of Forbes (2000) who applies similar econometric techniques in a similar panel data set in order to study the effect of inequality on growth. In order to reduce concerns about endogeneity of these variables with respect to growth, we enter each of them as an average over the 5 years prior to year $t - k$. We estimate the growth regression in eqn (2.3) using the same system estimator that combines information in the levels and differences of the data, although our choice of lags as instruments is slightly different from before.[22]

In the levels equation, we instrument for lagged income with growth in the preceding 5 years, and we do not need to instrument for the remaining growth determinants under the assumption that they are predetermined with respect to the error term v_{ct}. In the differenced equation we instrument for lagged growth with the twice-lagged log-level of income, and for the remaining variables with their twice-lagged levels.

The results of this growth regression are reported in the first column of Table 2.6. Most of the variables enter significantly and with the expected signs. Secondary education, financial development, and better rule of law are all positively and significantly associated with growth. Higher levels of government consumption and inflation are both negatively associated with growth, although only the former is statistically

[21] Since our panel is irregularly spaced, the coefficient on lagged income in the growth regression should in principle be a function of the length of the interval over which growth is calculated. There are two ways to address this issue. In what follows below, we simply restrict attention to the vast majority of our observations which correspond to growth spells between 5 and 7 years long, and then ignore the dependence of this coefficient on the length of the growth interval. The alternative approach is to introduce this dependence explicity by assuming that the coefficient on lagged income is $\rho^{k(c,\,t)}$. Doing so yields very similar results to those reported here.

[22] See, for example, Levine, Loayza, and Beck (2000) for a similar application of this econometric technique to cross-country growth regressions.

Table 2.6. *Growth and distribution effects*

	Growth regression		Income of poor regression		Standard deviation	Growth effect	Distribution effect
	Coef	Std. err.	Coef	Std. err.			
Income			1.140	0.101 ***			
Lagged income	0.668	0.169 ***					
Lagged inequality	−0.089	0.062					
Secondary education	0.097	0.057 *					
Trade volumes	0.045	0.074	0.024	0.056	0.280	0.035	0.012
Inflation	−0.145	0.131	−0.162	0.107	0.275	−0.104	−0.059
Government consumption	−0.973	0.415 **	−0.744	0.387 *	0.054	−0.143	−0.060
Financial development	0.374	0.167 **	−0.208	0.172	0.153	0.175	−0.007
Rule of law	0.180	0.082 **	−0.032	0.060	0.250	0.133	0.011

Notes: The first two columns report the results obtained from adding the indicated control variables to eqn (2.1) and applying the system estimator described in the text. The third and fourth columns report the results of applying the same system estimator to the growth regression in eqn (2.3). The remaining columns show the growth and distribution effects on incomes of the poor of a one-standard deviation increase in each of the explanatory variables, as discussed in the text. Standard errors are corrected for heteroskedasticity and for the first-order autocorrelation induced by first differencing using a standard Newey–West procedure. * (**) (***) denote significance at the 10 (5) (1) per cent levels.

Source: See text.

significant. Trade volumes are positively associated with growth, although not significantly so, possibly reflecting the relatively small sample on which the estimates are based (the sample of observations is considerably smaller than in Table 2.5 given the requirement of additional lags of right-hand-side variables to use as instruments). Interestingly, the log of the first quintile share enters negatively (although not significantly), consistent with the finding of Forbes (2000) that greater inequality is associated with higher growth.

We next combine these estimates with the estimates of eqn (2.1) to arrive at the cumulative effect of these growth determinants on incomes of the poor. From eqn (2.1) we can express the effect of a permanent increase in each of the growth determinants on the level of average incomes of the poor as

$$\frac{\partial y_{ct}^{\mathrm{P}}}{\partial X_{ct}} = \frac{\partial y_{ct}}{\partial X_{ct}} + \left((\alpha_1 - 1) \cdot \frac{\partial y_{ct}}{\partial X_{ct}} + \alpha_2 \right), \tag{2.5}$$

where $\partial y_{ct}/\partial X_{ct}$ denotes the impact on average incomes of this permanent change in X. The first term captures the effect on incomes of the poor of a change in one of the determinants of growth, holding constant the distribution of income. We refer to this as the 'growth effect' of this variable. The second term captures the effects of a change in one of the determinants of growth on incomes of the poor through changes in the distribution of income. This consists of two pieces: (i) the difference between the estimated income elasticity and one times the growth effect, that is, the extent to which growth in average incomes raises or lowers the share of income accruing to the poorest quintile; and (ii) the direct effects of policies on incomes of the poor in eqn (2.1).

In order to evaluate eqn (2.5) we need an expression for the growth effect term. We obtain this by solving eqns (2.1) and (2.3) for the dynamics of average income, and obtain

$$\begin{aligned} y_{ct} = \beta_0 + \beta_1 \cdot \alpha_0 + (\rho + \beta_1 \cdot \alpha_1) \cdot y_{c,\, t-k} + (\beta_1 \cdot \alpha_2 + \beta_2)' X_{c,\, t-k} \\ + \eta_c + \beta_1 \cdot \mu_c + v_{ct} + \beta_1 \cdot \varepsilon_{ct}. \end{aligned} \tag{2.6}$$

Iterating eqn (2.6) forward, we find that the estimated long-run effect on the level of income of a permanent change in one of the elements in X is:

$$\frac{\partial y_{ct}}{\partial X_{ct}} = \frac{\beta_1 \cdot \alpha_2 + \beta_2}{1 - (\rho + \beta_1 \cdot \alpha_2)}. \tag{2.7}$$

The remaining columns of Table 2.6 put all these pieces together. The second column repeats the results reported in the final column of Table 2.5. The next column reports the standard deviations of each of the variables of interest, so that we can calculate the impact on incomes of the poor of a one-standard deviation permanent increase in each variable.[23] The remaining columns report the growth and distribution effects of these changes, which are also summarized graphically in Fig. 2.2. The main story here is

[23] The only exception is the rule of law index which by construction has a standard deviation of one. Since perceptions of the rule of law tend to change only very slowly over time, we consider a smaller change of 0.25, which still delivers very large estimated growth effects.

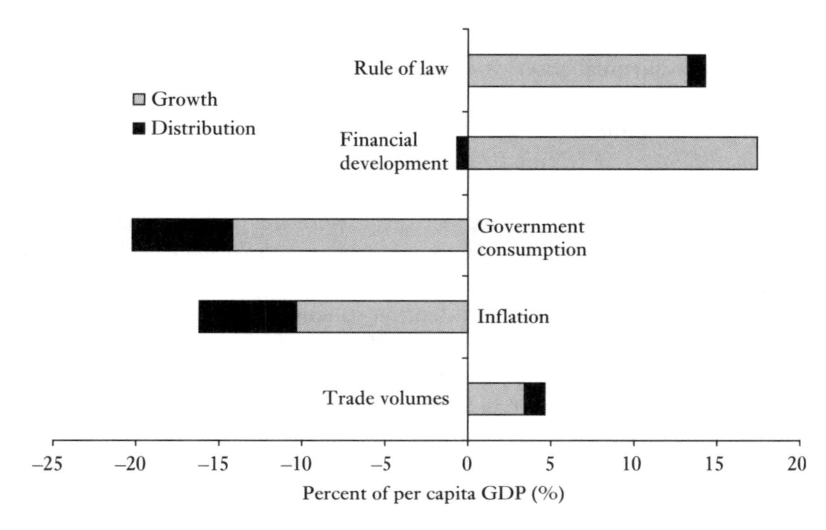

Figure 2.2. *Growth and distribution effects of policies*

that the growth effects are large and the distribution effects are small. Improvements in rule of law and greater financial development of the magnitudes considered here, as well as reductions in government consumption and lower inflation all raise incomes in the long run by 15–20 per cent. The point estimate for more trade openness is at the low end of existing results in the literature: about 5 per cent increase in income from a one standard deviation increase in openness. This should, therefore, be viewed as a rather conservative estimate of the benefit of openness on incomes of the poor. In contrast, the effects of these policies that operate through their effects on changes in the distribution of income are much smaller in magnitude, and with the exception of financial development work in the same direction as the growth effects.

2.3.3. *Globalization and the Poor*

One possibly surprising result in Table 2.5 is the lack of any evidence of a significant negative impact of openness to international trade on incomes of the poor. While this is consistent with the finding of Edwards (1997) who also finds no evidence of a relationship between various measures of trade openness and inequality in a sample of 44 countries, a number of other recent papers have found evidence that openness is associated with higher inequality. Barro (2000) finds that trade volumes are significantly positively associated with the Gini coefficient in a sample of 64 countries, and that the disequalizing effect of openness is greater in poor countries. In a panel data set of 320 irregularly spaced annual observations covering 34 countries, Spilimbergo, Londoño, and Székely (1999) find that several measures of trade openness are associated with higher inequality, and that this effect is lower in countries where land and capital are abundant and higher where skills are abundant. Lundberg and Squire (2000) consider a panel of 119 quinquennial observations covering thirty-eight countries and find that an increase from 0 to 1 in the Sachs–Warner openness index is associated with a 9.5 point increase in the Gini index, which is significant at the 10 per cent level.

Several factors may contribute to the difference between these findings and ours, including (i) differences in the measure of inequality (all the previous studies consider the Gini index while we focus on the income share of the poorest quintile, although given the high correlation between the two this factor is least likely to be important); (ii) differences in the sample of countries (with the exception of the paper by Barro, all of the papers cited above restrict attention to considerably smaller and possibly non-representative samples of countries than the seventy-six countries which appear in our basic openness regression, and in addition the paper by Spilimbergo *et al.* uses all available annual observations on inequality with the result that countries with regular household surveys tend to be heavily overrepresented in the sample of pooled observations); (iii) differences in the measure of openness (Lundberg and Squire 2000, for example, focus on the Sachs–Warner index of openness which has been criticized for proxying the overall policy environment rather than openness *per se*[24]); (iv) differences in econometric specification and technique.

A complete accounting of which of these factors contribute to the differences in results is beyond the scope of this short section. However, several obvious extensions of our basic model can be deployed to make our specification more comparable to these other studies. First, we consider several different measures of openness, some of which correspond more closely with those used in the other studies mentioned above. We first (like Spilimbergo, Londoño, and Székely 1999; Barro 2000) purge our measure of trade volumes of the geographical determinants of trade, by regressing it on a trade-weighted measure of distance from trading partners, and a measure of country size and taking the residuals as an adjusted measure of trade volumes.[25]

Since these geographical factors are time invariant, this will only influence our results to the extent that they are driven by the cross-country variation in the data and to the extent that these geographical determinants of trade volumes are also correlated with the share of income of the poorest quintile. Second, we use the Sachs–Warner index in order to compare our results more closely with those of Lundberg and Squire (2000). Finally, we also consider three other measures of openness not considered by the above authors: collected import taxes as a share of imports, a dummy variable taking the value one if the country is a member of the World Trade Organization (or its predecessor the GATT), and a dummy variable taking the value one if the country has restrictions on international capital movements as reported in the International Monetary Fund's Report on Exchange Arrangements and Exchange Controls.

We also consider two variants on our basic specification. First, in order to capture the possibility that greater openness has differential effects at different levels of

[24] See, for example, the criticism of Rodriguez and Rodrik (2000), who note that most of the explanatory power of the Sachs–Warner index derives from the components that measure the black market premium on foreign exchange and whether the state holds a monopoly on exports.

[25] Specifically, we use the instrument proposed by Frankel and Romer (1999) and the logarithm of population in 1990 as right-hand-side variables in a pooled OLS regression.

development, we introduce an interaction of the openness measures with the log-level of real GDP per capita in 1990 for each country. Given the high correlation in levels between per capita income and capital per worker, this interaction may be thought of as capturing in a very crude way the possibility that the effects of trade on inequality depend on countries' relative factor abundance. The second elaboration we consider is to add an interaction of openness with the logarithm of arable land per capita, as well as adding this variable directly. This allows a more general formulation of the hypothesis that the effects of openness depend on countries' factor endowments.

The results of these extensions are presented in Table 2.7. Each of the columns of Table 2.7 corresponds to a different measure of openness, and the three horizontal panels correspond to the three variants discussed above. Two main results emerge from this table. First, in all of the specifications considered below, we continue to find that average incomes of the poor rise proportionately with average incomes: in each regression, we do not reject the null hypothesis that the coefficient on average incomes is equal to one. This indicates that our previous results on the lack of any significant association between average incomes and the log first quintile share are robust to the inclusion of these additional control variables. Second, we find no evidence whatsoever of a significant negative relationship between any of these measures of openness and average incomes of the poor. In all but one case, we cannot reject the null hypothesis that the relevant openness measure is not significantly associated with the income share of the bottom quintile, holding constant average incomes. The only exception to this overall pattern is the measure of capital controls, where the presence of capital controls is significantly (at the 10 per cent level) associated with a *lower* income share of the poorest quintile. Overall, however, we conclude from this table that there is very little evidence of a significant relationship between the income share of the poorest quintile and a wide range of measures of exposure to the international economy. The only other finding of interest in this table is unrelated to the question of openness and incomes of the poor. In the bottom panel where we include arable land per capita and its interaction with openness measures, we find some evidence that countries with greater arable land per worker have a lower income share of the poorest quintile. This is consistent with Leamer *et al.* (1999) who find that cropland per capita is significantly associated with higher inequality in a cross section of forty-nine countries.

2.3.4. *Other Determinants of Incomes of the Poor*

Finally, we consider a number of other factors that may have direct effects on incomes of the poor through their effect on income distribution (Table 2.8). We consider four such variables: primary educational attainment, social spending, agricultural productivity, and formal democratic institutions. Of these four variables, only the primary education variable tends to be significantly correlated with economic growth, and even here recent evidence suggests that much of this correlation reflects reverse causation from growth to greater schooling (Bils and Klenow 2000).

However, these policies may be especially important for the poor. Consider for example primary enrolment rates. Most of the countries in the sample are developing countries in which deviations from complete primary school enrolments are most likely

Table 2.7. *Openness and incomes of the poor*

	Trade volumes		Adjusted trade volumes		Sachs–Warner trade policy index		Import taxes as share of imports		Dummy for WTO membership		Dummy for capital controls	
	Coef	Std. err.	Coef	Std. err.	Coef	Std. err.	Coef	Std. err.	Coef	Std. err.	Coef	Std. err.
Basic												
ln(per capita GDP)	**1.094**	**0.108** ***	**1.047**	**0.133** ***	**1.077**	**0.092** ***	**0.936**	**0.136** ***	**0.917**	**0.104** ***	**0.869**	**0.116** ***
Openness measure	−0.039	0.088	−0.038	0.167	−0.071	0.065	−0.161	0.358	0.021	0.043	−0.090	0.051 *
P-Ho: $\alpha_1 = 1$	0.386		0.724		0.407		0.638		0.428		0.259	
P-OID	0.257		0.135		0.431		0.074		0.425		0.183	
T-NOSC	−0.751		−0.767		−0.677		1.263		−0.998		−1.084	
# Observations	223		213		234		137		269		208	
Interaction with per capita GDP												
ln(per capita GDP)	**1.102**	**0.092** ***	**0.991**	**0.126** ***	**1.066**	**0.076** ***	**1.013**	**0.082** ***	**1.012**	**0.078** ***	**0.969**	**0.084** ***
Openness measure	−0.323	1.363	1.188	1.601	0.237	0.573	0.604	3.133	−0.026	0.558	−0.515	0.587
Openness measure × ln(per capita GDP)	0.030	0.146	−0.123	0.169	−0.036	0.072	−0.085	0.396	0.002	0.070	0.052	0.064
P-Ho: $\alpha_1 = 1$	**0.267**		**0.942**		**0.386**		**0.873**		**0.876**		**0.708**	
P-OID	0.218		0.144		0.567		0.126		0.226		0.121	
T-NOSC	−0.742		−0.816		−0.696		1.253		−0.905		−1.005	
# Observations	223		213		234		137		269		208	
Interaction with per capita GDP and land												
ln(per capita GDP)	**1.120**	**0.105** ***	**0.901**	**0.099** ***	**1.046**	**0.084** ***	**1.063**	**0.083** ***	**1.101**	**0.072** ***	**1.009**	**0.081** ***
Openness measure	0.304	1.780	1.161	1.485	0.109	0.605	2.552	2.858	0.513	0.569	−0.574	0.607
ln(arable land/worker)	−0.090	0.031 ***	−0.086	0.023 ***	−0.018	0.032	−0.037	0.029	−0.054	0.039	−0.038	0.025
Openness measure × ln(per capita GDP)	−0.036	0.198	−0.074	0.170	−0.024	0.075	−0.378	0.385	−0.066	0.072	0.050	0.066
Openness measure × ln(arable land/worker)	0.061	0.070	0.245	0.111 **	−0.041	0.035	−0.366	0.262	0.016	0.039	−0.023	0.031
P-Ho: $\alpha_1 = 1$	0.253		0.322		0.582		0.443		0.163		0.915	
P-OID	0.030		0.062		0.267		0.082		0.208		0.095	
T-NOSC	−0.755		−0.896		−1.134		0.421		−1.019		−1.492	
# Observations	207		207		219		131		243		193	

Notes: All regressions include regional dummies. The row labelled P-Ho: $\alpha_1 = 1$ reports the p-value associated with the test of the null hypothesis that $\alpha_1 = 1$. The row labelled P-OID reports the p-value associated with the test of overidentifying restrictions. The row labelled T-NOSC reports the t-statistic for the test of no second-order serial correlation in the differenced residuals. Standard errors are corrected for heteroskedasticity and for the first-order autocorrelation induced by first differencing using a standard Newey–West procedure. * (**) (***) denote significance at the 10 (5) (1) per cent levels.

Source: See text.

Table 2.8. *Other determinants of incomes of the poor*

	Years primary education		Social spending		Agricultural productivity		Voice		Voice with macro controls	
	Coef	Std. err.	Coef	Std. err.	Coef	Std. err.	Coef	Std. err.	Coef	Std. err.
ln(per capita GDP)	**1.067**	**0.088** ***	**1.025**	**0.101** ***	**0.985**	**0.104** ***	**0.933**	**0.095** ***	**1.117**	**0.098** ***
Years primary education	0.014	0.031								
Government consumption/GDP			−1.553	0.547 ***						
Social spending/total public spending			−0.664	0.429						
Agricultural relative productivity					0.060	0.081				
Voice							0.095	0.053 *	0.029	0.058
P-Ho: $\alpha_1 = 1$	**0.448**		**0.803**		**0.886**		**0.480**		**0.233**	
P-OID	0.213		0.028		0.166		0.302		0.419	
T-NOSC	−0.384		0.594		−0.837		−0.970		−0.767	
# Observations	222		111		197		265		207	

Notes: All regressions include regional dummies. The row labelled P-Ho: $\alpha_1 = 1$ reports the p-value associated with the test of the null hypothesis that $\alpha_1 = 1$. The row labelled P-OID reports the p-value associated with the test of overidentifying restrictions. The row labelled T-NOSC reports the t-statistic for the test of no second-order serial correlation in the differenced residuals. Standard errors are corrected for heteroskedasticity and for the first-order autocorrelation induced by first differencing using a standard Newey–West procedure. * (**) (***) denote significance at the 10 (5) (1) per cent levels.

Source: See text.

to reflect the low enrolment among the poorest in society. This, in turn, may be an important factor influencing the extent to which the poor participate in growth. Similarly, depending on the extent to which public spending on health and education is effective and well-targeted towards poor people, a greater share of social spending in public spending can be associated with better outcomes for poor people. Greater labour productivity in agriculture relative to the rest of the economy may benefit poor people disproportionately to the extent that the poor are more likely to live in rural areas and derive their livelihood from agriculture. And finally, formal democratic institutions may matter to the extent that they give voice to poor people in the policy-making process.

Table 2.8 reports the results we obtain adding these variables to the basic specification of Table 2.4. We find that while years of primary education and relative productivity in agriculture both enter positively, neither is significant at conventional levels. In the regression with social spending, we also include overall government consumption in order to capture both the level and compositional effects of public spending. Overall government spending remains negatively associated with incomes of the poor, and the share of this spending devoted to health and education does not enter significantly. This may not be very surprising, since in many developing countries, these social expenditures often benefit the middle class and the rich primarily, and the simple share of public spending on the social sectors is not a good measure of whether government policy and spending is particularly pro-poor.[26] Finally, the measure of formal democratic institutions enters positively and significantly (although only at the 10 per cent level). However, this result is not very robust. In our large sample of developed and developing countries, measures of formal democratic institutions tend to be significantly correlated with other aspects of institutional quality, especially the rule of law index considered earlier. When we include the other growth determinants in the regression, the coefficient on the index of democratic institutions is no longer significant.

2.4. CONCLUSIONS

Average incomes of the poorest fifth of a country on average rise or fall at the same rate as average incomes. This is a consequence of the strong empirical regularity that the share of income of the poorest fifth does not vary systematically with average incomes, in a large sample of countries spanning the past four decades. This relationship holds across regions and income levels, and in normal times as well as during crises. We also find that a variety of pro-growth macroeconomic policies, such as low inflation, moderate size of government, sound financial development, respect for the rule of law, and

[26] Existing evidence on the effects of social spending is mixed. Bidani and Ravallion (1997) do find a statistically significant impact of health expenditures on the poor (defined in absolute terms as the share of the population with income below one dollar per day) in a cross-section of thirty-five developing countries, using a different methodology. Gouyette and Pestiau (1999) find a simple bivariate association between income inequality and social spending in a set of thirteen OECD economies. In contrast Filmer and Pritchett (1997) find little relationship between public health spending and health outcomes such as infant mortality, raising questions about whether such spending benefits the poor.

openness to international trade, raise average incomes with little systematic effect on the distribution of income. This supports the view that a basic policy package of private property rights, fiscal discipline, macroeconomic stability, and openness to trade on average increases the income of the poor to the same extent that it increases the income of the other households in society. It is worth emphasizing that our evidence does not suggest a 'trickle down' process or sequencing in which the rich get richer first and eventually benefits trickle down to the poor. The evidence, to the contrary, is that private property rights, stability, and openness contemporaneously create a good environment for poor households—and everyone else—to increase their production and income. On the other hand, we find little evidence that formal democratic institutions or a large degree of government spending on social services systematically affect incomes of the poor.

Our findings do not imply that growth is all that is needed to improve the lives of the poor. Rather, we simply emphasize that growth on average does benefit the poor as much as anyone else in society, and so standard growth-enhancing policies should be at the centre of any effective poverty reduction strategy. This also does not mean that the potential distributional effects of growth, or the policies that support growth, can or should be ignored. Our results do not imply that the income share of the poorest quintile is immutable—rather, we simply are unable to relate the changes across countries and over time in this income share to average incomes, or to a variety of proxies for policies and institutions that matter for growth and poverty reduction. This may be simply because any effects of these policies on the income share of the poorest quintile are small relative to the very substantial measurement error in the very imperfect available income distribution data we are forced to rely upon. It may also be due to the inability of our simple empirical models to capture the complex interactions between inequality and growth suggested by some theoretical models. In short, existing cross-country evidence—including our own—provides disappointingly little guidance as to what mix of growth-oriented policies might especially benefit the poorest in society. But our evidence does strongly suggest that economic growth and the policies and institutions that support it on average benefit the poorest in society as much as anyone else.

APPENDIX

Table 2A.1. *Variable definitions and data sources*

Variable	Source	Comments
Real GDP per capita	Summers and Heston (1991) Penn World Tables, World Bank Data	Constant 1985 US dollars. Extended to 1998 using constant price local currency growth rates. Extended cross-sectionally as described in Kraay, Loayza, Serven, and Ventura (2000).

Table 2A.1. *Continued*

Variable	Source	Comments
First quintile share	UNU-WIDER (2000), Deininger and Squire (1996), Chen and Ravallion (2000), Lundberg and Squire (2000)	Combination of data from different sources described in text.
Gini coefficient	UNU-WIDER (2000), Deininger and Squire (1996), Chen and Ravallion (2000), Lundberg and Squire (2000)	Combination of data from different sources described in text.
(Exports + Imports)/ GDP	World Bank Data, Summers and Heston (1991) Penn World Tables	Exports and imports are in constant 1985 US dollars at market exchange rates. Denominator is in constant 1985 dollars at PPP.
Government consumption/GDP	World Bank Data	Numerator and denominator are in current local currency units.
ln(1+inflation)	World Bank Data	Inflation is CPI-based where available, otherwise use growth of GDP deflator.
Commercial bank assets/ Total bank assets	Beck, Demirguc-Kunt, and Levine (1999)	
Rule of law	Kaufmann, Kraay, and Zoido-Lobatón (1999)	Index, greater values indicate better rule of law
Secondary education	Barro and Lee (2000)	Stock of years of secondary education.
Frankel–Romer distance measure	Frankel and Romer (1999)	Trade-weighted average of distance from trading partners.
Population	World Bank Data	
Sachs–Warner index	Sachs and Warner (1995)	
Import taxes/Total imports	World Bank Data	Data on import taxes in numerator originally from IMF Government Finance Statistics. Numerator and denominator in current local currency units.
WTO membership dummy	www.wto.org	
Capital controls dummy	International Monetary Fund Report on Exchange Arrangements and Exchange Controls, various issues.	

Table 2A.1. *Continued*

Variable	Source	Comments
Years primary education	Barro and Lee (2000)	Stock of years of primary education
Social spending/Total public spending	Government finance statistics	
Arable land per worker	World Bank Data	Total arable land in hectares divided by population aged 15–64.
Agricultural relative labour productivity	World Bank Data	Current price share of agriculture in GDP divided by share of workforce in agriculture.

REFERENCES

Ali, A. G. A. and Elbadawi, I. (2001). 'Growth Could Be Good for the Poor'. Manuscript, Arab Planning Institute and the World Bank.

Aitchinson, J. and Brown, J. A. C. (1966). *The Lognormal Distribution*. Cambridge University Press, Cambridge.

Agenor, P.-R. (1998). 'Stabilization Policies, Poverty, and the Labour Market'. Manuscript, International Monetary Fund and the World Bank.

Alesina, A. and Rodrik, D. (1994). 'Distributive Politics and Economic Growth'. *Quarterly Journal of Economics*, 109(2), 465–90.

Arellano, M. and Bover, O. (1995). 'Another Look at the Instrumental-Variable Estimation of Error-Components Models'. *Journal of Econometrics*, 68, 29–52.

Atkinson, A. B. and Brandolini, A. (1999). 'Promise and Pitfalls in the Use of 'Secondary' Data-Sets: Income Inequality in OECD Countries'. Manuscript, Nuffield College, Oxford and Banca d'Italia, Research Department.

Beck, T., Demirguc-Kunt, A., and Levine, R. (1999). 'A New Database on Financial Development and Structure'. *World Bank Policy Research Department Working Paper* 2146.

Banerjee, A. V. and Duflo, E. (1999). 'Inequality and Growth: What Can the Data Say?'. Manuscript, MIT.

Barro, R. J. (2000). 'Inequality and Growth in a Panel of Countries'. *Journal of Economic Growth*, 5, 5–32.

—— and Lee, J.-W. (2000). 'International Data on Educational Attainment: Updates and Implications'. *Harvard University Center for International Development Working Paper* 42.

Bidani, B. and Ravallion, M. (1997). 'Decomposing Social Indicators Using Distributional Data'. *Journal of Econometrics*, 77, 125–39.

Bils, M. and Klenow, P. (2000). 'Does Schooling Cause Growth?'. *American Economic Review*, 90(5), 1160–83.

Blundell, R. and Bond, S. (1998). 'Initial Conditions and Moment Restrictions in Dynamic Panel Data Models'. *Journal of Econometrics*, 87, 115–43.

Chen, S. and Ravallion, M. (1997). 'What Can New Survey Data Tell Us about Recent Changes in Distribution and Poverty?' *The World Bank Economic Review*, 11(2), 357–82.

—— and —— (2000). 'How Did the World's Poorest Fare in the 1990s?'. Manuscript, the World Bank. Data and paper available at http://www.worldbank.org/research/povmonitor/.

Datt, G. and Ravallion, M. (1999). 'When is Growth Pro-Poor?'. Manuscript, The World Bank, Washington DC.

Deininger, K. and Squire, L. (1996). 'A New Data Set Measuring Income Inequality'. *The World Bank Economic Review*, 10(3), 565–91.

Easterly, W. (1999). 'Life During Growth'. *Journal of Economic Growth*, 4, 239–76.

—— (2001). 'The Middle-Class Consensus and Economic Development'. *Journal of Economic Growth*, 6, 317–35.

—— and Fischer, S. (2000). 'Inflation and the Poor'. *World Bank Policy Research Department Working Paper* 2335.

—— and Rebelo, S. T. (1993). 'Fiscal Policy and Economic Growth: An Empirical Investigation'. *Journal of Monetary Economics*, 32(3), 417–58.

Edwards, S. (1997). 'Trade Policy, Growth, and Income Distribution'. *American Economic Review*, 87(2), 205–10.

Filmer, D. and Pritchett, L. (1997). 'Child Mortality and Public Spending on Health: How Much Does Money Matter?' *World Bank Policy Research Working Paper* 1864.

Fischer, S. (1993). 'The Role of Macroeconomic Factors in Growth'. *Journal of Monetary Economics*, 32(3), 485–512.

Forbes, K. J. (2000). 'A Reassessment of the Relationship between Inequality and Growth'. *American Economic Review*, 90(4), 869–97.

Foster, J. and Székely, M. (2001). 'Is Economic Growth Good for the Poor? Tracking Low Incomes Using General Means'. *Inter-American Development Bank Research Department Working Paper* 453.

Frankel, J. A. and Romer, D. (1999). 'Does Trade Cause Growth?'. *The American Economic Review*, 89(3), 379–99.

Gallup, J. L., Radelet, S., and Warner, A. (1998). 'Economic Growth and the Income of the Poor'. Manuscript, Harvard Institute for International Development, Cambridge, MA.

Galor, O. and Zeira, J. (1993). 'Income Distribution and Macroeconomics'. *Review of Economic Studies*, 60(1), 35–52.

—— and Moav, O. (2001). 'From Physical to Human Capital Accumulation: Inequality and the Process of Development'. *Brown University Working Paper* 99/27.

Gouyette, C. and Pestieau, P. (1999). 'Efficiency of the Welfare State'. *Kyklos*, 52, 537–53.

Johnston, N., Kotz, S., and Balakrishnan, N. (1994). *Continuous Univariate Distributions*, vol. 2, 2nd edn. Wiley, New York.

Kaufmann, D., Kraay, A., and Zoido-Lobatón, P. (1999). 'Governance Matters'. *World Bank Policy Research Department Working Paper* 2196.

Knack, S. and Keefer, P. (1995). 'Institutions and Economic Performance: Cross-Country Tests Using Alternative Institutional Measures'. *Economics and Politics*, 7(3), 207–27.

Kraay, A. and Ravallion, M. (2001). 'Measurement Error, Aggregate Growth, and the Distribution-Corrected Mean: A Comment on Foster-Székely'. Manuscript, The World Bank, Washington.

Kuznets, S. (1955). 'Economic Growth and Income Inequality'. *The American Economic Review*, 45(1), 1–28.

Leamer, E., Maul, H., Rodriguez, S., and Schott, P. (1999). 'Does Natural Resource Abundance Increase Latin American Income Inequality?' *Journal of Development Economics*, 59, 3–42.

Levine, R., Loayza, N., and Beck, T. (2000). 'Financial Intermediation and Growth: Causality and Causes'. *Journal of Monetary Economics*, 46, 31–77.

Li, H., Squire, L., and Zou, H.-F. (1998). 'Explaining International and Intertemporal Variations in Income Inequality'. *The Economic Journal*, 108, 26–43.

—— and Zou, H.-F. (1998). 'Income Inequality is not Harmful for Growth: Theory and Evidence'. *Review of Development Economics*, 2(3), 318–34.

Lundberg, M. and Squire, L. (2000). 'The Simultaneous Evolution of Growth and Inequality'. Manuscript, The World Bank, Washington.

Perotti, R. (1996). 'Growth, Income Distribution and Democracy: What the Data Say'. *Journal of Economic Growth*, 1, 149–87.

Persson, T. and Tabellini, G. (1994). 'Is Inequality Harmful for Growth?' *American Economic Review*, 84(3), 600–21.

Ravallion, M. (1997). 'Can High-Inequality Countries Escape Absolute Poverty?' *Economics Letters*, 56(1), 51–7.

—— (2001*a*). 'Measuring Aggregate Welfare in Developing Countries: How Well do National Accounts and Surveys Agree?'. *World Bank Policy Research Department Working Paper* 2665.

—— (2001*b*). 'Growth, Inequality, and Poverty: Looking Beyond Averages'. *World Development*, 29(11), 1803–15.

Rodriguez, F. and Rodrik, D. (2000). 'Trade Policy and Economic Growth: A Skeptic's Guide to the Cross-National Evidence'. In B. Bernanke and K. Rogoff (eds), *Macroeconomics Annual 2000*. MIT Press for NBER.

Sachs, J. D. and Warner, A. (1995). 'Economic Reform and the Process of Global Integration'. *Brookings Papers on Economic Activity*, (1), 1–118.

Spilimbergo, A., Londoño, J. L., and Székely, M. (1999). 'Income Distribution, Factor Endowments, and Trade Openness'. *Journal of Development Economics*, 59(1) , 77–101.

Summers, R. and Heston, A. (1991). 'The Penn World Table (Mark 5): An Expanded Set of International Comparisons, 1950–88'. *Quarterly Journal of Economics*, 106(2), 327–68.

United Nations University World Institute for Development Economics Research (UNU/WIDER) (2000). World Income Inequality Database. Available online at www.wider.unu.edu/wiid/wiid.htm.

3

Growth, Inequality, and Poverty: Looking Beyond Averages

MARTIN RAVALLION

3.1. INTRODUCTION

The recent backlash against globalization has given new impetus to an old debate on whether the poor benefit from economic growth. The following quotes from *The Economist* represent well the two main opposing views on the matter:

> Growth really does help the poor: in fact it raises their incomes by about as much as it raises the incomes of everybody else . . . In short, globalization raises incomes, and the poor participate fully. *The Economist*, 27 May 2000: 94

> There is plenty of evidence that current patterns of growth and globalization are widening income disparities and hence acting as a brake on poverty reduction. Justin Forsyth, Oxfam Policy Director, Letter to *The Economist*, 20 June 2000: 6

Here, we seem to have irreconcilable positions about how much the world's poorest benefit from the economic growth that is fuelled by greater openness to foreign trade and investment. *The Economist*'s own article is adamant that such growth is poverty-reducing, drawing on a recent study by Dollar and Kraay (2002) which found that average incomes of the poorest quintile moved almost one-for-one with average incomes overall. In commenting on *The Economist*'s article, Oxfam's policy director seems equally confident that rising inequality is choking off the potential benefits to the poor, in seeming contradiction to the Dollar and Kraay results and earlier results in the literature pointing in the same direction.[1]

However, as this chapter will argue, there is some truth in both the quotes above. Indeed, it is not difficult to reconcile these two views, with important implications for

Reprinted from *World Development* Vol. 29, Martin Ravallion 'Growth, Inequality and Poverty: Looking Beyond Averages', pages 1803–15 (2001), with permission from Elsevier Science. Helpful comments on this chapter were received from Nancy Birdsall, Giovanni Andrea Cornia, Bill Easterly, Gary Fields, Paul Isenman, Ravi Kanbur, Aart Kraay, Branko Milanovic, Giovanna Prennushi, Dominique van de Walle, Nicolas van de Walle, Michael Walton, the Journal's referees and participants at presentations at the World Institute for Development Economics Research, the African Economic Research Consortium and the World Bank. These are the views of the author, and need not reflect those of the World Bank or any affiliated organization.

[1] Earlier contributions include Fields (1989), World Bank (1990: chapter 3), Squire (1993), Ravallion (1995), Ravallion and Chen (1997), and Bruno, Ravallion, and Squire (1998).

development policy. In critically reviewing the arguments in this debate, I will draw heavily on evidence from a new compilation of household-level data for developing countries. The following section discusses these data. Section 3 looks at what they show about how much the poor have benefited from rising average living standards in developing countries, and how much they have lost from contractions. Section 4 looks at how distribution has been changing, to see if there is evidence to support the second quote above. The section first looks at how aggregate distribution in the developing world has been changing in the 1990s, and then it looks at what has been happening at country level. The chapter then considers in more detail the ways in which distribution matters to the outcomes for the poor—both as an impediment to growth (Section 5) and as an impediment to poverty-reducing growth (Section 6). Section 7 then points to some potential pitfalls in drawing policy implications from the evidence of a weak correlation between growth and distributional changes across countries. Section 8 concludes with some observations about directions for future research.

3.2. NEW EVIDENCE ON AN OLD DEBATE

Data on poverty and inequality are obtained from household surveys, in which random samples of households are interviewed using a structured questionnaire. The main data I will draw on here relate to 'spells' defined by the periods of time spanning two successive household surveys for a given country. From the latest update of the database on which the World Bank's tabulations of income distribution are based (Chen and Ravallion 2001), one can assemble two or more household surveys over time for about fifty developing countries, to create 120 such spells, mostly in the 1990s.[2] The estimates of poverty and inequality measures were done from the primary data (rather than using secondary sources), so that it was possible to eliminate obvious inconsistencies in existing compilations from secondary sources. Comparisons over time between any two surveys use the same indicator of economic welfare, which was either income or expenditure per person; half the time it is expenditure, which is taken to be the preferred indicator. Imputed values are included for income or consumption-in-kind from own-farm output. All measures are population weighted (taking account of household size and sample expansion factors). The underlying household surveys are nationally representative.

The data are not without problems.[3] Amongst the concerns about the data used here, there are clearly underlying differences (between countries and over time) in the original household surveys that were the source of the data on household incomes and expenditures. There are also concerns about how best to deflate nominal values for changes in the cost-of-living; the available consumer price indices do not always reflect well the spending behaviour of the poor. On top of these problems, there is likely to be underestimation of incomes and spending in household surveys, particularly

[2] The latest version of the data set can be found at www.worldbank.org/research/povmonitor/. This web site is updated regularly; the results in this paper are based on the data set at mid-2000, as used in Chen and Ravallion (2001).

[3] For a critical review of the methods underlying the data set used here see Deaton (2001).

(but probably not only) by the rich, who often do not want to participate, or are hard to reach, or deliberately understate their incomes or spending. Nothing much can be done to fix these problems. However, one can still take partial account of the data problems by using methods of analysis that are not likely to be too sensitive to the errors in the data.

In examining the effect of growth on poverty there is also a question: 'growth of what?' We want to know whether the poor are sharing in the growth in average living standards. However, there are two quite distinct, and largely independent, sources of data on a country's average welfare, as measured by households' command over commodities. The level of private consumption expenditure (PCE) per capita from the national accounts (NAS) is widely used for this purpose. On the other hand, measures of average household living standards are available from the same household surveys used to measure poverty.

These two measures do not agree in general, either in the levels or in their growth rates. This is not surprising, given the differences in coverage, definitions, and methods. There are the aforementioned problems in survey data. But national accounts have their own data problems. For example, PCE is typically determined residually in the NAS, after accounting for other uses of domestic output and imports at the commodity level. In developing countries, there are concerns about how well both output and consumption by unincorporated ('informal sector') businesses are measured, though it is not clear how this would affect NAS consumption. A further problem is that it is not generally possible to separate the spending by non-profit institutions (such as NGOs, religious groups, and political parties) from that of households. In many developing countries, the non-household sectors that are implicitly lumped together with households appear to be sizeable and possibly growing, so PCE may well overstate the growth rate in household welfare. There are also consistency problems between the two sources, such as arising from imperfect matching between survey dates and the accounting periods used in the NAS.

There are differences in the extent of these data concerns both between regions and between types of surveys. India stands out as an unusual case in the 1990s. The growth rates in consumption that we have seen in the national accounts for India in the 1990s have not been reflected in the main national household survey of expenditures on consumption (the National Sample Survey). This divergence is naturally putting a brake on how much poverty reduction we are seeing in the survey data during this period of economic growth (Datt 1999). At the same time, there are signs that measured inequality is increasing, which is also slowing the rate of poverty reduction given the rate of growth (Ravallion 2000*b*).

How one interprets the data for India depends critically on why we are seeing this rising divergence between the two data sources on consumption. One interpretation assumes that all consumptions are being underestimated by the surveys, and so concludes that poverty is falling faster than the survey data suggest (Bhalla 2000). While agreeing that the surveys are probably missing a share of the aggregate consumption gains, an alternative interpretation is that the problem is more likely to be due to underestimation of consumption by the non-poor. The latter interpretation would appear to accord better with our limited knowledge of the problems of under-reporting and non-compliance in consumption and income surveys (see, for example, Groves and Couper 1998). The fact that the divergence is correlated with growth (over time, and across states) of India is also consistent with an income effect on survey underestimation, which one expects to hold also between households (Ravallion 2000*b*). If the problem is entirely due to under-reporting of consumption by the non-poor, who are, nonetheless, correctly weighted in the survey design, then one will still get the poverty measures right. However, there could well be problems of sample weighting and underestimation of consumption by the poor, leading to an underestimation of the rate of poverty reduction.

If one is willing to discount income (rather than expenditure) surveys for measuring average levels of economic welfare, and if one puts aside the (highly problematic) data from the transition economies of Central and Eastern Europe for growth rates, then the tests for bias reported in Ravallion (2000*a*) do not point to a systematic overall discrepancy between national accounts and survey-based estimates of aggregate consumption. (This holds in the aggregate across countries; large discrepancies can still be found for specific countries, in both directions.) Nonetheless, it is notable that in the aggregate, and for most regions, the elasticity of the survey mean to NAS consumption growth is less than 1 (even though the difference is often not statistically significant). This could well be an attenuation bias due to measurement error. By implication, elasticities of measured poverty to NAS growth will be less than those implied by the measured elasticities of poverty to growth in the survey mean.

The fact that the mean from the surveys is consistent with the data used to calculate poverty measures makes it an appealing candidate for measuring the growth rate. However, this creates a further problem, namely that survey measurement errors can create a spuriously high correlation between poverty measures and the means of the distributions on which those measures are based. The fact that there is measurement error in the surveys (probably creating a spurious negative correlation between measured poverty and the measured mean) speaks to the use of econometric methods that are robust to this type of problem. Examples will be given later.

3.3. POVERTY REDUCTION AND GROWTH IN AVERAGE LIVING STANDARDS

There is little or no correlation in these data between growth in average household income per person and the change in measured inequality. The correlation coefficient between the annualized change in the log of the Gini index and the annualized change in the log of the survey mean is -0.09 ($n = 115$). The correlation is even lower if one uses growth rates in consumption from the national accounts (a correlation coefficient of 0.01). This finding is consistent with previous research. Earlier versions of this data set also indicated that growth in average household income per person and the change in measured inequality are virtually orthogonal (Ravallion 1995; Ravallion and Chen 1997). Similarly, Dollar and Kraay (2002) find that, across countries, log mean income of the poorest quintile (inferred from distributional shares and GDP per capita) changes one-to-one with the overall log GDP per capita. This is equivalent to saying that the share of the poorest quintile is uncorrelated with log GDP per capita.

However, it does not follow that growth raises incomes of the poor 'by about as much as it raises the incomes of everybody else' (in the quote from *The Economist* at the beginning of this chapter). Finding that the share of income going to the poor does not change on average with growth does not mean that growth raises the incomes of the poor as much as for the rich. Given existing inequality, the income gains to the rich from distribution-neutral growth will, of course, be greater than the gains to the poor. For example, the income gain to the richest decile in India will be about four times higher than the gain to the poorest quintile; it will be nineteen times higher in Brazil.[4] The fact that, on average, the rich will tend to capture a much larger share of the increment to national income from growth than the poor is directly implied by the empirical results in the literature, including Dollar and Kraay (2002).

Of course, if distributional shares do not change on average then the poor will gain in absolute terms: Growth is poverty reducing, and contraction is poverty increasing. Figure 3.1 plots the proportionate changes in the poverty rate against the growth rate in average income. The poverty measure is the proportion of people living below $1/day (using 1993 purchasing power parity exchange rates), though other poverty lines show a similar pattern.[5]

The figure also gives the regression line that fits the data best. The line virtually passes through the origin, implying that the average rate of poverty reduction at zero growth is zero—consistent with the pattern of zero change in inequality on average. The line has a slope of −2.50 with a (heteroskedasticity corrected) standard error of 0.30 ($R^2 = 0.44$). This can be thought of as an overall 'growth elasticity' of poverty, since the two variables are proportionate changes. Thus, for every 1 per cent increase in the mean, the proportion of the population living below $1/day (at 1993 purchasing power parity) falls by an average of 2.5 per cent. For example, in a large enough sample of countries for which exactly half of the population lives below $1/day, a 3 per cent increase in the mean will bring that proportion down to about 0.46. And a 3 per cent fall in mean income will push the poverty rate up to about 0.54 on average.

There is no indication in the data that the elasticity is any different when the mean is increasing versus decreasing; one cannot reject the null hypothesis that the elasticity is the same in both directions (the *t*-statistic is 0.11). So there is no sign that distributional changes help protect the poor during contractions in average living standards.

[4] These are based on income shares for Brazil in 1996 and consumption shares for India in 1997; in both cases the ranking variable is per capita (World Bank 2000*a*).

[5] One possible concern is that the poverty line is fixed (in PPP terms) across countries. While this is valid for making comparisons of absolute poverty in terms of command over commodities, actual poverty lines tend to rise with mean consumption or income in a country (Chen and Ravallion 2001). However, comparisons of national poverty lines with mean consumption (both at PPP) indicate that the 'income' elasticity of the poverty line is very low amongst poor countries, only rising at middle to upper income levels (Chen and Ravallion 2001). Thus, the growth elasticity of poverty in low- and middle-income countries is unlikely to be affected much by using relative poverty lines consistent with the way national poverty lines vary.

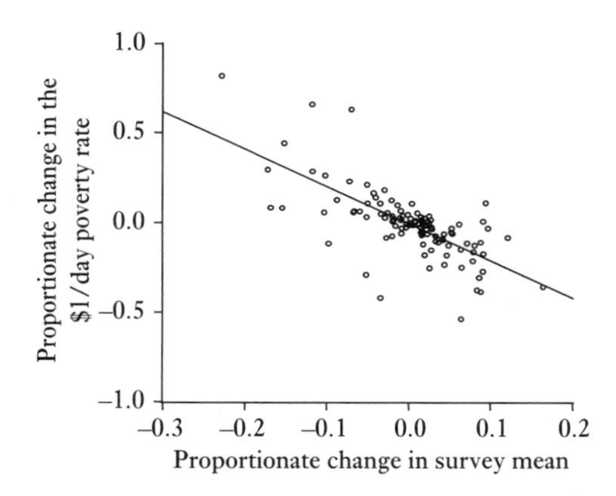

Figure 3.1. *Poverty tends to fall with growth in mean household income or expenditure*

Source: Based on data for forty-seven developing countries in the 1980s and 1990s (multiple spells for most countries). The horizontal axis is the annualized change in the log of the real value of the survey mean; the vertical axis is the annualized change in the log of the percentage of the population living below $1/day at 1993 Purchasing Power Parity. The figure has been trimmed of extreme values, but this does not alter the line of best fit indicated.

The relationship looks similar if one uses PCE per capita from the national accounts instead of the mean from the survey, although then the correlation is not as strong, and the elasticity is −1.96 with a considerably higher standard error of 0.89 (though still statistically significant at the 3 per cent level). This is partly because of measurement problems, such as the fact that survey periods do not match exactly the periods used in national accounts. And it is partly because changes in PCE can arise solely from the non-household sector of the economy (notably spending by non-profit organizations). Nor is there any sign that the elasticity to growth from the national accounts is any different in expansions versus contractions.

A possible concern about this estimate of the average growth elasticity of poverty reduction is that there may be negatively correlated measurement errors in the rate of poverty reduction and the rate of growth in the survey mean. If the second survey overestimated the mean for some reason (relative to the first survey) it will probably overestimate the rate at which poverty is falling. To check for a bias due to this problem, I used the growth rate in private consumption per capita from the national accounts as the instrumental variable for estimating the regression line in Fig. 3.1, that is, as the predictor of the growth rate in the survey mean. This assumes that the true values of the national accounts growth rates are correlated with the true growth rates based on the survey means, but that their respective errors are not correlated, so that the NAS growth rate purges the survey mean growth rate of its troublesome error components. The fact that national accounts are generally constructed quite independently of household surveys makes this assumption plausible (though common errors in the deflators used would lead one to question the assumption). This instrument is not, however, valid for the countries of Eastern Europe and Central Asia for which there is no correlation between the growth rates from the surveys and those from the national accounts (Ravallion 2000*a*). So I dropped the data for that region. This estimation method gave a growth elasticity of −2.07 with a standard error of 0.72 (significant at the 1 per cent level).

Therein lies the truth in the first quote at the start of this chapter. The incidence of absolute poverty in developing countries tends to fall with growth. This is not a new point; indeed, the empirical relationship has been well known for some time (Bruno, Ravallion, and Squire 1998, provide a survey). But it is worth emphasizing in the context of the recent debate.

Looking behind the averages, however, the experience is diverse as is evident in Fig. 3.1. Even ignoring extreme values, the 95 per cent confidence interval of the last estimate above of the growth elasticity implies that 1 per cent rate of growth in average household income or consumption will bring anything from a modest drop in the poverty rate of 0.6 per cent to a more dramatic 3.5 per cent annual decline. We will now try to better understand this variance in growth elasticities of poverty.

3.4. IS RISING INEQUALITY IMPEDING POVERTY REDUCTION?

Let us look first at distribution in the developing world as a whole in the 1990s. In the same way that rising inequality in one country can clearly put a brake on prospects for poverty-reducing growth, rising inequality in the developing world as a whole can inhibit overall poverty reduction. Has that been happening?

The proportion of the population of the developing world living in households with consumption per capita less than about $1 per day in 1998 (at 1993 purchasing power parity) is estimated to be 23 per cent which was only four percentage points lower than in 1987 (Chen and Ravallion 2001). The total number of poor by this standard was about the same in 1998 as in 1987, with roughly 1.2 billion people living below $1 per day. Chen and Ravallion (2001) try to assess what role worsening distribution played in explaining this disappointing performance in aggregate poverty reduction during the 1990s. They simulate what would have happened if there had been no change in the overall interpersonal distribution for developing and transitional countries between 1987 and 1998. In other words, all household consumptions and incomes grow at the same rate, given by the growth rate in the (population-weighted) survey mean over their entire data set. The 1987 Lorenz curve of interpersonal consumption for the developing world as a whole would, thus, remain fixed over the period. If it were true that distribution is worsening over time in the developing world as a whole then this distribution-neutral simulation would give lower poverty in 1998 than actually observed. However, Chen and Ravallion find that the poverty rate in 1998 would have been 24.4 per cent in the distribution neutral case, instead of 23.4 per cent as calculated from the data.

It can be inferred from this that there was no worsening in the overall interpersonal distribution from the point of view of the poor. Indeed, the actual distributional changes were slightly pro-poor, since the measured poverty rate in 1998 is slightly lower than the simulated rate without any change in distribution. However, on investigating this finding more closely, one finds that the difference is almost entirely attributable to growth in China. If one takes China out of the above calculation then the simulated poverty rate in 1998 is 25.9 per cent, which is almost exactly the same as the actual rate (25.2 per cent, excluding China). So income distribution has not been deteriorating overall in the 1990s, from the point of view of the poor.[6]

But this aggregate picture hides more than it reveals. The previous section pointed to the heterogeneity in the gains to the poor from a given rate of growth. Underlying this heterogeneity lies the fact that during spells of growth or contraction one sees changes in inequality over time within most developing economies—changes in both directions.

Table 3.1 divides the data points of Fig. 3.1 (each spell representing two surveys for a given country) into four groups, according to whether the mean is increasing or not, interacted with whether inequality is increasing or not. Even in the countries in which inequality is rising with growth in average living standards, poverty is falling on average. But it typically falls at a much slower rate than in countries experiencing more equitable growth. There can be little surprise in this fact, or the general qualitative pattern in Table 3.1. But the quantitative magnitudes are striking. The median rate of decline in the proportion of the population living below $1 per day amongst countries with both rising average income and rising inequality was 1.3 per cent per

Table 3.1. *Diverse impacts on poverty coexist with aggregate distribution neutrality*

What is happening to inequality between the surveys?	**What is happening to average household income between the surveys?**	
	Falling	**Rising**
Rising	(*16% of spells*) Poverty is rising at a median rate of 14.3% per year	(*30% of spells*) Poverty is falling at a median rate of 1.3% per year
Falling	(*26% of spells*) Poverty is rising at a median rate of 1.7% per year	(*27% of spells*) Poverty is falling at a median rate of 9.6% per year

Notes: Based on 117 spells between two household surveys covering forty-seven developing countries in the 1980s and 1990s. Poverty is measured by the percentage of the population living below $1/day at 1993 Purchasing Power Parity. Inequality is measured by the Gini index.

Source: See text.

[6] Here, I am only referring to distribution in the developing world as it affects poverty. There is evidence of rising overall interpersonal inequality in the world (developing and developed); see Milanovic (2002) for the period 1987–93.

year (Table 3.1). By contrast, the median rate of poverty reduction was seven times higher, at about 10 per cent per year, amongst the countries that combined growth in average living standards and falling inequality. Amongst contracting economies it also mattered greatly what was happening to inequality; when inequality was rising while average living standards fell, the poverty rate was rising by a dramatic 14 per cent per year on average, while with falling inequality the poverty rate rose by less than 2 per cent.

There have been plenty of cases of rising inequality during spells of growth. Indeed, inequality increases about half the time (Table 3.1, also see Ravallion and Chen 1997). Therein lies the truth in the second quote at the beginning of this paper. The first quote implicitly averages over this diversity; the second looks not at the averages, but the cases in which the poor are sharing little in the gains from growth.

However, the fact that we are seeing plenty of cases of rising inequality during spells of growth does not imply that the rising inequality is putting a brake on the rate of poverty reduction (as the second quote at the beginning of this chapter suggests). It cannot be concluded from the information in Table 3.1 that the growing economies with rising inequality could have achieved something like a 9.6 per cent rate of poverty reduction—instead of 1.3 per cent on average—if only inequality had been falling. For that to hold one requires the assumption that the growth rate would have been no lower with falling inequality. Possibly there is an aggregate trade-off between growth and inequality reduction. That depends critically on exactly how the reduction in inequality is achieved. The next section considers this point further.

3.5. INEQUALITY AS AN IMPEDIMENT TO GROWTH

One way inequality can matter to the rate of poverty reduction is through the rate of growth in average income. There are a number of arguments that have been made as to why greater equality can actually be good for growth, belying the presumption of an aggregate trade-off (see, for example, Benabou 1996; Aghion, Caroli, and Garcia-Penalosa 1999; Bardhan, Bowles, and Gintis 1999). A seemingly plausible argument points to the existence of credit market failures such that people are unable to exploit growth-promoting opportunities for investment in (physical and human) capital. With declining marginal products of capital, the output loss from the market failure will be greater for the poor. So the higher the proportion of poor people there are in the economy the lower the rate of growth.[7]

Cross-country comparisons of growth rates provide some support for the claim that countries with higher initial inequality in incomes experienced lower rates of growth

[7] Banerjee and Duflo (1999) sketch a simple but elegant model of the inter-generational accumulation of wealth in which individuals start with an endowment from the previous generation but face a borrowing constraint. In this model, individual wealth at one date is a concave function of the individual's endowment, given declining marginal products of capital. Thus mean wealth in the economy at one date is a quasiconcave function of the vector of endowments left over from the previous period. It follows from well-known properties of concave functions that higher initial inequality will entail lower future mean wealth for any given initial mean wealth.

controlling for other factors such as initial average income, openness to trade and the rate of inflation.[8] The robustness of this finding has been called into question in some studies. There are difficult problems in identifying this relationship empirically, and the results in the literature have not been robust to alternative specifications, such as allowing for country fixed effects (Forbes 1997; Li and Zou 1998; Barro 2000).

Again, there are a number of concerns about the data and methods used. There are measurement errors in both the levels and changes in measured income inequality, including comparability problems between countries and over time arising from survey error (sampling and non-sampling) and heterogeneity in survey design and processing (see, for example, Atkinson and Brandolini 1999). One expects that this will matter more to tests which allow for country fixed effects than to standard growth regressions, since the signal-to-noise ratio could well be quite low for changes in measured inequality in existing data sets. Greater attenuation bias should be expected in the fixed-effects regressions of growth on inequality. Using a pooled regression of growth on inequality, Knowles (2001) finds that trimming the data set to reduce the comparability problems changes the results obtained in important ways. However, Knowles finds that using more recent and more comparable measures of inequality in consumption expenditures does indicate significant negative effects of inequality on growth.

Another concern is that spurious inequality effects in an aggregate growth regression can arise from the assumptions made in aggregating across micro-relationships, given credit market failures. In theory, the direction of this bias could go either way, though empirical results for China in Ravallion (1998) indicate that regional aggregation hides the adverse effect of inequality on growth. The validity of the common assumption that initial inequality has a linear effect on aggregate growth is also questionable; Banerjee and Duflo (1999) find evidence that changes in income inequality are bad for growth, whichever way the changes go. The choice of control variables in identifying the relationship is also open to question; for example, past tests of the effect of inequality on growth have controlled for the human capital stock, yet reducing investment in human capital is presumably one of the ways that inequality matters to growth.

On balance, the existing evidence using cross-country growth regressions appears to offer more support for the view that inequality is harmful to growth than the opposite view, which was the prevailing view in development economics for decades. However, that does not imply that any reduction in inequality will enhance growth; indeed, it can have the opposite effect if it comes at the expense of other factors that are also known to matter to growth. Reducing inequality by adding further distortions to external trade or domestic economy will have ambiguous effects on growth and poverty reduction.

Given the concerns about past tests based on cross-country aggregates, it is of interest to ask if there might be some other way of testing for an effect of initial distribution on growth. Returning to the various theories about why initial distribution might matter, one finds that many of the proposed models share some strong and testable implications for micro data. An example is the common feature of a number of the

[8] Examples include Persson and Tabellini (1994), Alesina and Rodrik (1994), Birdsall, Ross, and Sabot (1995), Clarke (1995), Perotti (1996), Deininger and Squire (1998), and Deininger and Olinto (2000).

theoretical models based on credit market failures that individual income or wealth at one date is an increasing concave function of its own past value. This implication of the class of models of distribution-dependent growth based on credit market failures is testable on micro panel data; Lokshin and Ravallion (2001) provide supportive evidence in panel data for Hungary and Russia and Jalan and Ravallion (2002) find a similar result using panel data for China.[9]

As with macro tests of whether inequality is bad for growth, finding the appropriate non-linearity in household-level income dynamics would not constitute a case for public redistribution as a means of stimulating aggregate growth. However, with the right data, dynamic micro models of income or consumption can be augmented to allow for (possibly endogenously placed) public programmes.[10] Microstructural modelling of growth in the presence of specific redistributive interventions may offer hope of a deeper understanding of the policy implications.

3.6. INEQUALITY AS AN IMPEDIMENT TO PRO-POOR GROWTH

Even when inequality is not rising, a high initial level of inequality can stifle prospects for pro-poor growth. In an economy where inequality is low and does not subsequently rise, one can expect that the poor will tend to obtain a higher share of the gains from growth than in an economy in which inequality is high. This expectation will not necessarily be borne out by the data if inequality tends to rise when it is low, and there is some evidence of such 'inequality convergence' (Benabou 1996, Ravallion 2001*a*, *b*).[11] It is, thus, an empirical issue whether in fact high inequality attenuates the growth elasticity of poverty.

The evidence suggests that it does. An important determinant of the rate of poverty reduction is the *distribution-corrected rate of growth* in average income, given by a measure of initial equality (100 minus the measure of inequality) times the rate of growth. Indeed, the distribution-corrected growth rate knocks out the ordinary growth rate when both are used in a regression for the rate of poverty reduction (Ravallion 1997). It is not the rate of growth that matters, but the distribution-corrected rate of growth. One can represent this in the form of a very simple model in which the proportionate rate of change in the incidence of poverty (P) between surveys is directly proportional to the distribution-corrected rate of growth; on adding an error term, this can be written as

$$\Delta \ln P_{it} = \gamma(1 - G_{i,\,t-\tau})\Delta \ln Y_{it} + \varepsilon_{it}, \tag{3.1}$$

[9] Distribution-dependent growth is possible without non-linear income or wealth dynamics at the micro level. Such models that have been driven instead by their assumptions about political economy, notably the way initial distribution influences the balance of power over public spending (Alesina and Rodrik 1994; Persson and Tabellini 1994).

[10] For example, research on government anti-poverty programmes in China suggests that there have been dynamic consumption gains from the programme at farm-household level (Jalan and Ravallion 1998).

[11] Ravallion (2001) includes tests for inequality convergence that allow for serially independent measurement error in initial inequality (given that measurement error can generate spurious signs of convergence).

where the difference is taken between surveys that are τ years apart (which varies between countries and over time), $G_{i,t-\tau}$ is the Gini index (between zero and one) for country i at the beginning of the spell, Y_{it} is real value of the survey mean at date t, and γ is a parameter to be estimated. Using the same data as in Fig. 3.1, I obtained an estimate of -3.74 for γ, with standard error of 0.68 (this is very close to the estimate in Ravallion 1997, on the earlier and smaller data set). Again a possible concern about this estimate is that there may be (negatively) correlated measurement errors in the changes in P and Y. Using the growth rate in PCE per capita from the national accounts as the instrumental variable for the growth rate in the survey means and dropping the observations for Eastern Europe and Central Asia (where the instrument fails) I found a lower estimate of γ, namely—2.94, with standard error of 1.18.

The elasticity of poverty to growth declines appreciably as the extent of initial inequality rises. Consider a per capita growth rate of (say) 2 per cent per annum (roughly the mean for low-income countries in the 1990s). With $\gamma = -3$ a country with high inequality (a Gini index of 60 per cent, say) can expect to see a rate of poverty reduction of 2.4 per cent per year. By contrast, a relatively low-inequality country, with a Gini of 30 per cent, can expect a rate of poverty reduction of 4.2 per cent per year.

The above results are unrevealing about what specific aspects of inequality matter. The theoretical arguments based on credit market failures point to the importance of asset inequality, not income inequality per se. There is evidence of adverse effects of asset inequality in growth (see Birdsall and Londoño 1997, and Deininger and Olinto 2000, both using cross-country data, and Ravallion 1998, using regional data for China).

Some clues have been found by comparing rates of poverty reduction across states of India, for which we can compile a long series of reasonably comparable survey data back to about 1960. The analyses of these data confirm that economic growth has tended to reduce poverty in India. Higher average farm yields, higher public spending on development, higher (urban and rural) non-farm output and lower inflation were all poverty-reducing (Ravallion and Datt 2002). However, the response of poverty to non-farm output growth in India has varied significantly between states. The differences reflected systematic differences in initial conditions. Low farm productivity, low rural living standards relative to urban areas, and poor basic education, all inhibited the prospects of the poor participating in growth of the non-farm sector. Rural and human resource development appear to be strongly synergistic with poverty reduction though an expanding non-farm economy.

3.7. 'NO CORRELATION' DOES NOT MEAN 'NO IMPACT'

We have seen that the data suggest little or no correlation between growth and changes in inequality across countries. The same holds for indicators of growth promoting policies for which significant correlations with inequality have rarely been found, one way or the other. This is confirmed by Dollar and Kraay (2002), who find negligible correlation between changes in inequality and indicators of policy reform, including greater openness.[12] If there is no effect on inequality, then the outcomes for the poor depend solely on the growth effects.

There are three main reasons to be cautious in drawing implications for policy from this lack of correlation between growth and changes in inequality. First, this apparent distribution-neutrality of reform (on average) could simply reflect the fact that changes in inequality are not well measured. For example, it should be emphasized again that although the main data set used above has been constructed to try to eliminate as many of the problems as possible, there are still changes in survey design that can add considerable noise to the measured changes in inequality.

Second, the data relate to averages within countries. Aggregate inequality or poverty may change relatively little over time, and yet there are both gainers and losers at all levels of living. Indeed, in cases in which the survey data have tracked the same families over time ('panel data'), it is quite common to find considerable churning under the surface; Baulch and Hoddinott (2000) compile evidence of this for a number of countries. Some of this reflects measurement error, but probably not all, since the changes seen in the data are partially explicable in terms of observable characteristics and measurable shocks (see, for example, Jalan and Ravallion 2000, using data for rural China).

One can find that many people have escaped poverty while others have fallen into poverty, even though the overall poverty rate may move rather little. For example, comparing household incomes immediately after the 1998 financial crisis in Russia with incomes of the same households 2 years earlier, one finds a seemingly small two percentage point increase in the poverty rate. However, this was associated with a large proportion of the population (18 per cent) falling into poverty, while a slightly smaller proportion (16 per cent) escaped poverty over the same period (Lokshin and Ravallion 2000). Panel data and qualitative observations often reveal welfare losses for some households even when the aggregate outcomes are favourable. It is important to know the aggregate balance of gains and losses, but it will be of little consolation to those suffering to be told that poverty is falling on average.

A third reason why the low correlations found between policy reform and changes in overall inequality can be deceptive is that starting conditions vary a lot between reforming countries. Averaging across this diversity in initial conditions can readily hide systematic effects. This argument warrants further elaboration since it holds lessons for policy.

One obvious way that countries differ is in their initial level of economic development. It has been argued that greater openness to external trade will have very different effects on inequality depending on the level of economic development—increasing inequality in rich countries and decreasing it in poor ones (Wood 1994, makes a qualified argument along these lines). However, the opposite outcome is possible when economic reforms, including greater openness to external trade, increase

[12] Dollar and Kraay do find that stabilizing against inflation is associated with lower inequality. This is consistent with other evidence that inflation hurts the poor (including Easterly and Fischer 2001, using cross-country data, and Datt and Ravallion 1998, using data for India).

demand for relatively skilled labour, which tends to be more inequitably distributed in poor countries than rich ones.[13] Geographic disparities in access to infrastructure also impede prospects for participating in the growth generated by reform, and these disparities tend to be correlated with incomes.

A simple test for the effect of openness on inequality is suggestive. Using the same data set as Li, Squire, and Zou (1998), I found no significant effect of exports as a share of GDP on the Gini index across fifty countries (100 observations). The regression included controls for schooling, financial sector development, urbanization and the black-market premium (the same explanatory variables used by Li *et al.*). However, I found a strong *negative* interaction effect with initial GDP per capita (with openness entering positively on its own in the same regression). This suggests that openness is associated with *higher* inequality in poor countries. Barro (2000) also reports a significant negative interaction effect between GDP per capita and openness in a regression for inequality, using different controls.

Heterogeneity might also be expected at given levels of economic development. Suppose that reforming developing countries fall into two categories: Those in which prereform controls on the economy were used to benefit the rich, keeping inequality artificially high, and those in which the controls had the opposite effect, keeping inequality low. The reforms may well entail sizeable redistribution between the poor and the rich, but in opposite directions in the two groups of countries. Then one should not be surprised to find that there is zero correlation between growth and changes in inequality, or that the average impact of policy reform on inequality is not significantly different from zero. Yet, there could well be non-random distributional change going on under the surface of this average impact calculation. This can arise when policy reforms shift the distribution of income in different directions in different countries. And it is not implausible that they would do so, given the diversity in initial conditions across developing countries at the time reforms begin.

There is evidence to support this interpretation. As noted already, using the same data set underlying Fig. 3.1, one finds virtually zero correlation between changes in the Gini index of inequality and growth in mean income or consumption. However, suppose that the true relationship is one in which initial inequality interacts with growth, such that the growth attenuates inequality when it is initially high, but it increases inequality when it is low. Using the same set of developing countries as used for Fig. 3.1, one finds evidence for such an interaction effect by regressing the change in the log of the Gini index on the growth rate in PCE and the product of that growth rate with initial inequality. More precisely, the test regression takes the form:

$$\Delta \ln G_{it}/\tau = (\beta_0 + \beta_1 \ln G_{it-\tau})\Delta \ln Y_{it}/\tau + \mu_{it}, \tag{3.2}$$

where G_{it} is the Gini index in country i at date t, and Y_{it} is the private consumption per capita of country i at date t and τ is the time between surveys. The estimate of β_0

[13] Disparities in returns to schooling need not favour the poor either. For evidence on this point see van de Walle's (2000) results for Vietnam.

is significantly positive (6.03, with a standard error of 2.14), while β_1 is significantly negative (a regression coefficient of -1.60 with a standard error of 0.57). (Again, the standard errors are heteroskedasticity-consistent). Thus, one finds a significant *negative* interaction effect between growth and initial inequality.[14] At a value of the log Gini index of $-\beta_0/\beta_1$, growth has no effect; this occurs at a Gini index of 0.433, which is very close to the median Gini index in the sample of 0.425.

A possible concern about this test is that the interaction effect with initial inequality might be due to measurement error in the latter variable. If the Gini index is over- (under-) estimated this year then the growth rate in the Gini index will tend to be under (over-) estimated, which will be reflected in a negative interaction effect with growth in the above test (a version of a problem known as 'Galton's Fallacy'). However, the negative interaction effect remained significant (at the 2 per cent level) when I used a higher lag of the inequality measure as the instrument for 'initial' inequality.[15] This will eliminate any bias due to measurement error as long as the errors are serially independent. The turning point was almost the same (a Gini index of 0.432). So, for roughly the lower half of countries in terms of inequality, growth tends to come with higher inequality, while for the upper half, growth tends to attenuate inequality.

This pattern in the data is suggestive, though hardly conclusive. Strong serial dependence in inequality measurement errors could well invalidate this test. Better data are clearly needed to be confident that the patterns emerging in the data are robust. Caution is also needed with regard to the policy interpretations. None of this denies that growth-oriented reforms have an important role in fighting poverty, or that policies can intervene to alter the distributional outcomes. But these observations do point to the need for a deeper understanding of the heterogeneity in the impacts on poverty, and what role other policies have played. This requires further research on the role of initial conditions (including distribution) and how they interact with policy changes.

Economic reforms in developing countries can create opportunities for poor people. But only if the conditions are in place for them to take advantage of those opportunities will absolute poverty fall rapidly. Given initial inequalities in income and non-income dimensions of welfare, economic reforms can readily bypass the poor. The conditions for pro-poor growth are this closely tied to reducing the disparities in access to human and physical capital, and sometimes also to differences in returns to assets, that create income inequality and probably also inhibit overall growth prospects.

Policy discussions have often emphasized the need to combine policies conducive to growth with investments in the human and physical assets of poor people.[16] However, many questions remain unanswered. What specific interventions should

[14] This test has used the data for developing market economies. The negative interaction effect vanishes if one includes the transition economies of Eastern Europe and Central Asia. This is not too surprising given that these economies are going through a transition process to a market economy in which the economies are tending to contract, and inequality is rising, which may well be confounding the true relationship.

[15] Naturally the number of observations drops considerably, to $n = 69$.

[16] Arguments along these lines can be found in World Bank (1990, 2000*b*), Bruno, Ravallion, and Squire (1998), and Kanbur and Squire (1999) amongst others.

have priority in specific circumstances? Should reform be redesigned or delayed when initial conditions are not favourable, and take time to change?

3.8. CONCLUSIONS

The seemingly opposing positions taken in this ongoing debate are not as hard to reconcile as it might seem at first sight. The poor typically do share in the benefits of rising aggregate affluence, and they typically do suffer from economic contraction. However, there is a sizeable variance around the 'typical' outcomes for the poor. One source of variance is that 'economic growth', as measured in the national accounts, is not always reflected in average household living standards as measured in surveys, at least in the short run.

But the sources of the heterogeneity in outcomes for the poor go deeper than that. Finding zero average impact on inequality of growth-oriented policy reforms does not mean that reforms are generally distribution-neutral. An average is just that, and it is deceptive when one averages over large differences across countries in their starting points. There are important differences in initial inequalities, with implications for how much the poor share in aggregate growth, and contraction. The churning that is found under the surface of the aggregate outcomes also means that there are often losers during spells of growth, even when poverty falls on average. While various papers in the literature have found that growth-promoting policies have little or no average impact on inequality, that finding is perfectly consistent with sizeable distributional impacts in specific countries, albeit in different directions. Average neutrality is consistent with strong distributional effects at the country level. There is truth in both the quotes at the beginning of this chapter, though each is deceptive on its own.

These observations point to the importance of more micro, country-specific, research on the factors determining why some poor people are able to take up the opportunities afforded by an expanding economy—and so add to its expansion—while others are not. Individual endowments of physical and human capital have rightly been emphasized in past work, and suggest important links to policy. Other factors that may well be equally important have received less attention, such as location, social exclusion, and exposure to uninsured risk.

While good policy-making for fighting poverty must obviously be concerned with the aggregate impacts on the poor, it cannot ignore the diversity of impacts underlying the averages, and it is here that good micro-empirical work can help. That diversity also holds potentially important clues as to what else needs to be done by governments to promote poverty reduction, on top of promoting economic growth.

REFERENCES

Aghion, P., Caroli, E., and Garcia-Penalosa, C. (1999). 'Inequality and Economic Growth: The Perspectives of the New Growth Theories'. *Journal of Economic Literature*, 37(4), 1615–60.

Alesina, A. and Rodrik, D. (1994). 'Distributive Politics and Economic Growth'. *Quarterly Journal of Economics*, 108, 465–90.

Atkinson, A. B. and Brandolini, A. (1999). 'Promise and Pitfalls in the Use of "Secondary" Data Sets: Income Inequality in OECD Countries'. Nuffield College, Oxford, mimeo.

Banerjee, A. and Duflo, E. (1999). 'Inequality and Growth: What Can the Data Say?' Department of Economics, MIT, mimeo.

Bardhan, P., Bowles, S., and Gintis, H. (1999). 'Wealth Inequality, Wealth Constraints and Economic Performance'. In A. B. Atkinson and F. Bourguignon (eds), *Handbook of Income Distribution*, vol. 1. North-Holland, Amsterdam.

Barro, R. (2000). 'Inequality and Growth in a Panel of Countries'. *Journal of Economic Growth*, 5, 5–32.

Baulch, R. and Hoddinott, J. (2000). 'Economic Mobility and Poverty Dynamics in Developing Countries'. *Journal of Development Studies*, 36(6), 1–24.

Benabou, R. (1996). 'Inequality and Growth', in B. Bernanke and J. Rotemberg (eds), *National Bureau of Economic Research Macroeconomics Annual*. MIT Press: Cambridge MA.

Bhalla, S. (2000). 'Growth and Poverty in India–Myth and Reality'. Available from http://www.oxusresearch.com/economic.asp.

Birdsall, N. and Londoño, J. L. (1997). 'Asset Inequality Matters: An Assessment of the World Bank's Approach to Poverty Reduction'. *American Economic Review, Papers and Proceedings*, 87(2), 32–7.

——, Ross, D., and Sabot, R. (1995). 'Inequality and Growth Reconsidered: Lessons from East Asia'. *World Bank Economic Review*, 9(3), 477–508.

Bruno, M., Ravallion, M., and Squire, L. (1998). 'Equity and Growth in Developing Countries: Old and New Perspectives on the Policy Issues'. In Vito Tanzi and Ke-young Chu (eds), *Income Distribution and High-Quality Growth*. MIT Press, Cambridge, MA.

Chen, S. and Ravallion, M. (2001). 'How Did the World's Poorest Fare in the 1990s?' *Review of Income and Wealth*, 47(3), 283–300.

Clarke, G. R. G. (1995). 'More Evidence on Income Distribution and Growth'. *Journal of Development Economics*, 47, 403–28.

Datt, G. (1999). 'Has Poverty in India Declined since the Economic Reforms?' *Economic and Political Weekly*, 34.

—— and Ravallion, M. (1998). 'Farm Productivity and Rural Poverty in India'. *Journal of Development Studies*, 34, 62–85.

Deaton, A. (2001). 'Counting the World's Poor: Problems and Possible Solutions'. *World Bank Research Observer*, 16(2), 125–47.

Deininger, K. and Olinto, P. (2000). 'Asset Distribution, Inequality and Growth'. *Policy Research Working Paper* 2375. The World Bank, Washington DC.

—— and Squire, L. (1998). 'New Ways of Looking at Old Issues: Inequality and Growth'. *Journal of Development Economics*, 57(2), 259–87.

Dollar, D. and Kraay, A. (2002). 'Growth is Good for the Poor'. *Journal of Economic Growth*, 7(3), 195–225, reprinted with kind permission as Chapter 2 of this volume.

Easterly, W. and Fischer, S. (2001). 'Inflation and the Poor'. *Journal of Money Credit and Banking*, 33(2), 160–79.

Economist, The (various issues).

Fields, G. (1989). 'Changes in Poverty and Inequality in Developing Countries'. *World Bank Research Observer*, 4, 167–86.

Forbes, K. J. (1997). 'A Reassessment of the Relationship Between Inequality and Growth'. Department of Economics, MIT, mimeo.

Groves, R. M. and Couper, M. P. (1998). *Nonresponse in Household Surveys*. Wiley, New York.

Jalan, J. and Ravallion, M. (1998). 'Are There Dynamic Gains from a Poor-Area Development Program?' *Journal of Public Economics*, 67(1), 65–86.

—— and —— (2000). 'Is Transient Poverty Different? Evidence for Rural China'. *Journal of Development Studies*, 36, 82–99.

—— and —— (2002). 'Household Income Dynamics in Rural China'. *WIDER Discussion Paper* 2002/10. UNU/WIDER, Helsinki.

Kanbur, R. and Squire, L. (1999). 'The Evolution of Thinking about Poverty: Exploring the Interactions'. *Department of Agricultural, Resource and Managerial Economics Paper*, 24. Cornell University.

Knowles, S. (2001). 'Inequality and Economic Growth: The Empirical Relationship Reconsidered in the Light of Comparable Data'. Paper prepared for the WIDER Conference on Growth and Poverty. UNU/WIDER, Helsinki.

Li, H. and Zou, H. F. (1998). 'Income Inequality is not Harmful to Growth: Theory and Evidence'. *Review of Development Economics*, 2(3), 318–34.

——, Squire, L., and Zou, H. F. (1998). 'Explaining International and Intertemporal Variations in Income Inequality'. *Economic Journal*, 108, 26–43.

Lokshin, M. and Ravallion, M. (2000). 'Welfare Impacts of Russia's 1998 Financial Crisis'. *Economics of Transition*, 8(2), 269–95.

—— and —— (2001). 'Nonlinear Household Income Dynamics in Two Transition Economies'. Development Research Group, World Bank, mimeo.

Milanovic, B. (2002). 'True World Income Distribution: 1988 and 1993: First Calculations Based on Household Surveys Alone'. *Economic Journal*, 112(476), 51–92.

Perotti, R. (1996). 'Growth, Income Distribution and Democracy: What the Data Say'. *Journal of Economic Growth*, 1(2), 149–87.

Persson, T. and Tabellini, G. (1994). 'Is Inequality Harmful for Growth?' *American Economic Review*, 84, 600–21.

Ravallion, M. (1995). 'Growth and Poverty: Evidence for Developing Countries in the 1980s'. *Economics Letters*, 48, 411–17.

—— (1997). 'Can High Inequality Developing Countries Escape Absolute Poverty?' *Economics Letters*, 56, 51–7.

—— (1998). 'Does Aggregation Hide the Harmful Effects of Inequality on Growth?' *Economics Letters*, 61(1), 73–7.

—— (2000*a*). 'Do National Accounts Provide Unbiased Estimates of Survey-Based Measures of Living Standards?' *Policy Research Working Paper*. The World Bank: Washington. (http://econ.worldbank.org/files/2384_wps2665.pdf)

—— (2000*b*). 'Should Poverty Measures be Anchored to the National Accounts?' *Economic and Political Weekly*, 35(35/36), 3245–52.

—— (2001). 'Inequality Convergence'. Policy Research Working Paper. The World Bank: Washington. (http://econ.worldbank.org/resource.php?type=5).

—— and Chen, S. (1997). 'What Can New Survey Data Tell Us about Recent Changes in Distribution and Poverty?' *World Bank Economic Review*, 11(2), 357–82.

—— and Datt, G. (2002). 'Why Has Economic Growth Been More Pro-Poor in Some States of India than Others?' *Journal of Development Economics*, 68(2), 381–400.

Squire, L. (1993). 'Fighting Poverty'. *American Economic Review, Papers and Proceedings*, 83(2), 377–82.

van de Walle, D. (2000). 'Are Returns to Investment Lower for the Poor? Human and Physical Capital Interactions in Rural Vietnam'. *Policy Research Working Paper* 2425. The World Bank, Washington.

Wood, A. (1994). North–South Trade, Employment and Inequality: Changing Fortunes in a Skill-Driven World. Clarendon Press, Oxford.

World Bank (1990). *World Development Report: Poverty*. Oxford University Press, New York.

—— (2000*a*). *World Development Indicators*. The World Bank, Washington.

—— (2000*b*). *World Development Report: Attacking Poverty*. Oxford University Press, New York.

4

The Growth Elasticity of Poverty

RASMUS HELTBERG

4.1. INTRODUCTION

Social scientists have long debated the relationship between growth and poverty. One side in this discussion is represented by growth optimists, who believe in 'trickle down', that is, the notion that growth in average incomes automatically sinks down to benefit the poor. The opposing view puts the distribution of income and wealth at the centre stage, and argues that reductions in inequality are required to combat poverty. This includes adherents of the notion of 'immiserizing growth', that is, the idea that growth in average incomes may well occur at the same time as large groups of people are being increasingly impoverished. During the 1990s, the proliferation of quality data on income distribution from a number of countries has allowed rigorous empirical testing of standing debates such as this one.

Datt and Ravallion (1992) developed a method to decompose changes in poverty into a 'growth effect', stemming from change in average income, and a 'distribution effect', caused by shifts in the Lorenz curve holding average income constant. Using data from India and Brazil, they found the growth effect to explain the largest part of observed changes in poverty. Similar results have been found in a number of other developing countries by other researchers. White and Anderson (2001), looking, not at poverty, but at the income of the bottom 20 per cent, also found growth to be, on average, much more important than distributional change. Significant work has also been done based on cross-country comparisons of data 'spells', meaning instances where two or more comparable household surveys are available from the same country at different points of time. Such spells provide the data needed for detailed household-level analysis of growth, poverty, and inequality. Analyses based on spells have found that increases (decreases) in mean income tend to be strongly and significantly associated with falling (increasing) poverty rates (e.g. Ravallion 1995, 2001).

Fields (2001: 97–8) summarizes the literature this way: 'twenty years of research has shown convincingly that in a cross section of countries, those with higher per capita income or consumption have less poverty. The cross-sectional version of the absolute impoverishment hypothesis has been thoroughly discredited'. Moreover, there is substantial evidence to indicate that, usually, distributional change is too little and too slow to be relied upon for poverty reduction. Growth is, in practice, the main tool for fighting poverty (Bruno, Ravallion, and Squire 1998; Squire 1993). However, the imperative of growth for combating poverty should not be misinterpreted to mean that 'growth is all that matters'. Growth is a necessary condition for poverty alleviation, no doubt, but inequality also matters and should also be 'on the agenda' (Kanbur and Lustig 1999). Growth and distribution are interconnected in numerous ways, and the effectiveness with which growth translates into poverty reduction depends crucially on initial inequality. Although emphasized by Ravallion (1997), this simple and obvious fact is too often overlooked. For example, poverty projection studies by Hanmer and Naschold (1999) and Collier and Dollar (2001) are based on a constant elasticity linking poverty reduction to the rate of growth. Such projections yield imprecise results because they fail to take account of how the growth elasticity of poverty depends on initial inequality and level of development (poverty line relative to mean income). This chapter surveys the literature on the growth–poverty relationship, seeking to synthesize empirical and theoretical work in this important and still emerging field. I argue that the growth-versus-distribution dichotomy is false: the growth elasticity of poverty is non-constant, and depends on factors such as initial inequality and the level of development. Inequality, therefore, does matter to poverty alleviation.

4.2. ANALYTICS OF THE GROWTH ELASTICITY OF POVERTY

There are some precise analytical results on the growth elasticity of poverty provided one is willing to make the rather drastic assumption that the Lorenz curve is constant, that is, that inequality does not change. Alternatively, some analytical results are also possible if one imposes simplifying assumptions about either the nature of change in the income distribution or the shape of the distribution. This section reviews the major insights on the growth elasticity of poverty that appear from literature that embodies these assumptions. In Section 3, I review empirical results based on spell data, in which no assumptions on the nature of the distribution or its change are imposed.

Let $F(x)$ denote the distribution function of individual income. If z is a poverty line, then $H = F(z)$ is the proportion of poor in the society. H is usually called the headcount ratio, and is the most popularly used measure of income/consumption poverty. As a poverty measure, H has some drawbacks because it fails to take into account both the size of the aggregate income shortfall of the poor and the distribution of income among the poor. A more general class of poverty measures can be written

$$\theta = \int_0^z P(z,x)f(x)\,\mathrm{d}x, \tag{4.1}$$

where $f(x)$ is the density function of x and $\partial P/\partial x < 0, \partial^2 P/\partial^2 x > 0, P(z,z) = 0$ and $P(z,x)$ is homogenous of degree zero in z and x (Kakwani 2001). The most famous incarnation of eqn (4.1) is the P_a measure proposed by Foster, Greer, and Thorbecke (FGT) (1984). The FGT P_a measure is given by

$$P_a(z,x) = \int_0^z ((z-x)/z)^{\alpha} f(x)\,\mathrm{d}x. \tag{4.2}$$

If the inequality aversion parameter, α, equals zero, we have $P_0 = H$, that is, the headcount measure. P_1 is termed the poverty gap measure, and indicates the aggregate income shortfall, or depth of poverty, of those below the poverty line. P_2 is referred to as the squared poverty gap measure, or severity of poverty, because it places greater weight on those far below the poverty line.

4.2.1. *Analytical Elasticities*

For any poverty measure that satisfies eqn (4.1), Kakwani (1993) derived its elasticity with respect to mean income, while holding the distribution constant (i.e. assuming a growth process in which the entire Lorenz curve is shifted in a constant proportion). The elasticity is

$$\eta_\theta = \frac{1}{\theta} \int_0^z x \frac{\partial P}{\partial x} f(x)\, \mathrm{d}x. \tag{4.3}$$

This is always negative. For headcount poverty, this implies an elasticity of $\eta_H = zf(x)/H$, which shows the percentage of the poor who will cross the poverty line if all incomes increase by 1 per cent (Kakwani 1993, 2001). For the FGT-measures with $\alpha \neq 0$, the elasticity is

$$\eta_\alpha = -\frac{\alpha(P_{\alpha-1} - P_\alpha)}{P_\alpha}, \tag{4.4}$$

which will always be negative. For the poverty gap measure, $\alpha = 1$, this gives $\eta_1 = -\mu^*/(z - \mu^*)$, where μ^* is the average income of the poor. Since μ^*/z is the inverse of the depth of poverty, this shows that the poverty elasticity increases (decreases) in absolute value the lower (higher) is the depth of poverty. Chen and Ravallion (2001) use this formula to calculate the elasticity of P_1 poverty, and find a global average of -2.39 for the \$1/day line. The corresponding regional averages range from -4.4 for the Middle East and North Africa to just -1.67 for sub-Saharan Africa, probably reflecting differences in the incidence of poverty.

4.2.2. *An Illustration*

It may be useful to illustrate these elasticities using real world income distributions. This helps bring out the magnitudes and the non-linearities involved in the growth elasticity of poverty for specific developing countries. To do so, I used household survey data from Mozambique, Vietnam, and South Africa. Mozambique was chosen for its high level of poverty; Vietnam for its equal distribution and rapid poverty reduction during the 1990s; and South Africa for its high degree of inequality. Table 4.1 summarizes for each country its headcount rate (based on national poverty lines, and therefore not comparable across countries), Gini coefficient, sample size, and the source of the data. All data come from nationally representative household surveys. The income variable used here is total real per capita daily expenditure in line with most of the literature.

I simulated the impact of distribution-neutral growth by maintaining the income distribution fixed, and calculating the growth elasticity for a range of artificial poverty lines spanning from the 1st percentile (where 99 per cent are poor) to the 99th percentile, where just 1 per cent is poor.

In Figs 4.1–4.4, the horizontal axis shows the location of the poverty line, with the movement from left to right mimicking the impact of distribution-neutral growth in terms of reducing $z/\bar{x}$. Elasticities are shown on the vertical axes. Figure 4.1 compares the elasticities for headcount poverty, η_H, for these three countries, Fig. 4.2 compares P_1 elasticities, η_{P_1}, and Fig. 4.3, η_{P_2}. The figures show that for a given income distribution, the absolute value of the poverty elasticity increases as average income grows relative to the poverty line. Thus, poverty is more (less) elastic to growth the lower (higher) is poverty. For any given location of the poverty line and P_α, poverty elasticities are largest (in absolute value) in Vietnam, which has the most equal income distribution, and lowest in South Africa, which is the most unequal of these countries. The dependence of the poverty elasticity on $z/\bar{x}$ appears even more pronounced for

Table 4.1. *Summary statistics for income data*

	Mozambique	Vietnam	South Africa
Headcount ratio	0.69	0.37	0.25
Gini index	0.396	0.345	0.586
Sample size	8,250	5,999	8,783
Data source	IAF 1996–97	VLSS 1997–98	Integrated household survey 1993–94

Source: Author's compilation.

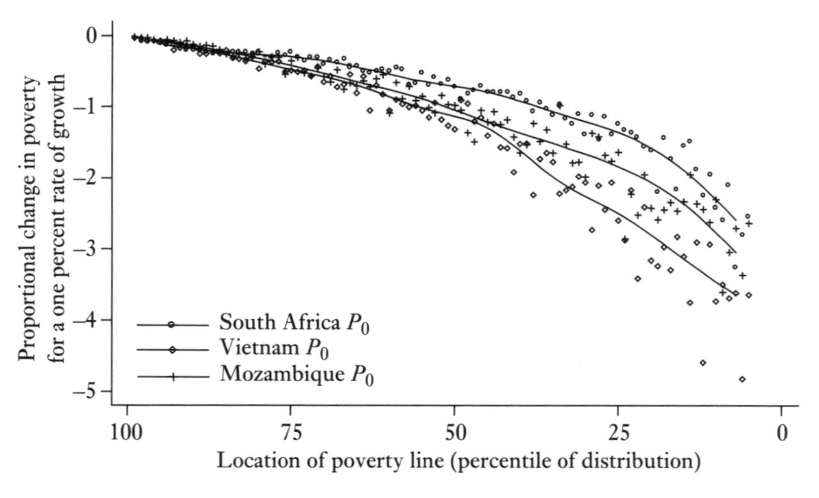

Figure 4.1. *Growth elasticities of P_0 for three countries compared*

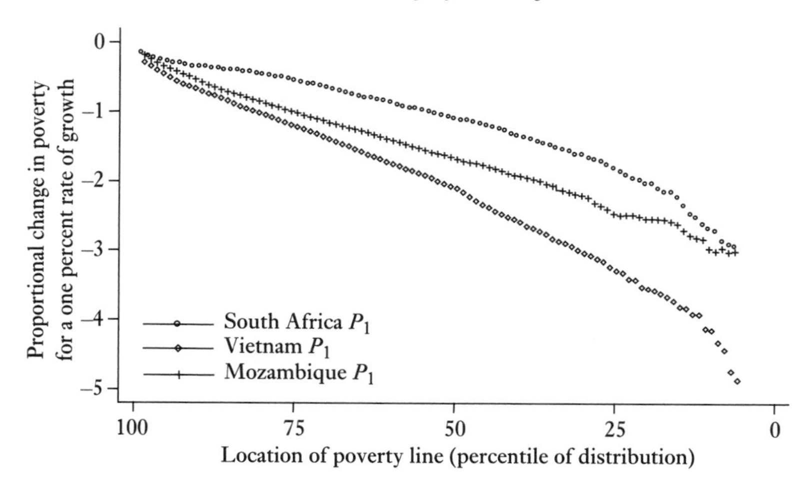

Figure 4.2. *Growth elasticities of P_1 for three countries compared*

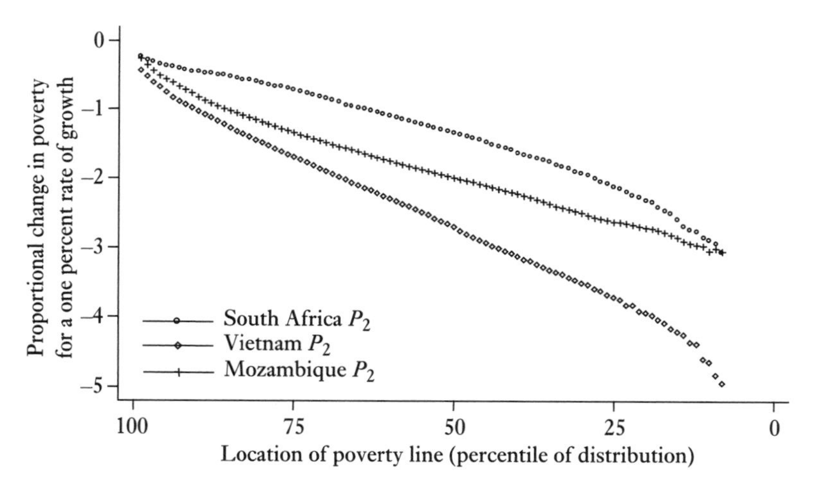

Figure 4.3. *Growth elasticities of P_2 for three countries compared*

Vietnam than for the other countries. This is because Vietnam is also more equal, at the bottom of the distribution than Mozambique and South Africa. It can be seen that the poverty elasticity increases with α: depth and severity of poverty responds more elastically to growth than the headcount.

These results may be hard to understand intuitively. One may ask, rightly, if the impact of growth on poverty does not depend on the location of the poverty line *vis-à-vis* the bulk of the income distribution? After all, if many people are located at, or slightly below, the poverty line, economic growth should have a large impact. The key to understand the above results is that they refer to the *percentage change* in poverty,

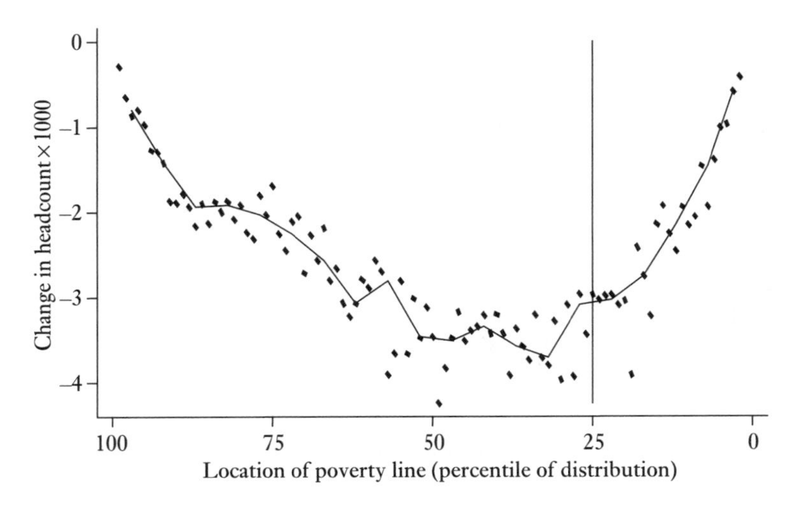

Figure 4.4. *Headcount poverty: Absolute change for South Africa*

not the *absolute change* in the number of poor. To illustrate this point, I plot in Fig. 4.4, the change in headcount level (i.e. the number of people moving from below to above the poverty line) for South Africa in response to changes in mean income. It can be seen that at the location of the current national poverty line (indicated by a vertical bar), a substantial number of people will be shifted out of poverty by distribution-neutral growth. Yet the impact on the headcount rate will quickly reduce in absolute magnitude if growth in mean income is sustained. If, on the other hand, mean incomes were to fall, a large number of people would be moving into poverty in South Africa.

The Development Assistance Committee (DAC) of the OECD has set some official development targets, one of which is to cut global poverty by half between 1990–2015. Existing projection studies (Hanmer and Naschold 1999; Collier and Dollar 2001) use constant elasticities to answer that question. The approach adopted in this section can be used to provide a more precise answer. Based on the actual data for these three countries, I calculated how much growth in mean household income is required to reduce poverty by half (relative to the survey year) in 25 years. I assume constant distribution and constant share of household income to GDP. The result is shown in Table 4.2. Mozambique needs 2.1 per cent real annual per capita growth to halve poverty in 25 years. For Vietnam just 1.1 per cent growth will suffice, whereas for South Africa 1.8 per cent is required.

Given their past growth records, achieving the target of halving headcount poverty in 25 years seems feasible for Vietnam and Mozambique. South Africa will need substantial improvement in the rate of growth, in distribution, or in both, to achieve the development target. This clearly illustrates the importance of inequality—Vietnam's highly equal income distribution means that economic growth in that country translates into poverty reduction in a very effective manner. To achieve a comparable rate of poverty reduction, countries with unequal income distribution have to grow a lot

Table 4.2. *Actual and required growth rates*

	Annual real per capita growth rates		
	Mozambique	**Vietnam**	**South Africa**
Needed to halve poverty in 25 years	2.1	1.1	1.8
Actual GDP growth rate 1995–99	6.0	5.96	0.43

Source: Author's calculations.

faster. In this context, poverty alleviation in South Africa is facing the double hurdle of sluggish growth in income and unequal distribution.

4.2.3. *A Log-Linear Approximation*

Inequality can change in countless ways, hence, it is hard to say anything general about the growth–poverty relationship when the distribution is allowed to change during growth. Kakwani (1993) developed a formula for the inequality elasticity of poverty under the assumption of an equal proportionate change in the Lorenz curve. Another road ahead is to assume a particular functional form for the income distribution, and work out the growth–inequality–poverty relationship for that distribution. Bourguignon (2000) does this, assuming incomes follow the lognormal distribution. He derives an explicit formula linking the growth-elasticity of headcount poverty to mean income and inequality in the lognormal case

$$\tilde{\eta}_H = -\frac{\Delta H}{H_t}\frac{1}{\Delta\log(\bar{x})} = \frac{1}{\sigma}\lambda\left[\frac{\log(z/\bar{x})}{\sigma} + \frac{\sigma}{2}\right], \tag{4.5}$$

where $\Delta\log(\bar{x})$ is the proportionate change in income, $\Delta H/H_t$ is the proportionate change in headcount poverty, σ is the standard deviation of log income and λ is the ratio of the density to the cumulative function, or hazard rate, of the standard normal distribution. Expression (5) shows that the growth elasticity of poverty is an increasing function of development—the inverse of $z/\bar{x}$—and a decreasing function of income inequality as measured by σ. Bourguignon (2000) also develops a formula for the elasticity of P_1 poverty. Both these formulae provide explicit proof, in the case where income follows the lognormal distribution, for the points made above, namely that the growth elasticity of poverty increases with development and decreases with rising inequality.

4.3. REGRESSION ESTIMATES OF THE GROWTH ELASTICITY OF POVERTY

In reality, inequality can and does change in numerous ways in response to growth and multiple other factors. How responsive is poverty to growth in mean income when the Lorenz curve is free to vary? Clearly, this is an empirical issue. One might naively try to address this issue by regressing the rate of poverty on mean income for a range of countries. However, such level-based poverty comparison across countries suffers from numerous shortcomings, and could potentially be misleading due to problems arising from currency conversions, measurement errors and omitted country-specific fixed effects correlated with income (Ravallion 1995). Differencing provides a solution because it removes any country-specific fixed effects.

Therefore, as mentioned in the Introduction, data on growth spells from multiple countries are appropriate for helping to determine the size of the average poverty elasticity in actual growth experiences, i.e. without imposing distributional assumptions. Data on spells can also help determine if there is symmetry in the way that increasing and decreasing average incomes affect the poor. Moreover, differencing will also help address any potential endogeneity problem that would occur if growth is endogenously influenced by inequality, because differencing removes country-specific effects in the levels (such as the level of initial inequality). During the 1990s, there has been a rapid expansion in the number of nationally representative household surveys, and many countries now have two or more surveys available. This has resulted in a much better understanding of the poverty–inequality–development nexus (Fields 2001).

Ravallion (1995) regressed changes in headcount (based on the $1/day purchasing power parity international poverty line used by the World Bank and others) on growth for a sample of sixteen countries with observations at two or more points in time, and found an elasticity of -2.4 ($R^2 = 0.64$). The squared poverty gap, P_2 was found to be more elastic, as theory predicts, at -4. Squire (1993) used a data set consisting of twenty-one spells to regress the change in the headcount index on growth in mean income while controlling for the initial headcount index. Growth was found to be significant and have an elasticity equal to -2.4 ($R^2 = 0.70$). Ravallion and Chen (1997) used data on sixty-four spells. Based on the $1/day poverty line, they found an (highly significant) elasticity of -3.12 ($R^2 = 0.37$). When instead they fixed the poverty line at 50 per cent of the mean, the elasticity was -2.6 ($R^2 = 0.84$). When Eastern Europe and Central Asia are excluded the elasticity drops in absolute value to -1.57 ($N = 43; R^2 = 0.58$). Since Eastern Europe and Central Asia are, or at least used to be, low inequality countries, it is unsurprising that their growth elasticity is larger in absolute value. Ravallion and Chen (1997) also experimented with even higher poverty lines, and found, as one would expect, that the elasticity drops: it was -1.29 for a poverty line at 75 per cent of mean income for the full sample, and -0.69 when the poverty line was 100 per cent of mean income. The sample of household survey spells continues to grow. Based on 115 spells, Ravallion (2001) reports $\eta_0 = -2.5$ ($R^2 = 0.44$) based on the $1/day international poverty line.

An implication of these studies is symmetry of the manner in which rising and falling mean income affects the poor. Equal economies have a high absolute value of the growth elasticity, implying that the poor gain a larger share of growth and lose more from contraction. Conversely, unequal societies have a small absolute η, and this protects the income of the poor during contraction.

The above regressions likely suffer from misspecification because they treat the growth–poverty relationship as governed by some fixed elasticity, ignoring its dependency on inequality and level of development. Recent literature has, therefore, moved on to address directly the dependence of the growth elasticity on inequality. Ravallion (1997) regressed the rate of poverty reduction (based on a \$1.50/day PPP line) on an encompassing model including growth, inequality as measured by the Gini index, interaction terms between them, and all of their squared terms. He found a statistically acceptable restricted form of the general model to be

$$\frac{\Delta H}{H_t} = 4.435(1 - Gini_t)\frac{\Delta x}{x_t} + \text{residual}, \quad N = 41; R^2 = 0.36. \tag{4.6}$$

Based on this, Ravallion (1997) concludes that it is the *distribution-corrected rate of growth* ([1 − Gini] · growth rate) that matters. The estimates imply that, at the lowest Gini in his sample (0.25), the growth elasticity of \$1.5/day headcount poverty is −3.3, while at the highest Gini (0.59) it is −1.8. At the mean Gini index (0.41), the elasticity is −2.6. Ravallion (2001) repeated the exercise on a larger data set, and found a quite similar result,

$$\Delta \log P_0 = -3.74(1 - Gini_t)\Delta \log(x) + \text{residual}, \quad N = 115; R^2 \text{ not reported.} \tag{4.7}$$

The distribution-corrected rate of growth is an interesting concept that helps us understand better how inequality shapes the impact of growth on poverty. Since the distribution-corrected rate of growth does not explicitly take into account the dependence of the growth elasticity of poverty on the level of development ($z/\bar{x}$), it is potentially vulnerable to the misspecification of imposing a constant elasticity to a more complex non-linear relationship. Ravallion (1997) tested for this and found eqn (4.6) statistically acceptable. Future studies seeking to apply the distribution-corrected rate of growth as an explanatory variable will also need to pay careful attention to this issue.

Bourguignon (2000) explored various models based on a data set comprised of 116 growth spells from 52 different countries. The best fit was obtained by the following model

$$\frac{\Delta H}{H_t} = 0.05 + 5.23\Delta Gini_t - 1.14x_t\tilde{\eta}_H + \text{residual}, \quad N = 116; R^2 = 0.508, \tag{4.8}$$

where $\tilde{\eta}_H$ is the theoretically expected value of the growth–poverty elasticity that can be obtained from eqn (4.5), that is, based on assuming incomes are lognormal. Bourguignon (2000) refers to this as an 'identity check' on the logical identity linking growth and poverty eqn (4.5) under the assumption that incomes are lognormal. This identity is 'confirmed' by finding a parameter not significantly different from unity. Unfortunately, Bourguignon (2000) did not directly compare his model to the distribution-corrected rate of growth, $(1 - Gini_t)\Delta \log(x)$. However, although the regression in eqn (4.8) incorporates the lognormal growth–poverty 'identity', it does not give a perfect fit, with 50 per cent of the variation in the data unaccounted for.

It, therefore, appears that real world distributions and distributional changes are more complex than what is captured by the lognormal. The best fit is likely to incorporate non-linearities and interactive terms between the poverty line relative to average income, inequality, and growth.

4.4. CONCLUSIONS

Summing up, the conclusions of this study are the following. First, the magnitude of the poverty elasticity of distribution neutral changes in mean income depends on the location of the poverty line, and hence should not be treated as a constant across countries or time. It increases monotonically with increasing mean income, holding the poverty line constant. Second, as Ravallion (1997) emphasized, the poverty elasticity depends strongly on the degree of inequality. An unequal income distribution is a serious impediment to effective poverty alleviation. Third, as a consequence of this the 'growth versus redistribution' dichotomy is false. One needs to be careful when decomposing poverty changes into growth and distribution components, because the growth effect is itself a function of the degree of inequality. The manner in which growth and inequality interact to shape poverty is not additive.

It is true that redistribution often has limited potential and that growth is a necessary condition for poverty alleviation. Yet, the level of inequality, and changes therein, still matters. This is because (i) for any given level of average income, the level of inequality affects the degree of poverty; (ii) inequality strongly affects the growth elasticity of poverty, and lower inequality contributes to an acceleration of poverty reduction for a given rate of growth; (iii) if recent cross-country regression studies are true, initial inequality, especially asset inequality, is harmful for growth (see, for example, Deininger and Olinto 2000). For these reasons, inequality still matters, and the search for effective policies for reducing inequalities, or at least preventing them from rising, goes on.

REFERENCES

Bourguignon, F. (2000). 'The Pace of Economic Growth and Poverty Alleviation'. The World Bank and Delta, Paris, unpublished.

Bruno, M., Ravallion, M., and Squire, L. (1998). 'Equity and Growth in Developing Countries: Old and New Perspectives on the Policy Issues'. In Vito Tanzi and Ke-young Chu (eds), *Income Distribution and High-Quality Growth*. MIT Press, Cambridge, MA.

Chen, S. and Ravallion, M. (2001). 'How did the World's Poorest Fare in the 1990s?' *Review of Income and Wealth*, 47(3), 283–300.

Collier, P. and Dollar, D. (2001). 'Can the World Cut Poverty in Half? How Policy Reform and Effective Aid Can Meet International Development Goals'. *World Development*, 29(11), 1787–802.

Datt, G. and Ravallion, M. (1992). 'Growth and Redistribution Components of Changes in Poverty Measures: A Decomposition with Applications to Brazil and India in the 1980s'. *Journal of Development Economics*, 38(2), 275–95.

Deininger, K. and Olinto, P. (2000). 'Asset Distribution, Inequality, and Growth'. *Policy Research Working Papers* 2375. The World Bank, Washington.

Fields, G. (2001). 'Distribution and Development: A New Look at the Developing World'. MIT Press, Cambridge MA.

Foster, J., Greer, J., and Thorbecke, E. (1984). 'A Class of Decomposable Poverty Measures'. *Econometrica*, 52(3), 761–6.

Hanmer, L. and Naschold, F. (1999). 'Attaining the International Development Targets: Will Growth Be Enough?' *Journal of International Development*, 11(4), 547–64.

Kakwani, N. (1993). 'Poverty and Economic Growth with Application to Côte D'Ivoire'. *Review of Income and Wealth*, 39(2), 121–39.

—— (2001). 'A Note on Growth and Poverty Reduction'. Unpublished. Asian Development Bank, Manila.

Kanbur, R. and Lustig, N. (1999). 'Why is Inequality Back on the Agenda?' Paper presented at the Annual World Bank Conference on Development Economics, World Bank.

Ravallion, M. (1995). 'Growth and Poverty: Evidence for Developing Countries in the 1980s'. *Economics Letters*, 48, 411–17.

—— (1997). 'Can High-Inequality Developing Countries Escape Absolute Poverty?' *Economics Letters*, 56, 51–7.

—— (2001). 'Growth, Inequality and Poverty: Looking Beyond Averages'. *World Development*, 29(11), 1803–15.

—— and Chen, S. (1997). 'What Can New Survey Data Tell Us about Recent Changes in Distribution and Poverty?' *World Bank Economic Review*, 11(2), 357–82.

Squire, L. (1993). 'Fighting Poverty'. *American Economic Review*, 83(2), 377–82.

White, H. and Anderson, E. (2001). 'Growth versus Distribution: Does the Pattern of Growth Matter?'. *Development Policy Review*, 19(3), 267–89.

5

Education is Good for the Poor: A Note on Dollar and Kraay

ERICH GUNDLACH, JOSÉ NAVARRO DE PABLO, AND NATASCHA WEISERT

5.1. INTRODUCTION AND BACKGROUND

A recent study by Dollar and Kraay (2002) finds that growth is good for the poor, but that the income of the poor does not respond systematically to supposedly 'pro-poor' policies such as public expenditure on education. Using a sample covering 137 countries over the period 1950–99, they report that the income of the poor rises one-for-one with average income. However, the primary educational attainment of the workforce (and the level of primary enrolment, as in an earlier version of their study) does not seem to have a measurable effect on the income of the poor beyond its effect on average income. Hence, their work tends to suggest that a focus on education rather than on growth might be misplaced as an essential component of any poverty-reduction strategy.

We test the robustness of the findings by Dollar and Kraay by using a broader measure of human capital, which considers all levels of education and accounts for international differences in the quality of education. Contrary to Dollar and Kraay, we find that a higher stock of human capital increases the income of the poor, not only through its effect on average income, but also through its effect on the distribution of income. Our results appear to be robust to a number of alternative specifications. We interpret our findings as suggesting that effective education policies would be a first-best poverty reduction strategy.

Our interpretation of the empirical evidence seems to be more in line with a policy strategy favoured by the Development Report 2000 (World Bank 2000*a*) than the paper we seek to criticize, which in fact emanated from the World Bank's research department. With its focus on attacking poverty, the Development Report goes significantly beyond the message conveyed by Dollar and Kraay (2002) in that economic growth is merely considered to be a necessary condition for achieving development and reducing poverty, but it is not deemed a sufficient force. Effective anti-poverty strategies are meant

We thank Bert Hofman for basic ideas and two anonymous referees and participants of the WIDER Development Conference on Growth and Poverty for constructive comments on an earlier version.

to focus on three additional issues: strengthening the participation of poor people in local decision-making and fighting discrimination; reducing vulnerability of the poor to economic and natural shocks, sickness and violence; and lastly, expanding economic opportunity and access to assets, such as education, capital, and land. An additional study by the World Bank on growth and poverty (World Bank 2000*b*) further emphasized the centrality of education in the development process. This study argues that human capital appears to be the main asset of most poor people. Hence, investment in the human capital of the poor should be a powerful way to augment their assets, redress asset inequality, and reduce poverty.

Recent analyses of international differences in output per worker and growth rates have also raised the awareness of the role of human capital in development, either as a direct or as an indirect factor.[1] The endogenous growth literature emphasizes the centrality of human capital for innovation and technological progress. Most empirical cross-country studies of long-run growth now include some measure of human capital. Regardless of the underlying model, it is a fairly robust empirical finding that a country's human capital is almost always identified as an essential ingredient for achieving growth.[2] However, the quantitative impact of human capital on growth has not been precisely estimated up to now.

The centrality of education in poverty-reduction policies stems from the belief that education is a powerful equalizer. However, this belief cannot command strong theoretical support. Ram (1989) reviews several theoretical frameworks linking the level of schooling and its dispersion with income inequality, such as human capital or dual-economy-type models. He finds that these models do not generate any clear theoretical hypotheses about the effect of education on income inequality or absolute poverty.

For instance, traditional human-capital models of earnings provide two opposing insights with regard to the relationship between education and income-distribution. First, holding other things equal these models imply a partial positive relation between the mean level of schooling and earnings inequality, such that if the mean level of schooling rises, wages of educated workers go up relative to wages earned by non-educated workers. But these models also feature a partial positive relation between schooling inequality and earnings inequality in that a more equal distribution of schooling leads to a more equal distribution of earnings.

Knight and Sabot (1983) show these effects in a dual-economy version of the human capital model. Educational expansion has again two different effects on the distribution of earnings and thus on overall income inequality as it raises the supply of educated labour. On the one hand, the composition effect (or Kuznets' effect) increases the relative size of the group with higher education (and higher earnings) and thus tends to increase inequality. On the other hand, the wage compression effect resulting from the relatively greater supply of educated labour reduces inequality. Which effect dominates

[1] See, for example, Mankiw, Romer, and Weil (1992), Benhabib and Spiegel (1994), and Hall and Jones (1999).

[2] See, for example, Temple (1999) and Krueger and Lindahl (2000).

is again unclear and will ultimately depend on the country's level of development, the relative size of the different educational groups, the degree of substitutability between workers with different levels of education, and the wider social, political, and economic aspects that affect the structure of relative wages for different educational groups and the demand for labour.

To the extent that formal schooling is a significant component of human capital investment, the recent endogenous growth literature might provide a more conclusive theoretical framework regarding the relationship between educational expansion and income distribution. Tamura (1991) explains income convergence in the developed world by an endogenous growth model with human capital spillovers and heterogeneous agents. In his model, human capital convergence results in income convergence. Human capital convergence can be induced by educational expansion and the promotion of research activity, and arises because for a given stock of existing knowledge, agents with below average human capital have a higher rate of return to human capital investment.

With a more explicit focus on the formal schooling component of human capital investment, Glomm and Ravikumar (1992) construct an overlapping generations model with heterogeneous agents that provides similar results. The human capital possessed by each individual agent is a function of the parents' stock of human capital, the level of schooling acquired, and the quality of education provided, which is modelled as an increasing function of tax revenue and determined endogenously by majority-voting. Furthermore, they assume that the learning technology exhibits at least constant returns to the quality of schools and the parents' stock of human capital. While they are mainly interested in comparing the effects of public and private investment in human capital on growth and the distribution of income, they also show that income inequality unambiguously declines over time in an economy with a public education sector where the quality of schooling is homogenous. Since the growth rate of any agent's income is inversely related to his initial level, income convergence results in their model.

By contrast, the endogenous growth model suggested by Lucas (1988) does not predict income convergence. In this model, the human capital is supposed to generate internal and external effects, where the latter means that the average level of education also contributes to the productivity of all other factors of production. Assuming that a given percentage increase in human capital requires the same effort independent of the level of human capital already attained, the model generates sustainable growth through the accumulation of human capital. Due to the presumed linearity in the production of human capital, the model is capable of predicting permanent income differences of any size. Incomes would not converge because the incentive to invest in human capital, as measured by the rate of return to education, would be the same across all levels of income and human capital.

Given the various theoretical possibilities, it is probably not surprising that it has proved to be difficult to identify a clear empirical link between education and income inequality up to now. Intertemporal studies are rare in number and, as Ram (1989) notes, also do not appear to point to general conclusions regarding the relationship between education and inequality.[3] Fields (1980) and Psacharopoulos and Woodhall (1985) provide extensive surveys of the empirical literature. Some older cross section studies tend to confirm the equalizing function of education. Ram (1984) challenges these findings by pointing out that the empirical evidence appears generally inconclusive. More recently, a study by De Gregorio and Lee (1999) based on international panel data finds that higher educational attainment (and a more equal distribution of education) plays a significant role in making the distribution of income more equal. Their finding appears to be in conflict with the results by Dollar and Kraay (2002).

Our chapter is structured as follows. Section 2 presents the data and the basic specification for our empirical analysis. Section 3 presents our empirical results. Section 4 summarizes our argument and points out directions for future research.

5.2. DATA AND SPECIFICATION OF VARIABLES

5.2.1. *Income Distribution*

As the source for internationally comparable data on the distribution of income, we draw on the data set initially provided by Deininger and Squire (1996). This data set contains Gini coefficients and cumulative quintile shares for 111 countries over a period of 40 years. In line with Dollar and Kraay (2002), we define the average per capita income of the poor as the average per capita income of the poorest 20 per cent of the population.

At this point, it is worth stressing that this definition does not provide a very homogenous measure of poverty, neither across countries nor across time. For example, in Indonesia it was only in 1997, just before the Asian crises, that absolute poverty (as defined by the World Bank) was reduced to 20 per cent of its population. In this case, our measure would be an appropriate indicator of absolute poverty. However, countries such as Bangladesh have 60 per cent of their population living on less than one dollar a day. In that case, our measure would only reflect how the poorest of the poor are faring without capturing the extent of absolute poverty. Another drawback of this measure is that its capacity to register changes in the mass of the desperately poor across time is not very accurate. Again, if extraordinary growth in Bangladesh were to halve absolute poverty, our measure may not reflect any change at all. These ambiguities should be kept in mind when we use the term incomes of the poor. Our approach focuses on relative poverty rather than on absolute poverty.

The poverty data we use are taken from an updated version of the Deininger and Squire (1996) data set. As a first step, we derive a sample of 102 countries for which 'high quality' Gini coefficients are available. In order to be included in their 'high quality' data set, an observation must be drawn from a published household survey,

[3] There may also exist several indirect mechanisms which influence the relation between educational expansion and reduced inequality. In particular, there appears to be some empirical evidence for the favourable impact of female education on reducing inequality. For instance, Ram (1989) notes that the expansion of female schooling may improve the income distribution through increasing female labour force participation as well as through reducing fertility.

provide comprehensive coverage of the population and be based on a comprehensive measure of income or expenditure. We only use data around 1990 and restrict our sample to one observation per country. For eighty-nine of the 102 countries with high-quality Gini coefficients, there is also information about the share of income accruing to the poorest 20 per cent of the population (quintile 1). For these countries, we measure average per capita income of the poor as average per capita income times the share of income accruing to the poorest quintile divided by 0.2, where data for average per capita income are taken from the Penn World Tables (PWT 1994).

We estimate the average per capita income of the poor for the remaining thirteen countries in our sample under the assumption that the distribution of income is log-normal. The missing quintiles for these countries can then be approximated on the basis of Gini coefficients using

$$\ln y_{\mathrm{p}} = -0.036G + \ln y, \tag{5.1}$$

where $\ln y_{\mathrm{p}}$ denotes the natural logarithm of average per capita income in the poorest quintile of the population, G denotes the Gini coefficient, and $\ln y$ denotes the natural logarithm of average per capita income in the entire population.[4] The results for the average per capita income of the poor based on eqn (5.1) are shown in Appendix Table 5A.1, where the thirteen countries considered in our sample are indicated by footnote (b). Appendix Table 5A.1 also includes all other variables used in the analysis.

With our data set, we find that income of the poor and average income of the total population are highly correlated. Regressing per capita income of the poor on average per capita income yields an adjusted R-squared of 0.86 and a slope coefficient of 1.06 (with a standard error of 0.04). Our result comes very close to the result of Dollar and Kraay (2002) for their basic specification in levels, which they estimate for a sample of 269 pooled cross-country and time series observations. Hence, using the same initial specification but a much smaller sample which only includes one observation per country, we also find that growth is good for the poor: higher average income would translate one-for-one into higher income of the poor.[5] The question is whether other variables could have an additional positive impact on the income of the poor. Our focus is on education.

5.2.2. *Education*

In the empirical growth literature, it has been common practice to use enrolment rates or average years of education as proxies for the change and the level in the stock of human capital. Dollar and Kraay (2002), for instance, focus on years of primary education (and on primary enrolment rates in an earlier version of their study) as their

[4] The coefficient on G was obtained as a result of a regression reported in the March 2000 version of Dollar and Kraay (2002).

[5] This result does not change if we exclude countries with a population of less than one million persons in 1990 countries, if we exclude the thirteen countries for which we estimated the income of the poor according to eqn (5.1), or if we exclude formerly socialist countries. In all cases, the estimated slope coefficient remains statistically significantly indifferent from 1. This also holds if we exclude all three subsamples together.

measure of differences in education across countries because deviations from complete primary school enrolments are most likely to reflect the low enrolment among the poorest in society. But given that international variation in primary education tends to be small relative to broader measures of education, their finding of insignificant effects of education on incomes of the poor may not be robust when compared with other measures of education which cover a larger degree of international variation.

As discussed in Wößmann (2000), the standard specification of human capital in macroeconomic production functions is problematic for methodological and empirical reasons. For instance, a large body of microeconometric evidence based on the Mincerian wage equation would suggest a semi-logarithmic and not a log-linear relation between output per worker and average years of education, which, restricted to primary education, is the measure used in the level equations of Dollar and Kraay (2002). In addition, rates of return to education tend to decline with rising levels of schooling (Psacharopoulos 1994), and the quality of a year of education may differ substantially across countries. All these aspects should be taken into account when constructing an empirical measure of the stock of human capital.

Hall and Jones (1999) address these problems by specifying the stock of human capital (H) in a way that is consistent with a microeconomic Mincerian wage equation. Their measure of human capital is given by

$$H_i = e^{\sum r_j \cdot S_{ij}} L_i, \tag{5.2}$$

where r_j is the world average of the Mincerian rate of return to investment in the j-th level (primary, secondary, or higher) of education, S_{ij} is average years of schooling taken from Barro and Lee (1996) at the j-th level of education in country i, and L_i is the number of working-age persons in country i.

Gundlach, Rudman, and Wößmann (2002) improve this empirical measure of human capital by using social rates of return to education derived on the basis of the so-called elaborate method as reported in Psacharopoulos (1994) and by accounting for country-specific duration of each level of education as reported in UNESCO's Statistical Yearbook. In addition, Gundlach, Rudman, and Wößmann (2002) use an index of schooling quality calculated by Hanushek and Kimko (2000) on the basis of international cognitive achievement tests of students in mathematics and natural sciences to account for international differences in the quality of education. The resulting measure of human capital per working-age person in country i, which we also use in this chapter, is given by

$$\ln(H_i/L_i) = \begin{cases} r^{\text{Pri}} \cdot S_i \cdot Q_i & \text{if } S_i \leq \text{Pri}_i \\ (r^{\text{Pri}} \cdot \text{Pri}_i + r^{\text{Sec}} \cdot (S_i - \text{Pri}_i)) \cdot Q_i & \text{if } \text{Pri}_i < S_i \leq \text{Pri}_i + \text{Sec}_i \\ (r^{\text{Pri}} \cdot \text{Pri}_i + r^{\text{Sec}} \cdot \text{Sec}_i & \\ \quad + r^{\text{High}} \cdot (S_i - \text{Pri}_i - \text{Sec}_i)) \cdot Q_i & \text{if } S_i > \text{Pri}_i + \text{Sec}_i, \end{cases} \tag{5.3}$$

where r^{Pri}, r^{Sec} and r^{High} are world-average social rates of return to primary, secondary, and higher education (20, 13.7, and 10.7 per cent, respectively); Pri_i and Sec_i are country-specific measures of the duration of the primary and the secondary level of schooling; S_i is average years of educational attainment in country i taken from Barro and Lee (1996), and Q_i is an index of schooling quality in country i, measured on a 0–1 scale.[6]

At first sight, our measure of quality-adjusted human capital per worker may be criticized for being unnecessarily complicated because the effect of quality in education could be already picked up by a correctly measured country-specific rate of return variable. However, many empirical estimates of country-specific rates of return as surveyed by Psacharopoulos (1994) appear implausible. Like Hall and Jones (1999), we therefore use world average rates of return for the three levels of education for each country. But their approach by definition fails to account for any international differences in the quality of schooling. Hence, eqn (5.3) should be read as attempting to make the best of the available empirical evidence: it captures both the quantity and the quality of education at the country level by multiplying country-specific years of schooling with world-average rates of return and country-specific estimates of schooling quality. The resulting measure of human capital is certainly not perfect, but it may be preferable to previously used measures, because it is based on a functional form in line with a large microeconometric literature, and because it considers that the quality of education differs across countries.

5.3. EMPIRICAL RESULTS

To estimate the potential impact of quality-adjusted human capital on the incomes of the poor, we estimate an OLS-regression which controls for the impact of average per capita income. Accordingly, our regression equation reads

$$\ln y_p = c + a_1 \ln y + a_2 \ln (H/L) + a_i X_i, \tag{5.4}$$

where X_i denotes a set of further possible control variables. Without including any further control variables, we find that the regression coefficients are statistically significant and have the expected sign (Table 5.1 column 1). The coefficient a_1 is statistically not different from one, which preserves the finding that growth in average income is translated one-for-one in growth of income of the poorest quintile of the population. But in contrast to Dollar and Kraay (2002) we find that the income of the poor increases with rising quality-adjusted human capital. This distributional effect comes on top of the growth effect of rising quality-adjusted human capital, which works through higher average income. Our point estimates suggest that a 10 per cent increase in the stock of quality-adjusted human capital per worker would increase the average income of the poor by an additional 3.2 per cent.

To test the robustness of our basic result, we include further variables in our regression eqn (5.4). In most empirical growth studies, a measure of physical capital

[6] For details of the calculation, including the imputation of missing values for selected countries, see Gundlach, Rudman, and Wößmann (2002). Their data set includes 1990 data, while our data set is adjusted where appropriate to match as closely as possible the distribution data from Deininger and Squire (1996) for different years.

Table 5.1. *OLS estimates*

	Dependent variable: $\ln y_p$				
	(1)	(2)	(3)	(4)	(5)
c	−0.85	−1.00	−0.88	−0.70	−1.00
	(0.46)	(0.06)	(0.46)	(0.49)	(0.65)
$\ln y$	0.90	0.90	0.90	0.88	0.91
	(0.07)	(0.07)	(0.07)	(0.07)	(0.07)
$\ln (H/L)$	0.32	0.34	0.30	0.32	0.31
	(0.10)	(0.11)	(0.10)	(0.10)	(0.11)
ln INV	—	−0.04	—	—	−0.05
		(0.09)			(0.10)
MINING	—	—	−0.48	—	−0.56
			(0.65)		(0.66)
MALFAL	—	—	—	−0.02	−0.01
				(0.02)	(0.02)
Sample	$n = 101$	$n = 101$	$n = 99$	$n = 91$	$n = 89$
Adjusted R^2	0.87	0.87	0.87	0.88	0.88
s.e.e.	0.43	0.44	0.43	0.43	0.42

Source: See text.

accumulation is found to be a robust variable (Levine and Renelt 1992). We measure physical capital accumulation (INV) as the average share of real investment in GDP in 1960–90.[7] In our specification, this variable yields a statistically insignificant negative regression coefficient (column 2). This result most likely reflects that the inclusion of average income as a conditioning variable already accounts for the potential distributional effect of physical capital accumulation on the income of the poor. But conditioning for average income obviously does not fully account for the distributional effects of human capital accumulation, since the estimated regression coefficient remains statistically significant and more or less unchanged in size.

In further specifications, we include poverty-related variables such as the share of mining in GDP (MINING) and the incidence of malaria in a country (MALARIA) as further checks of the robustness of our results.[8] A high share of mining in GDP may lead to a relatively unequal distribution of income due to rent seeking activities, and hence to slower growth (Rodriguez and Sachs 1999). The incidence of malaria may limit economic development through poor health, high mortality, and absenteeism of the workforce. Accordingly, Bloom and Sachs (1998) have argued for the importance of malaria in explaining African poverty. However, we find statistically insignificant regression coefficients both for MINING (column 3) and for MALARIA (column 4).

[7] The share of real investment in GDP is taken from the Penn World Tables (PWT 1994).

[8] The share of mining in GDP is taken from Hall and Jones (1999); the proportion of a country's population at risk of falciparum malaria transmission is taken from McArthur and Sachs (2001).

Our basic result also remains intact if we enter all additional variables together (column 5). We still find that quality-adjusted human capital has a statistically significant positive effect on the income of the poor in addition to the one-for-one effect of higher average income on the income of the poor. To compare the effects of the two statistically significant variables on the income of the poor more directly, the different units of measurement have to be accounted for. Beta coefficients measure changes in all variables in units of standard deviations. With a standard deviation of 1.21 of the dependent variable ($\sigma_{yp} = 1.21$), our point estimates imply beta coefficients of 0.176 for quality-adjusted human capital and of 0.512 for average income. This suggests that improving quality-adjusted human capital by one standard deviation could generate about one-third of the effect on the income of the poor that would result from changing average income by one standard deviation.

We also consider the possibility that OLS-estimation of eqn (5.4) might lead to upward biased coefficients because the stock of quality-adjusted human capital is an endogenous variable which depends, through the political process, on the level of the income of the poor. For instance, in countries where the income of the poor is relatively high, relatively more resources may be available for investment in education. In that case, the causality could run from the income of the poor to the stock of quality-adjusted human capital, and not the other way round as presumed in eqn (5.4). A similar reasoning could also be applied with respect to average per capita income, as discussed in Dollar and Kraay (2002). However, they find that the possible endogeneity of average per capita income ($\ln y$) does not cause an upward bias in the estimated regression coefficient.

Since we estimate basically the same regression coefficient on average per capita income of about one as do Dollar and Kraay, we impose their empirical result as restriction on eqn (5.4) such that

$$\ln y_p - \ln y = c + a_2 \ln (H/L), \tag{5.5}$$

which we estimate by using the absolute distance of a country from the equator (DISTANCE) and the mean temperature of a country (MEANTEMP) as instruments for our human capital variable.[9] These geographical variables can be considered as truly exogenous. They may be useful instruments for human capital accumulation in so far as they proxy for the institutional framework of a country, as suggested by Hall and Jones (1999), and Acemoglu, Johnson, and Robinson (2000). If so, these variables should be correlated with $\ln (H/L)$, but not with the error term of eqn (5.5).

The results of our IV-estimation are presented in Table 5.2. In all three specifications, the estimated effect of our human capital measure on the difference between the per capita income of the poor and the average per capita income is positive and statistically significant. When we use both instruments together, a chi-squared test on overidentifying restrictions does not reject the underlying hypothesis that both instruments are

[9] Absolute distance from the equator is taken from Hall and Jones (1999), mean temperature is taken from McArthur and Sachs (2001).

Table 5.2. *IV estimates*

Instruments	Dependent variable: $\ln y_p - \ln y$		
	MEANTEMP	DISTANCE	DISTANCE, MEANTEMP
c	−1.69	−1.79	−1.69
	(0.10)	(0.12)	(0.10)
$\ln(H/L)$	0.34	0.43	0.34
	(0.09)	(0.11)	(0.09)
Sample	$n = 86$	$n = 100$	$n = 86$
Adjusted R^2	0.08	0.08	0.08
s.e.e.	0.43	0.47	0.43
OverID test			
Test value	—	—	0.63
Test result	—	—	Accept

Source: See text.

uncorrelated with the error term (critical value for 1 degree of freedom at the 5 per cent level of statistical significance: 3.84).

On average, our three IV point estimates imply that a 10 per cent change in our measure of human capital would generate a 3.7 per cent increase in the average income of the poor relative to average income (which may also rise because of an increase of human capital). This distributional effect is larger than the effects estimated with OLS (see Table 5.1). A possible interpretation of the difference between IV- and OLS-results is that a potential positive effect of simultaneity on the estimated coefficient is outweighed by a potential negative effect of measurement error. Hence, taken together, our findings suggest that in addition to its growth effect, improving the stock of human capital may have a substantial distributional effect on the average income of the poor.

5.4. OUTLOOK

From a political economy perspective as well as according to some endogenous growth models, a more equal distribution of income should be conducive to growth if it reduces social conflict and guarantees a greater protection of private property rights. If, for instance, imperfect capital markets are responsible for observed inequality, then a certain amount of redistribution is believed to enhance growth and welfare because it would transfer resources to agents with potentially higher returns to investment. Redistribution through state-funded access to primary and secondary education for all children might be an efficient why to implement such a transfer of resources.

Overall, our empirical results confirm that education is not distribution-neutral. Education seems to improve the income distribution, and thus may allow the poor to benefit from growth to a greater extent. Accordingly, a focus of economic policies on education in order to reduce poverty and to speed up development appears to be justified. Our empirical findings indicate that improving the quality of education rather than merely expanding access to education should play a crucial role in development strategies.

Several issues for future research are immediately apparent from our analysis. First, the direction of causality between inequality and human capital accumulation somehow remains an open question. Notwithstanding our results in Table 5.2, more empirical research based on alternative instrumental variables is probably necessary to support the interpretation given in our chapter. Second, while our findings provide an encouraging impetus for the use of education policies as part of anti-poverty programmes, a rigorous theoretical framework supporting such a claim is still missing.

Third, and most importantly, highlighting the importance of education policy, as we do, should be accompanied by a more precise identification of effective education policies that would actually generate the expected effects. This is an important caveat because recent empirical evidence for OECD countries and for selected East Asian countries tends to suggest that additional schooling resources do not automatically guarantee improved schooling outcomes (Gundlach, Wößmann, and Gmelin 2001; Gundlach and Wößmann 2001). The international empirical evidence presented in Wößmann (2001) indeed reveals that schooling outcomes depend more on schooling institutions than on schooling resources. Hence, creating efficient schooling systems is probably more important for improving the stock of human capital than increasing schooling expenditure.

APPENDIX

Table 5A.1. *Country characteristics*

	Year	Income of the poor (int. $)	Average income (int. $)	Human cap. per worker (index)	Invest. share in GDP	Mining share in GDP	Malaria share in pop.	Mean temp. (Celsius)	Distance from equator (index)
Algeria	1988	941	2,769	1.400	0.214	0.053	0.000	19.30	0.408
Australia	1990	3,322	14,445	9.140	0.286	0.038	0.000	20.90	0.358
Bahamas[a]	1989	1,910	12,610	3.808	0.094	0.006	n.a.	n.a.	0.247
Bangladesh	1989	653	1,375	1.503	0.042	0.000	0.158	25.68	0.265
Barbados[a]	1979	717	6,373	5.297	0.123	0.006	n.a.	n.a.	0.131
Belgium	1988	5,610	13,232	6.636	0.238	0.000	0.000	8.40	0.565
Bolivia	1990	466	1,658	1.619	0.165	0.075	0.005	21.50	0.169
Botswana	1986	479	2,662	1.379	0.191	0.533	0.390	21.07	0.239
Brazil	1989	530	4,271	1.743	0.193	0.017	0.194	23.70	0.217
Bulgaria[c]	1990	3,269	6,203	4.543	0.411	n.a.	0.000	10.70	0.420
Burkina Faso	1994	203	514	1.462	0.076	0.001	1.000	28.10	0.134
Cameroon[b]	1983	230	1,342	1.427	0.085	0.088	1.000	24.43	0.119
Canada	1990	6,474	17,173	7.692	0.239	0.034	0.000	−0.20	0.486
Chile	1989	807	4,361	1.921	0.196	0.155	0.000	13.40	0.373

Table 5A.1. *Continued*

	Year	Income of the poor (int. $)	Average income (int. $)	Human cap. per worker (index)	Invest. share in GDP	Mining share in GDP	Malaria share in pop.	Mean temp. (Celsius)	Distance from equator (index)
China	1990	464	1,324	4.138	0.203	0.045	0.006	11.70	0.329
Colombia	1988	609	3,293	1.990	0.158	0.062	0.250	22.50	0.053
Costa Rica	1989	690	3,451	2.903	0.162	0.051	0.000	25.10	0.111
Côte d'Ivoire	1988	481	1,419	1.805	0.112	0.029	1.000	26.00	0.061
CSSR[c]	1988	2,445	4,110	8.234	0.276	0.040	0.000	n.a.	0.491
C. Afr. Rep.	1992	51	514	1.146	0.065	0.030	n.a.	n.a.	0.043
Denmark	1992	3,861	14,091	11.377	0.258	0.006	0.000	6.80	0.619
Djibuti[a,b]	1996	345	1,362	1.805	0.095	0.000	n.a.	n.a.	0.115
Dom. Rep.	1989	510	2,430	1.880	0.152	0.024	0.000	25.60	0.206
Ecuador	1994	859	3,206	2.532	0.220	0.098	0.137	19.10	0.023
Egypt	1991	833	1,913	1.503	0.046	0.034	0.000	22.60	0.333
El Salvador	1977	561	2,244	1.318	0.083	0.002	0.000	23.57	0.153
Ethiopia	1996	111	312	1.462	0.049	0.001	0.750	n.a.	0.100
Fiji[a,b]	1977	765	3,532	3.294	0.174	0.039	n.a.	n.a.	0.173
Finland	1991	4,926	12,663	8.598	0.348	0.004	0.000	0.20	0.669
France	1984	3,959	12,034	4.076	0.272	0.005	0.000	11.20	0.543
Gabon	1977	895	6,170	2.244	0.218	0.215	1.000	24.50	0.372
Gambia	1992	160	1,735	1.153	0.050	0.000	1.000	25.66	0.132
Germany	1984	4,054	12,302	4.323	0.279	0.005	0.000	7.20	0.535
Ghana	1989	314	902	1.359	0.062	0.016	1.000	26.35	0.074
Greece	1988	1,999	6,459	4.707	0.247	0.017	0.000	16.90	0.423
Guatemala	1989	224	2,137	1.551	0.091	0.003	0.012	21.70	0.163
Guinea[b]	1995	183	783	1.462	0.061	0.077	1.000	24.43	0.130
Guinea Bissau	1991	61	593	1.462	0.172	0.000	1.000	26.49	0.132
Guyana[a]	1993	343	1,095	3.259	0.242	0.087	n.a.	n.a.	n.a.
Honduras[b]	1990	197	1,377	1.571	0.139	0.014	0.011	25.40	0.158
Hong Kong	1991	3,814	15,601	10.327	0.199	0.001	0.000	22.60	0.252
Hungary[c]	1991	1,650	4,947	8.777	0.263	0.038	0.000	9.00	0.474
India	1990	575	1,264	1.372	0.138	0.017	0.281	25.90	0.281
Indonesia	1990	908	1,974	2.065	0.165	0.121	0.426	26.80	0.073
Iran[b]	1984	860	4,027	1.221	0.150	0.049	0.152	23.30	0.354
Ireland	1987	1,859	7,541	4.687	0.247	0.009	0.000	9.20	0.607
Italy	1989	5,214	12,488	3.397	0.280	0.002	0.000	13.40	0.505
Jamaica	1990	761	2,545	2.553	0.218	0.089	0.000	26.50	0.201
Japan[b]	1990	4,063	14,331	9.758	0.342	0.003	0.000	14.60	0.397
Jordan	1991	1,039	3,212	2.573	0.139	0.037	0.000	18.10	0.351
Kenya	1992	155	914	1.434	0.155	0.002	0.910	22.60	0.006
Korea, R.	1988	2,072	5,607	7.713	0.232	0.007	0.000	13.10	0.417
Laos	1992	678	1,420	1.963	0.024	n.a.	0.863	25.41	0.165
Lesotho	1987	136	949	2.024	0.111	0.003	0.000	n.a.	0.295
Luxembourg[a]	1985	5,764	13,175	4.289	0.297	0.003	n.a.	n.a.	0.498
Madagascar	1993	186	634	1.462	0.014	0.077	1.000	23.30	0.211
Malawi[b]	1993	58	543	1.475	0.098	0.081	1.000	22.00	0.176
Malaysia	1989	1,070	4,674	3.630	0.229	0.103	0.467	26.70	0.036
Mali[b]	1994	66	458	1.125	0.061	0.012	0.620	29.30	0.139
Mauritania	1988	139	788	1.462	0.151	0.069	25.300	25.30	0.199
Mauritius	1991	1,996	5,959	3.417	0.105	0.001	0.000	23.50	0.225
Mexico	1989	891	5,566	2.546	0.165	0.032	0.000	19.00	0.186

Table 5A.1. *Continued*

	Year	Income of the poor (int. $)	Average income (int. $)	Human cap. per worker (index)	Invest. share in GDP	Mining share in GDP	Malaria share in pop.	Mean temp. (Celsius)	Distance from equator (index)
Morocco	1991	736	2,241	1.832	0.090	0.029	0.000	18.50	0.373
Nepal	1984	424	930	1.146	0.053	0.001	0.047	19.00	0.308
Netherlands[b]	1989	4,508	13,029	6.059	0.247	0.027	0.000	8.60	0.576
New Zealand	1990	2,636	11,513	14.527	0.246	0.011	0.000	12.80	0.410
Nicaragua	1993	297	1,415	1.468	0.114	0.041	0.044	26.63	0.136
Niger	1992	189	1,043	1.091	0.087	0.076	0.660	28.40	0.154
Nigeria	1992	323	978	1.482	0.125	0.208	1.000	26.65	0.073
Norway	1991	4,063	15,047	7.507	0.310	0.079	0.000	3.20	0.666
Pakistan	1988	601	1,396	1.523	0.106	0.006	0.527	23.50	0.346
Panama	1989	279	2,785	4.097	0.203	0.001	0.138	27.50	0.102
Peru	1986	678	2,188	2.560	0.177	0.022	0.002	20.50	0.131
Philippines[b]	1991	455	1,749	2.539	0.153	0.019	0.617	26.50	0.155
Poland[c]	1990	1,818	3,820	12.173	0.327	0.043	0.000	6.40	0.502
Portugal	1990	2,131	7,478	1.976	0.227	0.033	0.000	16.00	0.431
Puerto Rico	1989	1,265	8,727	2.951	0.222	0.001	n.a.	n.a.	0.203
Romania[c]	1989	1,019	2,043	4.529	0.290	0.048	0.000	8.40	0.442
Rwanda	1983	404	834	1.235	0.039	0.002	1.000	n.a.	0.023
Senegal	1991	196	1,120	1.366	0.051	0.005	1.000	27.20	0.164
Seychelles[a,b]	1984	517	2,811	2.244	0.163	0.001	n.a.	n.a.	0.046
Sierra Leone	1968	151	1,097	1.084	0.015	0.061	1.000	26.20	0.097
Singapore[b]	1989	2,715	11,059	5.407	0.309	0.001	0.000	26.20	0.015
South Africa	1993	310	3,068	2.889	0.184	0.111	0.000	17.70	0.324
Soviet Union[c]	1989	3,449	7,741	6.080	0.384	0.015	n.a.	n.a.	0.556
Spain	1989	3,875	9,238	3.657	0.253	0.006	0.000	15.90	0.416
Sri Lanka	1990	935	2,096	2.614	0.091	0.014	0.200	27.60	0.076
Sudan	1968	337	2,420	1.064	0.135	0.000	0.810	28.50	0.140
Sweden	1990	5,462	14,762	7.644	0.235	0.003	0.000	2.40	0.659
Taiwan	1990	3,128	8,063	n.a.	0.220	0.043	0.000	23.30	0.252
Tanzania	1993	164	478	1.462	0.107	0.002	1.000	25.09	0.024
Thailand	1990	716	3,580	2.786	0.174	0.017	0.471	27.20	0.153
Trinidad	1981	2,013	11,738	3.705	0.124	0.157	0.000	25.90	0.116
Tunisia	1990	853	2,910	1.681	0.147	0.079	0.000	19.60	0.409
Turkey	1987	902	3,441	1.654	0.211	0.020	0.000	13.20	0.458
Uganda	1992	186	548	1.256	0.024	0.001	1.000	21.57	0.003
United Kingdom	1990	5,141	13,217	8.097	0.181	0.022	0.000	8.80	0.572
United States	1990	4,152	18,054	6.862	0.214	0.018	0.000	11.20	0.382
Venezuela	1990	1,093	6,055	2.264	0.178	0.110	0.070	24.80	0.109
Yugoslavia[c]	1990	1,665	4,541	3.980	0.298	0.025	0.000	n.a.	0.437
Zambia	1991	195	699	1.887	0.219	0.204	1.000	21.30	0.144
Zimbabwe	1990	235	1,182	1.482	0.172	0.060	0.700	16.90	0.199

Notes:
[a] Population of less than 1 million in 1990.
[b] Income of the poor estimated on the basis of eqn (5.1).
[c] Formerly socialist country. For definition of variables, see text.

Source: See text.

REFERENCES

Acemoglu, D., Johnson, S., and Robinson, J. A. (2000). 'The Colonial Origins of Comparative Development: An Empirical Investigation'. *MIT Working Papers* 00/22.

Barro, R. J. and Lee, J.-W. (1996). 'International Measures of Schooling Years and Schooling Quality'. *American Economic Review*, 86(2), 218–23.

Benhabib, J. and Spiegel, M. M. (1994). 'The Role of Human Capital in Economic Development: Evidence from Aggregate Cross-Country and Regional U.S. Data'. *Journal of Monetary Economics*, 34, 143–73.

Bloom, D. E. and Sachs, J. D. (1998). 'Geography, Demography, and Economic Growth in Africa'. *Brookings Papers on Economic Activity*, 2, 207–95.

De Gregorio, J. and Lee, J. -W. (1999). 'Education and Income Distribution: New Evidence from Cross-country Data'. *Harvard Institute for International Development Discussion Papers* 714.

Deininger, K. and Squire, L. (1996). 'A New Dataset Measuring Income Inequality'. *World Bank Economic Review*, 10, 565–91.

Dollar, D. and Kraay, A. (2002). 'Growth is Good for the Poor'. *Journal of Economic Growth*, 7(3), 195–225. Reprinted with kind permission as Chapter 2 of this volume.

Fields, G. S. (1980). 'Education and Income Distribution in Developing Countries: A Review of the Literature'. In Timothy King (ed.) *Education and Income*. The World Bank, Washington.

Glomm, G. and Ravikumar, B. (1992). 'Public versus Private Investment in Human Capital: Endogenous growth and Income Inequality'. *Journal of Political Economy*, 100, 818–34.

Gundlach, E. and Wößmann, L. (2001). 'The Fading Productivity of Schooling in East Asia'. *Journal of Asian Economics*, 12.

——, Rudman, D., and Wößmann, L. (2002). 'Second Thoughts on Development Accounting'. *Applied Economics*, 34, 1359–69.

——, Wößmann, L., and Gmelin, J. (2001). 'The Decline of Schooling Productivity in OECD Countries'. *Economic Journal*, 111, C135–47.

Hall, R. E. and Jones, C. I. (1999). 'Why Do Some Countries Produce So Much More Output per Worker than Others?' *Quarterly Journal of Economics*, 114, 83–116.

Hanushek, E. A. and Kimko, D. D. (2000). 'Schooling, Labor Force Quality, and The Growth of Nations'. *American Economic Review*, 90(5), 1184–208.

Knight, J. and Sabot, R. (1983). 'Educational Expansion and the Kuznets Effect'. *American Economic Review*, 73(5), 1132–6.

Krueger, A. B. and Lindahl, M. (2000). 'Education for Growth: Why and For Whom?' *NBER Working Papers* 7591.

Levine, R. and Renelt, D. (1992). 'A Sensitivity Analysis of Cross-Country Growth Regressions'. *American Economic Review*, 82(4), 942–63.

Lucas, R. E., Jr. (1988). 'On the Mechanics of Economic Development'. *Journal of Monetary Economics*, 22, 3–42.

Mankiw, N. G., Romer, D., and Weil, D. N. (1992). 'A Contribution to the Empirics of Growth'. *Quarterly Journal of Economics*, 107, 408–37.

McArthur, J. W. and Sachs, J. D. (2001). 'Institutions and Geography: A Comment on Acemoglu, Johnson, and Robinson (2000)'. *NBER Working Papers* 8114.

Penn World Tables (PWT) (1994). Version 5.6. Read-only file maintained by the NBER, Cambridge, MA, available at http://www.nber.org/pwt56.html.

Psacharopoulos, G. (1994). 'Returns to Investment in Education: A Global Update'. *World Development*, 22, 1325–43.

—— and Woodhall, M. (1985). *Education for Development: An Analysis of Investment Choices.* Oxford University Press, New York.

Ram, R. (1984). 'Population Increase, Economic Growth, Educational Inequality, and Income Distribution: Some Recent Evidence'. *Journal of Development Economics*, 14, 419–28.

—— (1989). 'Can Educational Expansion Reduce Income Inequality in Less-Developed Countries?' *Economics of Education Review*, 8, 185–95.

Rodriguez, F. and Sachs, J. D. (1999). 'Why Do Resource-Abundant Economies Grow More Slowly?' *Journal of Economic Growth*, 4, 277–303.

Tamura, R. (1991). 'Income Convergence in an Endogenous Growth Model'. *Journal of Political Economy*, 99, 522–36.

Temple, J. (1999). 'A Positive Effect of Human Capital on Growth'. *Economics Letters*, 65, 131–4.

World Bank (2000*a*). *World Development Report 2000/2001: Attacking Poverty*. The World Bank: Washington.

—— (2000*b*). *The Quality of Growth*. World Bank Research Department. The World Bank: Washington.

Wößmann, L. (2000). 'Specifying Human Capital: A Review, Some Extensions, and Development Effects'. *Kiel Institute of World Economics Working Papers* 1007.

—— (2001). 'Why Students in Some Countries Do Better: International Evidence on the Importance of Education Policy'. *Education Matters*, 1(2), 67–74.

6

Growth, Distribution, and Poverty Reduction: LDCs are Falling Further Behind

FELIX NASCHOLD

6.1. INTRODUCTION

Poverty levels in the developing world have been declining steadily over the 1990s (World Bank 2000*a*, 2001). However, this progress has been very unequally distributed. Some regions and groups of countries have made rapid progress, while poverty levels in others, particularly in the least developed countries (LDCs) have been stagnant or rising. Economic growth performance is one factor explaining these differences, but there may also be fundamental differences in the efficiency with which growth and distribution reduce poverty in different groups of countries.

This study has two main objectives. First, it explores whether there is a systematic relationship between the level of development, as proxied by the level of consumption per capita, and the income and inequality elasticities of poverty. Specifically, it looks at whether changes in consumption levels and distribution have different effects on poverty in LDCs compared to other low-income and middle-income countries.

Second, it examines whether different methods of estimation significantly affect the results. Poverty elasticities have often varied greatly across existing studies. The difference could be due to one or both of two factors: systematic differences between estimation methods, or differences resulting from using different data. This chapter tries to shed some light on this by using the same data set for all three methodologies.

The structure of the chapter is as follows. Section 2 reviews some of the recent literature on the interaction between consumption, inequality and poverty. Three different methodologies are introduced and their results discussed in Section 3. Section 4 then uses the results in a set of simulations to demonstrate their likely effects for poverty levels until 2015. Section 5 concludes with a summary of the main points, and implications for policy and further research.

The study was originally prepared as background paper for the UNCTAD Least Developed Countries Report 2002. The author would like to thank UNCTAD for financial support for this study, and the participants of the WIDER conference on Growth and Poverty for helpful comments on the work in progress. Views as well as any remaining errors are the author's alone.

6.2. ASSESSING THE RELATIONSHIP BETWEEN POVERTY, INEQUALITY, AND GROWTH

A large literature exists on the relationships between poverty, income distribution, and economic growth. The links between inequality and poverty, between growth and poverty, and their relative importance are the main areas of interest in this study.

6.2.1. *Inequality and Poverty*

Very small changes in distribution can have a large effect on poverty headcounts. White and Anderson (2001) demonstrate this using a simple arithmetic example. If the share of national income that goes to the poorest population quintile increased from 6 to 6.25 per cent, this would represent a 4 per cent increase in their total income.[1] Thus, a very small redistribution would have the same effect on poverty as a doubling the annual growth of national income from 4 per cent (which is the projected growth rate of many African countries) to 8 per cent (which is necessary to achieve the poverty Millennium Development Goal). When taking a broader view of consumption poverty to also include the depth and severity of poverty, changes in distribution have an even greater effect on poverty trends (Creedy 1998; Wodon 1999).

6.2.2. *Growth and Poverty*

As long as distribution is constant, consumption growth reduces aggregate poverty. The extent to which it does so varies between existing studies. A priori it is not possible to say whether this variation is because studies use different methods, or because they are based on different data sets.

Several studies derive poverty elasticities of growth through econometric analysis. Ravallion and Chen (1997) use a first difference specification to regress log poverty headcount ratios on log average consumption levels. Their sample represents an early form of the poverty data set based on household surveys that is now available on the World Bank poverty monitoring website.[2] It contains sixty-four poverty spells in forty-two transitional and developing economies, and includes episodes where income inequality increased as well as others where it fell. For the $1 a day poverty line they estimate a poverty growth elasticity of 3.1.[3] Hanmer *et al.*'s (1999) methodology differs slightly in that their bivariate econometric model contains separate equations for low, medium, and high inequality countries. Their data set is taken from various editions of the World Development Indicators (WDI); thus, there may be some overlap with the Ravallion and Chen data set. Hanmer *et al.*'s (1999) poverty elasticities are overall much lower, and vary between 0.5 for countries with Gini coefficients lower than 0.4, and 1.5 for countries with Ginis greater than 0.5.

[1] As 0.25 is about 4 per cent of 6.
[2] www.worldbank.org./research/povmonitor.
[3] Absolute values are reported for elasticities.

Multivariate econometric analysis tends to reduce the size of the growth poverty elasticity. Hanmer and Naschold (2000) use an expanded multivariate regression model which includes qualitative and structural variables to capture the characteristics of the growth path. The data is again taken from the WDI. While the total poverty elasticities, that is, the total effect of growth and other variables on poverty, remains around 1.5, the income poverty elasticity itself reduces to a maximum of 0.9. De Janvry and Sadoulet (2000) also include qualitative and structural factors in their econometric model, and find poverty elasticities of similar magnitude for a set of twelve Latin American countries.

Other studies try to estimate country specific poverty elasticities of growth. Demery, Sen, and Viswanath (1995) differentiate the cumulative distribution function of income or consumption in the region of the poverty line for thirty-nine developing countries. The resulting poverty elasticities show wide variations around the mean poverty elasticity of 1.89, and range from close to 0 (for Zambia) to over 4 (for Singapore), with higher values in Asia than in Africa, with Latin America in between. Bourguignon (2000) has developed a theoretical, identity-based method to calculate country specific poverty elasticities from Lorenz curves. Collier and Dollar (2001) apply this method to an unspecified data set and find mean and median poverty elasticities of around 2, which they use to project future poverty trends. They argue that average elasticities derived from global cross-country analysis are adequate for making worldwide projections of poverty, as variations in the poverty elasticity due to differences (and changes) in distribution will roughly cancel each other out.

Extending the analysis below the aggregate global level, however, requires us to verify whether we can indeed use a single elasticity. It is not possible to determine in the abstract how inequality in consumption will affect the consumption poverty elasticity, as this depends on changes in income distribution over time, and on the properties of the poverty measure used (Ravallion 1997). However, empirical evidence shows that the size of the consumption poverty elasticity varies systematically with income or consumption inequality (Ravallion and Sen 1996; Ravallion 1997; Hanmer *et al.* 1999). This variation can be considerable. Hanmer and Naschold (2000), for example, separate their sample of 121 observations into two groups: those with Ginis above 0.43, and those with Ginis below 0.43. They find that the high inequality countries need growth rates around three times as high as low inequality countries to achieve the same rate of poverty reduction.

In addition to this variation with distribution, Bourguignon (2000) and Heltberg (2003) show theoretically why the absolute value of the elasticity should increase with the level of per capita consumption. This relationship is based on the underlying assumption that past growth will have pulled the poor closer to the poverty line, so that any given extra growth will move more people out of poverty. Lipton (2001) challenges this assumption on two grounds. First, it ignores the fact that a large proportion of poor become poor in any given year, and second, those left in poverty during past growth periods are also those who are least likely to escape poverty through future growth. However, the positive relationship between average consumption and poverty elasticity of growth has been supported empirically across a large number of case studies

(Bourguignon 2000). It, therefore, makes sense to allow for different elasticities across income groups.

6.2.3. *The Relative Importance of Growth and Distribution*

A common conclusion has been that growth, rather than distribution, is what matters for poverty reduction. Conventional wisdom has it that inequality trends are stable, and that therefore not much can be done about changing the pattern of distribution (Deininger and Squire 1996; Li, Squire, and Zou 1998). This has meant that distribution was sometimes not a factor considered in analysing the relationship between growth and poverty. Where it was, the growth effect is typically found to outweigh the effect of changes in distribution on poverty. While this is true on average, this is clearly not the case always and for all countries. White and Anderson (2001) decompose changes in the income of the lowest income quintile into growth and distribution effects, and find that the inequality effect was greater than the growth effect for a quarter of the 143 growth episodes studied. Hanmer and Naschold (2000) simulate growth and distribution scenarios, which show that the inequality effect can dominate the growth effect in the case of highly unequal countries, particularly in poor regions with low past growth such as sub-Saharan Africa.

6.3. ACCOUNTING FOR CHANGES IN POVERTY IN THE 1980S AND 1990S

Most empirical studies examining the relationship between consumption growth, changes in distribution, and poverty reduction are based on one of three methodologies: estimating consumption and distribution elasticities either through econometric analysis, or by calculating them at a point on the cumulative consumption distribution function, or deriving arithmetic relationships from poverty spells[4] between two household surveys. This study uses all three; first, in order to determine whether the choice of methodology affects the results, and second, to project ranges of poverty levels in 2015.

6.3.1. *The Data*

All methodologies use the same data set, namely the poverty and distribution data available on the World Bank's poverty monitoring website,[5] which is based on the data compiled by Chen and Ravallion (2000). The 162 surveys in the sample are from between 1980 and 1998 and cover sixty countries and approximately three quarters of the population in developing countries (see Table 6.1). The data set excludes surveys for Eastern Europe and Central Asia, as recent poverty and inequality trends in this region

[4] A poverty spell represents poverty and distribution measures from a pair of household surveys at two points in time.

[5] www.worldbank.org./research/povmonitor as of May 2001.

Table 6.1. *Data set used*

	Total number of surveys in sample	Total number of countries in sample	Population covered by at least one survey (%)	Population in income group (in millions)
All developing countries	**162**	**60**	**76**	**5006**
LDCs	31	18	56	614
Other low income	50	13	94	2917
Middle income	84	29	51	1475

Source: See text.

are exceptional, and data quality highly variable (see, e.g. Mosley and Kalyuzhnova 2000; Luttmer 2001).

Consumption rather than income is used as a measure of poverty. The headcount index shows the percentage of the population consuming less than $1.08 per day in 1993 PPP. The Gini coefficient is used as a summary measure of national income distribution, as they are available for the widest range of countries.

Before proceeding to the analysis and interpretation of results it is important to bear in mind the intrinsic shortcomings of the data. Survey and price data can be out of date, the quality of the surveys varies across countries and over time, some household surveys measure consumption, others income,[6] and international comparability is affected by difficulties in estimating purchasing power parities across countries and over time. In addition, the limited availability of data for individual countries means that there is little alternative to using cross-country techniques to assess what are essentially country specific processes. Nevertheless, the improved coverage and accuracy of surveys means that aggregate results should be more reliable than in the past (World Bank 2000*b*).

6.3.2. *Econometric Analysis*

The regressions include consumption poverty headcount ratios as the dependent variable, and consumption per capita and income inequality as independent variables. A wide range of qualitative and structural variables to measure labour intensity in production, sources, and type of growth, and trade openness were included initially, but then dropped, partly due to multicollinearity, and partially on the basis of model specification tests. A side effect of using this more parsimonious regression is that the econometric results are more directly comparable with the other methodologies.

The final regressions reported in Table 6.2 control the initial level of consumption by allowing separate equations for each income group. Testing down confirmed that

[6] The income-based surveys were adjusted by multiplying the mean income by the share of consumption in GDP.

Table 6.2. *Poverty regressions: Results by income group*

Sample	Observations	Constant	Independent variables		
			LnCons/cap	Gini	Adj R^2
All	162	13.26 (24.87)*	−1.68 (−14.63)*	0.053 (9.92)*	0.75
LDCs	31	6.50 (7.07)*	−0.61 (−4.59)*	0.033 (7.79)*	0.69
Other low-income countries	50	18.35 (16.82)*	−2.07 (−14.12)*	0.028 (5.91)*	0.84
Middle-income countries	84	12.80 (9.33)*	−1.96 (−10.58)*	0.079 (9.02)*	0.67

Note: The equation for 'All' countries is only reported as a reference point for comparison with other studies. Dependent variable poverty headcount in logs.

Source: See text.

the groups cannot be pooled into one equation, and that there are distinct equations for LDCs, other low-income countries and middle-income countries.[7]

Growth clearly matters for poverty reduction. The consumption poverty elasticities have the expected negative sign (see Table 6.1), so that in all equations increasing consumption reduces poverty. What is immediately striking, however, is the large difference between LDCs and the other two groups. If consumption levels grow by 10 per cent the poverty headcount in LDCs falls by only 6 per cent, compared to around 20 per cent in other developing countries. Therefore, LDCs need around three times as much growth as other developing countries to achieve the same percentage reduction in poverty.

Sensitivity tests confirmed that consumption poverty elasticities are sensitive to the choice of the poverty line. Raising the poverty line by 10 per cent[8] reduces the poverty elasticities by between 16 and 63 per cent, with the percentage variation being higher the higher the average income.

The distribution of consumption also matters for poverty reduction. The positive coefficients in Table 6.2 show that for a given level of consumption, increases in inequality lead to higher levels of poverty. However, unlike for consumption there is no distinct pattern between the level of development and the size of the inequality regression coefficient. The inequality elasticity for other low-income countries is slightly lower than that for LDCs. From the results in Table 6.2 we cannot determine whether growth in consumption or changes in distribution are more important for reducing poverty. We return to this in Section 4.

[7] Model specification tests showed that lower and upper middle-income countries could be pooled and analysed in one regression.

[8] Alternatively, one can think of this as allowing for a 10 per cent measurement error in the survey.

6.3.3. *Calculating Income and Inequality Elasticities from the Distribution Function*

Another method of estimating the effect of growth in consumption and changes in income distribution on poverty is to calculate point elasticities from the cumulative distribution of per capita consumption from individual household surveys. This is done by differentiating the cumulative distribution function in the region of the poverty line. Estimates for consumption and inequality poverty elasticities were derived using the POVCAL software (Datt, Chen, and Ravallion 1993). The elasticities are based on the latest available household survey for each country. The consumption growth elasticities of poverty assume distributionally neutral growth, whereas the Gini elasticities assume constant mean income.

Table 6.3 summarizes the median elasticities for developing countries as a whole, as well as for the three income groups. The consumption growth elasticity with respect to the headcount (H0) for all developing countries is −1.57. Again, LDCs have by far the lowest consumption poverty elasticities (−0.91), with the estimates for other low-income and middle-income countries close together at around −1.7. When combining the estimates of poverty consumption elasticities by region, they display a similar pattern to (Demery, Sen, and Viswanath 1995), with sub-Saharan Africa having the lowest and East Asia Pacific and South Asia having the highest elasticities, with the other regions in between. The Gini elasticities all have the expected positive sign. Poverty increases as the distribution of income becomes more unequal. The Gini elasticities also increase from LDCs to middle-income countries.

6.3.4. *Calculating Income and Distribution Effects from Poverty Spells*

The third approach to derive poverty consumption elasticities is to calculate them arithmetically from the poverty spells. A poverty spell consists of two comparable surveys for a given country at two points in time, conducted using similar methodologies (e.g. consumption *or* income surveys). The spells analysis is based on a total of 102 spells, fifteen for LDCs, thirty-six for other low-income, and fifty-one for middle-income countries. Poverty elasticities were derived for each country by dividing the

Table 6.3. *Analytic consumption and Gini poverty elasticities*

	Cons growth elasticities H0	Gini elasticities H0
All developing countries	−1.57	1.90
LDCs	−0.91	0.75
Other low income	−1.63	1.43
Middle income	−1.74	5.80

Source: See text.

Table 6.4. *Comparison of consumption poverty elasticities*

	Econometric model	POVCAL	Poverty spells
All developing countries	−1.68	−1.57	−1.48
LDCs	−0.61	−0.91	−0.82
Other low income	−2.07	−1.63	−1.61
Middle income	−1.96	−1.74	−1.60

Note: The equation for 'All' countries is only reported as a reference point for comparison with other studies.

Source: See text.

log change in headcounts by the log change in mean consumption. The median values for each income group in the third column in Table 6.4 show the now familiar pattern of low elasticities in LDCs (−0.82), and much higher and similar elasticities for the other two groups (around −1.6).

6.3.5. *Comparing Results*

Comparing the results from the three methodologies it is immediately striking how similar the elasticities are (see Table 6.4).[9] Three main conclusions emerge. First, poverty elasticities in LDCs are much lower than in other developing countries. This empirical result confirms what we should expect from theory (Bourguignon 2000; Heltberg, this volume): that there is a systematic relationship between the level of development and the poverty-reducing effect of growth. The effectiveness of growth in reducing poverty could differ even more between LDCs and other developing countries than the results suggest. This is because the poverty elasticity of consumption growth is, if anything, larger during periods of recession, than during subsequent recoveries (Cornia 1994), and many LDCs recorded periods of negative growth in the years covered by the data set. Since fifteen out of eighteen LDCs in the sample are from sub-Saharan Africa, the findings also imply a strong regional difference between Africa and other world regions.

Second, inequality matters, but there is no direct link between the level of development and the importance of consumption inequality for poverty reduction. However, as poverty consumption elasticities are low in LDCs, the inequality effect on poverty is bound to be larger relative to growth effect than in other developing countries. Third, the choice of methodology does not significantly affect the conclusions. Different findings in previous studies are, therefore, most likely the result of using different data sets.

[9] The results also remain robust when using bivariate regressions of the log change in the real survey mean on the log change in poverty headcount ratios (Ravallion 2001), and when replacing the intercept by the number of years elapsed between the two surveys to account for the different intervals between surveys in the data set (Ravallion and Chen 1997).

6.4. POVERTY PROJECTIONS TO 2015

The results in the previous section have given some indication of the relative importance of growth and distribution in reducing poverty. However, it is difficult to draw any meaningful conclusions by simply comparing consumption elasticities with distribution elasticities of poverty. The main purpose of the poverty projections in this section is, therefore, to simulate the impact of changes in consumption and distribution for a range of plausible growth and inequality scenarios. Of course, the projections also produce distinct 'numbers' for the poverty headcount in 2015. As these are subject to various caveats (see Section 5) the discussion in this section focuses less on the exact headcounts projected for 2015, and more on the different projection patterns that emerge between the three income groups, and between different projection scenarios.

The poverty projection results are straightforward extrapolations and use the latest available headcount ratios as a baseline. The projections take the regression results from Table 6.4 and combine them with consumption growth forecasts and distribution scenarios to simulate poverty incidences for 2015. Estimates are presented for six scenarios, representing combinations of two consumption growth and three distribution scenarios. The higher consumption growth case uses the regional forecasts in consumption per capita from the *Global Economic Prospects 2001*. The base case assumes 1990s growth in regional consumption to continue in the future (see Table 6.8). For both scenarios, the consumption forecasts for each income group are constructed according to the weight of the regions in the income group.

The three distribution scenarios include a linear reduction in the Gini coefficient by five percentage points over 15 years to 2015, a linear increase in the Gini coefficient by the same amount, and a stable pattern of distribution. The magnitude of change for the Gini is somewhat arbitrary, but has some basis in the findings of studies investigating trends in Ginis. For example, Deininger and Squire (1996) find a 0.28 per cent average annual change in Gini coefficients using the standard Deininger and Squire data set. The five percentage point change is equivalent to roughly double that annual change. As the Deininger and Squire result reflects totally random movements in Gini, the doubling of the rate could be thought of as commitment to change income distribution. To some this may sound overambitious, but we should also remember that past distribution changes occurred without active policy intervention, as the focus of development policy and research was on growth, rather than distribution issues. Arguably, with greater attention to distribution issues more can be achieved in future. Furthermore, larger changes are not purely hypothetical; we do not have to look towards the transition economies to find distributional changes which are larger than the scenarios here and occurred over shorter time periods. For example inequalities increased in sub-Saharan Africa (Ali and Thorbecke 2000), and fell in Latin America during the 1970s, before rising again in the 1980s (Birdsall, Pinckney, and Sabot 1996).

The projections are presented as ranges (see Table 6.5). These show the spread of results between the different methodologies. Using ranges is, in any case, preferable for something as inexact as long-term projections. Each scenario in Table 6.5 contains an upper and a lower value, which reflect the highest and lowest forecast from the three

Table 6.5. *Incidence of poverty in 2015 as a percentage of incidence of poverty in 1990*

	In 1998 as % of 1990	Forecast growth						1990s growth					
		Increasing inequality		Stable		Reducing inequality		Increasing inequality		Stable		Reducing inequality	
		Min	Max	Min	Max	Min	Max	Min	Max	Min	Max	Min	Max
LDCs	98	70	90	66	81	63	73	89	101	84	91	80	83
Other low income countries	67	**14**	**21**	**13**	**19**	**12**	**17**	**28**	**36**	**29**	**32**	**24**	**28**
Middle income countries	51	**29**	**29**	**21**	**25**	**15**	**16**	61	72	**45**	**46**	**33**	**35**
Developing countries	75	**26**	**32**	**22**	**28**	**18**	**20**	**42**	**50**	**37**	**43**	**33**	**37**

Note: If value is lower or equal to 50, then poverty is halved (figures in bold print).

Source: See text.

sets of projections based on the three different methodologies used in Section 3.[10] Projections are based on the countries in the data set used in the analysis.

6.4.1. *Poverty Incidence and Numbers in 2015*

On the basis of these projections developing countries as a whole are on course to substantially reduce the proportion of people living under $1 per day. With forecast growth, headcount ratios are likely to reduce to between 18 and 32 per cent of their 1990 level. If future growth performance only matches growth rates from the 1990s, poverty will only reduce to between a third and a half of the 1990 level (see Table 6.5 bottom row). Due to population growth, reductions in the number of people living in absolute poverty are necessarily smaller, with likely reductions of between 50 and 60 per cent under high growth, and 20–40 per cent under low growth (see Table 6.6 bottom row).

These rather positive overall trends hide large variations between LDCs and the two other income groups. Middle-income countries are on track to halve the incidence of poverty by 2015 in all scenarios, except when worsening inequality coincides with growth continuing at 1990s rates. The absolute number of poor people in middle-income countries is only likely to fall in the optimistic growth case, or if distribution becomes more equal.

Other low-income countries are on schedule to reduce poverty to less than 50 per cent of its 1990 level in all scenarios, driven by strong performances in China and

[10] Each of the three methodologies produced its own projection tables of the kind presented in Tables 6.5 and 6.6. These are not reported separately, as they each show the same patterns as the summary Tables 6.5 and 6.6.

Table 6.6. *Number of poor*

In millions	Latest (late 1990s)	Forecast growth						1990s growth					
		Increasing inequality		Stable		Reducing inequality		Increasing inequality		Stable		Reducing inequality	
		Min	Max	Min	Max	Min	Max	Min	Max	Min	Max	Min	Max
LDCs	229	223	287	212	257	201	232	283	323	269	290	255	266
Other low income countries	701	196	288	178	260	162	230	385	490	351	467	322	388
Middle income countries	94	62	85	45	53	33	35	129	153	95	98	69	75
Developing countries	1024	537	632	471	553	415	489	838	943	736	817	655	716

Source: See text.

India. This is comparable to what Hanmer and Naschold (2000) find with a different data set. The total number of people below the poverty line falls under all scenarios, and quite dramatically under forecast growth. At these higher growth rates the total number of poor in other low-income countries in 2015 is projected to be similar to the total number of poor in LDCs, which have a far smaller total population. Effectively, this suggests that poverty is becoming increasingly concentrated in LDCs.

The positive outlook for middle and other low-income countries may appear overly optimistic for a number of reasons. First, the available data suggests that by the late 1990s other low-income countries and middle-income countries had already reduced poverty to 67 and 51 per cent of the 1990 level, respectively (see first column Table 6.5). Therefore, these two groups of countries are practically guaranteed to meet the poverty target, and would only miss it under very exceptional circumstances, such as prolonged periods of recession, or substantial redistribution away from the poor. Second, the projections may be optimistic, as the data set on which they are based contains poverty estimates which are unusually low for some large countries,[11] as well as extraordinary past trends, as, for example, the enormous reduction in poverty in China between 1990–93 (Lipton 2001). Third, the forecast growth rates seem on the optimistic side, both compared to what has been achieved in the past, and in view of recent events in the world economy. Fourth, poverty projections are for group averages, which may hide the fact that individual countries miss the target. Nevertheless, the outlook for other low-income and middle-income countries is positive.

In contrast, the prospects for reducing poverty in the LDCs are bleak. They are far from meeting the Millennium Development Goal of halving poverty under any growth

[11] For example, recent figures put the poverty level in Bangladesh well below two-thirds that in India, which does not fit the nutritional data and most observers' judgements (Lipton 2001).

and inequality scenario. At best poverty levels fall by around one-third compared to 1990. In the worst case poverty levels may be as high in 2015 as they were in 1990 (see Table 6.5). Combined with a population growth higher than in the other two groups, the number of people in absolute poverty in LDCs falls only marginally under the best case scenarios, but could increase by close to 50 per cent under the worst case scenarios (see Table 6.6).

Another key difference between the poverty projections for LDCs and those for other developing countries is the relative importance of income inequality for reducing poverty. For developing countries as a whole the growth effect dominates the inequality effect. Moving from, say, the stable inequality scenario to increasing inequality, the 2015 headcount projection rises by considerably less (i.e. from the range 22–28 to 26–32) than if moving from the low to the high growth scenario (i.e. from the range 22–28 to 37–43) (see Table 6.5 bottom row). In contrast, for LDCs the inequality effect is (almost) as strong as the growth effect (see Table 6.5 first row). The incidence of poverty in 2015 as a percentage of 1990 is between 66 and 81 per cent under forecast growth and stable income distribution. Under the same distribution scenario, but with past growth, this proportion rises to between 84 and 91 per cent. If on the other hand forecast growth coincides with a deterioration in income distribution, the ratio goes up by almost the same amount, that is, to between 70 and 90 per cent. Expressed differently,[12] over the 15-year forecast period a 5 per cent point change in the Gini makes as much a difference to poverty reduction as an additional 50 per cent growth in consumption per capita. On an annual basis this translates to an additional 1.3 per cent growth per capita, which is, of course, approximately the difference between the two growth scenarios. This striking finding further supports the idea that there is a structural difference between the ability of LDCs and that of other developing countries to reduce poverty. However, it is worth noting that the influence of distribution on poverty projections is not due to a larger *absolute* effect of the inequality variable, but due it being larger *relative* to the growth effect. Clearly, this suggests a need for making growth in LDCs more pro-poor and to increase the poverty elasticity of growth. At the same time, policies to create pro-poor growth must not neglect distribution issues in the short run for two reasons: increases in inequality are hard to reverse, and greater inequality reduces the poverty elasticity of growth. Given the rather dire prospects for poverty reduction in LDCs under *any* scenario, it could be argued that LDCs need to exploit all the available opportunities for reducing poverty, through higher growth as well as by reducing inequality.

6.4.2. *Crosschecking the Relative Importance of Consumption and Distribution*

The above results already provided some evidence on the relative importance of changes in consumption and distribution for poverty reduction. This section crosschecks

[12] Using the upper bounds of the ranges.

Table 6.7. *Decomposing annual changes in poverty headcount and the poverty bias of growth*

	Decomposition of change in headcount index			Normalized PBG (median)
	Change in headcount index	Explained by growth	Explained by inequality	
All developing countries	−0.47	−0.45	−0.02	0.02
LDCs	0.69	−0.17	0.86	−0.33
Other low income	−0.92	−0.62	−0.30	0.09
Middle income	−0.45	−0.41	−0.04	0.02

Source: See text.

the evidence through decomposition analysis, and by calculating the Poverty Bias of Growth (PBG).

The Kakwani decomposition method (Kakwani 1993)[13] makes it possible to separate changes in poverty between two periods into changes due to growth in consumption and changes due to shifts in income distribution. The growth component measures the change in poverty that would have occurred under actual consumption growth, with no change in income distribution, while the inequality component represents the change in poverty that would have occurred if the distribution of consumption had changed as observed, while consumption had remained constant.

$$H_{22} - H_{11} = \underbrace{\frac{1}{2}([H_{21} - H_{11}] + [H_{22} - H_{12}])}_{\text{(Growth component)}} + \underbrace{\frac{1}{2}([H_{12} - H_{11}] + [H_{22} - H_{21}])}_{\text{(Inequality component)}}, \tag{6.1}$$

where H is the headcount index. The first subscript indicates the period of the mean consumption figure, while the second subscript denotes the period of the income distribution.

Table 6.7 summarizes the decomposition results, showing the annualized change in poverty headcounts, and its breakdown into growth and inequality effects. Reported values are medians for each income group. It is important to remember that these are *actual* changes in poverty incidence in the past. They are therefore not directly comparable to the poverty elasticities in Table 6.4, which the projections use to simulate *potential* for changes in the headcount in the future. They do, however, provide a means of ground-truthing the results from the other methods.

The first column shows that in developing countries as a whole, the average poverty incidence fell by close to half a percentage point in each year during the spells included in the sample. The first row in columns two and three in Table 6.7 indicate that

[13] Another frequently used decomposition method, proposed in Datt and Ravallion (1992), is very similar. The Kakwani averages the growth and inequality components by using initial and final distributions as starting points, whereas Datt and Ravallion choose the initial distribution as their reference period, which results in a residual component that is not attributable to either growth or inequality. There is no a priori reason to prefer one choice of reference period over another.

most of the average change (−0.47) is explained by changes in levels of consumption (−0.45), and with only very little explained by changes in the distribution of income (−0.02). This result reflects that on average there were no changes in the distribution of consumption, as we know from pure arithmetic that this result is not due to a lack of impact of distribution changes on poverty (see the argument at the beginning of Section 2). Thus, the result for all developing countries in Table 6.7 seems to lend support to the common conclusion from cross-country regression studies that only growth matters for poverty reduction. However, this apparent result disappears when we look beyond the 'all developing countries' aggregate.

The first difference between LDCs and other developing countries is that poverty headcounts have gone up, rather than down, driven by both growth and distribution effects (see second row Table 6.7). The results also suggest that in LDCs the income distribution effect (0.86) has been the dominant factor for changes in poverty. This is partly due to the low levels of consumption growth experienced in LDCs. Again, one should not read too much into the exact size of the growth and inequality effects, but look at the pattern between LDCs and the other two groups of countries. The decomposition results are a further indication that (*a*) LDCs have found it much more difficult to reduce poverty in the past, and (*b*) changes in distribution have been instrumental in changing poverty levels in LDCs.

The decomposition findings are supported by estimations of the PBG. This measure proposed by McCulloch and Baulch (1998) subtracts the change in poverty that would have occurred under distributionally neutral growth from the change in poverty that actually happened.[14] A value of 0 means that growth has been distributionally neutral, so that incomes for all have gone up by the same proportion.[15] The last column in Table 6.7 shows that across all developing countries growth was distribution neutral. The median PBG for developing countries as a whole is very close to 0. Again, this hides the now familiar pattern of variation between the income groups. The negative PBG in LDCs suggests that growth has been anti-poor, whereas other low income and middle-income countries experienced marginally pro-poor growth. Of course, the poverty bias of growth also varies within each of the three income groups. Thus, analysis at the income group level cannot be used to draw policy conclusions for any particular country. Nonetheless, the results show that in the past the poor in LDCs have benefited less from a given amount of growth than the poor in other developing countries.

6.4.3. *Growth Rates Required to Halve Poverty by 2015*

Forecast growth rates are easily sufficient for developing countries as a whole to halve poverty by 2015 (see Table 6.8). Only the prospects of past growth combined with

[14] Note that this is also equivalent to the negative of the Kakwani inequality component.

[15] Definitions of pro-poor growth differ. Whether equal income growth rates across the population (which lead to an increase in the absolute differences in incomes between rich and poor) is an appropriate definition of pro-poor growth is an issue of debate. For a discussion of alternative pro-poor definitions see, for example, White and Anderson (2001).

Table 6.8. *Growth rates required to halve poverty by 2015*

	Growth rates required to halve poverty by 2015		Forecasts	
	Reducing inequality	Increasing inequality	2000–10 (GEP 2001 base case)	1990s growth
LDCs	4.3–6.2	5.2–8.6	2.0	0.7
Other low income countries	0–0.2	0.7–1.1	4.6	2.5
Middle income countries	0–0.1	2.1–3.0	3.3	0.3
Developing countries	0.2–0.4	1.7–2.1	4.0	1.7

Source: See text.

increasing inequality may not be enough to meet the poverty target at a global level. Middle-income countries either need to attain their optimistic growth scenario, or at least make sure that income distribution does not deteriorate. Other low-income countries should have no problems exceeding the required growth rate. In contrast, growth rates required in LDCs are completely out of reach. Even if inequality can be reduced, the growth rate required to halve poverty by 2015 is still more than double the optimistic growth forecast. The high performing Asian economies achieved an average growth rate of 5.5 per cent during their rapid industrialization between 1960 and 1990. This historical perspective gives an indication of the magnitude of the effort required in LDCs today.

6.5. CONCLUSIONS

The level of development as proxied by per capita consumption affects the poverty-reducing effect of growth. Consumption growth elasticities in LDCs are only between a third and half the size of elasticities in other developing countries. As a result growth has benefited the poor in LDCs far less. This has exacerbated the effect of low growth, and contributed to stagnant or rising poverty levels in this group of countries over the last 20 years.

The results from the various methodologies using the same data to assess the growth–poverty relationship have been very similar, suggesting that the choice of methodology does not significantly affect the conclusions. Different findings in previous studies are, therefore, most likely the result of using different data sets, rather than different methods.

There is no systematic link between the level of development and the importance of consumption inequality for poverty reduction. However, as poverty consumption elasticities are low in LDCs, the inequality effect on poverty is larger relative to the growth effect than in other developing countries. The econometric results suggest that the distribution effect could be as strong as the consumption effect.

Two main caveats limit how much we can read into these results. First, the regression analysis can only examine past relationships, and simulations assume that these hold in the future. Of course, the future can be different. Indeed, one of the key challenges is to break past relationships in LDCs. Second, cross-country analysis produces results for country averages. However, averages are just that. While some countries are 'average', most are not. This intrinsic shortcoming of cross-country analysis means that we must be very careful in interpreting the results at the country level.

The poverty projections indicate that developing countries as a whole are likely to achieve the Millennium Development Goal of halving poverty by 2015, and the number of people living on less than $1.08 a day is expected to fall. Halving poverty was conceived as a global target, but arguably it should apply to subgroups and individual countries, too. However, the large differences between income groups mean that many of the poorest countries will not reach the target. Particularly worrying is the trend that LDCs are likely to fall further behind other developing countries. Under the best scenario the number of poor in LDCs is constant, at worst, poverty incidence will increase significantly. While growth in consumption per capita is probably most important in reducing poverty in other low-income and middle-income countries, in LDCs distribution effects can be as important as growth. This group of countries needs to combine consumption growth with improvements in distribution to make any significant progress towards the MDG. In view of the caveats that apply to the analysis presented here, we should not take the exact levels of projected poverty too seriously. However, what the simulations show clearly is the distinctly different patterns between likely poverty trends in LDCs and in other developing countries.

What do the findings mean for policy? The main message in this chapter could be that changes in distribution matter for poverty reduction in LDC, and even more so when looking at measures for depth and severity of poverty, which are more sensitive to the distribution of income. Even if we were not to believe any of the findings in this chapter, and maintain that growth is what poverty reduction is all about in all countries at all times, we should still pay more attention to distribution, because higher inequality tends to depress economic growth.[16] Each of these reasons on their own suggests that if we are serious about reducing poverty, especially in the poorest countries, we need to pay attention to distribution issues. Together they add up to a compelling case to put distribution firmly at the heart of the poverty reduction agenda.

How should this change policy in practice? Cross-country analysis has identified inequality as an area that is important for poverty reduction, but it tells us little what to do about it. There is a lot that we still do not know about what determines the level of inequality. More country level work is needed to explore what drives changes in distribution, and which of these factors policy can and should target. Country case studies can also help us understand why growth in LDCs has a lower impact on poverty reduction.

[16] The literature has explained this either through political economy effects (Alesina and Perotti 1993; Alesina and Rodrik 1994; Bourguignon 1998, 1999; Rodrik 1997), or due to economic factors, such as capital market imperfections (Birdsall, Pinckney, and Sabot 1996; Kanbur 2000).

Finally, as in many other studies, the analysis here is limited to a consumption approach to poverty and inequality. Poverty is now widely recognized as multidimensional; in theory and policy, as well as in research. Inequality on the other hand is still primarily studied in its income dimension, so that we know relatively little about the determinants of non-income dimensions of inequality, presenting another area for further research.

REFERENCES

Alesina, A. and Perotti, R. (1993). 'Income Distribution, Political Instability and Investment'. *NBER Working Papers* 4486.

Alesina, A. and Rodrik, D. (1994). 'Distributive Politics and Economic Growth'. *Quarterly Journal of Economics*, 109, 465–90.

Ali, A. A. and Thorbecke, E. (2000). 'The State and Path of Poverty in Sub-Saharan Africa: Some Preliminary Results'. *Journal of African Economies*, 9, 9–41.

Birdsall, N., Pinckney, T., and Sabot, R. (1996). 'Why Low Inequality Spurs Growth: Savings and Investment by the Poor'. *Inter-American Development Bank Working Paper Series* 327.

Bourguignon, F. (1998). 'Crime as a Social Cost of Poverty and Inequality: A Review Focusing on Developing Countries'. DELTA, Paris.

—— (1999). 'Absolute Poverty, Relative Deprivation and Social Exclusion'. *Villa Borsig Workshop Series*. DSE, Berlin.

—— (2000). 'The Pace of Economic Growth and Poverty Reduction'. The World Bank and DELTA, Washington and Paris.

Chen, S. and Ravallion, M. (2000). 'How Did the World's Poorest Fare in the 1990s?' The World Bank, Washington.

Collier, P. and Dollar, D. (2001). 'Can the World Cut Poverty in Half? How Policy Reform and Effective Aid Can Meet International Development Goals'. *World Development*, 29, 1727–802.

Cornia, G. A. (1994). 'Poverty in Latin America in the Eighties: Extent, Causes and Possible Remedies'. *Giornale degli Economisti e Annali di Economia*, July–September.

Creedy, J. (1998). 'The Dynamics of Inequality and Poverty: Comparing Income Distributions'. Edward Elgar, Cheltenham.

Datt, G., Chen, S., and Ravallion, M. (1993). 'POVCAL: A Program for Calculating Poverty Measures from Grouped Data'. The World Bank, Washington, mimeo.

—— and Ravallion, M. (1992). 'Growth and Redistribution Components of Changes in Poverty Measures: A Decomposition with Applications to Brazil and India in the 1980s'. *Journal of Development Economics*, 38, 275–96.

de Janvry, A. and Sadoulet, E. (2000). 'Growth, Poverty, and Inequality in Latin America: A Causal Analysis, 1970–94'. *Review of Income and Wealth*, 46(3), 267–88.

Deininger, K. and Squire, L. (1996). 'A New Dataset Measuring Income Inequality'. *World Bank Economic Review*, 10.

Demery, L., Sen, A., and Viswanath, T. (1995). 'Poverty, Inequality and Growth'. Economic and Social Policy Discussion Paper. The World Bank, Washington.

Hanmer, L., deJong, N., Kurian, R., and Mooij, J. (1999). 'Are the DAC Targets Achievable? Poverty and Human Development in 2015'. *Journal of International Development*, 11, 547–63.

—— and Naschold, F. (2000). 'Attaining the International Development Targets: Will Growth be Enough?' *Development Policy Review*, 18, 11–36.

Kakwani, N. (1993). 'Poverty and Economic Growth with an Application to Côte d'Ivoire'. *Review of Income and Wealth*, 39, 121–39.

Kanbur, R. (2000). 'Income Distribution and Development'. In A. B. Atkinson and F. Bourguignon (eds) *Handbook of Income Distribution* (1). Elsevier, Amsterdam, pp. 791–841.

Li, H., Squire, L., and Zou, H.-F. (1998). 'Explaining International and Intertemporal Variations in Income Inequality'. *Economic Journal*, 108, 26–43.

Lipton, M. (2001). *2015 Poverty Targets: What Do the 1990–98 Trends Tell Us?* Sussex University Poverty Research Unit, Brighton.

Luttmer, E. F. P. (2001). 'Measuring Poverty Dynamics and Inequality in Transition Economies: Disentangling Real Events from Noisy Data'. *World Bank Policy Research Working Papers* 2549.

McCulloch, N. and Baulch, B. (1998). 'Assessing the Poverty Bias of Growth: Methodology and an Application to Andhra Pradesh and Uttar Pradesh'. *IDS Working Paper* 98. IDS, Brighton.

Mosley, P. and Kalyuzhnova, Y. (2000). 'Are Poverty and Social Goals Attainable in the Transition Region?' *Development Policy Review*, 18, 107–20.

Ravallion, M. (1997). 'Can High Inequality Developing Countries Escape Absolute Poverty?' *World Bank Policy Research Working Papers* 1775.

—— (2001). 'Growth, Inequality and Poverty: Looking Beyond Averages'. *World Development*, 29, 1803–15.

—— and Chen, S. (1997). 'What Can New Survey Data Tell Us about Recent Changes in Distribution and Poverty'. *World Bank Research Observer*, 11, 357–82.

—— and Sen, A. K. (1996). 'When Method Matters: Monitoring Poverty in Bangladesh'. *Economic Development and Cultural Change*, 44, 761–92.

Rodrik, D. (1997). *Where Did all the Growth Go? External Shocks, Social Conflict and Growth Collapses*. Kennedy School, Harvard University.

White, H. and Anderson, E. (2001). 'Growth Versus Distribution: Does the Pattern of Growth Matter?' *Development Policy Review*, 19(3), 267–89.

Wodon, Q. (1999). 'Growth, Poverty and Inequality: A Regional Panel for Bangladesh'. *World Bank Policy Research Working Papers* 2072.

World Bank (2000*a*). *World Development Report 2000/01 Attacking Poverty*. Oxford University Press, Oxford.

—— (2000*b*). *Global Economic Prospects 2001*. The World Bank, Washington.

—— (2001). *Global Economic Prospects 2002*. The World Bank, Washington.

7

Redistribution does Matter: Growth and Redistribution for Poverty Reduction

HŰLYA DAĞDEVIREN, ROLPH VAN DER HOEVEN, AND JOHN WEEKS

7.1. INTRODUCTION

In the late 1990s the bilateral and multilateral development agencies came to place increasing policy emphasis on poverty reduction in developing countries.[1] Some agencies went so far as to establish specific targets for poverty reduction. The achievement of targets requires policies, and policies are most effective within an overall, coherent strategy. We argue that the central strategy choice is between poverty reduction through faster economic growth and reduction through distribution, though the two may be complementary. This chapter develops an analytical framework to consider which of these would be the most effective in terms of resource allocation, given specific poverty targets, then proceeds to empirical investigation.

Following this introduction, we review recent literature on growth and distribution, and suggest that a consensus emerges that discards the previous trade-off conclusion. More and more analysts have moved to the view that an initial condition of greater asset and income equity enhances growth rates. This emerging view allows us to reject concerns that the redistribution strategy we consider need necessarily undermine poverty reduction in the long run by reducing per capita growth. The question then becomes, how effective would redistribution be in reducing poverty? We argue that this will vary by country, and the analytical framework to assess effectiveness is presented in Section 2. The framework formulates two abstract possibilities: poverty reduction through distribution-neutral growth, and poverty reduction through an

Research for this chapter was jointly done at ILO and SOAS. Hűlya Dağdeviren's research for this chapter was funded by the International Labour Organization.

[1] See, for example, the discussion of targets in DFID (1997). It would appear that there was some controversy over this emphasis within the World Bank. In June 2000, the convenor of the World Development Report, Ravi Kanbur, resigned from his participation in the report. Press reports attributed this to internal disagreements over the relative emphasis to place on growth and redistribution (see *The Financial Times*, 15 and 16 June 2000).

equal redistribution of each period's growth increment. These are compared to a conventional one-off redistribution of current income. In Section 3, these possibilities are simulated for a large number of countries. The conclusion is reached that redistribution at the margin is far more effective in poverty reduction than increases in economic growth that are distribution-neutral. In Section 4, the exercise in simulation is rendered concrete by discussion of specific policies that could be used to redistribute income, and this is followed by a summary of major conclusions.

7.2. GROWTH AND DISTRIBUTION

7.2.1. *Inequality and Poverty*

Of the many issues central to the development process, few have been characterized by the shifts, reversals and reaffirmations that have plagued the analysis of the interaction of growth, poverty, and inequality. Evidence that inequality and poverty have risen in many countries in the 1980s and 1990s,[2] including some of the OECD countries, rekindled the ever-smouldering controversies. The mainstream literature has not so much evolved as fluctuated over the past 50 years.[3] It is necessary to revisit the debates, in order to place the empirical discussion of a subsequent section in context.

From the 1950s into the 1970s emphasis was on probable trade-offs between growth and income distribution. This derived in part from the famous 'inverted U-hypothesis' (Kuznets 1955), which proposed that inequality rises in the initial phases of development, then declines after some crucial level is reached. Much research involved estimation of the so-called turning point (Fields 1980, Chapter 4). Growth theories could be cited that provided support for this trade-off. Kanbur (1998) pointed out the obvious correspondence between Kuznets' empirical results and Lewis' (1954) labour surplus model. The latter predicts that in a 'labour surplus' economy, with 'unlimited supply of labour', the profit share would rise relatively to the wage share until the labour surplus was exhausted. However, theoretical inconsistencies in the Lewis model undermine this conclusion (Weeks 1971). Other models, as suggested by Aghion, Caroli, and Garcia-Penalosa (1999), might explain a trade-off between growth and inequality. For example, Kaldor's well-known growth model, in which capitalists have higher marginal propensity to save than workers, implies, as in the Lewis model, that redistribution to profits raises the growth rate. However, this model is most appropriate for developed countries, in which the functional distribution of income largely consists of wages and profits, and of less relevance to the developing countries considered in this chapter.

In contrast, work in the 1970s sought to identify redistributive mechanisms for poverty reduction without hampering growth.[4] This was a short-lived focus of the literature, reversed with the rise of neoliberalism and the Washington Consensus in the early 1980s. For the latter, growth itself would be the vehicle for poverty reduction,

[2] See De Janvry and Sadoulet (1995), Ravallion and Chen (1997), Flemming (1998), Aghion, Caroli, and Garcia-Penalosa (1999), Cornia (1999), Chu, Davoodi, and Gupta (1999), McDonald, Schiller, and Ueda (1999), and Milanovic (1999).

[3] See Kanbur (1998) for a thorough review.

[4] See Chenery *et al.* (1974).

achieved through 'trickle down' mechanisms not always clearly specified. In the 1990s, both the neoliberal analysis and the earlier view of a trade-off between growth and equity were challenged by a number of studies. Accumulating empirical evidence suggested no consistent relationship among growth, inequality, and poverty across countries and over time.[5] At the same time, studies suggested that in many developing countries in Africa, in countries in transition, and in Latin America stabilization and adjustment policies had an adverse impact on poverty and inequality, or at best did not improve conditions of the poor (van der Hoeven 2002). Further, a consensus emerged that the high performing Asian countries, prior to the financial crisis of the late 1990s, combined rapid growth of per capita income with relatively stable and low inequality (World Bank 1993).

This recent literature that challenges the trade-off and trickle down approaches has roots, not always acknowledged, in the brief flowering of pro-distribution arguments of the 1970s. Ahluwalia and Chenery (1974*a*, *b*) constructed a model of 'distribution with growth', which distinguished social groups by asset ownership or mode of access to assets. Growth and distribution were related through income linkages between the groups; that is, through the linkages between the labour and commodity markets. The simulation experiments with this model indicated that redistribution led to substantial improvement in the incomes of not only poverty groups, but other income groups as well if aggregate productivity increased.[6] The general thrust of the Chenery and Ahluwalia work was that poverty *constrains* growth. The authors summarized the central conclusion of their work as follows:

> If [a poverty group] is provided with an appropriate mix of education, public facilities, access to credit, land reform, and so forth, investment in the poor can produce benefits in the form of higher productivity and wages in the organized sectors, as well as greater output and income for the self-employed poor. In the short run, there may be a reduction in the growth of other groups through this redirection of investment toward the poor, although this is by no means necessary. In the long run, however, it can be argued that the transformation of the poverty groups into more productive members of society is likely to raise the incomes of all. (1974*b*: 47)

Latter day contributions repeat this focus on how inequality and poverty reduce the capacity for growth, and vice versa. Bruno, Ravallion, and Squire (1998) confirmed that the effect of growth on inequality is indeterminate, based upon a sample of forty-five countries for which at least four or more surveys were available over a period of at least two decades covering the 1960s into the 1990s. They further concluded that lower initial inequality raises the likelihood that growth will reduce poverty. As shown in our simulations below, this conclusion follows almost by definition. Li, Squire, and

[5] A clear and thorough survey is found on a World Bank website (Ferreira 1999).

[6] Two of the experiments are especially worth noting. In the first, redistribution to lower income groups took the form of better nutrition, health, and access to education, which led to an increase in the output–capital ratio in the sectors using wage labour. In this case, consumption and income of all groups increased after redistribution. In the second experiment redistribution directly increased the earning capacity of the poor; for example, redistribution of the investment share of national income. This simulation led to an increase in the incomes of and the assets owned by the poor, as well as a substantial increase in the aggregate capital stock of the economy.

Zou (1998) demonstrated that income inequality is relatively stable within countries, a confirmation of almost every other cross-country study, but that it varies significantly among countries. Though obvious as well, the latter finding indirectly supports the pessimistic conclusion that poverty levels tend to persist as countries grow.

Of special interest to our study is the empirical work focused on the policy that considers the impact of different distributive measures on growth, inequality, and poverty. Two points emerge as important: the form of redistribution, and the cost and the incidence of redistributive programmes. With regard to impact, productivity-raising redistribution ensures, as shown in the insufficiently appreciated Chenery–Ahluwalia work of the 1970s, that distribution does not reduce poverty at the expense of growth, and produces sustainable poverty reduction. That is, those raised from poverty do not regress to their former deprivation. Enhancing asset ownership for the poor is the clearest way to accomplish this. Investment in infrastructure, credit targeted to the poor, land redistribution, and education emerge as important mechanisms to make growth 'pro-poor'. In the 1990s, considerable stress was placed on education, perhaps because of its non-controversial nature. The approach was that of the human capital framework, which treats the acquisition of skills on par with ownership of physical assets. This approach is dubious, since accumulated education as such cannot be sold by the 'asset holder', while land and other tangible property can. Thus, if a worker loses his or her job during a general fall in aggregate demand, education provides no asset that can serve as a safety net when sources of livelihood are temporarily lost (i.e. it is not 'liquid').

7.2.2. *Methods and Incidence of Redistribution*

If redistribution is used to reduce poverty, then key policy issues are redistribution from whom, to whom, and by what mechanism, which relate directly to the empirical work of this paper. The loss and gain of distributive programmes on income groups, and their reaction to these losses and gains, will depend on the nature of the programme. Similarly, the administrative burden will vary by programme.

Superficially, land redistribution and income redistribution would seem to be polar cases. It might be argued that redistributive land reform, from large landowners to landless peasants involves a one-off redistribution, which, once achieved, can be left to generate a more equal distribution and lower poverty levels. On the other hand, a redistribution of income, without asset redistribution, must be implemented by a continuous application of progressive taxation and equity-biased public expenditure. In practice, the alternatives are not so clear-cut. For example, land redistribution unaccompanied by rural development expenditure might generate a class of poverty stricken smallholders. Most of the land redistribution programmes in Latin America, even those that radically changed ownership patterns (as in Peru), proved in practice to be poverty generating rather than poverty reducing (Thiesenhusen 1989). Land redistribution that generates sustainable poverty reduction may require substantial current expenditure, which, in the medium term, could equal or exceed the cost of administering a progressive tax system and pro-poor distribution of expenditures.

Perhaps more importantly, the more equitable land distribution may prove to be unsustainable in the absence of permanent administrative restrictions on accumulation of land (ownership 'ceilings').

Like land redistribution, progressive income taxation would appear to be an obvious vehicle for redistribution. However, studies of tax incidence and impact have produced mixed conclusions. Some indicate that progressive taxation is a limited tool for reducing inequalities in income distribution, as a result of evasion by the rich. A study of Latin America concluded that tax systems did not contribute significantly to the reduction of inequality (Alesina 1998). Using a hypothetical data set, Harberger reached the same conclusion, suggesting that the redistributive effects of progressive and moderate taxation systems were quite similar (Harberger 1998). As an alternative, he proposed that broadly based taxes, such as a value added tax, could be modified to increase their equity by exemptions and exclusions. All such results are sensitive to the analytical framework made by each researcher, as can be shown by studies that conclude quite the opposite. For example, it would appear that the progressivity of income taxes during 1980–96 in Taiwan had 'positive influence in restricting the expansion of the income gap [between rich and poor]' (Jao 2000). A cross-country study of thirty-six developing countries found that in thirteen cases total taxation was progressive, was proportional in seven, and regressive in six. Income tax systems were progressive in twelve cases out of fourteen (Chu, Davoodi, and Gupta 1999). A survey by the ILO reached similar conclusions (ILO 1992).

Revenue raised *via* progressive taxation can generate a further redistributive impact via progressive expenditure, depending on targeting or incidence. Empirical work has adopted either a 'benefit incidence' or an 'expenditure incidence' approach. Expenditure incidence examines the effects of public spending on the *incomes* of the beneficiaries, while benefit incidence examines the comparative benefits of public goods for intended beneficiaries. The provision of public goods can be considered progressive if the benefits to the poorest quintile are larger than for the richest quintile. As an alternative measure, public spending can be considered progressive if the benefit–income ratio for the poorest quintile is larger than that for the richest quintile.

The studies of public education typically show that expenditure on primary and secondary education reduces inequality, and expenditure on tertiary education has a regressive impact.[7] In this context, Alesina (1998) maintained that subsidizing higher education at the expense of primary and secondary education reduces the redistributive impact of public spending, because these subsidies will accrue to the middle or high income. He went further and argued that most social welfare and benefit programmes favour the urban middle classes, rather than the poor, because provision of social services is more concentrated in the urban areas. The allegation that expenditure on tertiary education is regressive reflects a partial equilibrium, static perspective. It takes no great insight to point out that the middle and upper classes in almost every country take advantage of tertiary education, and the poor do not. This is not a serious

[7] See, for instance, Chu, Davoodi, and Gupta (1999), Hammer, Nabi, and Cercone (1995), Harberger (1998), van de Walle (1995).

argument against public funding of tertiary education, for the scientists, technicians, even entrepreneurs who will be crucial to growth typically require university education; that is, there are externalities to tertiary education. Further, a university system that is purely privately funded may reinforce the power rigidities that are the basic cause of inequality. That the poor do not go to universities is no more an argument against public funding than the absence of the poor from most legal cases is an argument against public funding of courthouses.

The perceived ineffectiveness of redistributive measures leads some to advocate targeting public expenditure to the poor, and to judge effectiveness by accuracy of that targeting.[8] However, targeting of expenditures in developing countries is fraught with difficulty. Sen (1995) emphasized information asymmetries, negative incentive effects and politically weak position of beneficiaries among some of the factors that render the sustainability of targeted programmes doubtful. To the list can be added the formidable problems of identification and measurement, and the burden of administrative costs.[9] Identification of the poor gives rise to what might be called the 'borderline problem'. If one assumes that the poor are identified accurately and programmes are delivered with equal accuracy, it follows by definition that the poor just below the borderline will be raised above the non-poor just above it. Recognition of this possibility by 'borderline' households can have a negative incentive effect.

Targeting public spending is more likely to be effective if the poor are a small proportion of population; that is, if poverty is not a major problem. For countries in which poverty is widespread, the administrative cost, identification, monitoring, and delivery of programmes may outweigh benefits. This is particularly the case if a country is or recently has experienced conflict such as civil war. In such countries targeting may serve to accentuate the tensions that generate conflict, since, by its nature, targeting seeks to discriminate among segments of the population (Cramer and Weeks 1997).[10] This problem was a major one in the sub-Sahara in the 1990s, where poverty was both widespread and created or intensified by conflict.

A further strand of theoretical arguments involves the so-called political economy arguments against inequality and, by implication, poverty. This analysis predicts a negative relationship between income inequality and growth on the grounds that higher initial inequality would (*a*) lead to increased public expenditure, because it prompts a demand for redistributive policies, and (*b*) incite political instability that undermines growth (Alesina and Rodrik 1994). This excursion into political science is somewhat dubious. For example, it is not at all clear how a society with the power relationships to generate inequality would, at the same time, produce an underclass with the political power to force redistributive policies upon a government (see Cramer 2000).

[8] For example, Milanovic (1999) introduces a concentration coefficient that measures the cumulative rate of social transfers when recipients are ranked by income.

[9] In a study of thirty social service programmes in Latin America, Grosh (1995) found a trade-off between administrative costs and the incidence of targeting programmes. That is to say, the more effective the targeting, the greater the cost, implying less expenditure for poverty reduction as such.

[10] To take but one example, attempts at identification of the poor by the authorities may be perceived as having a sinister agenda, identifying the political allegiances of households.

On somewhat firmer analytical ground, Aghion, Caroli, and Garcia-Penalosa (1999) argue that inequality has a negative impact on growth through imperfect capital markets, to which the poor have limited access. In other words, if capital markets discriminate against the poor, potentially profitable activities by the poor are constrained by lack of credit. This position harks back to Chenery *et al.* (1974), in which it was argued that growth would be enhanced if wealth were redistributed from the rich to the poor, because the marginal productivity of capital is higher for the poor. The Aghion *et al.* version adds arguments of 'moral hazard' and macroeconomic stability to the Chenery *et al.* advocacy of redistribution, to reach much the same conclusion.

Overall, the pro-redistribution literature of the 1990s was relatively limited in its theoretical contribution, and most striking in that it demonstrated, yet again, the ambivalence of economists towards the issues of inequality and poverty. On the one hand, the mainstream literature, with its emphasis upon the efficiency of markets, had a predilection to view inequality and poverty as accidental or occasional outcomes of a deregulated growth process. On the other hand, the persistence and severity of poverty in many, if not most, developing countries brought forth periodic arguments for their alleviation. The shifts in emphasis in the literature reflect the difficulty of reconciling these two.

From our review of the literature emerge several important points relevant to the empirical presentation below. Perhaps the most important is the growing consensus in the literature that countries with an 'initial condition' of relatively egalitarian distribution of assets and income tend to grow faster than countries with high initial inequality. For our purposes this is an extremely important conclusion because it means that reducing inequality 'cuts both ways'. On the one hand, a growth path characterized by greater equality at the margin directly benefits the poor in the short run. On the other, the resulting decrease in inequality creates in each period an 'initial condition' for the future which is growth enhancing. Thus, any growth path that reduces inequality deals poverty a double blow: through redistribution, and through trickle-down.

7.3. ANALYTICAL FRAMEWORK

The purpose of this section is to define our basic growth scenarios, which allow us in the subsequent section to compare poverty reduction through neutral distribution growth to an alternative in which growth incorporates a simple redistribution rule.

Income and asset redistribution are not necessary conditions for poverty reduction. Aggregate growth can also reduce poverty; and, equally, redistribution can achieve poverty reduction without growth (assuming that a portion of the population has incomes above the poverty line). To develop a poverty reduction strategy, the central issues are the relative effectiveness of growth and redistribution, and whether one enhances the other. It would seem clear, even on the most superficial analysis, that growth combined with redistribution would be more effective than either on its own. This truism gives no insight into the appropriate balance between the two for a concrete poverty target. Therefore, in order to determine an appropriate balance, 'growth' and 'redistribution' must be specified rigorously.

Let per capita GDP at time t be denoted by μ_t and suppose that it grows at rate g in period 1 so that

$$\mu_1 = \mu_0(1 + g). \tag{7.1}$$

If the population is constant and growth is distribution-neutral, then the income of the ith percentile also grows at rate g. In other words:

$$y_{1i} = y_{0i}(1 + g), \quad \text{for all } i, \tag{7.2}$$

where y_{ti} indicates the income of percentile i at time t. We think of this as the *primary distribution of income.* At various points in the discussion we refer to this pattern as 'distribution-neutral', 'trickle down', or 'status quo' growth.

In contrast, fiscal policy and other measures discussed below could be used to bias growth towards a more equal distribution. Specifically, we consider the case in which GDP growth is equally distributed in *absolute* terms. Since the per capita gain from growth is

$$\mu_1 - \mu_0 = \mu_0 g, \tag{7.3}$$

percentile i would end up with the post-transfer or *secondary distribution of income* given by

$$y_{1i}{}^{*} = y_{0i} + \mu_0 g. \tag{7.4}$$

This formulation provides a simple definition of growth and redistribution in the spirit of the *Redistribution with Growth* volume of the 1970s (Chenery *et al.* 1974). The proposed redistribution, equal absolute increments across percentiles, could be viewed as relatively minimalist. Alternative redistribution rules could be used, in which the allocation of the growth increment across percentiles was progressive.

A change in the primary distribution of income can be viewed as a tax. For each percentile ('household'), the implicit redistribution tax rate (relative to proportional gains from growth) is given by

$$t_i = (y_{1i} - y_{1i}^{*})/(y_{1i} - y_{0i}) = (y_{0i} - \mu_0)/y_{0i}. \tag{7.5}$$

The redistribution tax is negative (indicating a positive income transfer) up to the point of average per capita income, then positive above (a negative income transfer). If income is normally distributed, the tax is negative up to the fiftieth percentile. With more unequal (i.e. skewed) distributions, average per capita income is expected to be located above the fiftieth percentile.

Calculated by percentiles, the implicit redistribution tax is not out of line with income tax rates that have been applied in many developed countries. For example, the extremely unequal Brazilian distribution for the 1990s, with a Gini coefficient of 0.6, implies a *marginal* tax rate at the hundredth percentile of slightly more than 80 per cent. This is well below the maximum marginal tax rate of 91 per cent which operated in the United States from the Second World War until the early 1960s.

The proposed marginal redistribution has features that derive automatically from the nature of income distributions. First, and most obvious, equal absolute additions have a greater proportional effect as one moves down the income distribution. Second, as a consequence of the first feature, the lower the poverty line, the greater will be the poverty reduction. If different poverty lines are used to distinguish degrees of poverty, as is commonly done, the marginal redistribution will reduce severe poverty more than less severe poverty. Third, the more unequal the distribution of income below the poverty line, the less is the reduction in poverty associated with a (distribution-neutral) increase in per capita income, or a (equal absolute) redistribution of that rise in average income.

7.4. REDISTRIBUTION WITH GROWTH: EMPIRICAL EVIDENCE

In this section we inspect the impact on poverty in fifty countries of three simulation exercises, corresponding to different distributional outcomes: (1) a 1 per cent distribution-neutral increase in per capita GDP; (2) a 1 per cent increase in per capita GDP, distributed equally across income percentiles; and (3) a 1 per cent redistribution of income from the richest 20 per cent to the poorest 20 per cent. The effectiveness of the outcomes in reducing poverty is judged by the time period required to achieve a given target.

The necessary condition for a country to be included in the simulations is that there were statistics on the income share for quintiles,[11] and that the country was included in the World Bank's estimate of absolute poverty. The World Bank estimates were generated by converting each country's per capita income to constant US dollars for a base year, then setting a poverty line of US$ 1 a day.[12] The specified poverty percentile for $1 a day is implied by the assumptions made about the distribution of income within each quintile. To estimate the impact of a change in income on the percentage of households in poverty, it is necessary to make explicit the implicit intraquintile distribution of income. It was not necessary to know the intraquintile distribution for all quintiles, only for the quintile in which the poverty line fell, before and after the three simulations. The method of estimating intraquintile distribution is explained in the data appendix (Appendix A7.1). Our assumption is that in the relevant quintiles mean and median income are equal.

For an absolute poverty line, US$ 1 per day in this case, the percentage of households in poverty is strictly determined by per capita income and the degree of inequality. This is demonstrated in Table 7.1. Moving vertically down the table, the poverty line rises as a percentage of GDP; and moving across, the Gini coefficient rises. On the assumption of a continuous distribution function, such as a lognormal function with a given variance and a poverty line expressed as a fraction or multiple of the mean (van der Hoeven 2002), one can generate the implied percentage of households in poverty. In Table 7.1 these are the lower numbers in each cell, calculated by substituting the country's Gini coefficient and per capita income into the lognormal distribution. Since these numbers are generated from a continuous distribution function the intraquintile

[11] The major source was the WIDER income distribution database. See Appendix A7.1 for details by country.

[12] The World Bank also provides estimates of the population below $2 a day, but this measure is not used here.

Table 7.1. *Poverty levels by Gini coefficient and poverty line, estimated (in bold) and from functional form, fifty countries*

Gini (%)	**20–29**	**30–39**	**40–49**	**50–59**	**60 and above**
Pov. line, % of PCY					
10–19		**0.7**	**0.7**	**5.6**	
		0.5	0.8	4.8	
20–29	**0.7**	**2.7**	**7.7**	**18.6**	**23.2**
	0.7	2.6	7.1	18.8	25.4
30–39		**9.0**	**27.8**	**33.0**	**41.0**
		9.7	27.5	33.9	41.5
40–49	**3.6**	**15.5**	**28.6**	**50.5**	
		15.1	29.1	48.9	
50–59	**12.8**		**31.7**	**48.0**	**48.7**
			32.0	48.3	51.0
60–69	**17.9**			**54.5**	
	17.0			54.6	
70 and above		**47.2**	**50.7**	**77.9**	
		47.0	50.4	75.0	

Notes: The numbers in bold are the estimated one dollar poverty percentages from Table 7.2. The number below these is the poverty level generated from the functional relationship, $P_i = P(G_i, p_i)$ where P is the poverty percentage, G the Gini coefficient, p the poverty line as a percentage of per capita income, and i the country. The functional form is found in van der Hoeven (2002: 15–17), with a numerical example. The two measures are not the same due to differences across countries in the intraquintile distribution of income. Empty cells indicate no observations among the fifty countries.

Source: Authors' estimates based on the World Bank poverty estimates and World Income Inequality Database (WIID).

distribution of income for the poverty quintiles is given by the overall distribution function. The upper numbers in each cell, in bold, are the poverty percentages of the World Bank. For cells with more than one country, the simple average of poverty percentages is used. Table 7.1 shows that in most cases the poverty figures generated by the lognormal distribution, with the appropriate Gini coefficient and per capita income figures, compare reasonably well with the 'actual' estimates of the World Bank.

Prior to presenting the simulation results, a brief commentary is necessary on the particular definition we use for poverty reduction. Throughout the discussion, different growth and distribution scenarios will be assessed by their effectiveness in moving households out of poverty; that is, moving households from below to above the poverty line. This definition has two advantages. First, it corresponds to the poverty reduction targets of multilateral and bilateral donors. Second, and no doubt related to the first, it is easily calculated and compared across countries. However, it has a serious drawback, in that it excludes the improvement for all households whose incomes do not rise above the poverty line. This drawback of the approach becomes especially serious for comparing different growth scenarios when considering low-income countries.

Table 7.2 provides the basic statistics for the simulation exercises for the fifty countries: per capita income,[13] the Gini coefficient, and the percentage of the population with income per head below one US dollar (the poverty line), as estimated by the World Bank.

Table 7.2. *Distribution and poverty statistics for fifty countries, 1980s and 1990s*

Country by region	PCY	Gini (%)	Poverty: % of pop US$ 1
Latin America (12)	**1,391**	**53.5**	**26.0**
Brazil 1995	1,870	60.1	23.2
Chile 1992	1,585	50.7	15.0
Colombia 1991	2,400	57.2	7.8
Costa Rica 1989	1,350	42.0	19.0
Dom. Rep. 1989	1,390	50.5	19.9
Ecuador 1994	860	43.0	30.6
Guatemala 1989	658	59.1	53.5
Honduras 1992	660	52.6	46.7
Mexico 1992	1,620	50.3	14.9
Nicaragua 1993	685	50.3	43.8
Panama 1989	1,560	56.5	26.0
Venezuela 1990	2,050	53.8	11.9
N. Africa and ME (5)	**1,563**	**44.0**	**3.0**
Algeria 1995	1,757	35.3	0.8
Egypt 1991	905	32.0	7.6
Jordan 1992	1,700	40.7	2.4
Morocco 1991	1,845	39.2	0.8
Tunisia 1990	1,610	40.2	3.6
Sub-Sahara (13)	**746**	**51.1**	**46.5**
Botswana 1986	1,062	54.2	33.0
Guinea 1991	1,073	46.8	27.0
Kenya 1992	750	57.5	50.5
Lesotho 1987	675	56.0	48.7
Madagascar 1993	300	46.0	73.8
Mauritania 1988	690	42.4	31.7
Niger 1992	390	36.1	61.2
Nigeria 1993	840	45.0	31.1
Rwanda 1984	445	28.9	46.5
Senegal 1991	545	53.8	54.5
South Africa 1993	1,740	62.3	23.2

[13] Given the distribution of income by quintiles and the intraquintile distribution for the quintile in which the poverty level falls, a unique per capita income is implied. If the World Bank source gave a per capita other than this, the implied value was used in the table.

Table 7.2. *Continued*

Country by region	PCY	Gini (%)	Poverty: % of pop US$ 1
Zambia 1993	210	46.2	82.0
Zimbabwe 1990	977	56.8	41.0
Asia, not FSU (8)	**1,000**	**40.3**	**21.7**
China 1995	972	41.5	22.7
India 1992	460	32.0	47.9
Indonesia 1996	890	36.5	7.9
Nepal 1996	437	36.7	50.7
Pakistan 1991	850	31.2	11.8
Philippines 1994	862	42.9	26.6
Sri Lanka 1990	962	30.1	4.0
Thailand 1992	2,570	51.5	1.8
Former CP (12)	**1,249**	**33.1**	**5.9**
Belarus 1993	1,415	21.6	0.5
Bulgaria 1992	1,050	30.8	2.7
Czech Rep. 1993	780	26.6	3.6
Hungary 1993	1,520	27.9	0.6
Kazakhstan 1993	1,900	32.7	0.7
Kyrgyzstan Rep. 1993	881	35.3	18.9
Lithuania 1993	1,558	33.6	0.7
Moldova 1992	1,233	34.4	6.7
Romania 1992	680	25.5	17.8
Russian Fed. 1993	1,965	31.0	0.7
Slovak Rep. 1992	531	27.7	12.8
Turkmenistan 1993	1,480	35.8	4.6

Note: PCY, per capita income in indicated year; poverty measured as per cent of population.

Source: See Table 7.1.

In Table 7.3, the results of the simulations are given, for the two growth exercises, distribution-neutral growth (DNG in the table) and equal distribution growth (EDG). Columns one and two report the estimates of the percentage of households lifted out of US one dollar poverty as the result of 1 per cent growth, distribution-neutral and equal-distribution, respectively. Column three reports the 'effectiveness of redistribution' ratio. This is defined as the ratio of poverty reduction for EDG to DNG (column 2 divided by column 1). This ratio is greater than unity for forty-seven of the fifty countries. That is, for 94 per cent of the countries, the EDG strategy reduces poverty more in a given time period than a DNG strategy. This in itself is not surprising, for distribution-neutral growth is only more effective in reducing poverty for countries with 50 per cent or more of the population below the poverty line. Given our criterion of $1 a day these countries belong to the group with a very low per capita income. It is surprising how much more effective equally distributed growth proves to be in reducing poverty for most countries. For a large proportion of the countries, the ratio

Table 7.3. *Impact of two growth patterns on poverty, fifty countries*

Country by region	Percentage raised from poverty		Effectiveness of RedisY ratio	Redistribution tax rates	
	DNG 1%	EDG 1%		100th percentile	Average
Latin America (12)	**0.32**	**1.11**	**3.86**	**77.7**	**45.0**
Brazil 1995	0.24	1.28	5.33	82.0	38.6
Chile 1992	0.28	1.20	4.29	77.6	38.6
Colombia 1991	0.20	1.36	6.80	76.4	40.3
Costa Rica 1989	0.27	0.98	3.63	71.8	44.3
Dom. Rep. 1989	0.35	1.34	3.83	76.7	41.6
Ecuador 1994	0.51	1.08	2.12	75.2	39.2
Guatemala 1989	0.46	0.83	1.80	81.7	38.0
Honduras 1992	0.41	0.75	1.83	79.3	50.1
Mexico 1992	0.31	1.41	4.55	76.5	52.1
Nicaragua 1993	0.38	0.70	1.84	77.3	50.5
Panama 1989	0.17	0.77	4.53	79.1	54.1
Venezuela 1990	0.29	1.67	5.76	78.9	52.1
N Africa and ME (5)	**0.23**	**0.82**	**3.52**	**67.6**	**43.0**
Algeria 1995	0.01	0.03	3.00	64.7	38.2
Egypt 1991	0.55	1.37	2.49	63.7	35.2
Jordan 1992	0.30	1.39	4.63	72.6	47.9
Morocco 1991	0.01	0.03	3.00	69.3	47.3
Tunisia 1990	0.28	1.26	4.50	67.5	46.5
Sub-Sahara (13)	**0.46**	**0.87**	**2.05**	**74.3**	**46.8**
Botswana 1986	0.40	1.13	2.83	79.1	40.2
Guinea 1991	0.20	0.59	2.95	72.9	43.6
Kenya 1992	0.50	0.94	1.88	82.4	50.5
Lesotho 1987	0.37	0.69	1.86	79.2	52.3
Madagascar 1993	0.24	0.20	0.83	72.6	43.6
Mauritania 1988	0.44	0.84	1.91	69.1	48.4
Niger 1992	0.87	0.93	1.07	64.9	43.6
Nigeria 1993	0.40	0.95	2.38	71.0	50.8
Rwanda 1984	0.90	1.10	1.22	59.0	38.8
Senegal 1991	0.75	1.13	1.51	78.8	50.4
South Africa 1993	0.30	1.48	4.93	82.1	52.7
Zambia 1993	0.24	0.14	0.58	73.0	42.0
China 1995	0.37	0.99	2.68	69.7	44.4
India 1992	0.78	0.99	1.27	62.3	41.7
Indonesia 1996	0.52	1.27	2.44	62.3	41.7
Nepal 1996	1.00	0.94	0.94	66.1	39.2
Pakistan 1991	0.47	1.11	2.36	61.8	42.3
Philippines 1994	0.40	0.96	2.40	73.0	48.9
Sri Lanka 1990	0.51	1.35	2.65	61.8	40.8
Thailand 1992	0.31	0.79	2.55	79.0	51.5

Table 7.3. *Continued*

Country by region	Percentage raised from poverty		Effectiveness of RedisY ratio	Redistribution tax rates	
	DNG 1%	EDG 1%		100th percentile	Average
Former CP (12)	**0.29**	**0.67**	**2.19**	**57.2**	**37.1**
Belarus 1993	0.01	0.01	1.00	49.3	28.8
Bulgaria 1992	0.30	0.86	2.87	48.8	27.2
Czech Rep. 1993	0.70	1.50	2.14	56.6	30.3
Hungary 1993	0.01	0.01	1.00	59.6	39.8
Kazakhstan 1993	0.01	0.02	2.00	61.7	34.0
Kyrgyzstan Rep. 1993	0.37	0.90	2.43	64.1	45.5
Lithuania 1993	0.01	0.02	2.00	65.0	43.6
Moldova 1992	0.34	1.18	3.47	63.1	44.5
Romania 1992	0.45	0.84	1.87	56.2	37.5
Russian Fed. 1993	0.01	0.02	2.00	57.5	41.9
Slovak Rep. 1992	1.00	1.46	1.46	39.3	27.0
Turkmenistan 1993	0.30	1.22	4.07	64.9	45.5

Note: Effectiveness of RedisY (effectiveness of redistributive growth) is the ratio of EDG to NDG. The average redistribution tax rate is the rate across percentiles with positive tax rates.

Source: See Table 7.1.

is in excess of three; that is, EDG raises three times as many households from poverty than DNG.

Inspection of the effectiveness ratios reveals the obvious point that the benefits of equal distribution growth are greater the higher is a country's per capita income, and the higher its Gini coefficient. The two together account for about 60 per cent of the variation in the effectiveness ratio, with most of the remainder explained by the distribution of income within the quintile in which the poverty level falls.

The results imply that growth with redistribution would be particularly appropriate for the Latin American countries and those of North Africa and the Middle East. Its poverty reducing advantage would be less for the sub-Saharan countries (except South Africa), because of their low per capita incomes. It would also be less effective for the former centrally planned countries, despite their middle-income status, because of their relatively low inequality.

As the poverty line rises up a country's income distribution, the effectiveness of redistribution ratio becomes less and less sensitive to measures of inequality. However, it is always the case, no matter what a country's per capita income or degree of inequality,[14] that redistribution with growth is more efficient than DNG in reducing the intensity poverty. This is because the relative benefit of EDG increases as one moves

[14] That is, for any distribution that is not equal.

down the income distribution, independently of a country's per capita income or degree of inequality.

As discussed above, the redistribution with growth outcome implies a tax on all households whose income is above the mean. The percentile in which mean income is located depends on the skewness of the overall income distribution. The final two columns (columns 4 and 5) of Table 7.3 report the implied tax rate for the highest percentile, and the average rate across all percentiles whose income is redistributed towards the poorer percentiles. This is a *marginal* rate, referring to the increase or growth increment in per capita income. Inspection of the table shows, as expected, the maximum and average rates are positively correlated with the Gini coefficient. Whether the implicit tax rates should be judged as high depends on the mechanism to bring about the outcome. If DNG represents the primary (pre-tax) outcome, and EDG the secondary (post-tax) outcome, then there is a straight forward disincentive effect for those taxed, to be weighted against the incentive effect of the beneficiaries. We make the reasonable assumption that if positive tax rates create a disincentive to earn further income, then negative tax rates create an incentive to earn income and contribute to higher national growth. If the income distribution is skewed, then the number of households enjoying an incentive to earn will outnumber those suffering a disincentive, and the impact on growth should be positive.

These growth simulations can be compared to the more conventional exercise, a direct redistribution from the rich to the poor. This redistribution is simulated in Table 7.4, where it is assumed that 1 percentage point of total national income is shifted

Table 7.4. *Impact of income redistribution on poverty by country*

Country by region	Poverty after RY % pop	Pov. red (% initial level)	Tax rate, top quintile, %
Latin America (12)	**21.9**	**29.1**	**1.8**
Brazil 1995	18.4	20.7	1.6
Chile 1992	8.7	41.9	1.8
Colombia 1991	1.0	87.3	1.8
Costa Rica 1989	14.4	24.0	2.0
Dom. Rep. 1989	14.0	29.7	1.8
Ecuador 1994	30.6	0.2	1.9
Guatemala 1989	53.4	0.1	1.6
Honduras 1992	46.6	0.2	1.8
Mexico 1992	7.1	52.3	1.8
Nicaragua 1993	43.4	0.8	1.8
Panama 1989	23.9	8.1	1.7
Venezuela 1990	1.9	84.1	1.7
N. Africa and ME (5)	**0.8**	**55.0**	**2.2**
Algeria 1995	0.6	25.0	2.3
Egypt 1991	1.0	87.4	2.4
Jordan 1992	0.8	65.1	2.1

Table 7.4. *Continued*

Country by region	Poverty after RY % pop	Pov. red (% initial level)	Tax rate, top quintile, %
Morocco 1991	0.6	22.1	2.2
Tunisia 1990	0.9	75.2	2.2
Sub-Sahara (13)	**45.8**	**2.5**	**1.9**
Botswana 1986	32.9	0.3	1.7
Guinea 1991	25.8	4.3	2.0
Kenya 1992	50.4	0.1	1.6
Lesotho 1987	48.7	0.0	1.7
Madagascar 1993	73.8	−0.1	1.9
Mauritania 1988	31.1	2.0	2.2
Niger 1992	61.1	0.2	2.3
Nigeria 1993	31.1	0.1	2.0
Rwanda 1984	46.4	0.3	2.6
Senegal 1991	53.4	1.9	1.7
South Africa 1993	17.8	23.1	1.5
Zambia 1993	82.3	−0.3	2.0
Zimbabwe 1990	41.0	0.1	1.6
Asia, not FSU (8)	**18.8**	**37.4**	**2.2**
China 1995	19.4	14.5	2.1
India 1992	47.8	0.1	2.4
Indonesia 1996	1.0	87.7	2.2
Nepal 1996	50.3	0.8	2.2
Pakistan 1991	5.3	55.0	2.5
Philippines 1994	25.0	6.1	2.0
Sri Lanka 1990	0.9	77.3	2.5
Thailand 1992	0.7	57.7	1.7
Former CP (12)	**3.2**	**41.8**	**2.6**
Belarus 1993	0.5	0.0	3.0
Bulgaria 1992	0.9	66.3	2.6
Czech Rep. 1993	0.9	74.9	2.7
Hungary 1993	0.5	16.7	2.6
Kazakhstan 1993	0.6	21.4	2.5
Kyrgyzstan Rep. 1993	15.1	20.2	2.4
Lithuania 1993	0.6	16.7	2.4
Moldova 1992	1.0	85.7	2.4
Romania 1992	14.1	20.7	2.9
Russian Fed. 1993	0.5	23.1	2.6
Slovak Rep. 1992	3.1	75.8	2.8
Turkmenistan 1993	0.9	80.4	2.3

Note: RY: redistribution of income of one percentage point from highest to lowest quintile; Pov. red: poverty reduction from initial (pre-redistribution) level of poverty. One per cent of national income redistributed from the top 20 per cent to the bottom 20 per cent.

Source: See Table 7.1.

from the top quintile to the bottom quintile, and distributed equally among those households.[15] The table shows for each country the reduction in the poverty measure for the 1 per cent redistribution in column two, and can be compared to column three in Table 7.2, where pre-redistribution poverty is given. The outcome is summarized in column three of Table 7.4, which reports the percentage reduction in poverty as the result of the redistribution. For example, pre-redistribution poverty in Brazil was measured as 23.2 per cent of the population, and is simulated to be 18.4 per cent after redistribution, for a fall of 20.7 per cent (4.8 percentage points). The final column of the table gives the implicit tax rate on the highest quintile resulting from the redistribution. These prove to be quite low, varying from less than 2 per cent to a high of 3 per cent, and inversely related to inequality (i.e. the share of pre-redistribution income accruing to the top quintile).

Inspection of Table 7.4 shows that the poverty reductions associated with redistribution *without growth* vary dramatically across countries. In general, the lower the per capita income of a country, the less is the poverty reduction, demonstrated most obviously for the twelve Latin American countries, among which the reduction for the Central American states and Ecuador is virtually nil. The other obvious influence is inequality. The lower the inequality, holding per capita income constant, the greater the poverty reduction from a redistribution, because those below the poverty line are 'packed' close together. Comparing the middle-income Latin American countries to the former centrally planned countries reveals this.

These results suggest a typology of countries differentiated by the general strategy that is most conducive to poverty reduction, and this is done in Table 7.5. In this table, we calculate in columns two and three the number of years required for DNG and EDG to achieve the same poverty reduction as a transfer of 1 per cent of national income from the highest to the lowest quintile. To take the first country, Venezuela, as an example, neutral distribution growth would require over 34 years to reduce poverty by the same amount as the 1 percentage point redistribution, and EDG would require 6 years.

On the basis of these calculations, the fifty countries fall into three categories. In category 1, the 'income redistribution countries', both growth strategies require more than 1 year to reduce poverty as much as a straight redistribution. The countries are listed in descending order of the number of years required for DNG to match the impact of the 1 per cent redistribution on poverty. For thirty-four of the fifty countries (68 per cent), straight redistribution is the most effective method of poverty reduction.

In category 2 are thirteen 'redistribution with growth' countries, for which redistribution is not the most effective poverty reduction strategy, and equal distribution growth is more effective than distribution-neutral growth. For these countries one or both of the growth strategies at least matches the redistribution poverty reduction in less than a year, and the time period for equal distribution growth is the shorter. The latter point is emphasized by inclusion of the 'effectiveness ratio' a final column, taken from Table 7.3. These countries are characterized either by low per capita income

[15] At the poverty boundary, this redistribution shifts some households above the ones with slightly higher pre-redistribution incomes, but this does not affect the conclusions reached in the text.

Table 7.5. *Growth equivalents of 1 per cent redistribution from highest to lowest quintile*

Country by most effective policy		Years to reduce poverty as much as 1% redistribution		Effectiveness ratio
		DNG 1%	EDG 1%	
I. Income redistribution countries (34)				
1	Venezuela 1990	34.4	6.0	5.76
2	Colombia 1991	34.1	5.0	6.80
3	Mexico 1992	25.1	5.5	4.55
4	Algeria 1995	20.0	6.7	3.00
5	Brazil 1995	20.0	3.8	5.33
6	South Africa 1993	17.9	3.6	4.93
7	Morocco 1991	17.0	5.7	3.00
8	Dom. Rep. 1989	16.9	4.4	3.83
9	Russian Fed. 1993	15.0	7.5	2.00
10	Kazakhstan 1993	15.0	7.5	2.00
11	Panama 1989	12.4	2.7	4.53
12	Turkmenistan 1993	12.3	3.0	4.07
13	Egypt 1991	12.1	4.8	2.49
14	Lithuania 1993	12.0	6.0	2.00
15	Hungary 1993	10.0	10.0	1.00
16	Tunisia 1990	9.8	2.2	4.50
17	Bulgaria 1992	6.0	2.1	2.87
18	Jordan 1992	5.2	1.1	4.63
19	Philippines 1994	4.1	1.7	2.40
20	Czech Rep. 1993	3.9	1.8	3.57
21	Thailand 1992	3.3	1.3	2.55
22	Mauritania 1988	1.4	0.7	1.91
23	Chile 1992	22.5	5.2	4.29
24	Costa Rica 1989	16.9	4.6	3.63
25	Moldova 1992	16.9	4.9	3.47
26	Kyrgyzstan Rep. 1993	10.4	4.3	1.43
27	Romania 1992	8.2	4.4	1.87
28	China 1995	8.9	3.3	2.68
29	Sri Lanka 1990	6.1	2.3	1.31
30	Guinea 1991	5.8	2.0	2.95
31	Pakistan 1991	13.8	5.8	2.30
32	Indonesia 1996	13.4	5.5	2.74
33	Slovak Rep. 1992	9.7	6.6	1.15
34	Senegal 1991	1.4	0.9	1.49

Table 7.5. *Continued*

Country by most effective policy	Years to reduce poverty as much as 1% redistribution		Effectiveness ratio
	DNG 1%	EDG 1%	
II. Equal distribution growth countries (13)			
35 Botswana 1986	0.3	0.1	2.83
36 Zimbabwe 1990	0.1	0.0	2.69
37 Nigeria 1993	0.1	0.0	2.38
38 Ecuador 1994	0.1	0.1	2.12
39 Lesotho 1987	0.0	0.0	1.86
40 Kenya 1992	0.1	0.1	1.88
41 Nicaragua 1993	0.9	0.5	1.84
42 Honduras 1992	0.2	0.1	1.83
43 Guatemala 1989	0.2	0.1	1.80
44 India 1992	0.1	0.1	1.27
45 Rwanda 1984	0.1	0.1	1.22
46 Niger 1992	0.1	0.1	1.07
47 Belarus 1993	0.0	0.0	1.00
III. Distribution-neutral growth countries (3)			
48 Nepal 1996	0.4	0.4	0.94
49 Madagascar 1993	neg.	neg.	0.83
50 Zambia 1993	neg.	neg.	0.58

Note: Criteria for policy categories: I Income redistribution: The poverty reduction achieved by a 1 per cent redistribution requires more than 1 year of distribution-neutral and equal-distribution growth. II Equal distribution growth: EDG in 1 year reduces poverty more than either redistribution or distribution-neutral growth. III Distribution-neutral growth: DNG reduces poverty in 1 year more than redistribution or EDG.

Source: See Table 7.1.

or relatively equal distribution (or some combination of the two). Finally, there is category 3, the three 'trickle down' countries, for which growth as such is the most effective vehicle for poverty reduction. The defining characteristic of the trickle down countries is that they have more than 50 per cent of their population in poverty as a result of their low per capita income. However, it does not follow that all low income countries would fall into this category. If low income is combined with a relatively equal distribution, as for Niger, EDG may be more effective in reducing poverty, if only marginally so.

Thus, the simulation exercises demonstrate that for the overwhelming majority of middle-income countries, poverty reduction is most effectively achieved by a redistribution of current income. For these same countries, redistribution with growth would be the second-best option, and distribution-neutral, or status quo growth, a poor third. Low-income countries require a growth strategy, and for most redistribution with growth would be more effective than status quo growth. With these generalizations in mind, we consider poverty reduction policies in the following section.

7.5. CONDITIONS FOR POLICIES FOR REDISTRIBUTION WITH GROWTH

The major element required to introduce and effectively implement a redistributive strategy in any country is the construction of a broad political coalition for poverty reduction. The task of this coalition would be the formidable one of pressuring governments for redistribution policies, on the one hand, while neutralizing opposition to those policies from groups whose self-interest rests with the status quo. How such a political coalition might come about is beyond the scope of this chapter. We focus on a less fundamental, but crucially practical issue: the policies that could bring about a redistribution strategy. To be policy relevant, our consideration of redistribution mechanisms must move beyond a listing of possibilities to an analysis of the likely effectiveness of these.

Perhaps the most important determinant of the effectiveness of the various measures and specifics of each redistribution strategy is the structure of an economy. This structure will depend on the level of development, which will to a great extent condition the country's production mix, the endowments of socio-economic groups, the remuneration to factors, direct and indirect taxes on income and assets, prices paid for goods and services, and transfer payments. These elements of the distribution system are initial conditions that delineate the scope for redistributive policies. In this analytical context, the implementation requirements of redistributive policies are summarized in a simple theoretical framework (see Hamner, Pyatt, and White 1997). First, define the following terms: Y denotes the income of a household, V is transfer payments, T is taxes, k is a vector of assets (including human capital), w is a vector of rates of return (including wages), p is the price vector of those goods and services, q is the vector of goods and services purchased by the household, and S is household saving. Then, by definition it follows:

$Y =$	wk	$+(V - T)$	$= pq$	$+S$
Policy options	Minimum wages, low-wage subsidies, other labour market regulations, public employment schemes (w); credit programmes for the poor; land reform, education (k)	Transfer payments (unemployment compensation, pensions, child benefits, aid to disabled) and progressive taxes (on income and wealth)	Subsidies for basic needs goods, public sector infrastructure investment (p); child nutrition programmes (q)	Facilitate future asset acquisition: 'village banks' and other financial services for the poor
	Some effective in low-income countries	Effective in middle-income countries	Effective in most countries	Effective in most countries

The effectiveness of tax and expenditure policies (V and T) to generate secondary and tertiary distributions more equitable than the primary distribution depends upon the relative importance of the formal sector. All empirical evidence shows that the formal sector wage bill and profit share increase with the level of development. It is wage employment and corporate profits to which governments can most effectively apply progressive taxation. Along with the importance of the formal sector goes a high degree of urbanization, and working–poor urban households are more easily targeted than either the rural poor or urban informal sector households. The experience of a number of middle-income countries has demonstrated the effectiveness of basic income payments for poverty reduction, with an effective example being the basic pension paid to the elderly in South Africa.[16]

As shown in the previous section, the redistribution strategy is most appropriate for middle-income countries, because their per capita incomes are high relatively to the absolute poverty line. These are also the countries whose economic structures make taxation and expenditure instruments effective for redistribution. Thus, the thirty-seven 'income redistribution' countries, and others at similar levels of development, qualify for the redistributive strategy both in terms of its intrinsic effectiveness and the institutional capacity to implement it. Such countries would include the larger ones in Latin America (Argentina, Brazil, Chile, Mexico, and Venezuela), several Asian countries (the Republic of Korea, Thailand, and Malaysia), and virtually all of the former socialist countries of Central and Eastern Europe.

To a certain extent, specific economic structures allow for effective use of taxation for redistribution in a low-income country that would typically be relevant only for middle-income countries. If the economy of a low-income country is dominated by petroleum or mineral production, then a large portion of national income may be generated by modern sector corporations. This allows for effective taxation even though administrative capacity of the public sector may be limited. The tax revenue can be redistributed through poverty-reduction programmes, though not through transfer payments if the labour force is predominantly rural. Examples of mineral-rich, low-income countries with the potential to have done this, albeit unrealized, were Nigeria (oil), Liberia (bauxite), and Zambia (copper).

Interventions to change the distribution of earned income (wk in the equation above), which, in effect, alter market outcomes, will also tend to be more effective in middle-income countries. The most common intervention is a minimum wage, though there are many other policies to improve earnings from work (see Rodgers 1995). Other mechanisms include public employment schemes and tax subsidies to enterprises to hire low-wage labour. It is unlikely that any of these would be effective in low-income countries, because of enforcement problems (minimum wage), targeting difficulties (employment schemes), and narrowness of impact (wage subsidies).

Land reform might achieve poverty reduction for rural households, but the relationship between land redistribution and level of development is a complex one. On the

[16] While relatively low, the pension in the 1990s was an important income source for the rural poor, especially for female-headed households (see Standing *et al.* 1997, ch. 6).

one hand, low-income countries are predominantly rural, so if land ownership is concentrated, its redistribution could have a substantial impact on poverty. Further, the more underdeveloped a country, the less commercialized the poor rural households tend to be. Therefore, the benefits to the poor from land redistribution in low-income countries are less likely to be contingent on support services. On the other hand, lack of administrative capacity and the so-called traditional tenure systems represent substantial constraints to land redistribution in many low-income countries, and especially in the sub-Saharan countries. The usual approach to land redistribution presupposes private ownership, such that it is clear from whom the land will be taken and to whom it will be given. There are few sub-Saharan countries in which private ownership is widespread, making redistribution difficult or impossible without prior clarification of ownership claims (Platteau 1992, 1995). While land redistribution is probably not an effective poverty reducing measure for most low-income countries, a few notable exceptions in Asia (e.g. India and Vietnam), suggest that it should not be ruled out in all cases.

For middle-income countries, experience in Latin America has shown that governments can effectively implement a land redistribution. However, the high degree of commercialization of agriculture in middle-income countries requires that redistribution be complemented by a range of rural support services, including agricultural extension, marketing facilities, and other measures. Perhaps more serious, the relevance of land reform for poverty reduction tends to decline as countries develop and the rural population shrinks relatively and absolutely. For example, at the end of the twentieth century in the five most populous Latin American countries, barely 20 per cent or less of the labour force was in agriculture. Further, when seeking to reduce poverty among the landless and near-landless in such countries, minimum wages may be more relevant than land redistribution. These considerations suggest that while land redistribution may be an effective and feasible mechanism for some countries, other mechanisms may be more effective in both low and middle-income countries.

Interventions that directly affect the prices and access to goods and services (pq) could potentially be quite powerful instruments for poverty reduction. Public subsidies to selected basic consumer products have the administrative advantage of not requiring targeting, only identification of those items that carry a large weight in the expenditure of the poor. Multilateral adjustment programmes typically require an end to such subsidies on grounds of allocative efficiency or excessive budgetary cost. However, among multilateral agencies there is no consensus on subsidies. The rules of the World Trade Organization do not prohibit consumer subsidies, as long as they do not discriminate between domestic production and imported substitutes. Whether subsidies would generate excessive fiscal strain would depend on their extent and how they were financed. Again, the level of development of a country is of central importance for the effectiveness of subsidies. In low-income countries with the majority of the poor in the countryside, consumer subsidies are unlikely to have a significant impact on the poor outside urban areas. Basic goods provision in kind can be an effective instrument for poverty reduction even in very low-income countries, by delivering such items as milk to school children. To do so with a non-targeted programme would require a progressive tax system, which would be more likely in a middle-income country, as discussed above.

The poor in all countries suffer from poor health and inadequate education in relation to the non-poor. Education and health have two great practical advantages for poverty reduction: (1) the programmes that would help the poor are easily identified (though the specifics would vary by country); and (2) unlike for asset or income redistribution, their provision to the poor is not controversial at the rhetorical level. Provision of health care and education that would improve the lives of the poor requires skilled workers. Since these workers would be in short supply in the public sector, effective provision might necessitate either their reallocation from delivering those services to the non-poor, or substantially increased expenditure to increase total provision. In practice delivering health and education services to the poor might prove as difficult politically as implementing direct redistribution of income and assets. The same point applies to infrastructure programmes directed to poverty reduction. To the extent that these would reduce public investment in projects favoured by the non-poor, especially the wealthy, they may be no easier to implement than measures that appear superficially to be more radical.

Table 7.6 provides a summary of the discussion, with poverty reducing measures listed by rows, and the three categories of countries across columns. Table 7.6 indicates that for the 'redistribution' countries, a redistribution of current income and assets is the most effective means of poverty reduction, and the methods to achieve this are

Table 7.6. *Summary of feasibility of redistribution instruments by category of country*

Country category: Redistributive instrument	**Redistribution of current income + assets (middle-income countries)**	**Growth with redistribution policies (middle + most low-income countries)**	**Growth without redistribution policies (very low-income countries)**
Progressive taxation	Yes	Yes, for some countries	No
Transfer payments	Yes	Yes, for some countries	No
Consumer subsidies	Yes	Yes	Yes, for some countries
Public employment schemes	Yes	Yes	No
Land reform	Yes, but not always relevant	Yes	Not for most countries
Education + health	Yes	Yes	Yes
Infrastructure + public works	Yes	Yes	Yes

Source: Authors' classification.

feasible. For the 'redistribution with growth' countries, the measures for redistribution of current income and assets are less feasible, but instruments to achieve the more modest goal of redistribution of the growth increment would be feasible. Finally, most redistribution instruments would not be feasible, or only to a limited degree, for very low-income countries; but for these countries, a growth strategy with no redistributive mechanisms may be the most poverty-reducing path.

While moving from the principle of redistribution to successful implementation involves major problems, these problems should not be exaggerated. In many countries they might prove no more intractable than the problems associated with implementation of other economic policies. For example, an effective orthodox monetary policy is difficult to implement if a country is too small or underdeveloped to have a bond market. The absence of a bond market leaves the monetary authorities unable to 'sterilize' foreign exchange flows. Similarly, replacing tariffs by a value-added tax would be a daunting task in a country whose commerce was primarily through small traders. Lack of public sector capacity would also limit the ability to carry out a range of the so-called supply-side policies: privatization, 'transparency' mechanisms, and decentralization of central government service delivery (van der Hoeven and van der Geest 1999). The multilateral agencies have recognized these constraints to adjustment programmes, and typically made the decision that constrained implementation represented action preferable to non-implementation. The same argument can be made for a redistributive growth strategy: for poverty reduction and sustainable growth, it might be preferable to implement redistributive growth imperfectly than to implement the status quo imperfectly.

7.6. CONCLUSION

Poverty reduction has always been a priority of development policy, albeit sometimes only at the rhetorical level. The end of the 1990s brought increased emphasis on bringing the benefits of growth to the poor. However, growth alone is a rather blunt instrument for poverty reduction, since the consensus of empirical work suggests that it is distribution-neutral. Along with emphasis on poverty reduction, a shift occurred in the policy literature towards a more favourable view of policies to redistribution income and assets. An integration of distributional concerns and a priority on poverty reduction could be the basis for a new policy agenda to foster both growth and equity. This new agenda would be based on three analytical generalizations:

(1) that greater distributional equality provides a favourable initial condition for rapid and sustainable growth;
(2) that redistribution of current income and assets, or redistribution of an economy's growth increment are the most effective forms of poverty reduction for most countries; and
(3) the mechanisms to achieve the redistributions are feasible for most countries. These generalizations imply that the new agenda could focus upon specific policies and instruments of redistribution, with the goal of substantial reductions in urban and rural poverty in the medium term.

APPENDIX: METHOD AND SOURCES

As shown in the text (see Table 7.1 and accompanying discussion), the percentage of households in poverty, with an absolute poverty line, can be estimated using two parameters, the poverty line as a percentage of per capita income, and the Gini coefficient. This estimate of poverty is not sufficient for carrying out the simulations. For the simulations, one must have an estimate of the distribution of income in the immediate range below the poverty line. This requires an estimate of the intraquintile distribution of income. For the vast majority of the countries, the poverty line fell in the first or second quintile. The procedure for estimation was the following:

(1) average income was calculated for the poverty quintile, and the quintile above and below (in the case in which the poverty quintile was the first, see below);
(2) within each quintile it was assumed that mean income equalled the median;[17] this assumption locates within each quintile the percentile for mean income; and
(3) between each mean income, income was assumed to rise at a constant rate.

For example, the rate of increase of income between mean income in quintile one (P_{m1}) and quintile two (P_{m2}) would be:

$$P_{m2} = (1 + r)^{20}(P_{m1})$$

If P_{m1} were at the fourteenth percentile, the income of the twentieth percentile would be $P_{20} = (1 + r)^6(P_{m1})$. If the poverty line lies within the first quintile, the value of r between the first and second quintile means it is used to calculate downwards to the first percentile. On the basis of this method, the percentile for the absolute poverty line for each country can be found by generating the income for each percentile until $P_i =$ US$ 365 is reached (Table 7A.1).

Table 7A.1. *Country-wise tabulation of percentage of Gini coefficients*

Country	Gini (%)	Definition	Reference unit	Coverage
Latin America (12)	**52.2**			
Brazil 1995	60.1	Income	Household per capita	All
Chile 1992	50.7	Income	Person	All
Colombia 1991	57.2	Income	Person	All
Costa Rica 1989	42.0	Income	Person	All
Dom. Rep. 1989	50.5	Income	Person	All
Ecuador 1994	43.0	Expenditure	Person	All
Guatemala 1989	59.1	Income	Person	All
Honduras 1992	52.6	Income	Person	All
Mexico 1992	50.3	Expenditure	Household per capita	All

[17] The authors wish to thank Malte Lubker for pointing out the empirical validity of this assumption for the lowest two quintiles.

Table 7A.1. *Continued*

Country	Gini (%)	Definition	Reference unit	Coverage
Nicaragua 1993	50.3	Expenditure	Household per capita	All
Panama 1989	56.5	Income	Person	All
Venezuela 1990	53.8	Income	Person	All
N. Africa and ME (5)	**37.5**			
Algeria 1995	35.3	Expenditure	Household per capita	All
Egypt 1991	32.0	Expenditure	Household per capita	All
Jordan 1992	40.7	Expenditure	Person	All
Morocco 1991	39.2	Expenditure	Household per capita	All
Tunisia 1990	40.2	Expenditure	Household per capita	All
Sub-Sahara (13)	**48.6**			
Botswana 1986	54.2	Expenditure	Household	All
Guinea 1991	46.8	Expenditure	Household per capita	All
Kenya 1992	57.5	Expenditure	Household per capita	All
Lesotho 1987	56.0	Expenditure	Household per capita	All
Madagascar 1993	46.0	Expenditure	Household per capita	All
Mauritania 1988	42.4	Expenditure	Household per capita	All
Niger 1992	36.1	Expenditure	Household per capita	All
Nigeria 1993	45.0	Expenditure	Household per capita	All
Rwanda 1984	28.9	Expenditure	Household per capita	All
Senegal 1991	53.8	Expenditure	Household per capita	All
South Africa 1993	62.3	Income	Person	All
Zambia 1993	46.2	Expenditure	Household per capita	All
Zimbabwe 1990	56.8	Expenditure	Household per capita	All
Asia, not FSU (8)	**32.6**			
China 1995	41.5	Income	Household per capita	All
India 1992	32.0	Expenditure	Person	All
Indonesia 1996	36.5	Income	Household per capita	All
Nepal 1996	36.7	Expenditure	Household per capita	All
Pakistan 1991	31.2	Expenditure	Household per capita	All
Philippines 1994	42.9	Expenditure	Household per capita	All
Sri Lanka 1990	30.1	Expenditure	Household per capita	All
Thailand 1992	51.5	Income	Household	All
Former CP (12)	**30.2**			
Belarus 1993	21.6	Income	Household per capita	All
Bulgaria 1992	30.8	Income	Person	All
Czech Rep. 1993	26.6	Income	Household per capita	All
Hungary 1993	27.9	Income	Household per capita	All
Kazakhstan 1993	32.7	Income	Household per capita	All
Kyrgyzstan Rep. 1993	35.3	Income	Household per capita	All
Lithuania 1993	33.6	Income	Household per capita	All
Moldova 1992	34.4	Income	Household per capita	All

Table 7A.1. *Continued*

Country	Gini (%)	Definition	Reference unit	Coverage
Romania 1992	25.5	Income	Household per capita	All
Russian Fed. 1993	31.0	Income	Household per capita	All
Slovak Rep. 1992	27.7	Income	Household	All
Turkmenistan 1993	35.8	Income	Household per capita	All

Source: World Income Inequality Database (WIID).

REFERENCES

Aghion, P., Caroli, E., and Garcia-Penalosa, C. (1999). 'Inequality and Economic Growth: The Perspective of the New Growth Theories'. *Journal of Economic Literature*, 37(4), 1615–60.

Ahluwalia, M. S. and Chenery, H. (1974*a*). 'The Economic Framework'. In H. Chenery, M. S. Ahluwalia, C. L. G. Bell, J. H. Duloy, and R. Jolly (eds), *Redistribution with Growth*. Oxford University Press, Oxford.

—— and —— (1974*b*). 'A Model of Redistribution and Growth'. In H. Chenery, M. S. Ahluwalia, C. L. G. Bell, J. H. Duloy and R. Jolly (eds), *Redistribution with Growth*. Oxford University Press, Oxford.

Alesina, A. (1998). 'The Political Economy of Macroeconomic Stabilizations and Income Inequality: Myths and Reality'. In V. Tanzi and K. Chu (eds), *Income Distribution and High-Quality Growth*, MIT Press, Cambridge, MA.

—— and Rodrik, D. (1994). 'Distributive Politics and Economic Growth'. *Quarterly Journal of Economics*, 109(2), 465–90.

Bruno, M., Ravallion, M., and Squire, L. (1998). 'Equity and Growth in Developing Countries: Old and New Perspectives on the Policy Issues'. In V. Tanzi and K. Chu (eds), *Income Distribution and High-Quality Growth*. MIT Press, Cambridge, MA.

Chenery, H., Ahluwalia, M. S., Bell, C. L. G., Duloy, J. H., and Jolly, R. (1974). *Redistribution with Growth*. Oxford University Press, Oxford.

Chu, K., Davoodi, H., and Gupta, S. (1999). 'Income Distribution and Tax and Government Spending Policies in Developing Countries'. Draft paper prepared for WIDER Project Meeting on Rising Income Inequality and Poverty Reduction, 16–18 July 1999, Helsinki.

Cornia, G. A. (1999). 'Liberalization, Globalization and Income Distribution'. *WIDER Working Papers* 157. UNU/WIDER, Helsinki.

Cramer, C. (2000). 'Inequality, Development and Economic Correctness'. *SOAS Department of Economics Working Papers* 105. SOAS, London.

—— and Weeks, J. (1997). 'Analytical Foundations of Employment and Training Programmes in Conflict-affected Countries'. *ILO Action Programme on Skills and Entrepreneurship Training for Countries Emerging from Armed Conflict*. ILO, Geneva.

DFID, Department for International Development (1997). *Eliminating World Poverty: A Challenge for the 21st Century*. The Stationery Office, London.

De Janvry, A. and Sadoulet, E. (1995). 'Poverty, Equity and Social Welfare in Latin America: Determinants of Change Over Growth Spells'. Issues in Development Discussion Paper. Development and Technical Co-operation Department, ILO, Geneva.

Dyer, G. (1997). *Class, State and Agricultural Productivity in Egypt. A Study of the Inverse Relationship between Farm Size and Land Productivity*. Frank Cass, London.

Fields, G. (1980). *Poverty, Inequality and Development*. Cambridge University Press, Cambridge.

Ferreira, F. H. G. (1999). 'Inequality and Economic Performance'. World Bank, www.worldbank.org/poverty/inequal/index.htm.

Flemming, J. (1998). 'Equitable Economic Transformation'. In V. Tanzi and K. Chu (eds), *Income Distribution and High-Quality Growth*, MIT Press, Cambridge, MA.

Grosh, M. E. (1995). 'Towards Quantifying the Trade-off: Administrative Costs and Incidence in Targeted Programs in Latin America'. In D. van de Walle and K. Neat (eds), *Public Spending and the Poor*. Johns Hopkins University Press for the World Bank, Baltimore.

Hammer, J. S., Nabi, I., and Cercone, J. A. (1995). 'Distributional Effects of Social Sector Expenditures in Malaysia: 1974–1989'. In D. van de Walle and K. Neat (eds), *Public Spending and the Poor*. Johns Hopkins University Press for the World Bank, Baltimore.

Hamner, L., Pyatt, G., and White, H. (1997). *Poverty in Sub-Saharan Africa. What can be Learnt from the World Bank's Poverty Assessments?* ISS, The Hague.

Harberger, A. (1998). 'Monetary and Fiscal Policy for Equitable Economic Growth'. In V. Tanzi and K. Chu (eds), *Income Distribution and High-Quality Growth*. MIT Press, Cambridge, MA, pp. 203–41.

ILO (1992). *Incomes Policies in the Wider Context: Wage, Price and Fiscal Initiatives in Developing Countries*. F. Paukert and D. Robinson (eds) ILO, Geneva.

Jao, C. C. (2000). 'The Impact of the Tax Revenue and Social Welfare Expenditure on Income Distribution in Taiwan'. *Journal of the Asia Pacific Economy*, 5(1,2), 73–90.

Kanbur, R. (1998). 'Income Distribution and Growth'. *World Bank Working Papers* 98/13.

Kuznets, S. (1955). 'Economic Growth and Income Inequality'. *American Economic Review*, 45, 1–28.

Lewis, W. A. (1954). 'Economic Development with Unlimited Supplies of Labour'. *Manchester School of Economics and Social Studies*, 22, 139–81.

Li, H., Squire, L., and Zou, H. (1998). 'Explaining the International and Intertemporal Variations in Income Inequality'. *The Economic Journal*, 108, 26–43.

McDonald, C., Schiller, C., and Ueda, K. (1999). 'Income Distribution, Informal Safety Nets, and Social Expenditures in Uganda'. *IMF Working Papers* 163.

Milanovic, B. (1999). 'Explaining the Increase in Inequality During the Transition'. *World Bank Policy Research Department Papers* 1935.

Platteau, J.-P. (1992). 'Land Reform and Structural Adjustment in Sub-Saharan Africa: Controversies and Guidelines'. *FAO Economic and Social Development Papers* 107. FAO, Rome.

—— (1995). 'Reforming Land Rights in Sub-Saharan Africa: Issues of Efficiency and Equity', *Research Institute for Social Development Discussion Paper* 60. UNRISD, Geneva.

Ravallion, M. and Chen, S. (1997). 'What Can New Survey Data Tell Us About Recent Changes in Distribution and Poverty'. *World Bank Review*, 11(2), 357–82.

—— and Sen, B. (1994). 'Impacts on Rural Poverty of Land-Based Targeting: Further Results for Bangladesh'. *World Development*, 22(6), 823–38.

Rodgers, G. (ed.) (1995). *The Poverty Agenda and the ILO: Issues for Research and Action*. ILO, Geneva.

Sen, A. (1995). 'The Political Economy of Targeting'. In D. van de Walle and K. Neat (eds), *Public Spending and the Poor*. Johns Hopkins University Press for the World Bank, Baltimore.

Standing, G., Sender, J., and Weeks, J. (1997). *Restructuring the Labour Market: The South African Challenge*. ILO, Geneva.

Thiesenhusen, W. H. (1989). *Searching for Agrarian Reform in Latin America*. Unwin Hyman, Winchester.

van de Walle, D. (1995). 'Incidence and Targeting: An Overview of Implications for Research and Policy'. In D. van de Walle and K. Neat (eds), *Public Spending and the Poor*, Johns Hopkins University Press for the World Bank, Baltimore.
van der Hoeven, R. (2002). 'Poverty and Structural Adjustment. Some Remarks on the Trade-off between Equity and Growth'. In P. Mosley and A. Booth (eds), *New Poverty Strategies, What Have They Achieved, What Have We Learned?* Palgrave, London.
—— and van der Geest, W. (1999). 'Africa's Adjusted Labour Markets. Can Institutions Perform?'. In W. van der Geest and R. van der Hoeven (eds), *Adjustment, Employment and Missing Institutions in Africa*, James Currey, London.
Weeks, J. (1971). 'The Political Economy of Labour Transfer'. *Science and Society*, 35(4), 463–80.
World Bank (1993). *The East Asian Miracle*. Oxford University Press, Oxford.

8

Producing an Improved Geographic Profile of Poverty: Methodology and Evidence from Three Developing Countries

GABRIEL DEMOMBYNES, CHRIS ELBERS, JEAN O. LANJOUW, PETER LANJOUW, JOHAN MISTIAEN, AND BERK ÖZLER

8.1. INTRODUCTION

Poverty maps provide detailed descriptions of the spatial distribution of poverty. These can be extremely valuable to governments, non-governmental organizations and multilateral institutions that want to strengthen the impact that their spending has on the poor. For example, many developing countries use poverty maps to guide the division of resources among local agencies or administrations as a first step in reaching the poor. Poverty maps can also be an important tool for research. Recent theoretical advances have brought income and wealth distributions back into a prominent position in growth and development theories.[1] Distributions of well-being are also considered determinants of specific socio-economic outcomes, such as individual health or levels of violence.[2]

Construction of detailed geographic poverty profiles and empirical testing of the importance of theoretical relationships, however, has been held back by the poor quality

We are grateful to the Instituto Nacional de Estadistica y Census (INEC), Ecuador, Statistics South Africa, and Institut National de la Statistique (INSTAT), Madagascar, for access to their unit record census data and the Bank Netherlands Partnership Program (BNPP) for financial support. Useful comments were received from Jesko Hentschel, Jose Lopez-Calix, and Martin Ravallion. We also thank Uwe Deichmann and Piet Buys for GIS/mapping assistance. The views in this study are our own and should not be taken to reflect those of the World Bank or any of its affiliates. All errors are our own.

[1] See, for example, Murphy, Schleifer, and Vishny (1989), Galor and Zeira (1993), Banerjee and Newman (1993), Aghion and Bolton (1997), Alesina and Rodrik (1994), Persson and Tabellini (1994) for early contributions to this rapidly growing literature.

[2] Deaton (1999) argues that it is most reasonable to search for a relationship between individual health outcomes and local, rather than national, income inequality. Demombynes and Özler (2001) explore the relationship between local inequality and crime in South Africa.

of distributional data. Detailed household surveys which include reasonable measures of income or consumption are samples, and thus are rarely representative or of sufficient size at low levels of disaggregation to yield statistically reliable estimates. In the three developing countries examined here, the lowest level of disaggregation possible using sample data is to regions that encompass hundreds of thousands of households. At the same time, census (or large sample) data of sufficient size to allow disaggregation either have no information about income or consumption, or measure these variables poorly.[3]

This chapter describes briefly, a recently developed statistical procedure to combine data sources so as to take advantage of the detailed information available in household sample surveys and the comprehensive coverage of a census (Elbers, Lanjouw, and Lanjouw 2002). Using a household survey to impute missing information in the census we estimate (as opposed to directly measure) poverty and inequality at a disaggregated level based on a household per capita measure of expenditure, y. The idea is straightforward. First a model of y is estimated using the sample survey data, restricting explanatory variables to those either common to both survey and census, or variables in a tertiary data set that can be linked to both of those data sets. Then, letting W represent an indicator of poverty or inequality, we estimate the expected level of W given the census-based observable characteristics of the population of interest using parameter estimates from the 'first stage' model of y. The same approach could be used with other household measures of well-being, such as assets, income, or employment. A recent study using data from Brazil extends the approach to combine a detailed but small sample survey with a much larger sample survey data set rather than the full unit record level census (Elbers, Lanjouw, and Lanjouw 2002).

Drawing on evidence from three different countries—Ecuador, Madagascar, and South Africa—we illustrate that the method generates reliable estimates of poverty at a very disaggregated level. Our estimates, for instance, of headcount rates of poverty for 'counties' of around 1000–2000 households have 95 per cent confidence intervals approximately the same size as those of stratum (region) level estimates in the household surveys. The last have populations well over 100,000 and often run to millions of households. With good welfare estimates for groups the size of towns, villages, or even neighbourhoods, policy-makers have a valuable tool for targeting purposes, and researchers are able to test a variety of hypotheses at levels of disaggregation where assumptions about stable underlying structures are more tenable than at a cross-country level. That the method performs satisfactorily in three settings as dissimilar as the countries considered in this chapter suggests that the approach will be useful in many contexts.

8.2. AN OVERVIEW OF THE METHODOLOGY

The survey data are first used to estimate a prediction model for consumption and then the parameter estimates are applied to the census data to derive poverty statistics.

[3] For example, a single question regarding individuals' incomes in the 1996 South African census generates an estimate of national income just 83 per cent the size of the national *expenditure* estimate derived from a representative household survey, and a per capita poverty rate 25 per cent higher, with discrepancies systematically related to characteristics such as household location (Alderman *et al.* 2002).

Thus, a key assumption is that the models estimated from the survey data apply to census observations. This is most reasonable if the survey and census years coincide. In this case, simple checks can be carried out by comparing the estimates to basic poverty or inequality statistics in the sample data. If different years are used but the assumption is considered reasonable, then the welfare estimates obtained refer to the census year, whose explanatory variables form the basis of the predicted expenditure distribution.

An important feature of the approach applied here involves the explicit recognition that the poverty or inequality statistics estimated using a model of income or consumption are statistically imprecise. Standard errors must be calculated. The following subsections briefly summarize the discussion in Elbers, Lanjouw, and Lanjouw (2002).

8.2.1. *Definitions*

Per-capita household expenditure, y_h, is related to a set of observable characteristics, $\mathbf{x}_h$:[4]

$$\ln y_h = \mathrm{E}[\ln y_h|\mathbf{x}_h] + u_h. \tag{8.1}$$

Using a linear approximation, we model the observed log per capita expenditure for household h as

$$\ln y_h = \mathbf{x}_h^T \boldsymbol{\beta} + u_h, \tag{8.2}$$

where $\boldsymbol{\beta}$ is a vector of parameters and u_h is a disturbance term satisfying $\mathrm{E}[u_h|\mathbf{x}_h] = 0$. In applications we allow for location effects and heteroskedasticity in the distribution of the disturbances.

The model in eqn (8.2) is estimated using the household survey data. We are interested in using these estimates to calculate the welfare of an area or group for which we do not have any, or insufficient, expenditure information. Although the disaggregation may be along any dimension—not necessarily geographic—we refer to our target population as a 'county'. Household h has m_h family members. While the unit of observation for expenditure is the household, we are more often interested in welfare measures based on individuals. Thus, we write $W(\boldsymbol{m}, \mathbf{X}, \boldsymbol{\beta}, \boldsymbol{u})$, where $\boldsymbol{m}$ is a vector of household sizes, $\mathbf{X}$ is a matrix of observable characteristics and $\boldsymbol{u}$ is a vector of disturbances. Because the disturbances for households in the target population are always unknown, we estimate the expected value of the indicator given the census households' observable characteristics and the model of expenditure in eqn (8.2).[5] We denote this expectation as

$$\mu = \mathrm{E}[W|\boldsymbol{m}, \mathbf{X}, \xi], \tag{8.3}$$

[4] The explanatory variables are observed values and need to have the same degree of accuracy in addition to the same definitions across data sources.

[5] If the target population includes sample survey households then some disturbances are known. As a practical matter we do not use these few pieces of direct information on y.

where ξ is the vector of all model parameters. In constructing an estimator of μ we replace the unknown vector ξ with consistent estimators, $\hat{\xi}$, from the first stage expenditure regression. This yields $\hat{\mu} = \mathrm{E}[W|\boldsymbol{m}, \mathbf{X}, \hat{\xi}]$. This expectation is generally analytically intractable so we use Monte Carlo simulation to obtain our estimator, $\tilde{\mu}$.

8.2.2. *Estimation Error Components*

The difference between $\tilde{\mu}$, our estimator of the expected value of W for the county, and the *actual* level of welfare for the county may be written

$$W - \tilde{\mu} = (W - \mu) + (\mu - \hat{\mu}) + (\hat{\mu} - \tilde{\mu}). \tag{8.4}$$

Thus, the prediction error has three components: the first due to the presence of a disturbance term in the first stage model which implies that households' actual expenditures deviate from their expected values (idiosyncratic error); the second due to variance in the first stage estimates of the parameters of the expenditure model (model error); and the third due to using an inexact method to compute $\hat{\mu}$ (computation error).[6]

Idiosyncratic error The variance in our estimator due to idiosyncratic error falls approximately proportionately in the number of households in the county. That is, the smaller the target population, the greater is this component of the prediction error, and there is, thus, a practical limit to the degree of disaggregation possible. At what population size this error becomes unacceptably large depends on the explanatory power of the expenditure model and, correspondingly, the importance of the remaining idiosyncratic component of the expenditure.

Model error The part of the variance due to model error is determined by the properties of the first stage estimators. Therefore, it does not increase or fall systematically as the size of the target population changes. Its magnitude depends on the precision of the first stage coefficients and the sensitivity of the indicator to deviations in household expenditure. For a given county its magnitude will also depend on the distance of the explanatory variables for households in that county from the levels of those variables in the sample data.

Computation error The variance in our estimator due to computation error depends on the method of computation used and can be made as small as desired with sufficient resources.

8.3. DATA

In all three of the countries examined here, household survey data were combined with unit record census data. In Ecuador the poverty map is based on census data from 1990, collected by the National Statistical Institute of Ecuador (Instituto Nacional de Estadistica y Census, INEC) combined with household survey data from 1994.

[6] Elbers, Lanjouw, and Lanjouw (2002) use a second survey in place of the census which then also introduces sampling error.

The census covered roughly 2 million households. The sample survey (Encuesta de Condiciones de Vida, ECV) is based on the Living Standards Measurement Surveys approach developed by the World Bank, and covers just under 4500 households. The survey provides detailed information on a wide range of topics, including food consumption, non-food consumption, labour activities, agricultural practices, entrepreneurial activities, and access to services such as education and health. The survey is clustered and stratified by the country's three main agroclimatic zones and a rural–urban breakdown. It also oversamples Ecuador's two main cities, Quito and Guayaquil. Hentschel and Lanjouw (1996) develop a household consumption aggregate adjusted for spatial price variation using a Laspeyres food price index reflecting the consumption patterns of the poor. The World Bank (1996) consumption poverty line of 45,476 sucres per person per fortnight (approximately $1.50 per person per day) underlies the poverty numbers reported here. Although the 1994 ECV data were collected 4 years after the census, we maintain the assumption that the model of consumption in 1994 is appropriate for 1990. The period 1990–94 was one of relative stability in Ecuador. Comparative summary statistics on a selection of common variables from the two data sources support the presumption of little change over the period. Details on these data and the poverty mapping application in Ecuador can be found in Hentschel *et al.* (2000).

Three data sources were used to produce local-level poverty estimates for Madagascar. First, the 1993 unit record population census data collected by the Direction de la Démographie et Statistique Social (DDSS) of the Institut National de la Statistique (INSTAT). Second, a household survey, the Enquête Permanente Auprès des Ménages (EPM), fielded to over 4508 households between May 1993 and April 1994, by the Direction des Statistique des Ménages (DSM) of INSTAT. Third, we made use of a variety of spatial and environmental outcomes at the *fivondrona* level (e.g. representing a collection of 'firaisanas' or communes).[7] The welfare indicator underpinning the Madagascar poverty map includes components such as an imputed stream of consumption from the ownership of consumer durables. Further details are provided in Mistiaen *et al.* (2002).

Three data sets were also combined to create the South African poverty map. The first is the OHS (October Household Survey), an annual survey which focuses on some key indicators of living patterns in South Africa. It focuses on employment, internal migration, housing, access to services, individual education, and vital statistics. In the 1995 round of the survey, 29,700 households were interviewed. The Income and Expenditure Survey (IES) is the source of information on the income and expenditure of households. It was designed for use with the OHS. In all, 28,710 households remained in the merged data set. The third source of data, the population census of 1996, covers over 8.3 million households. It collected both information on household composition and some details on housing and services in a manner that paralleled the OHS. Further details can be found in Alderman *et al.* (2002).

[7] These data were provided to this project by the non-governmental organization CARE.

8.4. IMPLEMENTATION

The first stage estimation is carried out using the household sample survey. For each of the three countries considered in this chapter, the household survey is stratified into a number of regions and is representative at that level. Within each region there are one or more levels of clustering. At the final level, households are randomly selected from a census enumeration area. Such groups we refer to as 'cluster' and denote by a subscript c. Expansion factors allow calculation of regional totals.

Our first concern is to develop an accurate empirical model of household consumption. Consider the following model:

$$\ln y_{ch} = \mathrm{E}[\ln y_{ch} | x_{ch}^T] + u_{ch} = x_{ch}^T \boldsymbol{\beta} + \eta_c + \varepsilon_{ch}, \tag{8.5}$$

where η and ε are independent of each other and uncorrelated with observables. This specification allows for an intracluster correlation in the disturbances. One expects location to be related to household income and consumption, and it is certainly plausible that some of the effect of location might remain unexplained even with a rich set of regressors. For any given disturbance variance, σ_{ch}^2, the greater the fraction due to the common component η_c, the less one benefits from aggregating over more households. Welfare estimates become less precise. Further, failing to account for spatial correlation in the disturbances would result in underestimated standard errors on poverty estimates.

Since unexplained location effects reduce the precision of poverty estimates, the first goal is to explain the variation in consumption due to location as far as possible with the choice and construction of explanatory variables. We tackle this in four ways.

1. We estimate different models for each stratum in the country's respective survey.
2. We include in our specification household-level indicators of connection to various networked infrastructure services, such as electricity, piped water, networked waste disposal, telephone, etc. To the extent that all or most households within a given neighbourhood or community are likely to enjoy similar levels of access to such networked infrastructure, these variables might capture unobserved location effects.
3. Third, we calculate means at the enumeration area (EA) level in the census (generally corresponding to the 'cluster' in the household survey) of household-level variables, such as the average level of education of household heads. We then merge these EA means into the household survey and consider them for inclusion in the first stage regression specification.[8]
4. Finally, in the case of Madagascar we have merged a *fivondrona*-level data set provided by CARE and also consider the spatially referenced environmental variables contained in that data set for inclusion in our household expenditure models.

[8] In Madagascar the EA in the household survey is not the same as that in the census. The most detailed spatial level at which we can link the two data sets is the firaisana ('commune'). Thus, firaisana-level means were used. In South Africa, means were calculated at the magisterial district level.

To select location variables (EA means and for Madagascar, the CARE variables), we regress the total residuals, $\hat{u}$, on cluster fixed effects. We then regress the cluster fixed effect parameter estimates on our location variables and select a limited number that best explain the variation in the cluster fixed effects estimates. These location variables are then included in the first stage regression model.

A Hausman test described in Deaton (1997) is used to determine whether to estimate with household weights. $\bar{R}^2$'s for our models are generally high, ranging between 0.45 and 0.77 in Ecuador, 0.24 to 0.64 in Madagascar, and 0.47 to 0.72 in South Africa.[9]

We next model the variance of the idiosyncratic part of the disturbance, $\sigma^2_{\varepsilon,ch}$. The total first stage residual can be decomposed into uncorrelated components as follows:

$$\hat{u}_{ch} = \hat{u}_{c.} + (\hat{u}_{ch} - \hat{u}_{c.}) = \hat{\eta}_c + e_{ch} \tag{8.6}$$

where a subscript '.' indicates an average over that index. Thus, the mean of the total residuals within a cluster serves as an estimate of that cluster's location effect. To model heteroskedasticity in the household-specific part of the residual, we choose between 10 and 20 variables, z_{ch}, that best explain variation in e^2_{ch} out of all potential explanatory variables, their squares, and interactions.[10]

Finally, we determine the distribution of η and ε using the cluster residuals $\hat{\eta}_c$ and standardized household residuals $e^*_{ch} = \frac{e_{ch}}{\hat{\sigma}_{\varepsilon,\,ch}} - \left[\frac{1}{H}\sum_{ch}\frac{e_{ch}}{\hat{\sigma}_{\varepsilon,\,ch}}\right]$, respectively where H is the number of households in the survey. We use normal or t distributions with varying degrees of freedom (usually 5), or the actual residual distributions when taking a semi-parametric approach. Before proceeding to simulation, the estimated variance–covariance matrix is used to obtain final GLS estimates of the first stage consumption model.

At this point we have a full model of consumption that can be used to simulate any expected welfare measures with associated prediction errors. For a description of different approaches to simulation see Elbers, Lanjouw, and Lanjouw (2002).

8.5. RESULTS

In this section we examine the success of the approach outlined in previous sections in our three case study settings: Ecuador, Madagascar, and South Africa. We begin by examining the degree to which our census-based poverty estimates match estimates from the countries' respective surveys at the level at which those surveys are representative (usually the stratum). We then ask how far we can disaggregate our census-based poverty estimates, when we take the survey-based sampling errors to

[9] Again, see Elbers, Lanjouw, and Lanjouw (2002), Mistiaen *et al.* (2002), and Alderman *et al.* (2002) for details.

[10] We limit the number of explanatory variables to be cautious about overfitting and use a bounded logistic functional form.

indicate acceptable levels of precision. We then turn to the ultimate goal of the analysis, namely, to produce disaggregated spatial profiles of poverty. We illustrate how projecting poverty estimates onto maps produces a quick and appealing way in which to convey a considerable amount of information on the spatial distribution of poverty to users. We also show that conclusions as to the spatial heterogeneity of poverty are directly dependent on the degree of disaggregation. By their very nature, sample surveys are likely to lead analysts to understate the significance of spatial variation in poverty.

8.5.1. *How Well do Survey and Census Estimates Match?*

Tables 8.1–8.3 present stratum-level estimates of the poverty headcount in our three countries. Table 8.1 illustrates that estimates of the incidence of poverty in Ecuador at the stratum-level are reasonably close to those from the census. Except for Guayaquil and Rural Sierra, the pairs of poverty estimates are statistically indistinguishable at better than a 5 per cent level of significance and are close to coinciding in several instances. The differences in estimates for Guayaquil and Rural Sierra can reasonably be traced to changes between the 1990 census and the

Table 8.1. *Stratum-level poverty rates in Ecuador (headcount)*

Stratum	Household survey (s.e.)	Census (s.e.)
Rural Costa	0.50	0.501
	(0.042)	(0.024)
Urban Costa	0.25	0.258
	(0.03)	(0.015)
Guayaquil	0.29	0.380
	(0.027)	(0.019)
Rural Sierra	0.43	0.527
	(0.027)	(0.019)
Urban Sierra	0.19	0.211
	(0.026)	(0.027)
Quito	0.25	0.223
	(0.033)	(0.022)
Rural Oriente	0.67	0.590
	(0.054)	(0.025)
Urban Oriente	0.20	0.189
	(0.05)	(0.021)

Note: Standard errors on poverty estimates from the household survey reflect 2-stage sampling.

Source: ECV (1994), Ecuador Census (1990).

Table 8.2. *Stratum-level poverty rates in Madagascar** *(headcount)*

Stratum	Household survey (s.e.)	Census (s.e.)
Antananarivo Urban	0.544	0.462
	(0.048)	(0.015)
Antananarivo Rural	0.767	0.738
	(0.037)	(0.019)
Fianarantsoa Urban	0.674	0.646
	(0.059)	(0.027)
Fianarantsoa Rural	0.769	0.820
	(0.049)	(0.025)
Taomasina Urban	0.599	0.599
	(0.086)	(0.018)
Taomasina Rural	0.810	0.786
	(0.035)	(0.026)
Mahajanga Urban	0.329	0.378
	(0.072)	(0.028)
Mahajanga Rural	0.681	0.695
	(0.065)	(0.039)
Toliara Urban	0.715	0.713
	(0.086)	(0.036)
Toliara Rural	0.817	0.800
	(0.042)	(0.027)
Antsiranana Urban	0.473	0.344
	(0.087)	(0.031)
Antsiranana Rural	0.613	0.581
	(0.073)	(0.046)

Note: Standard errors on poverty estimates from the household survey reflect 2-stage sampling.
*Madagascar estimates are preliminary, see Mistiaen *et al.* (2002).
Source: EPM (1994); Madagascar Census (1993).

1994 household survey in the exogenous variables underpinning the consumption regressions.[11]

In Madagascar the sample and census data refer to the same period. In this country, the main source of concern is that the sample-based estimates have large standard errors. In addition, in one or two of the strata the explanatory power of the first stage regressions is not particularly high (an adjusted R^2 of 0.24 for rural Antsiranana is the

[11] Other factors could play a role when survey and census years differ: changes in the definition of urban/rural, or of metropolitan boundaries; non-sampling errors in data entry and data collection; non-applicability of our maintained assumption that stratum-level regression parameters are applicable for sub-stratum localities, etc.

Table 8.3. *Stratum-level poverty rates in South Africa (headcount)*

Stratum	Household survey (s.e.)	Census (s.e.)
Western Cape	0.12	0.11
	(0.011)	(0.006)
Eastern Cape	0.45	0.40
	(0.014)	(0.009)
Northern Cape	0.38	0.35
	(0.030)	(0.014)
Free State	0.51	0.53
	(0.022)	(0.010)
Kwazulu-Natal	0.24	0.25
	(0.014)	(0.008)
Northwest Province	0.37	0.41
	(0.024)	(0.011)
Mpumalanga	0.26	0.22
	(0.022)	(0.011)
Northern Province	0.36	0.35
	(0.021)	(0.015)

Note: Standard errors on poverty estimates from the household survey reflect two-stage sampling. Gauteng is not included because the survey data in that stratum was not from a representative sample.

Source: IES/OHS (1995); South Africa Census (1996).

lowest obtained in any of our models). This gives relatively high standard errors on our census-level predicted poverty estimates. Together the errors make it difficult to reject that point estimates are the same. However, for all strata, the census and survey point estimates are reasonably close.[12]

South African results are also satisfactory (Table 8.3). Point estimates across the two data sources match closely at the stratum-level so that again we cannot reject equality at a 5 per cent significance level. Once again, stratum-level standard errors in the IES survey are not small, despite a sample size which is several times larger than the typical LSMS-style household survey.

Three points can be taken from these tables. First, in all three countries examined here, our estimates typically match household survey-based estimates closely and are statistically indistinguishable from them. Second, the precision of the survey-based estimates is not terribly high. Third, standard errors on our estimators at the stratum-level are uniformly lower than those obtained with household survey data alone. This implies that errors introduced by applying the statistical procedure outlined above are

[12] Mistiaen *et al.* (2002) document that the figures are similarly close for FGT1 and FGT2 poverty measures (Foster, Greer, and Thorbecke 1984).

more than offset by the removal of sampling error when producing poverty estimates in the population census. We shall show next that it is possible to produce estimates of poverty with census data at levels of disaggregation far below what is possible with household survey data alone without paying any additional price in terms of statistical precision.

8.5.2. *How Low can we go?*

The question of how far one can disaggregate in the population census depends on what is judged to be an acceptable level of statistical precision. As discussed in Section 2.2, the idiosyncratic component of the error in our estimator increases as the number of households in the target population falls. Thus, any attempt to identify individual poor households in the census, for example, would be very ill-advised because confidence bounds on household-level poverty estimates would likely encompass the entire range between 0 and 1. However, the idiosyncratic error declines sharply as one aggregates across households, such that overall standard errors quickly become quite reasonable when estimates are made at the level of towns or districts. In Figs 8.1–8.6, it is shown that if one takes as a benchmark the precision which is achieved with household survey data at the representative stratum-level, then in all three countries examined here, it is possible to produce estimates of poverty at the third administrative level (corresponding to 1000–2000 households on average in Ecuador and Madagascar, and 20,000 or so in

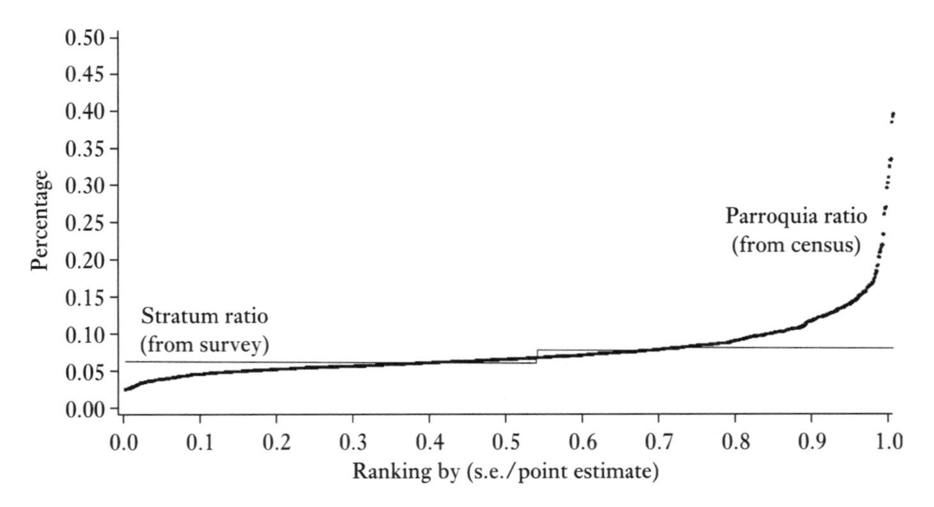

Figure 8.1. *Standard error as percentage of point estimate: Rural Ecuador, headcount*

Note: Comparing survey based stratum-level estimates to census based parroquia-level estimates (915 Parroquias with on average 1050 households).

Source: Authors' calculations.

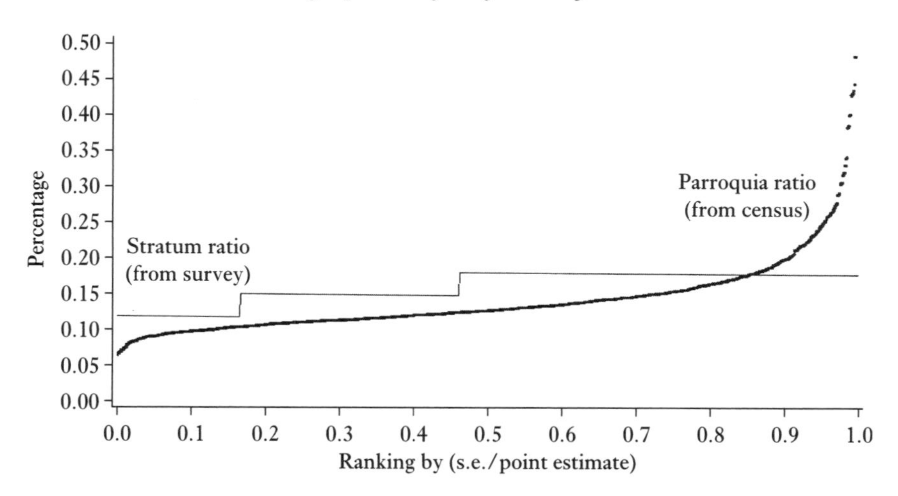

Figure 8.2. *Standard error as percentage of point estimate: Rural Ecuador, FGT2*

Note: Comparing survey based stratum-level estimates to census based parroquia-level estimates (915 Parroquias with on average 1050 households).

Source: Authors' calculations.

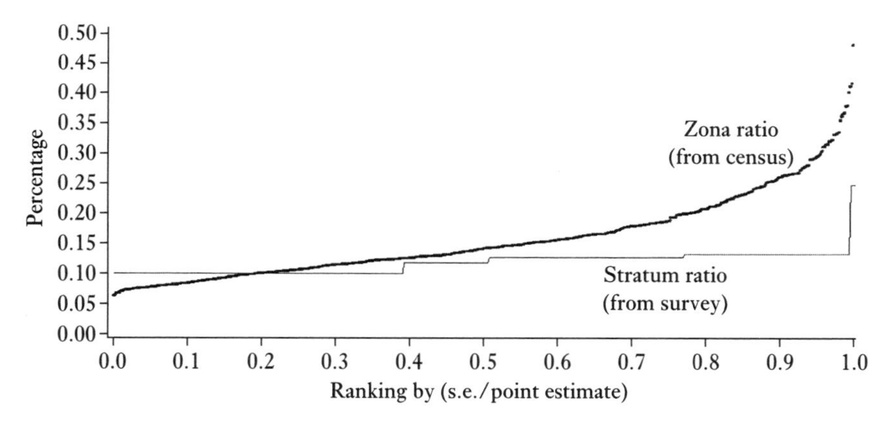

Figure 8.3. *Standard error as percentage of point estimate: Urban Ecuador, headcount*

Note: Comparing survey based stratum-level estimates to census based zona-level estimates (453 Zonas with on average 1360 households).

Source: Authors' calculations.

South Africa) with similar levels of precision. These are a tenth to a hundredth the size of the populations in the corresponding strata.

Figure 8.1 illustrates the case for the headcount in rural Ecuador. We calculate the ratio of the standard error to the point estimate for each of the 915 'parroquias' in rural Ecuador. The value of this ratio is represented by the vertical axis, and parroquias are

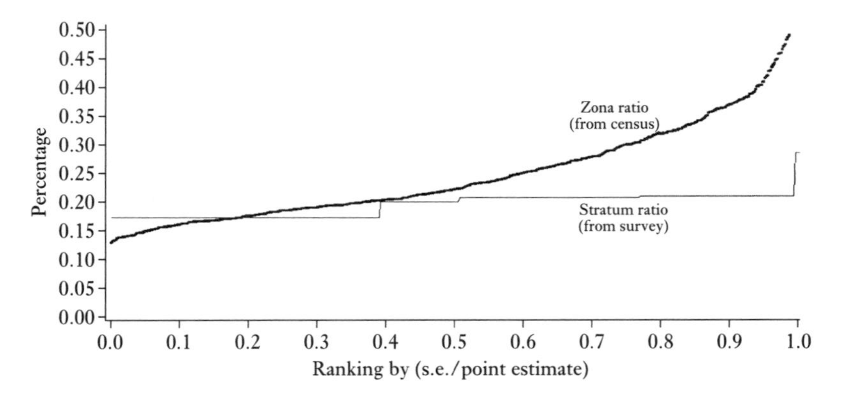

Figure 8.4. *Standard error as percentage of point estimate: Urban Ecuador, FGT2*

Note: Comparing survey based stratum-level estimates to census based zona-level estimates (453 Zonas with on average 1360 households).

Source: Authors' calculations.

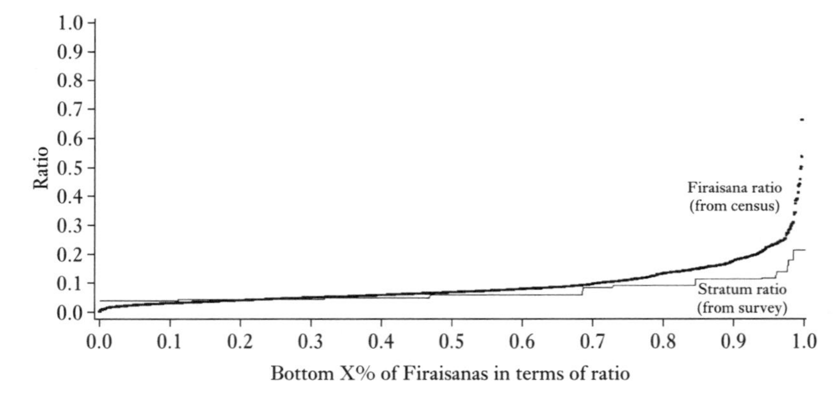

Figure 8.5. *Ratio of estimated standard error to point estimate: headcount*

Note: Firaisana-level estimates in Madagascar (1248 Firaisanas; average number of households per Firaisana: 1950).

Source: Authors' calculations.

ranked from lowest to highest along the horizontal axis. We overlay in this graph the value of the ratio from the survey estimates for the three strata covering rural Ecuador.[13] From Fig. 8.1 we can see that for nearly 80 per cent of parroquias the standard error as a share of the parroquia-level poverty estimate is no higher than that typically found in household surveys. If we take the survey-based stratum-level precision as a

[13] We compare ratios rather than absolute standard errors because we want to abstract away from the much greater variation in poverty estimated at the parroquia level compared to estimates at the stratum level from the household survey. Parroquias with very high estimated poverty tend to have larger standard errors, and the converse is the case for those with low poverty.

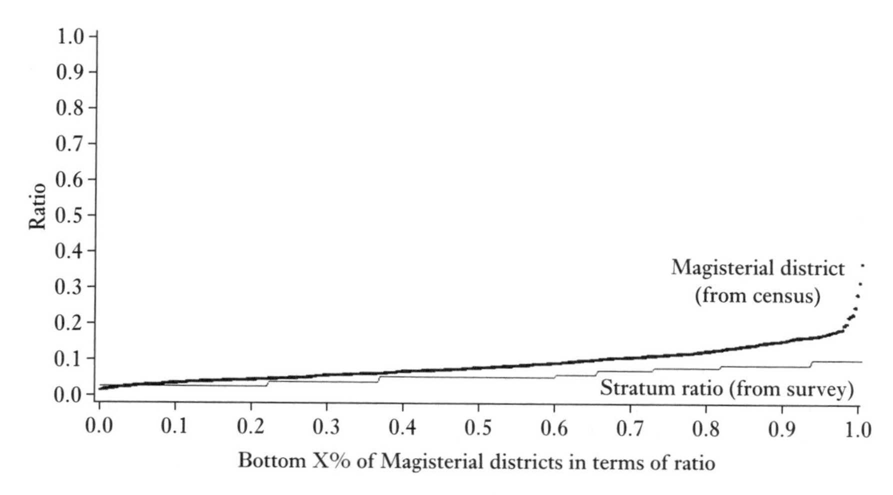

Figure 8.6. *Ratio of estimated standard error to point estimate: headcount*

Note: Magisterial District-level estimates in South Africa (354 Magisterial Districts; average number of households per MD: 24,000).

Source: Authors' calculations.

benchmark, such that the zone of acceptability is up to the highest ratio value from survey estimates, we find that estimating poverty at this level of disaggregation does not result in particularly noisy estimates for the large majority of parroquias in the country. It should also be noted that parroquias for which the ratio is well above the survey-level threshold usually have particularly low poverty rates. (Standard errors decline as estimates decline, but not as sharply.)

Figure 8.2 shows that the percentage of parroquias with lower ratios than observed from the household survey increases for poverty measures with greater distributional sensitivity than the headcount (here FGT2). This is not because the FGT2 measure is estimated with greater precision in the census, but rather that survey-based estimates of this measure are less precise than they are of the headcount. It is remarkable that for the FGT2 nearly 90 per cent of parroquia estimates of poverty are more precise than the corresponding stratum-level estimates of the FGT2 in the sample survey.

In urban Ecuador the lowest administrative level is the 'zona' (roughly a neighbourhood). With one exception (the Urban Oriente stratum—see Table 8.1) survey-level standard error ratios are lower than for most zonas (Figures 8.3 and 8.4). Despite their small populations, however, for a fairly large number of zonas the standard error ratios are hardly higher than their stratum-level counterparts in the survey. If one were to find these ratios excessive, neighbouring zonas could be joined into slightly larger groupings. While the picture is somewhat better with higher order FGT measures, the message remains that the zona is probably too low a level of disaggregation to apply our methodology for urban areas in Ecuador.

In Fig. 8.5, we reproduce for Madagascar a picture similar to Fig. 8.1. The firaisana is now the level of disaggregation (average number of households: 2000). Given that the sample estimates have ratios of standard error to point estimate as high as 20 per cent (see Table 8.2) the vast majority of firaisana-level estimates look at least as good. Once again, if analysts are satisfied with the stratum-level precision obtainable with the EPM survey in Madagascar, then there should be no concern in working with firaisana-level estimates from the census.

The situation in South Africa is somewhat different. Disaggregating to the police-station level, with an average of 7500 households, the ratio of standard error to point estimates lies well above the ratio that obtains with the household survey at the stratum-level.[14] Going down to police stations would require a price in terms of statistical precision of poverty estimates. Disaggregating to the Magisterial District level (of which there are 354 in South Africa, with an average of 20,000 households in each) the price is modest (see Fig. 8.6). It is important to note, however, that the stratum-level estimates available with the South African IES survey are remarkably precise, because of the survey's large sample size (nearly 30,000 households). If one were to apply in South Africa the same standards of acceptability that are usually applied to settings where LSMS-style surveys are the only source of information, even police station estimates of poverty would be viewed as acceptable.

8.5.3. *Geographic Profiles: Poverty in Ecuador, Madagascar, and South Africa*

The previous subsection has shown that reasonable estimates of poverty can be produced in our three example countries at levels of spatial disaggregation representing groupings of 1000–20,000 households. Clearly, intermediate levels of spatial disaggregation are also possible. The question often arises how best to present information on the spatial distribution of poverty in a country once the number of estimates is large. A convenient manner in which to present the geographic poverty profile is in the form of maps where shadings are used to depict different degrees of poverty. Recent advances in digitized geographic information systems (GIS) have greatly facilitated the process of producing maps and offer great opportunities to combine the spatially referenced poverty information with other similarly referenced data. We illustrate here with a few examples some of the ways in which the spatially disaggregated poverty estimates produced with this methodology can be represented in map form.

Figure 8.7 displays the spatial distribution of estimated rural poverty in Ecuador at the cantonal level (second administrative level representing around 5000–10,000 households). Comparisons between the Costa, the coastal region of Ecuador, and the Sierra, the central mountainous region, feature highly in popular political debate in Ecuador.[15] The top two maps in Fig. 8.7 depict the spatial distribution of poverty on

[14] The police station does not correspond to a government administrative level, but comes closest to the third administrative level identified in Ecuador and Madagascar in terms of population size.

[15] See, for example, 'Under the Volcano', *The Economist*, 27 November 1999, 66.

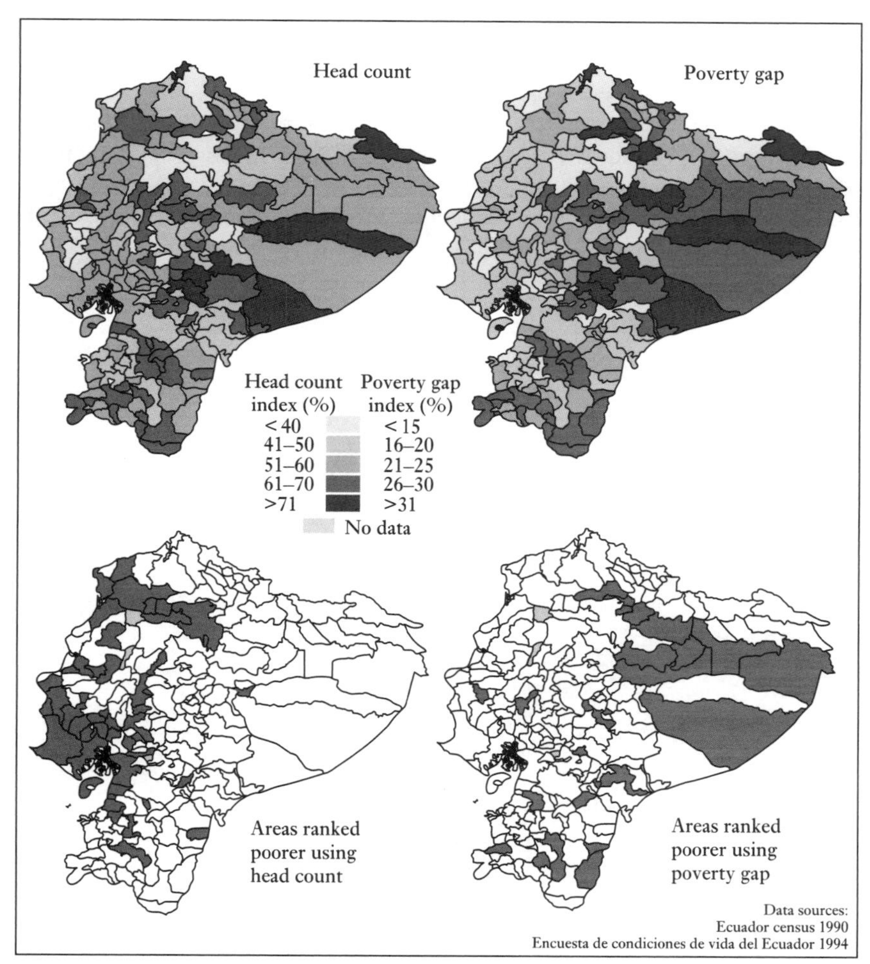

Figure 8.7. *Rural poverty by canton: headcount and poverty gap*

Source: Authors' calculations.

the basis of two common measures: the headcount and the poverty gap (FGT1). The bottom two maps in Fig. 8.7 indicate those instances where the two alternative poverty measures differ in their ranking of cantons. The map on the lower left shows that in the Costa a number of cantons are ranked poorer under the headcount criterion than under the poverty gap. In contrast, in the Sierra and the less populated east (Oriente), numerous cantons are ranked more poor under the poverty gap criterion than under the headcount. Clearly, views about the relative poverty of the regions will be affected by the measure of poverty employed.

The discussion in this chapter has placed considerable emphasis on statistical precision of poverty estimates produced with the methodology outlined here. As one thinks about drawing maps describing the spatial distribution of poverty, it is also important to convey information about statistical precision in those maps. Figures 8.8 and 8.9 are an attempt to do so for Madagascar. Figure 8.8 displays our geographic poverty profile for 1248 firaisanas in Madagascar. In Fig. 8.9 we present a similar profile, but we highlight those firaisanas that have headcount rates significantly different from their

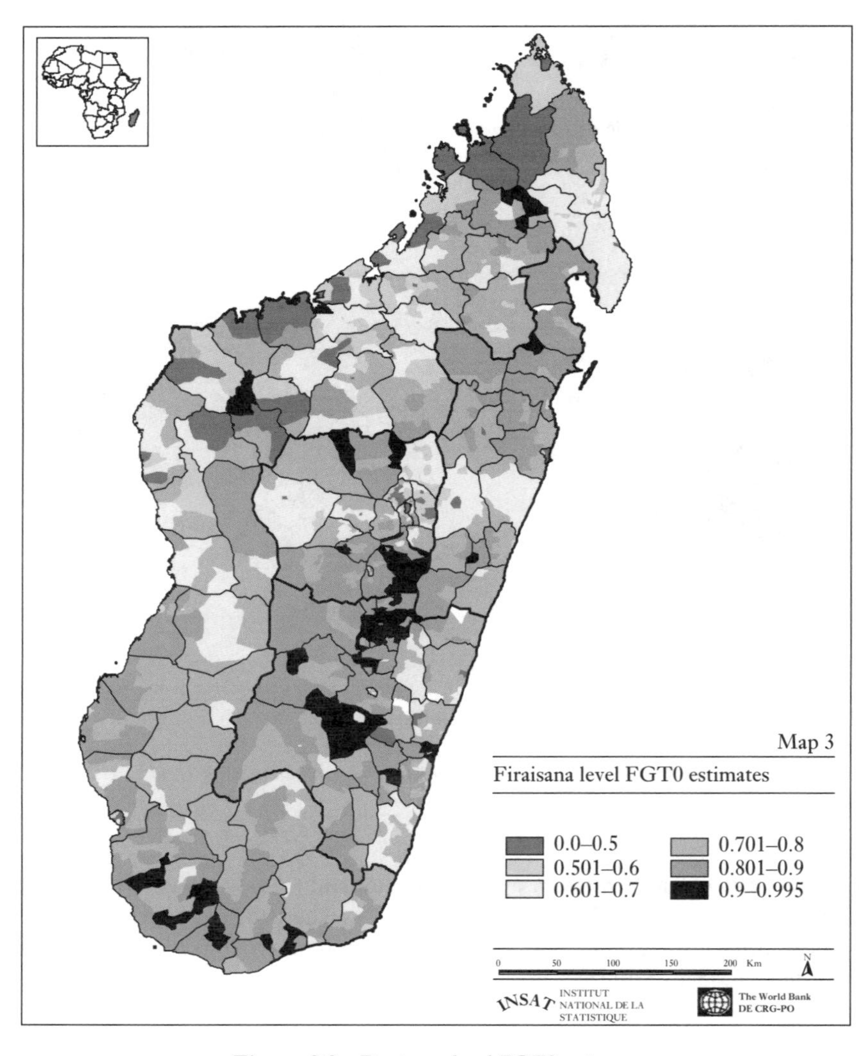

Figure 8.8. *Firaisana level FGT0 estimates*

Source: Authors' calculations.

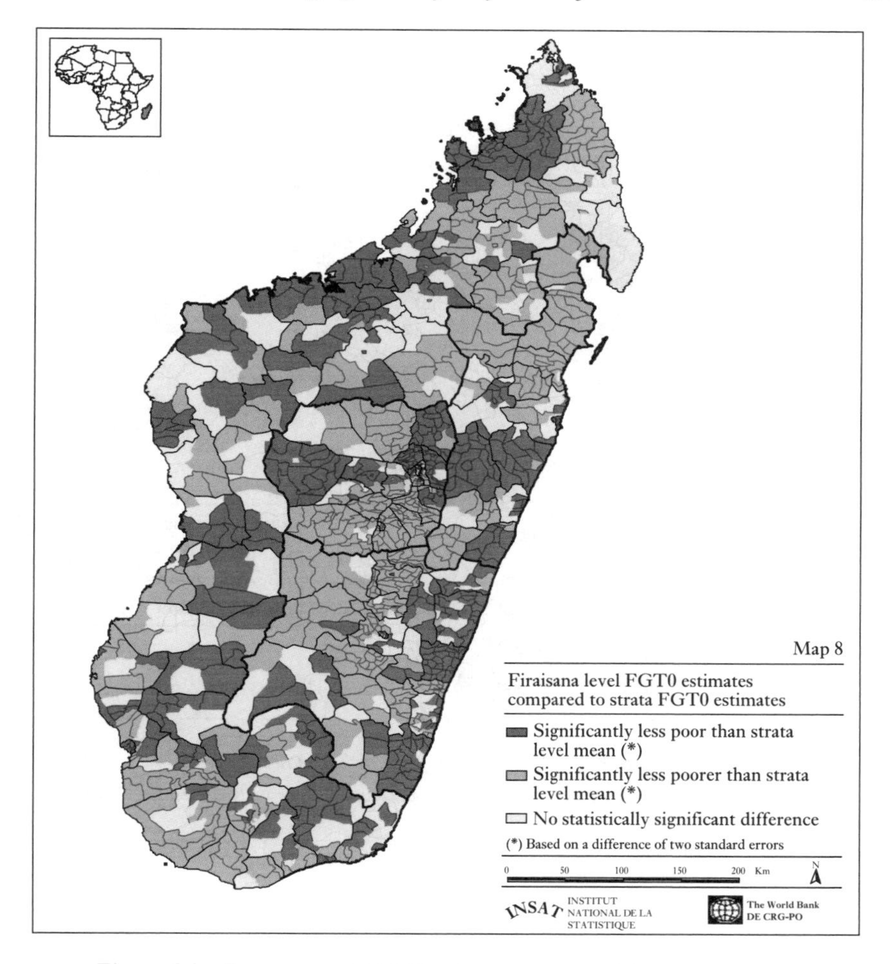

Figure 8.9. *Firaisanas with FGT0 different than the FGT0 in their faritany*

Source: Authors' calculations.

corresponding stratum-level estimates. The figures show that nearly four-fifths of all firaisanas in Madagascar have headcount rates that are significantly different than the headcount rate for the stratum to which they belong.

Similarly, Fig. 8.10 indicates that within South Africa's poorest province, Free State Province, poverty is not homogeneously distributed. A number of Magisterial Districts (MD) within this province record an incidence of poverty that is significantly lower than that of the province overall and others are considerably more poor. This observation follows directly from the fact that poverty measures such as the headcount, poverty gap (FGT1) and squared poverty gap (FGT2) all belong to a class of subgroup decomposable poverty measures (Foster, Greer, and Thorbecke 1984). The poverty

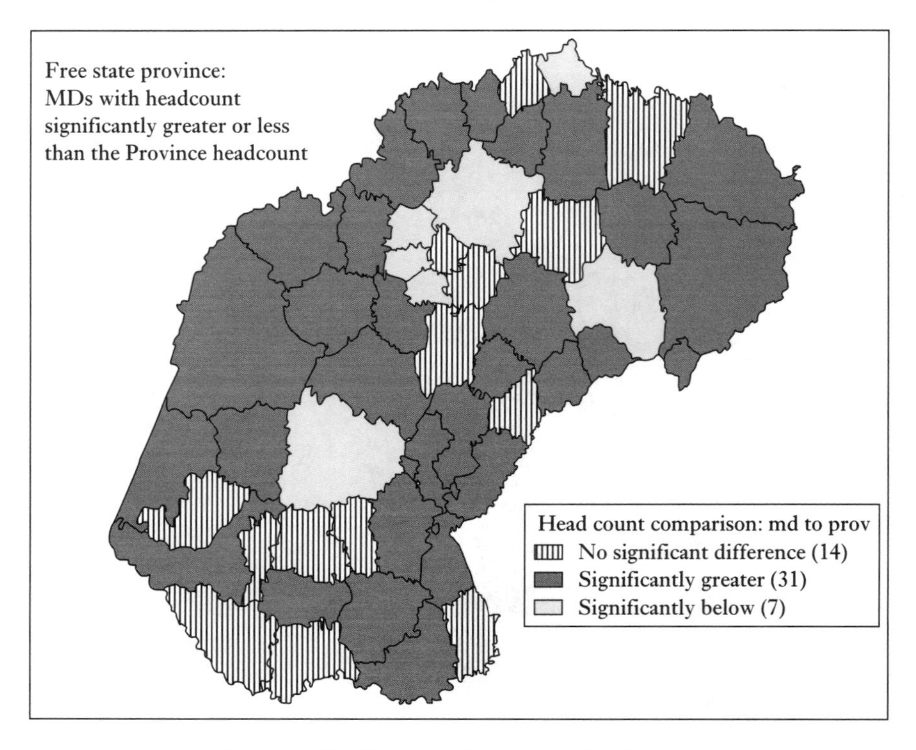

Figure 8.10. *Poverty within poverty: South Africa*

Note: Free State Province: MDs with headcount significantly greater or less than the Province headcount

Source: Authors' calculations.

rate for a given locality is equal to the population weighted average of poverty rates of sublocalities located within that area. Because the poverty rate for the given locality is an average, it is clear that some sublocalities will be more poor than the area in question and others will be less poor. From this it follows that the spatial heterogeneity of poverty will rise, the greater the level of disaggregation that one can confidently disaggregate to. In other words, when one is constrained in the degree of disaggregation, as is the case when one works with household survey data, one will be led to understate the true extent of spatial variability of poverty in a country.

Figures 8.11–8.13 illustrate the importance of this observation in Ecuador, Madagascar, and South Africa. Figure 8.11 ranks localities in rural Ecuador by incidence of poverty—in turn provinces, cantons and parroquias—and examines the spread of poverty of localities around the national level. This spread is lowest for provinces,

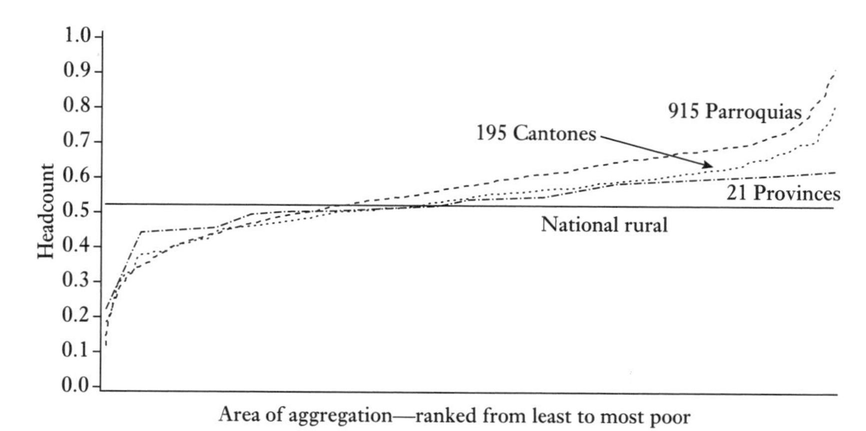

Figure 8.11. *Poverty by area of aggregation: Headcount, rural Ecuador*

Note: Comparing Parroquia versus Cantonal versus Provincial-level estimates in rural Ecuador. Areas of aggregation ranked from least poor to most poor.

Source: Authors' calculations.

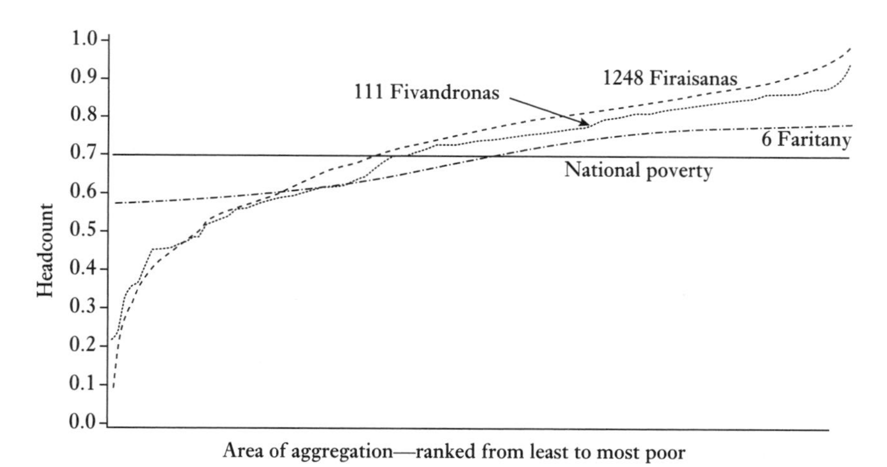

Figure 8.12. *Poverty by area of aggregation: Headcount, Madagascar*

Note: Comparing Firaisana versus Fivandrona versus Faritany-level estimates in Madagascar Areas of aggregation ranked from least poor to most poor.

Source: Authors' calculations.

then cantons and parroquias.[16] The same pattern obtains for Madagascar and South Africa.

[16] Note that we are working with *expected* poverty. The *true* spread of poverty, for any given level of disaggregation, is likely to be larger than that depicted.

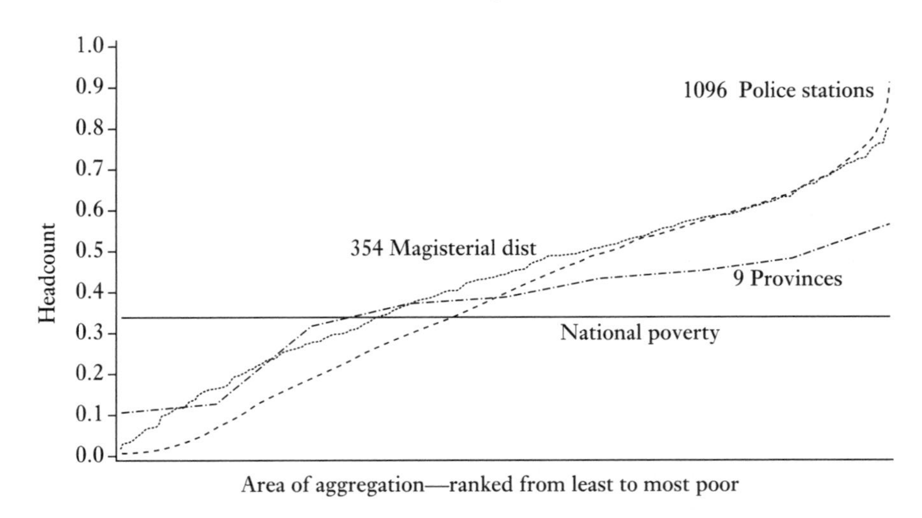

Figure 8.13. *Poverty by area of aggregation: Headcount, South Africa*

Note: Comparing police station versus Magisterial District versus Province-level estimates in South Africa. Areas of aggregation ranked from least poor to most poor.

Source: Authors' calculations.

8.6. CONCLUSIONS

This chapter has taken three developing countries, Ecuador, Madagascar, and South Africa, and has implemented in each, a methodology to produce disaggregated estimates of poverty. The countries are very unlike each other—with different geographies, stages of development, quality and types of data, and so on. The methodology works well in all three settings and produces valuable information about the spatial distribution of poverty within those countries—information that was previously not available.

The methodology is based on a statistical procedure to combine household-survey data with population census data, by imputing into the latter a measure of economic welfare (consumption expenditure in our examples) from the former. Like the usual sample-based estimates, the poverty rates produced are also *estimates* and subject to statistical error. The chapter has demonstrated that the poverty estimates produced from census data match well the estimates calculated directly from the country's surveys (at levels of disaggregation that the survey can bear). The precision of the poverty estimates produced with this methodology depends on the degree of disaggregation. In all three countries considered here our poverty estimators allow one to work at a level of disaggregation far below that allowed by surveys.

We have illustrated how the poverty estimates produced with this method can be represented in maps, thereby conveying an enormous amount of information about the spread and relative magnitude of poverty across localities, as well as the precision of estimates, in a way which is quickly and intuitively absorbed also by non-technical audiences. Such detailed geographical profiles of poverty can inform a wide variety of debates and deliberations, amongst policy-makers as well as civil society.

We have finally noted that perceptions as to the importance of geographical dimensions of poverty are themselves dependent on the degree of spatial disaggregation of available estimates of poverty. The smaller the localities into which a country can be broken down, the more likely it is, that one will conclude that geography matters.

REFERENCES

Aghion, P. and Bolton, P. (1997). 'A Theory of Trickle Down Growth and Development'. *Review of Economic Studies*, 64(2), 151–72.

Alderman, H., Babita, M., Demombynes, G., Makhatha, N., and Özler, B. (2002). 'How Low Can You Go? Combining Census and Survey Data for Mapping Poverty in South Africa'. *Journal of African Economies*, 11(2), 169–200.

Alesina, A. and Rodrik, D. (1994). 'Distributive Politics and Economic Growth'. *Quarterly Journal of Economics*, 109, 465–90.

Banerjee, A. and Newman, A. (1993). 'Occupational Choice and the Process of Development'. *Journal of Political Economy*, 101(1), 274–98.

Deaton, A. (1997). *The Analysis of Household Surveys: A Microeconometric Approach to Development Policy*. The Johns Hopkins University Press for the World Bank, Washington.

—— (1999). 'Inequalities in Income and in Health'. *NBER Working Papers* 7141.

Demombynes, G. and Özler, B. (2001). 'Inequality and Crime in South Africa?' DECRG-World Bank, Washington, Mimeo.

Elbers, C., Lanjouw, J. O., and Lanjouw, P. (2002). 'Micro-Level Estimation of Welfare'. *World Bank Policy Research Working Papers* 2911.

Foster, J., Greer, J., and Thorbecke, E. (1984). 'A Class of Decomposable Poverty Measures'. *Econometrica*, 52(3), 761–66.

Galor, O. and Zeira, J. (1993). 'Income Distribution and Macroeconomics'. *Review of Economic Studies*, 60, 35–52.

Hentschel, J. and Lanjouw, P. (1996). 'Constructing an Indicator of Consumption for the Analysis of Poverty: Principles and Illustrations with Reference to Ecuador'. *LSMS Working Papers* 124. DECRG-World Bank, Washington.

——, Lanjouw, J. O., Lanjouw, P., and Poggi, J. (2000). 'Combining Census and Survey Data to Trace the Spatial Dimensions of Poverty: A Case Study of Ecuador'. *World Bank Economic Review*, 14(1), 147–65.

Mistiaen, J. A., Özler, B., Razafimanantena, T., and Razafindravonona, J. (2002). 'Putting Welfare on the Map in Madagascar'. DECRG-World Bank, Washington, Mimeo.

Murphy, K. M., Schleifer, A., and Vishny, R. (1989). 'Income Distribution, Market Size and Industrialization'. *Quarterly Journal of Economics*, 104, 537–64.

Persson, T. and Tabellini, G. (1994). 'Is Inequality Harmful for Growth'. *American Economic Review*, 84, 600–21.

World Bank (1996). 'Ecuador Poverty Report'. *World Bank Country Study*. Ecuador Country Department. The World Bank, Washington.

9

Twin Peaks: Distribution Dynamics of Economic Growth across Indian States

SANGHAMITRA BANDYOPADHYAY

9.1. INTRODUCTION

There are few questions more compelling to economists than to explain why some countries grow faster than others. Understanding different patterns of cross-county or cross-regional growth is important—persistent disparities in income across countries and across regions lead to wide disparities in welfare and is often a source of social and political tension, particularly so within national boundaries. The existence of regional inequalities of incomes across Indian states has been well documented. It is well known that western states are industrially advanced, while the northwest is agriculturally prosperous. There are pockets of relative success in agriculture and industry in the south and the north, while the northeastern states are yet to excel in either.

Recording that regional inequalities exist is just the starting point; what is of concern is that they continue to persist even after five decades of concerted state-led planning. Such differential development, given widespread interstate socioethnic and political differences, risks unleashing highly destructive centrifugal political forces. It is, therefore, vitally important that policies for containing and counteracting regional disparities are implemented in the early rapid phase of development.

This study documents the dynamics of growth and convergence of real per capita incomes across Indian states over the period 1965–97, and attempts to find some factors underpinning such income dynamics. There are a number of specific goals. First, we are interested in the dynamics of equality of incomes across Indian states. In other words, is there any tendency towards equality in the cross section income distribution across the Indian states? If not, what distribution pattern do they exhibit?

Second, if cohesive tendencies are not obtained, we would like to characterize the possibilities for inter-regional mobility: are there any signs of poorer regions overtaking

I would like to thank Henry Overman, Danny Quah, and Diana Weinhold for guidance, and participants at various seminars, the WIDER Growth and Development conference, Helsinki 2001 and an anonymous referee for helpful suggestions. Funding from the Economic and Social Research Council, UK, and London School of Economics is gratefully acknowledged.

the rich in the future? Are there any signs of initially rich regions falling behind? For example, we would like to know whether a region initially within the poorest 10 per cent of the country can catch up with the rest, or converge to within 20 per cent of the median. These facts are important for policy purposes. Characterizing the presence of other distribution patterns, for example, those of convergence clubs or stratification, will enable the researcher to identify the economic forces governing their formation and their persistence.

Finally, the causes of persistent unequal growth performances will be investigated. To examine for conditional convergence properties a number of explanatory factors will be considered. In particular, attention will be given to the role of the disparate distribution of infrastructure across the states, and to the role of macroeconomic variables in explaining the divergent growth performances.

This exercise follows from the new wave of empirical growth analyses, following the studies of Barro and Sala-i-Martin (1992), Desdoigts (1994), Quah (1996*a*, *b*), and, for the Indian case, Bajpai and Sachs (1996) and Nagaraj, Varoudakis, and Véganzonès (1998), to name a few. These empirical studies of income dynamics have made powerful and controversial claims, which have instigated yet further empirical techniques of analysing cross-country income dynamics. The ensuing stylized facts of growth dynamics have telling implications for widely accepted theoretical claims. Also, the questions which are addressed in the new empirical growth literature differ from those in earlier empirical works of Kaldor's stylized facts (1963), or of Solow (1957) in a production function accounting exercise. The primary focus is to understand the cross-country patterns of income, rather than to explain only within-country dynamics. The new empirical literature also uses auxiliary explanatory factors to explain the stylized facts, as opposed to analyzing the production function residual, as was done earlier.

Here, we intend to examine interstate income inequalities in terms of the behaviour of the entire cross-sectional distribution. When the cross-sectional distribution shows signs of collapsing to a point mass, one can conclude that there are tendencies towards convergence. If, on the other hand, there is movement towards limits which have other properties—normality or twin peakedness, or a continual spreading apart—these too will be revealed. In essence, this approach endeavours to describe a law of motion of the cross-sectional income distribution over the period of study. Appropriately named, the distribution dynamics approach exposes instances of economies overtaking, or falling behind, and reveals the existence of intradistributional mobility, or persistence. Finally, the model allows the researcher to study not just the likelihood, but also the potential causes, of poorer economies becoming richer than those currently rich, and that of the rich regressing to become relatively poor.

The distribution dynamics approach to studying convergence (Bianchi 1995; Desdoigts 1994; Jones 1997; Lamo 1996; Quah 1996*a*, *b*) improves on the approaches employed earlier. Standard (i.e. beta convergence) regression analysis only considers average or representative behaviour, and says nothing about what happens to the entire distribution (Barro and Sala-i-Martin 1992; Bajpai and Sachs 1996; Cashin and Sahay 1996; Nagaraj, Varoudakis, and Véganzonès 1998 for the Indian case, among many others). Nor are beta and sigma convergence analyses able to inform the researcher of any prospects of inter-regional mobility. They are unable to uncover the long-run aspects of the evolving distributional pattern. Such is also the case with time series applications to regional analyses (Carlino and Mills 1993).

The methodology employed in this study goes beyond point estimates of dispersion and unit root analyses to highlight two vital aspects of how a distribution evolves over time—intradistributional mobility and the long-run prospects of the distribution (ergodicity). It encompasses both time series and cross-sectional properties of the data simultaneously and presents itself as an ideal approach for large data sets. Moreover, this method can be extended to identify factors governing the formation of these convergence clubs.

This study uncovers the relevant stylized facts of the Indian interstate income distribution over the period 1965–97 and different subperiods. The main finding is that strong polarizing tendencies are found to exist, resulting in the formation of two income 'convergence clubs'—one at 50 per cent of the national average, another at 125 per cent of the national average. Examining the subperiods reveals that while cohesive tendencies were observed in the late 1960s, these were considerably weakened over the following decades with increasingly polarizing tendencies. Further analysis shows that the disparate distribution of infrastructure strongly explains the observed polarization, particularly for the lower income club. Indicators of macroeconomic stability provide some explanation for the lack of convergence. Of the different macroeconomic indicators observed, capital expenditure and fiscal deficits explain part of the polarization. This contrasts with the results obtained using standard techniques (i.e. panel regressions) where the role of both of the above in explaining the lack of convergence are found to be inconclusive.[1]

The rest of the study is organized as follows. Section 2 introduces the distribution dynamics approach. Section 3 presents new stylized facts of the observed polarization. Section 4 briefly discusses the existing empirical literature on the role of various macroeconomic indicators in explaining disparate cross-country economic growth. Section 5 presents results of the various conditioning schemes and techniques to explain the observed stylized facts. Section 6 concludes.

9.2. THE DISTRIBUTION DYNAMICS APPROACH

The approach of distribution dynamics originates from recent empirical research on patterns of cross-country growth. The focus of research in the new empirical growth literature no longer concerns the behaviour of per capita income or per worker output of a single representative economy but rather asks questions like, why do some countries grow faster than others?

The traditional approach to convergence examines whether an economy will converge to its own steady state (income). Here, however, we are interested in a more useful notion of convergence—that of catch-up—which indicates whether the poorest

[1] See Bandyopadhyay (2000*b*) for standard regression results.

economies will stagnate, remaining permanently distant from the richest ones, or whether they will catch-up with the rest.

If the cross section of economies do not converge, divergence can take many forms. While intradistributional inequality may be increasing, economies may converge within individual convergence clubs, resulting in patterns of polarization or even stratification. Extant approaches used to study convergence remain silent on such patterns of distribution dynamics. Convergence as a notion of 'catch-up' is, thus, rendered defunct when studied using standard regression techniques as they capture only representative behaviour and regard convergence as the tendency of the representative economy to converge to its own steady-state income. It is, therefore, uninformative, in general, about the dynamics of the distribution of income across countries (Friedman 1992; Leung and Quah 1996). Similarly, while time series analyses of univariate dynamics do not utilize the cross-sectional information, it is also the case that the evolution of income dispersion (for instance, in terms of the standard deviation), does not tell us anything about the underlying cross-sectional growth dynamics.

What existing standard techniques fail to inform the researcher about is the *intra-distributional dynamics* of the income distribution and hence, of a distribution pattern other than convergence. These goals have necessitated going beyond the extant technical tools used to study convergence.

The distribution dynamics approach[2] tracks the evolution of the entire income distribution over time. Markov chains are used to approximate and estimate the laws of motion of the evolving distribution. The intradistribution dynamics information is encoded in a transition probability matrix, and the ergodic (or long-run) distribution associated with this matrix describes the long-term behaviour of the income distribution. Such an approach has revealed empirical regularities such as convergence clubs, polarization, or stratification—of cross-economy interaction that endogenously generates groups of economies; of countries catching up with one another, but only within subgroups (Bernard and Durlauf 1996; Bianchi 1995; Quah 1997).

9.2.1. *Random Fields and the Random Element*

The distribution dynamics approach is based on treating a single income distribution as a *random element* in a field of income distributions. Figure 9.1 presents the entire distribution of state incomes (relative per capita) in India for the period 1965–88. Such structures where both time series and cross-sectional dimensions are large and of equal magnitude are called *random fields* in probability theory. At each point in time, the income distribution is a *random element* in the space of distributions. This approach involves estimating the density function of the income distribution at each point in time and then observing how it evolves over time. These dynamics account for the change in the shape of the distribution and for intradistribution dynamics, which are

[2] See Quah (1996*a*, *b*). Similar studies which have focused on the behaviour of the entire distribution include Bianchi (1997), where he uses the bootstrap test to detect multimodality, and Bernard and Durlauf (1996), where they identify 'multiple regimes' across economies.

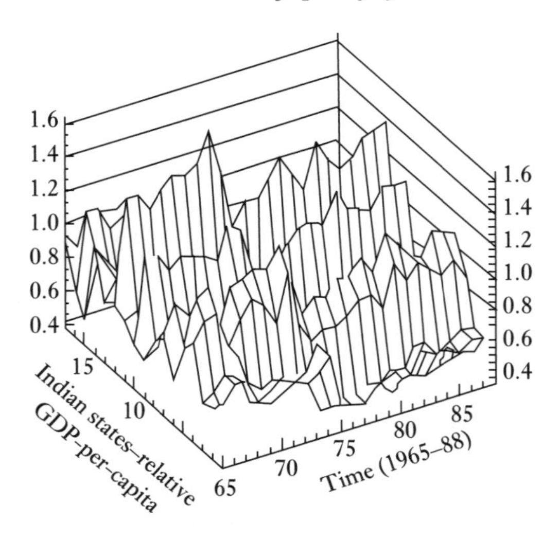

Figure 9.1. *Relative GDP per capita of Indian states, 1965–88*

notable characteristics of convergence. In our analysis, we shall estimate a density function of the given data non-parametrically as it does not impose a fixed structure on the distribution, allowing us to detect structures different from parametric forms. To study the distribution dynamics of the Indian income distribution, we shall be using transition probability matrices and stochastic kernels to estimate the density function and to observe its evolution.

9.2.2. *Models of Intradistribution Churning*

The two main models which highlight the distribution dynamics of an income distribution are stochastic kernels and transition probability matrices.[3] The transition probability matrix is the discrete model, while the stochastic kernel is its continuous version.[4] Both stochastic kernels and transition matrices provide an estimate of the intradistribution mobility taking place. In each case, it is assumed that an economy (in our case, a state) over a given time period (say, 1 year or 5 years) either remains in the same position, or changes its position in the income distribution. Such a change in position of an economy in the income distribution is called a transition. Our task is to observe how many such transitions take place in the given time period.

[3] See Bandyopadhyay (2000*a*) and Quah (1996*b*) for the use of other models to highlight the distribution dynamics. Transition probability matrices and stochastic kernels are, however, the main tools used to describe the distribution dynamics; see Quah (1996*a*, *b*).

[4] See Quah (1996*b*) for the underlying formal structure of these models as a law of motion of the cross section distribution of income.

Table 9.1. *Interstate relative (per capita) income dynamics, 1965–97, first order transition matrix, time stationary*

Number	Upper end point				
	0.640	0.761	0.852	1.019	1.393
5	0.40	0.00	0.40	0.00	0.20
5	0.00	0.40	0.20	0.20	0.20
2	0.00	0.00	0.50	0.00	0.50
4	0.00	0.00	0.25	0.25	0.50
1	0.00	0.00	0.00	1.00	0.00
Ergodic	0.00	0.00	0.22	0.44	0.33

Source: See text.

First, what needs to be identified is the position of the economy in the income distribution in the starting period. This is done by dividing the income distribution into 'income classes' comprising a range of income intervals, for example, between a fifth and a half of the weighted average of the country. Then we observe how many of the economies which are in an income class say, (0.2, 0.5) in the initial period land up in that same class, or elsewhere, in the next time period. If they do end up in another income class there is said to be mobility. If they end up in the same class, there is persistence.

In our exercise for India, we have measured these transitions and the results are tabulated in Tables 9.1 and 9.2 as *transition probability matrices*. The figure reported in row i and column j indicates the percentages of Indian states in class i initially that are found in class j at the later date. So all the row probabilities add up to 1. A diagonal of the transition matrix with high values indicates high probabilities of persistence—a high likelihood of remaining in a particular class. Conversely, smaller elements indicate greater intradistribution mobility.

The transition probability matrix also allows us to take a long-run view of the evolution of the income distribution. This is tabulated in the row labelled the 'ergodic distribution'. One drawback with this approach is the arbitrariness in the selection of income classes—different choices of intervals may lead to different results. The *stochastic kernel* improves on the transition probability matrix by replacing the discrete income classes by a continuum of classes. We now have an infinite number of rows and columns replacing the transition probability matrix.

The stochastic kernel is interpreted as follows. Any slice running parallel to the horizontal axis (i.e. $t + k$ axis) describes a probability density function describing the transitions from one part of the income distribution to another over k periods. The location of the probability mass provides information about the distribution dynamics and, thus, about any tendencies towards convergence. Concentration of the probability mass along the upward sloping diagonal indicates persistence in the states' relative position, and therefore low mobility. The opposite pattern, that is, concentration along

Table 9.2. *Interstate relative (per capita) income dynamics, 1965–70, 1971–80, and 1981–89 first order transition matrix, time stationary*

Number	Upper end point				
(a) 1965–70	0.640	0.761	0.852	1.019	1.393
5	0.40	0.00	0.40	0.00	0.20
5	0.00	0.40	0.20	0.20	0.20
2	0.00	0.00	0.50	0.00	0.50
4	0.00	0.00	0.25	0.25	0.50
1	0.00	0.00	0.00	1.00	0.00
Ergodic	0.00	0.00	0.22	0.44	0.33
(b) 1971–80	0.680	0.730	0.795	1.010	1.489
5	0.40	0.60	0.00	0.00	0.00
1	0.00	1.00	0.00	0.00	0.00
3	0.00	0.67	0.33	0.00	0.00
4	0.00	0.00	0.75	0.25	0.00
4	0.00	0.00	0.00	0.50	0.50
Ergodic	0.00	1.00	0.00	0.00	0.00
(c) 1981–1989	0.533	0.628	0.795	1.010	1.489
6	0.17	0.50	0.33	0.00	0.00
4	0.00	0.00	0.25	0.75	0.00
3	0.00	0.67	0.33	0.67	0.00
2	0.00	0.00	0.00	0.00	1.00
2	0.00	0.00	0.00	0.00	1.00
Ergodic	0.00	1.00	0.00	0.00	0.00

Source: See text.

the negative sloping diagonal, would imply overtaking of the states in their rankings. Concentration of the probability mass parallel to the $t + k$ axis indicates that the probability of being in any state at period $t + k$ is independent of their position in period t; that is, evidence for low persistence. Finally, convergence is indicated when the probability mass runs parallel to the t axis.

9.3. WHAT HAS BEEN HAPPENING TO THE INTERSTATE INCOME DISTRIBUTION IN INDIA?

We now look at the distribution dynamics of incomes across Indian states from 1965 to 1997. Figures 9.2(a)–(d) represent the stochastic kernels for relative per capita income of 1-year transitions for four subperiods 1965–70, 1971–80, 1981–89, and 1990–97.

Observation of the stochastic kernels and the contour plots reveals that the later years provide increasing evidence of persistence and low probabilities of changing positions. Over the periods 1965–70, 1971–80, 1981–89, 1990–97 we observe in Figs 9.2(a)–(d)

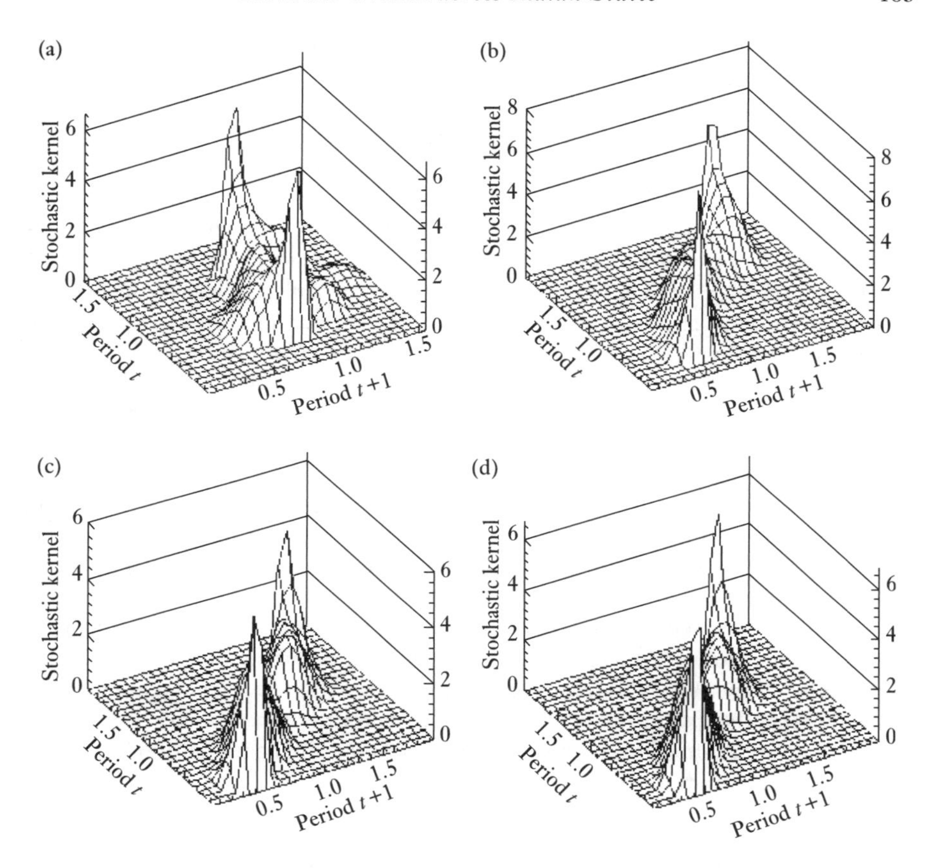

Figure 9.2. *Relative income dynamics across Indian states, 1-year horizon, (a) 1965–70, (b) 1971–80, (c) 1981–89, and (d) 1990–97*

the probability mass lengthening and shifting totally in line with the positive diagonal, the two peaks still at the two ends of the mass. The cluster of states at the two peaks consist of some low-income states at around 50 per cent of the all India average and another group at 125 per cent of the average. Thus, though an overall view of the entire sample period 1965–98 shows some signs of cohesion, the sub-sample periods, particularly during the later years, have shown cohesive forces substantially dissipating in influence. The results show the rich states forging ahead, the poor states making little progress, and a dispersing middle income group.

The long-run view of whether the states will converge over the long run is addressed by estimating the transition probability matrices. The results are tabulated in Tables 9.1 and 9.2(a)–(c). Interpretation of the tables is as follows. The defined classes for each table are chosen such that each distribution is uniform at the beginning year of the sample period. The first column of the table indicates the number of transitions originating in each class. The subsequent columns present the calculated probabilities of transition from one specified class to another. Like the stochastic kernel, a 'heavy' main diagonal indicates persistence.

Table 9.1 reports results for 1965–97 and they are quite similar to those obtained for the stochastic kernel—the values in the main diagonal are around 0.5 per cent, which indicates that the probability that a state remains in its own income class is around 50 per cent. The off-diagonal values reflect mobility, on the whole low, although evident and obvious for groups with above average incomes. Low-income states in the initial period are revealed to have forged ahead, particularly those in the first two income classes. We also have an estimator of the long-run tendencies—the ergodic distribution—shown in the last row of Table 9.1. This gives the long-run tendency of a state to end up in a given income range. The results suggest that over the long run, the probability that a state ends up in the fourth class is the highest, a little over 40 per cent. What is encouraging is that the two lowest income groups are non-existent in the ergodic distribution.

Tables 9.2(a)–(c) give us estimates of the transition matrix for the subperiods. The second period again reveals tendencies of both persistence and mobility. Persistence is high in the clusters of the high-income group states and low-income group states. However, signs of any intradistributional mobility are scant—a state belonging to the first two income classes or the last two income classes has zero probability of moving to any other class. However, there is some evidence of inter-club movement, particularly in the high-income club. This trend continues in the next two periods. It is important to remember that these estimates are based on time stationary transition matrices (i.e. the probabilities are assumed to remain the same over time), and hence may not be reliable over long time periods due to structural economic changes.

9.4. WHAT EXPLAINS THE POLARIZATION?

Why would one expect to observe such income dynamics? In the empirical growth literature, numerous sources study the links between macroeconomic stability and cross-regional economic growth. It is widely accepted that a stable macroeconomic environment is required (though is not sufficient) for sustainable economic growth. That taxation, public investment, inflation, and other aspects of fiscal policy can determine an economy's growth trajectory has been articulated in the growth literature for the last three decades. Recent cross-country studies also provide evidence that the direction of causation runs from good macroeconomic policy to growth (Fisher 1993, 1991; Easterly and Rebelo 1993; Barro 1995).

The relationship between short-run macroeconomic management and long-run growth, however, remains one of the most controversial areas in the cross-country literature. A number of regression studies show significant correlations with the expected signs, though it has been difficult to isolate any particular policy variable and to demonstrate a robust correlation with growth, irrespective of endogeneity concerns and other variables. While Levine and Renelt (1992) show that high-growth countries tend to have lower inflation, smaller governments, and lower black market premia, their results highlight the fact that the relationship between growth and other macroeconomic indicators (with the exception of the investment ratio) is fragile and not robust to different control variables being employed in the regressions. Fisher's (1991) extension of the basic Levine and Renelt regression shows that growth is significantly negatively associated with inflation and positively related to budget surplus as a ratio of GDP. Easterly and Rebelo (1993) also present convincing evidence of fiscal deficits being negatively related to growth.

The relationship between inflation and growth has been difficult to isolate. Levine and Zervos (1993) show that inflation is significant, though this finding is not robust and applies only to high-inflation countries. Their composite indicator of macroeconomic performance—a function of inflation and fiscal deficit—is shown to be positively related with growth performance (lower inflation, lower fiscal deficit). Bruno and Easterly (1998) also take a short-run approach and find that high inflation crises are associated with output losses, but that output returns to the same long-run growth path once inflation has been reduced. This may be the reason for the weak inflation and growth relationship.

Another common explanation for disparate development across regions is differing levels of infrastructure development. This is particularly pertinent for developing countries like India where poor states, being unable to raise sufficient funds themselves, are often heavily dependent on transfers from the centre. Infrastructure development of poorer states is, thus, circumscribed by the nature of the centre–state relationship, and this is often distorted due to conflicting party politics between the centre and the state. Recent political economy literature on fiscal federalism highlights the existence of such 'favouritism' of the central governments towards states which are ruled by the same political party. Though the traditional literature assumes that the central government is a benevolent planner, interested in maximizing social welfare, policy-makers, typically politicians, are increasingly viewed as opportunists who will implement policies that favour their re-election. Empirical studies of Case (2001) and Johanssen (1999), and theoretical studies by Dixit and Londregan (1996, 1998) and Lindbeck and Weibull (1987), describe how political parties design their policy platforms in order to maximize their chances of re-election. Dasgupta, Dhillon, and Dutta (2001) study on India using state-level Indian data detects the influence of the same political parties at the state-level government and the centre working in favour of allotting greater central government grants to the state.

We will empirically investigate the role of the distribution of infrastructure and a number of macroeconomic indicators in explaining the observed polarization in the following section. But let us first extend the distribution dynamics approach for our conditioning exercise.

9.4.1. *The Conditioning Methodology Under Distribution Dynamics*

The non-parametric tools used are those proposed by Quah (1996*a*). While the auxiliary factors in standard regression models explain average behaviour, the distribution dynamics method explains the evolution of the entire distribution, hence exposing and explaining behaviour at different parts of the distribution. In other words, while standard methods compare $E(Y)$ and $E(Y|X)$, thus determining whether X explains Y, this approach maps the entire distribution of Y to $Y|X$. If there is no change in the distributions, conditioned and unconditioned, we then conclude that the auxiliary factor does not explain the polarization (or any other observed distribution pattern). However, if it does explain the polarization, leading to conditional convergence, all economies in the conditioned distribution will have the same income—in our case, the national average income. This will be revealed in the two models described in the following section.

9.4.2. *How to Read the Stochastic Kernels and Transition Probability Matrices?*

The mappings obtained earlier to capture the distribution dynamics characterize transitions over time. It can further be shown (see Quah 1996*b*) that just as stochastic kernels (and transition matrices) provide information about how distributions evolve over time, they can also describe how a set of conditioning factors alter the mapping between any two distributions. Hence, to understand if a hypothesized set of factors explains a given distribution we can simply ask if the stochastic kernel transforming the unconditional one to the conditional one removes those same features.

One extreme situation is where the mapping from the unconditional to the conditional distribution has the probability mass running parallel to the original axis at value 1. This would indicate that all states, irrespective of their income, have their income conditioned by the auxiliary factor close to 1. Since all incomes here are relative to the national average, this would mean that income, once conditioned, leads to 'conditional convergence'—where all incomes converge to the national average. The conditioning factor would, therefore, be deemed as a factor explaining the observed polarization. This, of course, is the desired outcome.

Another extreme is where the stochastic kernel mapping the unconditional income distribution to that conditioned has its probability mass running along the diagonal. Unlike the previous case, this now implies the opposite possibility: when conditioned by the auxiliary factor, the income of each state, irrespective of its position, remains unchanged. The conditioning factor is then seen as one which does not explain the observed polarization.

While the stochastic kernels describe continuous movements, transition matrices are the discrete version of such kernels and map the unconditioned to the conditioned distribution. Here again, each element indicates intradistribution mobility between the respective income classes. Like the stochastic kernel, a heavy diagonal indicates persistence, while higher probabilities of movement into the national average income class (i.e. 1) indicates conditional convergence. The auxiliary factor used to derive the conditioned distribution will hence be a factor which explains the observed polarization.

9.5. THE RESULTS

9.5.1. *Conditioning on Infrastructure*

The precise linkages between infrastructure and economic growth and development are still open to debate. But it is widely agreed that the adequacy of infrastructure helps determine one country's success and another's failure—in diversifying production, expanding trade, coping with population growth, reducing poverty, or improving environmental conditions. Good infrastructure raises productivity and lowers costs, but it has to expand fast enough to accommodate growth,[5] and it must adapt to support the changing patterns of demand.

How far does the distribution of infrastructure explain disparate economic growth performance in the Indian case? In this section we will show that the changing pattern of the distribution of infrastructure serves to explain much of the evolution of disparities in economic performance across Indian states.

Construction of an index of general infrastructure

The infrastructure indicators[6] (panel data) which we use for the analysis are the following:

per capita electricity consumption (in kilowatt hours)
per capita industrial consumption of electricity
percentage of villages on electricity grid
percentage of gross cropped area irrigated
road length (in km per 1000 sq. km)
number of motor vehicles per 1000 population
rail track length (in km per 1000 sq. km)
literacy rates (in percentage of the age group)
primary school enrolment (age 6–11, in percentage of the age group)
secondary school enrolment (age 11–17, in percentage of the age group)
infant mortality (in percentage)
number of bank offices per 1000 population
bank deposits as a percentage of the SDP
bank credit as a percentage of the SDP

[5] Infrastructure capacity grows step for step with economic output—a 1 per cent increase in the stock of infrastructure is associated with a 1 per cent increase in GDP across all countries in the world (World Bank 1994).

[6] The infrastructure indicators' data set has been provided by the India team, Development Centre, OECD, Paris. The author thanks Drs A. Varoudakis and M. Véganzonès for kindly providing the data set.

Table 9.3. *Results of factor analysis*

Components	Eigenvalue	Cumulative R^2	
f_1	12.41	0.83	
f_2	1.22	0.91	
f_3	1.00	0.97	
Factor loadings	f_1	f_2	f_3
Total power consumption	0.97	−0.16	0.10
Power consumption in industrial sector	0.95	−0.12	0.04
Percentage of villages electrified	0.99	0.04	−0.08
Percentage of net area operated with irrigation	0.95	−0.20	0.18
Length of road network per 1000 sq km	0.97	−0.12	0.10
Number of motor vehicles per 1000 inhabitants	0.89	0.07	−0.37
Length of rail network per 1000 sq km	0.61	−0.47	0.60
Literacy rate of adult population	0.98	−0.04	−0.15
Primary school enrolment rate	0.97	0.04	−0.08
Secondary school enrolment rate	0.98	−0.13	−0.02
Infant mortality rate	−0.96	0.05	0.22
Bank offices per 1000 people	0.91	0.24	−0.30
Bank deposits as a percentage of SDP	0.75	0.57	0.28
Bank credit as a percentage of SDP	0.58	0.68	0.40

Source: See text.

The states covered by the analysis are listed[7] and the period of study is 1977–93. There are no missing observations.

To obtain a general idea of the overall provision of infrastructure across the states, and to observe the role of economic and social infrastructure as a whole in explaining the evolution of the income distribution, we construct a single index accounting for the each of the state's infrastructure base. One is also faced with the problem of multi-collinearity because of a large number of infrastructure variables, which may result in inconsistent estimates. To obtain the general index of infrastructure we use factor analysis, a technique which represents the indicators as linear combinations of a small number of latent variables.[8]

The results of the factor analysis are tabulated in Table 9.3. We accept the first factor (f_1, which we will call INFRA) to be the general index of infrastructure, which

[7] States used in the study: Andhra Pradesh, Assam, Bihar, Delhi, Gujarat, Haryana, Jammu and Kashmir, Karnataka, Kerala, Madhya Pradesh, Maharashtra, Orissa, Punjab, Rajasthan, Tamil Nadu, Uttar Pradesh, West Bengal. Other states were excluded from the study due to the incomplete data available over the given period.

[8] This method was first used in development economics by Adelman and Morris (1967) in an ambitious project to study the interaction of economic and non-economic forces in the course of development, with data on 41 social, economic, and political indicators for 74 countries. For further discussion, see Adelman and Morris (1967), and for more on factor analysis, see Everitt (1984).

takes an eigenvalue of over 12. This means that this factor accounts for twelve (out of seventeen) variables of infrastructure. Our results suggest that the indicator INFRA accounts for over 87 per cent of the variation in the 17 infrastructure variables. We will be using this indicator for our analyses.

Conditioning on infrastructure

Does the provision of infrastructure have a role to play in explaining the polarization of income across the states? Our results suggest yes. Figure 9.3(a)(i) plots the stochastic kernel mapping each state's income (relative to the national average) to that relative to the average income of states with the same level of infrastructure.[9] The stochastic kernel is constructed using six groups of states which have the same level of infrastructure, based on the general index of infrastructure constructed earlier. The mapping obtained is encouraging, particularly so for the higher income and lower income group states. For the middle income states, however, one finds that the mass lies close to the diagonal, implying that one does not observe a 'group effect'. Level of infrastructure, therefore, does not appear to explain cross-section disparity in middle-income states.

States with incomes above 1.2 times the national average, and those below the national average, stand out from the rest. This is clearly revealed in the contour in Fig. 9.3(a)(ii) as here we observe a vertical spread of the probability mass centred around 1. This suggests that these states experience similar outcomes. The spike at around 0.5 of the national average corresponds to the states of Bihar, Orissa, Rajasthan and Uttar Pradesh, Madhya Pradesh, and Rajasthan, while the spike at around 1.2 of the national average corresponds to the higher income states of Punjab, Haryana, Gujarat, and Maharashtra. Our conclusion is that infrastructure explains club formation at low-income levels but does little to explain the higher income club. Thus, infrastructure has differing roles in explaining different group dynamics. It is also worth noting that this result would go unnoticed in standard methods of investigating conditional convergence using regression analyses.[10]

9.5.2. *Conditioning with Indicators of Macroeconomic Stability*

Obtaining the conditional distribution

The conditioning scheme used to derive our conditioned distribution will be slightly different to that used earlier. Unlike many standard convergence regressions, we do not assume here that the time varying auxiliary variables are exogenous. We confirm endogeneity of the variables by Granger causality tests. Thus, we cannot include

[9] Calculating *same level of infrastructure relative income* entailed calculating each state's income relative to the group average income to which they belong for each year.

[10] See Bandyopadhyay (2000*b*) for parametric tests confirming conditional convergence with infrastructure.

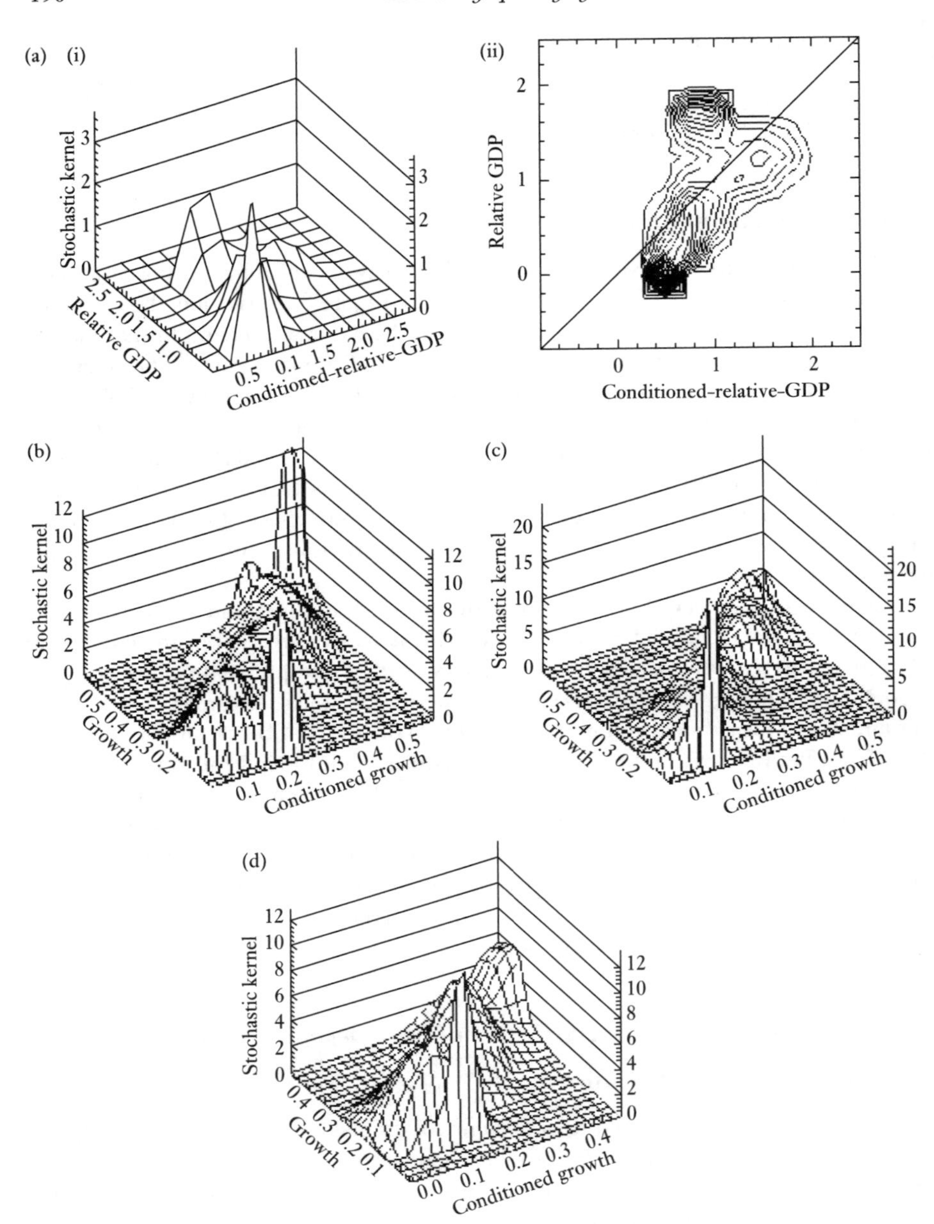

Figure 9.3. *Relative per capita incomes across Indian states, (a) infrastructure, (b) capital expenditure, (c) education, and (d) fiscal deficit conditionings*

Table 9.4. *Conditioning regressions (two-sided projections) of growth rate on capital expenditure*

Capital expenditure	Coefficients in two-sided projections		
Lead 4			0.00 (0.003)
3		0.010 (0.008)	0.012 (0.009)
2	0.013 (0.008)	−0.018 (0.01)	−0.019 (0.016)
1	0.020 (0.01)	0.021 (0.012)	0.024 (0.019)
Lag 1	−0.022 (0.016)	−0.024 (0.018)	−0.029 (0.019)
2	−0.021 (0.014)	−0.02 (0.016)	−0.022 (0.015)
3	−0.01 (0.010)	−0.01 (0.011)	−0.01 (0.011)
4			−0.00 (0.007)
Sum of coefficients	−0.01	−0.04	−0.014
R^2	0.10	0.10	0.11

Notes: Numbers in parentheses are OLS and White heteroskedasticity consistent standard errors.

Source: See text.

capital expenditure as an exogenous variable in our growth equations, but instead need to estimate the appropriate conditional distribution free from the feedback effects.

The conditioned distribution is obtained by regressing growth rates on a two-sided distributed lag of the time varying conditioning variables and then extracting the fitted residuals for subsequent analysis. This will result in a relevant conditioning distribution irrespective of the exogeneity of the right hand side variables. The method derives from that suggested by Sims (1972), as implemented in Quah (1996*b*), where endogeneity (or the lack of it) is determined by regressing the endogenous variable on the past, current and future values of the exogenous variables, and observing whether the future values of the exogenous variables have significant zero coefficients. If they are zero, then one can say that there is no feedback, or bidirection/al causality. Needless to say, the residuals resulting from such an exercise would constitute the variation of the dependent variable unexplained by the set of exogenous variables, irrespective of endogeneity. We present the results for these two-sided regressions in Table 9.4.

What is observed in all projections is that capital expenditure at lead 1 through lag 2 appears significant for predicting growth, but other leads and lags have less consistent effects. Fit does not seem to improve with increasing lags (or leads), and we appear to have a fairly stable set of coefficients of the two-sided projections. The residuals of the second lead–lag projections are used as the conditioned distribution of growth on capital expenditure.[11] Conditioning two-sided projections are also derived for the other auxiliary variables, namely, inflation, fiscal deficits, interest expenditure, own tax revenue, and education expenditure.

[11] Results are found to be unchanged if one uses residuals from other projections.

The results

Figures 9.3(b)–(d) present the stochastic kernels mapping the unconditioned to conditioned distributions using capital expenditure, education expenditure and fiscal deficits as the conditioning auxiliary factors. Figure 9.3(b) presents the conditioning stochastic kernel with capital expenditure. The relevant conditioned distribution indicates the residuals extracted from the two-sided regressions. The probability mass lies predominantly on the diagonal, though one can observe some local clusters running off the diagonal, parallel to the unconditioned axis at very low and high ends of the distribution. Since they run parallel to the original axis at different levels, they provide evidence of capital expenditure explaining polarization, quite similar to our earlier results with infrastructure.

Figure 9.3(c), mapping the conditioning stochastic kernel with education expenditure as the auxiliary variable, also runs mainly along the diagonal, with the upper and lower tails tending to run off parallel to the unconditioned axis. Thus, the conditioning exercises with capital and education expenditure seem to explain some of the cross-sectional distribution dynamics of growth across Indian states for high and low-income states.

Figure 9.3(d) maps the conditioning stochastic kernel with fiscal deficit. Though it lies predominantly on the diagonal, there appear to be a number of individual clusters running off the diagonal. Of these, a distinct cluster runs off the diagonal at a level of 0.5 of the national growth rate. This is suggestive of fiscal deficit serving to explain the observed distribution dynamics for the cluster of states identified at the observed level.[12]

Transition probability matrices results

The transition matrices estimates confirm the results from the previous section. The infrastructure matrix (Table 9.5) reveals tendencies of intradistributional mobility, particularly for the middle-income classes. The capital expenditure matrix (Table 9.6a) reveals a tendency of intradistributional mobility of the middle-income group towards lower and higher-income states. This confirms our earlier findings. Transition matrices for education expenditure and fiscal deficits (Tables 9.6b and c) exhibit similar signs of mobility for the middle income groups. The values for these income classes are smaller on the diagonals, with off-diagonal values increasing in value. There is, however, no tendency towards conditional convergence.[13]

[12] Additional calculations using inflation and interest expenditure as the conditioning variables provided no support in explaining the observed polarization.

[13] Again, estimates of intradistributional mobility using inflation and interest expenditure as the conditioning variables exhibit no signs of conditional convergence.

Table 9.5. *Interstate conditioning on infrastructure transition matrix*

Number	Upper end point				
	0.208	0.626	0.762	0.916	1.1
89	0.10	0.31	0.40	0.17	0.01
62	0.03	0.08	0.29	0.52	0.08
32	0.03	0.19	0.19	0.41	0.19
31	0.03	0.00	0.32	0.10	0.55
41	0.00	0.02	0.00	0.20	0.78
Ergodic	0.013	0.042	0.105	0.21	0.78

Source: See text.

Table 9.6. *Interstate conditioning on capital and education expenditures and fiscal deficit, transition matrix*

Number	Upper end point				
(a) Capital expenditure	0.173	0.234	0.276	0.396	0.547
110	0.82	0.18	0.00	0.00	0.00
300	0.73	0.23	0.03	0.00	0.00
310	0.10	0.16	0.35	0.35	0.03
180	0.00	0.06	0.11	0.56	0.28
220	0.00	0.00	0.00	0.27	0.73
Ergodic	0.731	0.179	0.015	0.036	0.038
(b) Education expenditure	0.190	0.227	0.273	0.400	0.572
170	0.76	0.12	0.06	0.06	0.00
220	0.36	0.36	0.23	0.05	0.00
290	0.21	0.38	0.14	0.28	0.00
230	0.04	0.09	0.14	0.28	0.00
210	0.00	0.00	0.00	0.05	0.95
Ergodic	0.305	0.129	0.093	0.126	0.346
(c) Fiscal deficit	0.172	0.235	0.272	0.388	0.536
100	1.00	0.00	0.00	0.00	0.00
320	0.72	0.19	0.09	0.00	0.00
250	0.08	0.20	0.48	0.20	0.04
220	0.00	0.09	0.18	0.50	0.23
230	0.00	0.00	0.04	0.30	0.65
Ergodic	1.00	0.00	0.00	0.00	0.00

Source: See text.

9.6. CONCLUSION

This study has examined the convergence of growth and incomes with reference to the Indian states using an empirical model of dynamically evolving distributions. The model reveals 'twin peaks' dynamics, or polarization across the Indian states, over 1965–97—empirics which would not be revealed under standard methods of cross-sectional, panel data, and time series econometrics. The dominant cross-state income dynamics is found to be associated with persistence, immobility, and polarization, with some cohesive tendencies in the 1960s, which dissipate over the following three decades. These findings contrast starkly with those emphasized in works of Aiyar (2000), Bajpai and Sachs (1996), Nagaraj *et al.* (1998), and Rao, Shand and Kalirajan (1999).

A conditioning methodology using the same empirical tools further reveals that such income dynamics are explained by the disparate distribution of infrastructure and to an extent by fiscal deficit and capital expenditure patterns. Unlike standard methods, this model allows us to observe the income dynamics at different levels of the distribution. Infrastructure explains the formation of the lower convergence club, while fiscal deficits and capital expenditure patterns explains club formation at higher income levels. By helping to uncover the forces which govern growth dynamics across the Indian states, such stylized facts are interesting for policy purposes.

REFERENCES

Adelman, I. and Morris, C. T. (1967). *Society, Politics and Economic Development—A Quantitative Approach*. Johns Hopkins Press, Baltimore.

Aiyar, S. (2000). 'Growth Theory and Convergence Across Indian States: A Panel Study'. In T. Callen, P. Reynolds, and C. Towe (eds), *India at the Crossroads: Sustaining Growth and Reducing Poverty*. IMF, Washington.

Bajpai, N. and Sachs, J. D. (1996). 'Trends in Interstate Inequalities of Income in India' *HIID Discussion Papers* 528, Harvard Institute for International Development, Cambridge, MA.

Bandyopadhyay, S. (2000*a*). 'Regional Distribution Dynamics of GDPs Across Indian States, 1965–1988'. *London School of Economics Working Paper Series* 00/06. LSE Development Studies Institute, London.

—— (2000*b*). 'Explaining Regional Distribution Dynamics of GDPs Across Indian States, 1977–1993'. London School of Economics. Unpublished manuscript.

Barro, R. J. (1995). 'Inflation and Growth', *NBER Working Papers* 5326. National Bureau of Economic Research, Cambridge, MA.

—— and Sala-i-Martin, X. (1992). 'Convergence'. *Journal of Political Economy*, 100(2), 223–51.

Bernard, A. and Durlauf, S. (1994). 'Interpreting Tests of the Convergence Hypothesis'. *NBER Technical Working Papers* 159. National Bureau of Economic Research, Cambridge, MA.

—— and —— (1996). 'Interpreting Tests of the Convergence Hypothesis', *Journal of Econometrics*, 71(1–2), 161–74.

Bianchi, M. (1997). 'Testing for Convergence: Evidence from Non-Parametric Multimodality Tests'. *Journal of Applied Econometrics*, 12(4), 393–409.

Bruno, W. and Easterly, W. (1998). 'Inflation Crises and Long-run Growth'. *Journal of Monetary Economics*, 41(1), 3–26.

Carlino, G. and Mills, L. (1993). 'Are US Regional Incomes Converging? A Time Series Analysis'. *Journal of Monetary Economics*, 32, 335–46.

Case, A. (2001). 'Election Goals and Income Redistribution—Recent Evidence from Albania'. Princeton University, New Jersey, Mimeo.

Cashin, P. and Sahay, R. (1996). 'Internal Migration, Centre-State Grants, and Economic Growth in the States of India'. *IMF Staff Papers*, 43(1).

Dasgupta, S., Dhillon, A., and Dutta, B. (2001). 'Electoral Goals and Centre-State Transfers in India', Warwick University, Warwick, Mimeo.

Desdoigts, A. (1994). 'Changes in the World Income Distribution: A Non-Parametric Approach to Challenge the Neoclassical Convergence Argument'. European University Institute: Florence, PhD dissertation.

Dixit, A. and Londregan, J. (1996). 'Determinants of Success of Special Interests in Redistribution Policy'. *The Journal of Politics*, 58(4), 1132–55.

—— and —— (1998). 'Ideology, Tactics and Efficiency in Politics'. *Quarterly Journal of Economics*, 113(2), 497–529.

Easterly, W. and Rebelo, S. (1993). 'Fiscal Policy and Economic Growth', *Journal of Monetary Economics*, 32(3), 417–58.

Everitt, B. (1984). *Graphical Techniques for Multivariate Data*. North Holland, New York.

Fischer, S. (1991). 'Growth, Macroeconomics, and Development'. In O. J. Blanchard and S. Fischer (eds), *NBER Macroeconomics Annual 1991*. MIT Press, Cambridge, MA.

—— (1993). 'The Role of Macroeconomic Factors in Growth'. *Journal of Monetary Economics*, 32(3), 485–512.

Friedman, M. (1992). 'Do Old Fallacies Ever Die'. *Journal of Economic Literature*, 30(4), 2129–32.

Galor, O. and Zeira, J. (1993). 'Income Distribution and Macroeconomics'. *Review of Economic Studies*, 60(1), 35–52.

Johanssen, E. (1999). 'Intergovernmental Transfers as a Tactical Instrument: Some Empirical Evidence from Swedish Municipalities'. Uppsala University, Uppsala, Mimeo.

Jones, C. I. (1997). 'On the Evolution of the World Income Distribution'. *Journal of Economic Perspectives*, 11(3), 19–36.

Kaldor, N. (1963). 'Capital Accumulation and Economic Growth'. In F. A. Lutz and D. C. Hague (eds), *Proceedings of a Conference held by the International Economics Association*. Macmillan, London.

Lamo, A. (1996). 'Cross Section Distribution Dynamics'. London School of Economics, London. PhD dissertation.

Leung, C. and Quah, D. T. (1996). 'Convergence, Endogenous Growth and Productivity Disturbances'. *Journal of Monetary Economics*, 38(3), 535–47.

Levine, R. and Renelt, D. (1992). 'A Sensitivity Analysis of Cross-country Growth Regressions'. *American Economic Review*, 76, 808–19.

—— and Zervos, S. (1993). 'What We Have Learned about Policy and Growth from Cross-Country Regressions'. *American Economic Review*, 83(2), 426–30.

Lindbeck, A. and Weibull, J. (1987). 'Balanced Budget Redistribution as the Outcome of Political Competition'. *Public Choice*, 52, 273–97.

Nagaraj, R., Varoudakis, A., and Véganzonès, M.-A. (1998). 'Long-Run Growth Trends and Convergence Across Indian States'. *OECD Development Centre Technical Paper* 131. OECD Development Centre, Paris.

Quah, D. T. (1996*a*). 'Convergence Empirics Across Economies with (Some). Capital Mobility'. *Journal of Economic Growth*, 1(1), 95–124.

Quah, D. T. (1996*b*). 'Twin Peaks: Growth and Convergence in Models of Distribution Dynamics'. *Economic Journal*, 106(437), 1045–55.
—— (1997). 'Empirics for Growth and Distribution: Stratification, Polarization and Convergence Clubs', *Journal of Economic Growth*, 2(1), 27–59.
Rao, G., Shand, R. T., and Kalirajan, K. P. (1999). 'Convergence of Incomes across Indian States: A Divergent View'. *Economic and Political Weekly*, 34(27), 769–78.
Solow, R. (1957). 'Technical Change and the Aggregate Production'. *Review of Economics and Statistics*, 39, 312–20.
Sims, C. A. (1972). 'Money, Income and Causality'. *American Economic Review*, 62(4), 540–52.
World Bank (1994). *World Development Report*. Oxford University Press, Oxford.

10

A Decomposition of Inequality and Poverty Changes in the Context of Macroeconomic Adjustment: A Microsimulation Study for Côte d'Ivoire

MICHAEL GRIMM

10.1. INTRODUCTION

After strong and sustained growth during the 1960s and 1970s in an environment of rising international commodity prices,[1] Côte d'Ivoire saw its average annual GDP per capita growth rate between 1978 and 1993 fall to −3.7 per cent. This period was marked by a sharp increase in the terms of trade, and thus a significant loss of competitiveness, as well as by a strong increase in external debt. Measures to stabilize the economy and structural reforms pursued by the Ivorian authorities since 1981 have not been sufficient to restore competitiveness or external viability (Bourguignon and Berthélemy 1996; Cogneau and Mesplé-Somps 2002; IMF 1998, 2000). The failure of the internal adjustment strategy in Côte d'Ivoire—one of the most significant economies of the fourteen member countries of the CFA[2] Franc Zone—led to a 50 per cent devaluation of CFA Franc parity in relation to the French Franc in January 1994. Numerous structural measures followed the devaluation in the framework of a fund-supported programme by the World Bank and the IMF. The growth rate of real GDP per capita

This study benefited greatly from very fruitful discussions with Denis Cogneau. I also thank Sandrine Mesplé-Somps, François Roubaud, and the two anonymous referees for their useful comments and suggestions, as well as the participants at the UNU/WIDER Development Conference on Growth and Poverty in Helsinki, the 18th Journées de Microéconomie Appliqueé in Nancy, the 15th Annual Conference of the European Society for Population Economics in Athens, the 16th Annual Congress of the European Economic Association in Lausanne, the 50th Congrès Annuel de l'Association Française de Science Economiques in Paris, the European Development Research Network Workshop in Bonn, and at research seminars in Ouagadougou and Abidjan. Furthermore, I am very grateful to the Institut National de la Statistique of Côte d'Ivoire and the World Bank for providing the data. I remain solely responsible for all errors and omissions that this study may contain.

[1] Côte d'Ivoire is the world's largest producer of cocoa, before Ghana and Indonesia.

[2] Communauté financière d'Afrique.

was −1.7 per cent in 1994, but attained over 3 per cent in the following 3 years. After the initial passage of higher import prices following devaluation, inflation has stabilized at under 6 per cent on average annually since 1996. Growth recovery was mainly due to a strong increase in the production of export crops (cocoa +62 per cent, coffee +107 per cent in volume) and cotton (+9 per cent), favoured by the devaluation and high world market prices, and due to a good performance in the manufacturing sector, agro-industry, and the energy sector.

From a political point of view, it is important to study how these profound economic changes as well as the accompanying high population growth (including immigration) affected the distribution of income and social welfare. Existing papers studying the evolution of inequality and poverty in the 1990s in Côte d'Ivoire (Jones and Ye 1997; World Bank 1997; Grimm, Guénard, and Mesplé-Somps 2002) are rich from a descriptive point of view, but they focus on consumption; therefore, they can tell us very little about the mechanisms through which the distribution of income may have been affected. Other studies used computable general equilibrium models to compare the distributional effects of different adjustment strategies open to Côte d'Ivoire (Bourguignon, de Melo, and Suwa-Eisenmann 1995; Calipel and Guillaumont Jeanneney 1996; Cogneau and Collange 1998). The advantage of these analyses is their macroeconomic closure, but by relying on the representative agent hypothesis they cannot tell us about individual responses to macroeconomic changes, and their implications for developments in overall income inequality.

In the present chapter, I use microsimulation techniques, developed by Bourguignon, Fournier, and Gurgand (2001), to analyse the respective effects of changes in the returns on the labour market, in occupational choices, and in the sociodemographic population structure, on the evolution of household income distribution in Côte d'Ivoire during the 1990s. The analysis is based on two household surveys carried out in 1992/3 and 1998, which constitute the most recent available microdata for Côte d'Ivoire. This study is, to my knowledge, the first application of this methodology to an African country, and to an economy characterized by a large agricultural sector.

This study also hopes to contribute to the general debate about the link between growth, inequality, and poverty alleviation. There is a rising consensus that results from cross-country studies (e.g. Dollar and Kraay 2002) are often not applicable to single countries and that data remain a serious problem. Therefore, more and more economists (e.g. Bourguignon 2000; Banerjee and Duflo 2001; Ravallion 2001) today argue that we can learn more from country specific case studies. This analysis offers such an approach.

The next section gives a brief description of the evolution of income distribution, poverty and some related economic and sociodemographic characteristics in Côte d'Ivoire. Section 3 explains the methodology and presents the econometric estimation of the occupational choice, wage, and profit functions. Section 4 presents various microsimulations and derives from them a decomposition of the change of income distribution and poverty ratios.

10.2. THE EVOLUTION OF INCOME DISTRIBUTION BETWEEN 1992/3 AND 1998: BASIC FACTS AND SOURCES OF CHANGE

10.2.1. *Evolution of Mean Household Income and its Components*

The following description, like the rest of the chapter, is based on two national representative household surveys that were jointly undertaken by the Institut National de la Statistique of Côte d'Ivoire (INS) and the World Bank. First, the Enquête Prioritaire (EP) which was started in 1992 (Abidjan), and finished in 1993 (other cities and rural areas). Second, the Enquête de Niveau de Vie (ENV) which was carried out in 1998. A two stage stratified design was used to sample a total of 9600 (57,433) and 4200 households (24,211 individuals) respectively, spread over five regions and 200 districts.

It can be seen in Table 10.1 that in the 1990s, real average household income declined in Abidjan (−1.6 per cent p.a.), the economic capital of Côte d'Ivoire, more or less stagnated in other cities (−0.3), and strongly increased in rural areas (+7.1).[3] The same can be said for mean household income per active household member. For all three strata, the evolution of average household income between 1992/3 and 1998 complies with the observed evolution of average household expenditures. However, the various income sources altered very differently. In Abidjan income from farm activities increased, whereas income from non-farm self-employment, transfer income, and income from other sources decreased. Wage income stagnated. The intensification of agricultural activity in Abidjan could indicate that households tried to cope with the downturn of market income by higher home-production. In contrast, in rural areas income increased from the three main sources as well as from transfers. The increase was particularly marked for income from export crops and wages. This pattern of change confirms that the sales of cocoa, coffee, and cotton have benefited from the devaluation of the CFA Franc and by the significant rise in world market prices, but also by an exceptional increase in cocoa production by historical standards.[4]

10.2.2. *Changes in Income Inequality and Poverty*

Table 10.2 summarizes some basic indicators of the distribution of household income per adult equivalent (Oxford Scale)[5] and some measures of poverty. For Abidjan, the data show an increase of 3.2 points in the Gini coefficient of the distribution of household income. The shares of households living with less than US$ 1 and 2 income per capita increased respectively.

[3] Unfortunately no reliable regional price index exits for the 1990s. The adjustment to Abidjan prices was thus undertaken before and after the devaluation of the CFA Franc by the same regional deflators (see notes to Table 10.1). However, it is likely that the devaluation affected regional price differences and especially the urban/rural price differential.

[4] The increase in income stemming from the production of export crops would have been even bigger if the CAISTAB had not taxed away a part of the surplus.

[5] The Oxford Scale gives a weight of one to the first adult in the household and a weight of 0.7 to all other adults. Children (younger than 14 years) receive a weight of 0.5. The robustness of the results has been tested using alternative equivalence scales. The distribution did not change significantly.

Table 10.1. *Evolution of mean household income from 1992/3 to 1998*

Weighted observation in thousands of 1998 CFAF, adjusted to Abidjan[a]	Abidjan			Other urban		
	1992	1998	$g_{p.a.}$ (%)	1993	1998	$g_{p.a.}$ (%)
Mean household income	2,488	2,264	−1.6	1,561	1,536	−0.3
Wage income[b]	1,370	1,444	0.9	636	766	3.8
Non-farm self-employment income[b]	612	509	−3.0	526	439	−3.6
Farm income[c]	10	17	9.6	106	116	1.8
Export crops (cotton, coffee, cocoa)	4	11	20.1	20	56	22.7
Food crops	3	12	27.9	25	25	−0.2
Cost of labour	7	9	5.0	13	12	−2.7
Self-consumption[d]	2	7	20.6	72	60	−3.6
Livestock, fishing, and hunting[e]	7	22	21.7	6	6	−0.7
Other income sources	237	123	−10.4	172	81	−14.0
Received transfers[f]	260	172	−6.6	121	135	2.2
Mean household income by active household member	1,686	1,418	−2.9	1,016	1,049	0.6
Mean household expenditure[g]	2,797	2,576	−1.4	1,588	1,606	0.2

	Rural			National		
	1993	1998	$g_{p.a.}$ (%)	1993	1998	$g_{p.a.}$ (%)
Mean household income	950	1,341	7.1	1,383	1,586	2.8
Wage income[b]	92	251	22.2	460	632	6.6
Non-farm self-employment income[b]	96	107	2.1	291	274	−1.2
Farm income[c]	675	888	5.6	420	513	4.1
Export crops (cotton, coffee, cocoa)	138	371	21.8	86	216	20.3
Food crops	123	110	−2.2	77	68	−2.7
Cost of labour	43	51	3.5	29	32	2.0
Self-consumption[d]	433	439	0.3	268	252	−1.2
Livestock, fishing, and hunting[e]	17	36	16.9	12	26	15.8
Other income sources	34	24	−6.6	104	59	−10.7
Received transfers[f]	53	70	6.0	108	108	0.1
Mean household income by active household member	421	614	7.8	788	886	2.4
Mean household expenditure[g]	1,094	1,415	5.3	1,532	1,710	2.2

Notes:

[a] The price deflator series 1992–98 published by the INS and the World Bank (2000) is used. To adjust incomes to the level of Abidjan, regional deflators constructed by Grootaert and Kanbur (1994) and revised by the INS (see Jones and Ye 1997) are used.

[b] In the EP 1992/3 individual earnings from dependent labour and non-farm self-employment were only collected from the first and second decision-maker in the household. Wages and profits for the other household members supplying labour in these activities are imputed to make the data of the two surveys comparable. The method used is described in Section 10.3.

[c] The four income sources minus the cost of labour do not exactly add up to the total farm income, because extreme values were omitted here and not replaced by imputed values.

[d] Self-consumption in the EP 1992/3 was corrected as proposed by Jones and Ye (1997).

[e] In the EP 1992/3 income from hunting was included in 'other income sources'.

[f] Including subsidies for education and transport, monetary aid, food aid and non-food aid received from individuals outside the household as well as pensions and insurance premiums.

[g] Including expenditure for durable and non-durable consumption items, self-consumption and transfers made to other households, but without taxes on wages and income. For house owners no rent was imputed here.

Source: EP 1992/3 and ENV 1998; computations by the author.

Table 10.2. *Evolution of the distribution of household income from 1992/3 to 1998*

Weighted observations 1998 CFAF, adjusted to Abidjan	Abidjan		Other urban		Rural		National	
	1992	1998	1993	1998	1993	1998	1993	1998
Household income per adult equivalent[a] *(Oxford scale)*								
Gini coefficient	0.497	0.529	0.489	0.487	0.417	0.480	0.494	0.508
Theil index	0.486	0.565	0.456	0.450	0.317	0.491	0.486	0.534
Mean logarithmic deviation	0.505	0.692	0.511	0.539	0.393	0.472	0.512	0.563
Atkinson ($e = 0.5$)	0.208	0.239	0.202	0.201	0.149	0.204	0.207	0.223
Atkinson ($e = 1$)	0.395	0.497	0.399	0.415	0.325	0.381	0.400	0.431
Household income per capita								
P0 (poverty line: US$ 1[b])	0.121	0.145	0.263	0.233	0.363	0.271	0.294	0.235
P0 (poverty line: US$ 2[b])	0.342	0.352	0.557	0.502	0.711	0.583	0.604	0.514
Household expenditure per adult equivalent (Oxford scale)								
Gini coefficient	0.396	0.424	0.392	0.387	0.349	0.371	0.417	0.412

Notes: See also notes of Table 10.1.

[a] Negative and zero incomes have been set to one.

[b] US$ 1 PPP1985: 110,700 CFAF 1998 (for details concerning the computation of the poverty lines, see DIAL 2000).

Source: EP 1992/3 and ENV 1998; computations by the author.

While in other cities the distribution of household income did not alter significantly between 1993 and 1998, absolute poverty decreased by 10 per cent when retaining the US$ 2 poverty line. In this context, it is important to note that the stratum 'other cities' is a very heterogeneous one, comprising more than sixty-five cities, ranging from 5000 to 550,000 habitants. In addition, the continuing urbanization process during the period under study may have led to a continuous expansion of this stratum. In contrast, in rural Côte d'Ivoire, income dispersion increased strongly and in 1998 reached a level comparable to that in urban areas. The Gini coefficient for 1998 was 6.3 points above the Gini coefficient for 1993. The Theil index shows that dispersion rose mainly at the top of the distribution. However, the rise in inequality was accompanied by a strong increase in average household income per capita, which was reflected by a remarkable reduction in absolute poverty. Whereas in 1993, 36 per cent of all households lived with less than US$ 1 per day per capita, this ratio fell to 27 per cent in 1998. Across all regions, the Gini coefficient increased slightly (+1.4 points).[6]

[6] The inequality measures for distribution of expenditure indicate a lower level of inequality than the measures for the distribution of income; this is a usual observation and stems generally from higher measurement error in the income variable, particularly for low-income groups, an underestimation of non-market income (e.g. transfers), and significant savings of high-income groups not taken into account by the expenditure variable. Likewise absolute poverty measured in terms of expenditure using the same data set is lower than in terms of income (see Grimm, Guénard, and Mesplé-Somps 2002). In what follows, I will assume that this statistical bias is constant over time, and within each category of household. This assumption may

10.2.3. *Variations in Occupational Structure*

In what follows I focus on the population of working age, which is defined here as individuals above 11 years of age. At age 12, school enrolment begins to decline, the share of working children reaches 20 per cent, and it can be assumed that 12-year-old children are able to contribute significantly to household production.

Table 10.3 shows that for men, the activity rate increased from 46.7 to 49.1 per cent in Abidjan (certainly signifying to a large extent a reduction in unemployment) and stagnated at around 50 per cent in other cities, and around 80 per cent in rural areas. In all zones wage labour increased, which complies with the observed rise in the share of wage income in other cities and in rural areas. An increase in employment in the modern private sector has also been noted by Cogneau and Mesplé-Somps (2002). A part of the increase in wage labour may also be due to an important number of immigrants from neighbouring countries who found jobs on the cocoa and coffee plantations in Côte d'Ivoire. Non-farm self-employment decreased in urban areas and stagnated in rural Côte d'Ivoire. The share of food crop farmers decreased, whereas the share of export crop farmers increased. However, the total proportion of farmers declined significantly. The shares of family workers in non-farm activity and in farm activity increased and decreased respectively. The activity rate of women increased in Abidjan (from 33.0 to 34.9 per cent), as did that for men, but decreased in other cities (from 41.7 to 40.2 per cent), and in rural areas (from 78.4 to 74.3 per cent). The proportion of female wage earners and non-farm self-employed increased and decreased respectively. The proportion of men and women with more than one professional activity rose (with exception of men in other urban areas).

10.3. METHODOLOGICAL FRAMEWORK: A DECOMPOSITION BY MICROSIMULATION

The chosen methodology was first proposed by Bourguignon and Martinez (1996), and was subsequently further developed and applied particularly by Bourguignon, Ferreira, and Lustig (1998), Bourguignon, Fournier, and Gurgand (1999, 2001), and Fournier (1999). Consider a simple household income function Y, where the income y_{ht} of household h observed at time t is assumed to depend on four sets of arguments: its observable sociodemographic characteristics, or those of its members i (x_{hit}), unobservable characteristics (ε_{hit}), a vector of remuneration rates of the observed (β_t) and unobserved earnings determinants (σ_t), and, finally, a set of parameters defining the participation and occupational choice behaviour of its members (λ_t):

$$y_{ht} = Y(x_{hit}, \varepsilon_{hit}; \beta_t; \sigma_t; \lambda_t). \quad (10.1)$$

The overall distribution of household income at time t, is then obtained by summarizing all y_{ht} and some demographic characteristics possibly included in x_{hit}, for example, the size or composition of the household at t, in one vector D_t. Accordingly, D_t can

be acceptable, in the sense that the evolution of the distribution of expenditures per adult equivalent between 1992/3 and 1998 complies completely with the evolution observed for the income variable.

Table 10.3. *Evolution of the socio-economic population structure, 1992/3 to 1998 (population 12 years and older)*

Weighted observations (proportions in %)	Abidjan		Other urban		Rural		National	
	1992	1998	1993	1998	1993	1998	1993	1998
Men								
Age								
12–14	11.5	9.8	15.5	15.0	14.4	13.5	14.0	13.0
15–24	30.5	35.2	33.5	35.6	27.8	30.3	29.7	32.8
25–44	43.9	40.3	32.0	32.4	29.6	33.0	33.2	34.5
45–64	12.7	13.2	15.0	13.4	20.3	16.4	17.5	14.9
65 and older	1.4	1.5	4.0	3.7	7.9	6.8	5.6	4.8
Non-Ivorian	27.6	26.7	25.0	20.1	18.6	16.1	22.0	19.6
Married	41.6	34.6	40.2	38.3	48.1	48.3	44.9	42.7
Schooling level								
No education	25.6	23.0	40.0	33.3	59.0	54.1	47.6	41.8
Primary school but no diploma	23.0	21.3	18.9	21.9	20.1	25.6	20.4	23.7
Primary school	28.8	27.0	25.6	28.0	16.5	15.4	21.2	21.2
Lower secondary	16.3	17.5	12.6	12.0	3.7	3.8	8.4	9.0
Higher secondary	3.0	6.7	1.5	2.2	0.6	0.6	1.3	2.4
Post-secondary	3.4	4.5	1.4	2.5	0.2	0.5	1.1	2.0
Occupation (main activity)								
Inactive (excluding enrolled/ trainees)	22.5	21.7	15.8	15.1	7.7	7.5	12.7	12.7
Enrolled or in training	30.8	29.2	33.6	35.9	13.0	13.8	21.6	22.8
Wage labour	32.0	36.0	20.4	25.9	5.7	12.2	14.6	21.1
Non-farm self-employed	12.5	11.3	14.2	12.2	2.7	2.9	7.5	7.1
Unpaid family work (non-farm)	1.3	0.9	1.9	2.6	0.4	4.3	0.9	3.1
Self-employed in agriculture	0.8	0.8	8.9	6.0	43.0	35.5	26.1	20.1
Food crop farmer			6.7	3.4	21.4	15.0	13.6	8.8
Export crop farmer[a]			2.1	2.6	21.6	20.5	12.5	11.4
Unpaid family work (farm)	0.1	0.1	5.2	2.3	27.6	23.9	16.6	13.0
Multi-activity (among actives)	4.0	5.9	12.8	10.1	9.9	13.5	9.6	11.5
Women								
Age								
12–14	13.8	13.2	14.5	14.1	11.6	10.3	12.7	11.9
15–24	36.4	36.9	33.5	38.1	26.1	29.3	30.0	33.2
25–44	41.1	39.2	36.4	33.5	37.7	38.4	38.1	37.4
45–64	7.7	9.5	13.3	12.0	20.1	16.9	15.9	14.0
65 and older	1.1	1.3	2.4	2.2	4.5	5.1	3.3	3.5
Non-Ivorian	24.3	22.5	23.2	17.3	16.6	11.7	19.8	15.6
Married	44.4	38.8	48.0	55.3	62.2	60.7	55.1	51.8
Schooling level								
No education	45.4	39.0	58.7	53.1	79.5	76.3	67.4	62.1
Primary school but no diploma	25.4	23.6	17.4	21.2	13.7	17.0	17.0	19.5
Primary school	20.2	25.4	18.7	20.9	6.1	5.9	12.1	14.0

Table 10.3. *Continued*

Weighted observations (proportions in %)	Abidjan		Other urban		Rural		National	
	1992	1998	1993	1998	1993	1998	1993	1998
Lower secondary	7.0	8.1	4.8	3.8	0.5	0.6	2.9	3.1
Higher secondary	1.2	2.8	0.3	0.6	0.1	0.2	0.4	0.9
Post-secondary	0.9	1.2	0.1	0.5	0.0	0.1	0.2	0.4
Occupation (main activity)								
Inactive (excluding enrolled/trainees)	47.3	44.3	40.5	38.2	17.1	18.8	29.0	29.4
Enrolled or in training	19.7	20.8	17.8	21.6	5.2	6.9	11.2	13.7
Wage labour	9.4	17.0	5.6	9.5	1.1	4.2	3.9	8.4
Non-farm self-employment	20.7	16.1	23.4	20.2	7.3	5.6	14.0	11.6
Unpaid family work (non-farm)	2.6	1.6	3.5	3.6	0.9	6.8	1.9	4.9
Self-employed in agriculture	0.0	0.1	1.9	1.6	6.0	5.8	3.8	3.5
Unpaid family work (farm)	0.3	0.1	7.3	5.3	62.4	51.9	36.3	28.5
Multi-activity (among actives)	1.1	1.9	3.8	5.3	3.2	4.1	3.1	4.0
All[b]								
Average household size	6.1	5.6	6.3	5.8	5.8	5.9	6.0	5.8

Notes:
[a] According to the definition used by the INS, farmers are considered here as export crop farmers, if the sales of cocoa, coffee, and cotton represent more than 50 per cent of the total value of agricultural production (33 per cent in the Savannah Region).
[b] Excluding visitors and domestics.

Source: EP 1992/3 and ENV 1998; computations by the author.

be written as a function H of the former parameters and of the distribution of the observable and unobservable household characteristics at date t:

$$D_t = H(\{x_{hit}, \varepsilon_{hit}\}, \beta_t, \sigma_t, \lambda_t). \tag{10.2}$$

where { } refers to the distribution of the corresponding variables in the population. Using this type of household income function, the difference between two distributions D_t and $D_{t'}$ observed over two distinct cross sections can be decomposed as resulting from four different causes: (i) a change in the remuneration rates of the observed earnings determinants; (ii) a change in the distribution of unobserved earnings determinants; (iii) a change in the occupational choice behaviour; and (iv) changes in the distribution of observed and unobserved individual sociodemographic characteristics. This decomposition can formally be written as:

$$\begin{aligned}
&\text{(i)} \quad B_{tt'}(\sigma_t, \lambda_t) = H(\{x_{hit}, \varepsilon_{hit}\}, \beta_{t'}, \sigma_t, \lambda_t) - H(\{x_{hit}, \varepsilon_{hit}\}, \beta_t, \sigma_t, \lambda_t),\\
&\text{(ii)} \quad S_{tt'}(\beta_t, \lambda_t) = H(\{x_{hit}, \varepsilon_{hit}\}, \beta_t, \sigma_{t'}, \lambda_t) - H(\{x_{hit}, \varepsilon_{hit}\}, \beta_t, \sigma_t, \lambda_t),\\
&\text{(iii)} \quad L_{tt'}(\beta_t, \sigma_t) = H(\{x_{hit}, \varepsilon_{hit}\}, \beta_t, \sigma_t, \lambda_{t'}) - H(\{x_{hit}, \varepsilon_{hit}\}, \beta_t, \sigma_t, \lambda_t),\\
&\text{(iv)} \quad P_{tt'} = H(\{x_{hit'}, \varepsilon_{hit'}\}, \beta_t, \sigma_t, \lambda_t) - H(\{x_{hit}, \varepsilon_{hit}\}, \beta_t, \sigma_t, \lambda_t).
\end{aligned} \tag{10.3}$$

Explained in words, this methodology assumes that the impact of a change in the remuneration rates of the observed earnings determinants can be quantified by comparing the observed distribution at date t with the hypothetical distribution obtained by simulating on the population observed at date t, the remuneration structure of the observed earnings determinants at date t'. In the same way we can evaluate variations in the other sets of parameters, or even in one single parameter (e.g. return to education). The change in the remuneration rates of the unobserved earnings determinants is measured by the change in the residual variance in earnings functions.[7] Of course, one cannot distinguish between changes in remuneration rates to unobserved characteristics and changes in their distribution. However, if we assume that the distribution of some of these unobserved characteristics (such as IQ) is 'unlikely' to have changed much, the changes in the variance of the residuals may rather reflect 'price' changes.

The population effect P can be estimated either, if panel data is available, by running the same type of simulation as for the different parameter sets, or by comparing the distribution at date t and the hypothetical distribution obtained by simulating on the population observed at date t' the remuneration structure and the behavioural parameters of period t. However, the evaluation of a change in any subset of the coefficients (β, σ, λ) depends on the value that is selected for the complementary subset. For instance, the occupational choice effect can be evaluated using the characteristics of the population at time t and the structure of earnings at time t, as done in eqns (10.3). But it can be also evaluated using the earnings structure of year t'. This is the meaning of the arguments of $B_{tt'}$, $S_{tt'}$, $L_{tt'}$ on the left-hand side of eqns (10.3). If $C_{tt'}$ is the overall change in the distribution between t and t' then the following identity holds:

$$C_{tt'} = B_{tt'}(\sigma_t, \lambda_t) + S_{tt'}(\beta_{t'}, \lambda_t) + L_{tt'}(\beta_{t'}, \sigma_{t'}) + P_{t't}, \tag{10.4}$$

where $P_{t't}$ is the population effect evaluated with the price structure and the occupational behaviour of t', rather than t.

It is important to note that these decompositions are path-dependent in two senses: First, it matters which basic population is used as point of departure (t or t'). Second, it matters which other parameters are used (e.g. λ_t or $\lambda_{t'}$) when a new set is simulated (e.g. $\beta_{t'}$). For example, a change in the return to education will have a different effect on the distribution of income whether it is applied to a highly-educated or a weakly educated population. This means, that generally $P_{tt'} \neq P_{t't}$, and likewise for B, S, and L. To assess the robustness of the results for each effect, the simulation will be performed in both directions, that is, using either the population at t or the population at t' as point of departure. However, I compute $B_{tt'}$, $S_{tt'}$ and $L_{tt'}$ effects as stated in eqns (10.3), and not sequentially. The population effect is simply computed as a residual. The assumed household income generating model can be summarized by the following set of equations, where k_h is the number of persons of working age (12 years

[7] The residual u_{hit} of each individual i is expanded by the ratio $\sigma_{t'}/\sigma_t$, which yields: $\tilde{u}_{hi}^{tt'} = \sigma_{t'}/\sigma_t \, u_{hit}$.

and over) in household h:

$$L_{hi}^{jt} = (x_{hi,j=1}^{t}, \ldots, x_{hi,j=\mathcal{J}}^{t}, z_{hi,j=1}^{t}, \ldots, z_{hi,j=\mathcal{J}}^{t}, \upsilon_{hi,j=1}^{t}, \ldots, \upsilon_{hi,j=\mathcal{J}}^{t}; \lambda_{x,j=1}^{t}, \ldots, \lambda_{x,j=\mathcal{J}}^{t}, \lambda_{z,j=1}^{t}, \ldots, \lambda_{z,j=\mathcal{J}}^{t}), \quad i = 1 \text{ to } k_h \forall h \text{ and } j = W, F, NF, H \forall i. \tag{10.5}$$

$$w_{hi}^{t,j=W} = w(x_{hi}^{t}, u_{hi}^{t}; \beta^{t}), \quad i = 1 \text{ to } k_h \forall h. \tag{10.6}$$

$$\prod_{hi}^{j=NF,F} = \prod(x_{hi}^{t}, z_{hi}^{t}, s_{hi}^{t}; \beta_{x}^{t}; \beta_{z}^{t}), \quad i = 1 \text{ to } k_h \forall h. \tag{10.7}$$

$$y_{h}^{t} = \sum_{i=1}^{k_h} L_{hi}^{Wt} w_{hi}^{t,j=W} + \sum_{i=1}^{k_h} L_{hi}^{NFt} \prod_{hi}^{t,j=NF} + \sum_{i=1}^{k_h} L_{hi}^{Ft} \prod_{hi}^{t,j=F} + y_{0h}^{t}. \tag{10.8}$$

Equation (10.5) describes the labour supply of each household member i, where the index j stands respectively for the labour supplied as a wage worker outside the family business (W), the labour supplied as manager of the family farm (F), the labour supplied as manager of a family non-farm business (NF),[8] and the labour supplied as family help (H) in either the family farm or the family non-farm business.[9] Besides these five occupational choices, I distinguish a sixth one, for household heads only, which is being a self-employed farmer *and* a wage worker. Multi-activity is, thus, explicitly modelled as a choice. However, for all other existing activity combinations only the principal activity is modelled. In the sample used there are very few household heads working as family help, therefore this opportunity is not modelled for household heads and the individuals concerned are coded as inactive.

The two surveys used in this study do not contain sufficient information about the allocation of time between different occupations, and, as a result, consideration is only given to whether individual i supplies labour or not in the corresponding activity j. I consider the population 12 years old and over, outside the educational system and professional training. Educational investment is, thus, taken as exogenous. If agent i makes choice j, it is assumed that U_{ij} is the maximum among the $\mathcal{J}$ utilities, $U_{ij} > U_{ik} \forall k \neq j$. The $\mathcal{J}$ disturbances υ_{ij} are supposed to be independent and identically distributed with Weibull distribution. Thus, the model can be estimated by a multinomial logit model

[8] The specification employed implicitly assumes that there is no fixed cost involved in switching from wage labour to non-farm self-employment, but no other assumption can be made in the absence of any information about capital goods relevant for non-farm self-employment.

[9] Individuals drawn from the simulation as family help are assigned to the family business as follows: If the household possesses a farm, the individual is assigned as family help to the farm. If the family possesses one or more family non-farm business the individual is assigned to the business which is conducted by the household member with the highest order number in the survey questionnaire. If the household possesses a non-farm business and a farm, a random number out of an uniform distribution is drawn and the individual is assigned with a probability 50 : 50 to one of the two. If two members of one household are drawn as farmers from the simulation, the one with the highest order number is assigned as farm manager and the other as family help.

(McFadden 1973, 1984). The labour supply of member i in household h is supposed to be a function of his/her personal characteristics x_{hi} (schooling, experience, sex, relation to household head, Ivorian nationality, religion, born in an urban area, region of residence) and some household characteristics z_{hi} (land size, household size, mean age, and mean schooling of other household members, household composition, for household members other than the household head: the household head's occupational choice [instrumented]).

The model is estimated for both surveys (1992/3 and 1998) and separately for the household head, his/her spouse, and the other household members. The estimations reveal that the most striking changes in preferences occurred for those associated with years of schooling, land, region of residence, and the occupational choice of the household head. For instance, the positive effect of schooling on the relative probability of being a wage worker was more pronounced in 1998 than in 1992/3. Access to land and its size were in 1992/3 more positively associated with self-employment in agriculture than in 1998. If the household head was working as an independent farmer, the probability of being family help for the spouse, children, nephews, or other relatives of the household head was stronger in 1998 than in 1992/3. Furthermore, the probability of being self-employed in a non-farm activity increased if the household head was a wage worker especially in 1998. The influence of regional location of the household on occupational choices was more important in 1998 than in 1992/3. For a complete tabulation of the estimated coefficients of eqn (10.5), see Grimm (2001).

Equation (10.6) is a typical semi-logarithmic Mincerian potential wage equation (Mincer 1974) whose arguments are human capital proxies and other personal characteristics. The dependent variable is the logarithm of the monthly wage w (before taxes and transfers).[10] The wage equation is estimated for 1992/3 and 1998, and separately for urban and rural men and women, using a tobit model to correct for self-selection in this activity (Heckman 1979).[11] The estimated coefficients of the wage equations show (Table 10.4) a general decrease in returns to schooling, and a narrowing of the wage differential between Ivorians and non-Ivorians over the period under study. Furthermore, a strong regional redistribution of returns in rural Côte d'Ivoire in favour of the West Forest Region can be noted. The dispersion of earnings due to unobserved wage

[10] Whereas in the ENV 1998 all wage workers and non-farm self-employed individuals were asked their earnings, in the EP 1992/3 only the first and second decision-maker of each household were asked. This means that earnings from very young household members are often unknown. This selection effect has to be corrected in addition to the usual (self-) selection bias. In the simulation model, earnings were imputed in both reference years (1992/3 and 1998), for self-employed and wage workers for whom earnings had not been observed using the estimated equations and by drawing residuals. Another difficulty in the 1992/3 survey stems from the fact that wage workers and non-farm self-employed individuals were not asked their exact earnings, but instead to specify one of nine different income classes and to give the corresponding period during which they were earned (month or year). To keep the analysis simple, the discrete observations are transformed into continuous ones by simulating residuals following the method described in Gourieroux *et al.* (1987) (for details see Grimm 2001).

[11] To be consistent with the occupational choice model, multiple choices should be taken into account in the selection model of the wage equation. However specifications along the lines of Lee (1983), with a selection process over multiple choices, rely on strong distributional assumptions about the error terms. Thus, to keep the model simple, the usual Heckman specification is used.

Table 10.4. *Wage equations, selection model (full MLE)*

Dependent variable: Log monthly wage	1992/3		1998	
Men, urban				
Schooling	0.125	(0.007)	0.094	(0.007)
Potential experience	0.057	(0.010)	0.048	(0.008)
Potential experience^2/100	−0.046	(0.015)	−0.034	(0.013)
Non-Ivorian	−0.244	(0.035)	−0.091	(0.056)
Multi-activity (IV)	−0.274	(0.066)	0.114	(0.134)
Abidjan	0.211	(0.031)	0.211	(0.050)
Intercept	9.605	(0.283)	10.094	(0.177)
ρ	−0.362	(0.163)	−0.725	(0.051)
$\hat{\sigma}_u$	0.684		0.924	
Number of observations	6,873		2,510	
Number of uncensored observations	2,222		1,057	
Men, rural				
Schooling	0.222	(0.023)	0.192	(0.017)
Potential experience	0.102	(0.023)	0.090	(0.017)
Potential experience^2/100	−0.118	(0.034)	−0.117	(0.027)
Non-Ivorian	0.551	(0.178)	0.414	(0.154)
Multi-Activity (IV)	−0.908	(0.162)	−0.149	(0.152)
East Forest (reference category)				
West Forest	−0.478	(0.144)	0.408	(0.123)
Savannah	0.421	(0.156)	−0.039	(0.142)
Intercept	7.022	(0.579)	7.796	(0.438)
ρ	0.014	(0.145)	0.042	(0.130)
$\hat{\sigma}_u$	1.304		1.162	
Number of observations	6,198		3,494	
Number of uncensored observations	558		521	
Women				
Schooling	0.192	(0.016)	0.134	(0.025)
Potential experience	0.080	(0.015)	0.090	(0.014)
Potential experience^2/100	−0.078	(0.023)	−0.126	(0.023)
Other urban (reference category)				
Abidjan	0.237	(0.075)	−0.112	(0.099)
Rural	−0.907	(0.134)	−0.477	(0.115)
Intercept	8.528	(0.379)	9.078	(0.688)
ρ	−0.081	(0.108)	−0.266	(0.269)
$\hat{\sigma}_u$	0.771		0.991	
Number of observations	15,985		6,784	
Number of uncensored observations	477		545	

Notes: Standard errors in parentheses. The explanatory variables in the selection model are schooling, age, square of age, matrimonial status, relationship to household head, square root of household size, dummy if migrated during the last 5 years, number of adult men in household, number of adult women in household, number of inactive adults in household (excluding the individuals themselves), and dummies for ethnic affiliation.

Source: EP 1992/3 and ENV 1998; estimations by the author.

Table 10.5. *Non-agriculture profit function, selection model (full MLE)*

Dependent variable: Log monthly profit	1992/3		1998	
Number of household members involved in business	0.185	(0.032)	0.127	(0.046)
Schooling	0.076	(0.006)	0.079	(0.008)
Potential experience	0.059	(0.006)	0.073	(0.011)
Potential experience^2/100	−0.070	(0.008)	−0.081	(0.015)
Women	−0.689	(0.035)	−0.729	(0.059)
Abidjan (reference category)				
Other urban	−0.188	(0.040)	−0.126	(0.063)
East Forest	−0.480	(0.086)	−0.558	(0.122)
West Forest	−0.892	(0.103)	−0.174	(0.099)
Savannah	−0.294	(0.076)	−0.630	(0.152)
Intercept	9.526	(0.146)	9.216	(0.253)
ρ	0.127	(0.041)	0.112	(0.084)
$\hat{\sigma}_u$	1.026		0.995	
Number of observations	29,056		12,888	
Number of uncensored observations	3,849		1,347	

Notes: Standard errors in parentheses. The explanatory variables in the selection model are: schooling, experience, square of experience, sex, religion, dummy for non-Ivorian, square root of household size, dummy for inactive adults in household (excluding the individuals themselves), mean age of other household members, dummy for land property, region of residence.

Source: EP 1992/3 and ENV 1998; estimations by the author.

determinants increased for men in urban areas and for women, and declined for men in rural areas.

Equation (10.7) is a profit function containing as arguments, in the case of non-farm self-employed workers, the number of (unpaid) household members involved in the business z_{hi} and the personal characteristics of the household member who runs the business x_{hi}. Unfortunately the data sets contain no usable information about potentially important productive assets in a firm. The dependent variable is the logarithm of the declared monthly individual earnings (before taxes and transfers) of the person who admitted running the business.[12] The usual Hausman specification test did not reject exogeneity of the supplied work by household members. The most striking feature emerging from the estimations (Table 10.5) is the decline in productivity of an additional person involved in the business between 1992/3 and 1998. Furthermore, the earnings differentials between regions show that the West Forest almost caught up with the earnings level in the stratum 'other cities' in 1998. In contrast, earnings in the Savannah region relatively lost ground. The residual variance remained more or less constant.

[12] Even if I refer to these functions as profit functions, it should be noted that declared earnings are not necessarily netted out of any imputed labour cost.

In the case of farmers, the dependent variable of eqn (10.7) is the logarithm of earnings derived from the sale and self-consumption of agricultural products (food crops, export crops, and livestock) during the previous 12 months minus the cost of hired labour from outside the household.[13] The profit includes the implicit wages of the family workers and the implicit cost of the cultivated land. Here, a Hausman specification test rejected exogeneity of the number of family members involved. Therefore, this variable is instrumented using household composition variables and the model is estimated with 2SLS. Besides the number of family members involved, the amount of available land (cultivated and left fallow),[14] some household and individual characteristics of the farmer are introduced as explanatory variables. The estimations show (Table 10.6) that despite the positive evolution of the export crop sector, the return to family members involved remained constant, and the return to land decreased, particularly for small-scale farmers, that is, mainly food crop farmers. However, it is obvious that the number of involved family members is only a very approximate measure of the amount of labour supplied. The participating household members may have reduced on average their supplied hours of work. Analysis of the data shows that the quantity of land held by households increased significantly between 1993 and 1998. Therefore, it seems that the increase in agricultural production (which took place as well as the price boost) was mainly due to an expansion in cultivated land and hired labour. However, further data has to be checked to verify if the increase in available land, observed in the data, is real or simply a measurement error.[15] The relative price increase of export crops is entirely reflected by the change of the coefficients associated to the regional dummies. The West Forest is the principal region for the cultivation of cocoa and coffee, so the evolution of the coefficients yields what can be expected.

The variables v_{hi}, u_{hi}, and s_{hi} are the usual residual terms of the corresponding econometric models. They can be interpreted as 'fixed' individual effects representing the influence of unobserved variables on occupational choice behaviour, wages, and profits. Naturally, these terms can only be estimated for the individuals who are engaged in the corresponding activity. Moreover, they are not observed for the discrete labour choice. As a result, for all non-participants these terms will be drawn randomly, but conditionally, on the estimated residual variance and the occupational choice that is observed (for details see Grimm 2001).

Equation (10.8) aggregates the different income sources over the household members. The term $y^t_{0\,h}$ summarizes income from other sources, including transfers, and income from wealth. It is assumed to be exogenous in the model.

[13] Whereas wages and non-farm profits are declared per month or per year (but used in a per month basis for the estimations), agricultural profits are systematically declared on a twelve month basis. This could create problems of comparability due to seasonal variations in wages and non-farm profits declared per month.

[14] The data from 1992/3 did not allow the separation of cultivated land from that left fallow.

[15] In harmony with this evolution, the Enquête de Niveau de Vie 1995 already shows an increase in the average amount of land held by households.

Table 10.6. *Agriculture profit function, 2SLS model*

Dependent variable: Log profit last 12 months	1992/3		1998	
Number of household members involved in business (IV)	0.153	(0.010)	0.148	(0.014)
Land: no land or less than 1 ha (reference category)				
Land: from 1 to 2 ha	0.498	(0.045)	0.176	(0.215)
Land: from 2 to 5 ha	0.723	(0.047)	0.663	(0.212)
Land: from 5 to 10 ha	1.074	(0.055)	0.932	(0.214)
Land: more than 10 ha	1.117	(0.061)	1.156	(0.213)
Homeowner	0.086	(0.034)	0.296	(0.055)
Potential experience	0.017	(0.004)	0.022	(0.006)
Potential experience^2/100	−0.025	(0.005)	−0.034	(0.007)
Women	−0.141	(0.040)	−0.323	(0.063)
Multi-activity (IV)	−0.071	(0.068)	−0.183	(0.115)
East Forest (reference category)				
Urban	−0.212	(0.042)	−0.234	(0.085)
West Forest	0.094	(0.038)	0.319	(0.056)
Savannah	0.327	(0.036)	0.016	(0.053)
Intercept	11.618	(0.088)	11.570	(0.231)
$\hat{\sigma}_u$	0.848		0.888	
Number of observations	4,454		1,899	
Adjusted R^2	0.359		0.298	

Notes: Standard errors in parentheses. The instrumental variables for 'number of household members involved in farm work' are, square root of household size, number of adult men in household, number of adult women in household, number of children 0–5 years old in household, number of children 6–14 years old in household, number of inactive adults in household, mean schooling of household members.

Source: EP 1992/3 and ENV 1998; estimations by the author.

10.4. DECOMPOSITION BY MICROSIMULATION OF THE EVOLUTION OF INCOME DISTRIBUTION

10.4.1. *Abidjan*

The simulation model suggests that the increase in inequality by 3.1 points in the Gini coefficient observed for Abidjan between 1992 and 1998 resulted from various forces which partly offset each other (Table 10.7). The simulation of income distribution for 1992 by applying the occupational preferences of 1998 suggests that modifications on the labour market contributed to a reduction in inequality. However, if the population of 1998 is used as the point of departure, the equalizing effect almost disappears. The activity rate (population 12 years old and over not at school or in training) rises from 52.8 to 59.1 per cent between 1992 and 1998, if one applies the 1988's preferences to 1992. The inflow into dependent wage work (+7 points) out of inactivity and

Table 10.7. *Decomposition by microsimulation of the change in the distribution of household income per adult equivalent (Oxford Scale)*

	Initial population 1992/3				Initial population 1998			
	Gini	dGini	E(0)	dE(0)	Gini	dGini	E(0)	dE(0)
Abidjan								
Initial values	0.497		0.505		0.529		0.692	
Observed change		0.031		0.187		0.031		0.187
Price observables (*B*)	0.472	−0.025	0.461	−0.044	0.570	−0.042	0.780	−0.089
Returns to schooling	0.475	−0.022	0.463	−0.042	0.578	−0.049	0.804	−0.113
Returns to experience	0.501	0.003	0.510	0.005	0.533	−0.005	0.706	−0.015
Ivorian/non-Ivorian wage difference	0.495	−0.002	0.501	−0.004	0.530	−0.002	0.695	−0.003
Residual variance (*S*)	0.520	0.022	0.553	0.048	0.491	0.038	0.621	0.071
Total price effects		−0.003		0.004		−0.004		−0.018
Occupational choice (*L*)	0.476	−0.021	0.439	−0.066	0.529	−0.001	0.649	0.042
Price and occupational choice		−0.024		−0.062		−0.005	0.024	
Population structure effect (*P*)		0.055		0.249		0.036		0.162
Other urban								
Initial values	0.489		0.511		0.487		0.539	
Observed change		−0.002		0.028		−0.002		0.028
Price observables (*B*)	0.476	−0.013	0.492	−0.019	0.503	−0.016	0.567	−0.028
Returns to schooling	0.473	−0.015	0.481	−0.030	0.515	−0.029	0.596	−0.057
Returns to experience	0.485	−0.004	0.503	−0.008	0.493	−0.006	0.554	−0.015
Ivorian/non-Ivorian wage difference	0.488	0.000	0.510	0.000	0.488	−0.001	0.541	−0.002
Returns to land	0.488	−0.001	0.511	0.000	0.484	0.003	0.533	0.006
Residual variance (*S*)	0.500	0.011	0.535	0.024	0.467	0.020	0.505	0.034
Total price effects		−0.002		0.005		0.004		0.006
Occupational choice (*L*)	0.489	0.000	0.501	−0.010	0.513	−0.026	0.555	−0.016
Price and occupational choice		−0.001		−0.005		−0.022		−0.010
Population structure effect (*P*)		−0.001		0.034		0.020		0.038
Rural areas								
Initial values	0.417		0.393		0.480		0.472	
Observed change		0.063		0.079		0.063		0.079
Price observables (*B*)	0.439	0.022	0.425	0.033	0.483	−0.003	0.485	−0.013
Returns to schooling	0.411	−0.006	0.385	−0.008	0.497	−0.017	0.501	−0.030
Returns to experience	0.412	−0.005	0.392	0.000	0.485	−0.006	0.481	−0.009
Ivorian/non-Ivorian wage difference	0.417	0.000	0.393	0.001	0.481	−0.001	0.474	−0.002
Returns to land	0.419	0.002	0.398	0.006	0.474	0.006	0.463	0.009
Residual variance (*S*)	0.431	0.014	0.420	0.028	0.458	0.021	0.435	0.037

Table 10.7. *Continued*

	Initial population 1992/3				Initial population 1998			
	Gini	dGini	E(0)	dE(0)	Gini	dGini	E(0)	dE(0)
Total price effects		0.036		0.060		0.018		0.023
Occupational choice (*L*)	0.421	0.004	0.387	−0.006	0.482	−0.003	0.472	0.000
Price and occupational choice		0.040		0.055		0.016		0.024
Population structure effect (*P*)		0.023		0.025		0.047		0.056
National								
Initial values	0.494		0.512		0.508		0.563	
Within-group inequality			0.441				0.537	
Between-group inequality			0.071				0.026	
Observed change		0.014		0.050		0.014		0.050
Price observables (*B*)	0.483	−0.011	0.497	−0.015	0.540	−0.032	0.630	−0.067
Returns to schooling	0.471	−0.023	0.473	−0.039	0.547	−0.039	0.640	−0.078
Returns to experience	0.476	−0.017	0.486	−0.026	0.512	−0.004	0.573	−0.010
Ivorian/non-Ivorian wage difference	0.495	0.001	0.515	0.003	0.508	0.000	0.562	0.001
Regional differential	0.484	−0.010	0.496	−0.016	0.511	−0.003	0.574	−0.011
Returns to land	0.489	−0.005	0.506	−0.006	0.500	0.008	0.550	0.013
Residual variance (*S*)	0.498	0.004	0.525	0.013	0.482	0.026	0.515	0.048
Total price effects		−0.007		−0.002		−0.006		−0.019
Occupational choice (*L*)	0.496	0.003	0.505	−0.007	0.515	−0.007	0.557	0.006
Price and occupational choice		−0.005		−0.010		−0.014		−0.013
Population structure effect (*P*)		0.019		0.060		0.028		0.064

Notes: E(0) is the mean logarithmic deviation. Positive change indicates a disequalizing effect from 1992/3 to 1998. Negative change indicates an equalizing effect from 1992/3 to 1998.

Source: EP 1992/3 and ENV 1998; simulations by the author.

non-farm self-employment is remarkable. The simulated transitions on the labour market are completely in line with the observed changes in the occupational structure between 1992 and 1998. These occupational changes suggest two things. First, a part of the involuntary unemployed individuals found jobs after 1994. Second, households tried to overcome declines in real income by an increase in labour market activity of former voluntary unemployed family members. The necessary supplementary jobs were provided, thanks to the recovery of private investment after the devaluation.

In the same way as the occupational choice effect, the price effect also tended towards a more equal distribution (−3.4 points in Gini on average over both simulations), mainly via a drop in the return to schooling and a decline in the wage differential between Ivorians and non-Ivorians. The major factor behind these two effects may be the freezing of wages in the public sector. In contrast, inequality increased due to changes in the distribution of unobserved earnings determinants, possibly reflecting more heterogeneity in working time among individuals. One can also assume that the major macroeconomic events (devaluation, rising world market prices for cocoa and coffee, adjustment policy) affected the different sectors of the economy in a very distinct way, and thus led to a higher residual variance.

Likewise, changes in the socio-economic population structure had a non-equalizing effect on income distribution. Factors behind this phenomenon may have been the rejuvenation of the population and longer school enrolment of the young. Indeed, natural population growth and immigration are still high in Côte d'Ivoire, so that each year, particularly in Abidjan, a large number of young people come onto the labour market, with no experience and hence potentially low wages. In the framework of the adjustment programme, the public administration stopped recruiting school graduates, which destroyed potentially favourable posts for the young. On average, younger cohorts also stay longer in school and so contribute little or nothing to the family income.[16] Another factor, included in the population effect, could be the higher mortality of adults of working age due to AIDS.

Decompositions not reported here using the two alternative poverty indicators reveal a quite similar picture in the sense that factors which reduced inequality also reduced poverty. Changes in returns to observed earnings determinants and changes in occupational preferences reduced poverty. Modifications in the residual variance of the different earnings functions and variations of the sociodemographic population structure increased poverty. However, it is interesting to see that a change in the returns to schooling had a decreasing effect on inequality, but an increasing effect on poverty. The direction and magnitude of household income changes due to modifications in occupational choices and returns to observables and unobservables can also be seen in Fig. 10.1, which shows the relative change of mean household income for each household income centile by performing the three counterfactual simulations.

10.4.2. *Other Urban*

Inequality remained constant in the other urban centres of Côte d'Ivoire. However, as the microsimulation exercise shows (Table 10.7), changes in the returns to different earnings determinants worked in favour of a more equal distribution. As in Abidjan, a drop in the return to education had a homogenizing effect on incomes. In contrast, changes in the distribution of unobserved earnings determinants contributed obviously to a higher dispersion of household incomes (approximately +1.5 points in Gini).

The simulation of occupational choices by taking one population as starting point and applying the occupational preferences of the other year, produces an increase in wage labour, a decrease in non-agricultural and agricultural independent activity,

[16] Of course, the long-term effects may be very positive.

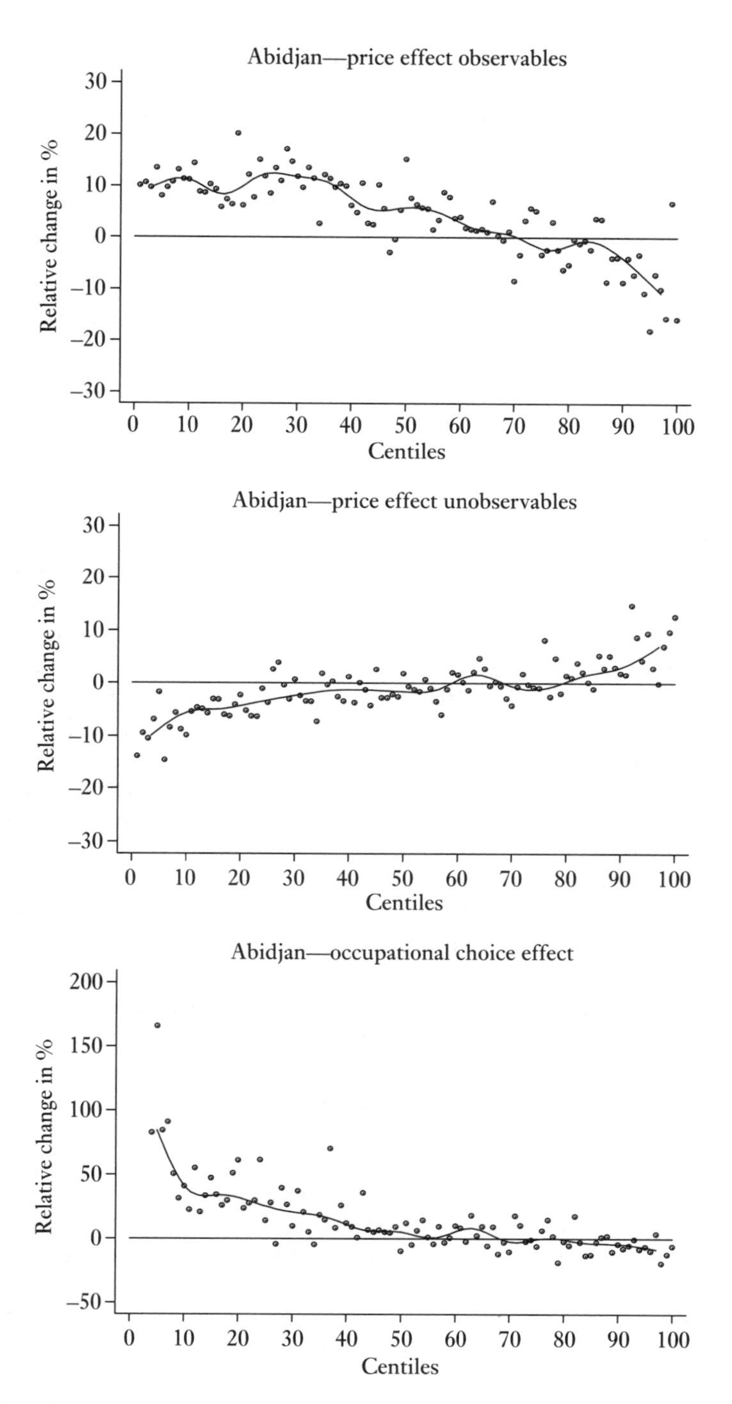

Figure 10.1. *Relative change of mean household income for each household income centile, when performing the three counterfactual simulations for Abidjan using 1992 as starting point (smoothing by a cubic spline)*

and a more or less constant share working as family help. These evolutions had an equalizing but weak effect on income distribution. Using the population of 1993 as the initial population even implies that the pure occupational choice effect was close to zero. As in Abidjan and rural areas (see below), changes in the population structure had a non-equalizing effect. Possible factors behind this phenomenon may be similar to those outlined above for Abidjan, including internal migration.

Whereas the degree of inequality remained constant between 1993 and 1998, other decompositions not reported here reveal that poverty decreased by 3 points using the US$ 1 poverty line, and by 5.5 points using the US$ 2 poverty line. This reduction was reached mainly by the channel of changes in the returns to observed earnings determinants, even if partly offset by a higher dispersion of unobserved earnings determinants.

10.4.3. *Rural Areas*

Rural areas experienced a strong increase in inequality with the Gini coefficient rising from 0.42 in 1993 to 0.48 in 1998 (Table 10.7). Changes in participation behaviour led to a higher proportion of the population becoming involved in dependent wage work and a lower proportion involved in independent non-farm, or farm activities. However, as the descriptive statistics in Table 10.3 show, even if the total share of farmers decreased (−7.5 percentage points among men), the share of export crop farmers remained more or less constant. That is what we can expect in the context of a devaluation and increasing international prices for coffee and cocoa. In particular, some of the food crop farmers became what I call ‘export crop farmers’ simply because of pure price effects (here, a farmer is considered as an export crop farmer, if sales of cocoa, coffee, and cotton represent more than 50 per cent of the total value of agricultural production [33 per cent in the Savannah region]), or by effectively substituting food crop production by export crop production. In addition, a significant share of food crop farmers reduced their labour supply on their own farms and started working as wage workers on cocoa or coffee plantations or in agro-industry (this is in line with the increase in multi-activity, +36 per cent among men). The share of wage workers may have also increased as a result of immigrants from neighbouring countries who found work on the Ivorian cocoa and coffee plantations.

The decrease in the returns to land, particularly for small-scale farmers (thus, mostly food crop farmers) as well as changes in the residual variance of the earnings functions had a non-equalizing effect on the income distribution. Important unobserved factors may be the use of fertilizers and market access. In contrast decreasing returns to schooling (concerns only wage workers and self-employed outside agriculture) and potential experience had an equalizing effect. Together, price changes had a strong non-equalizing effect. This can be clearly seen in Fig. 10.2, showing that the upper tail of the household income distribution knew significant income gains.

Concerning the effect of isolated changes in occupational preferences on income inequality, the two simulation variants might seem ambiguous. Taking the population of 1993 as the initial population implies a slightly more unequal income distribution.

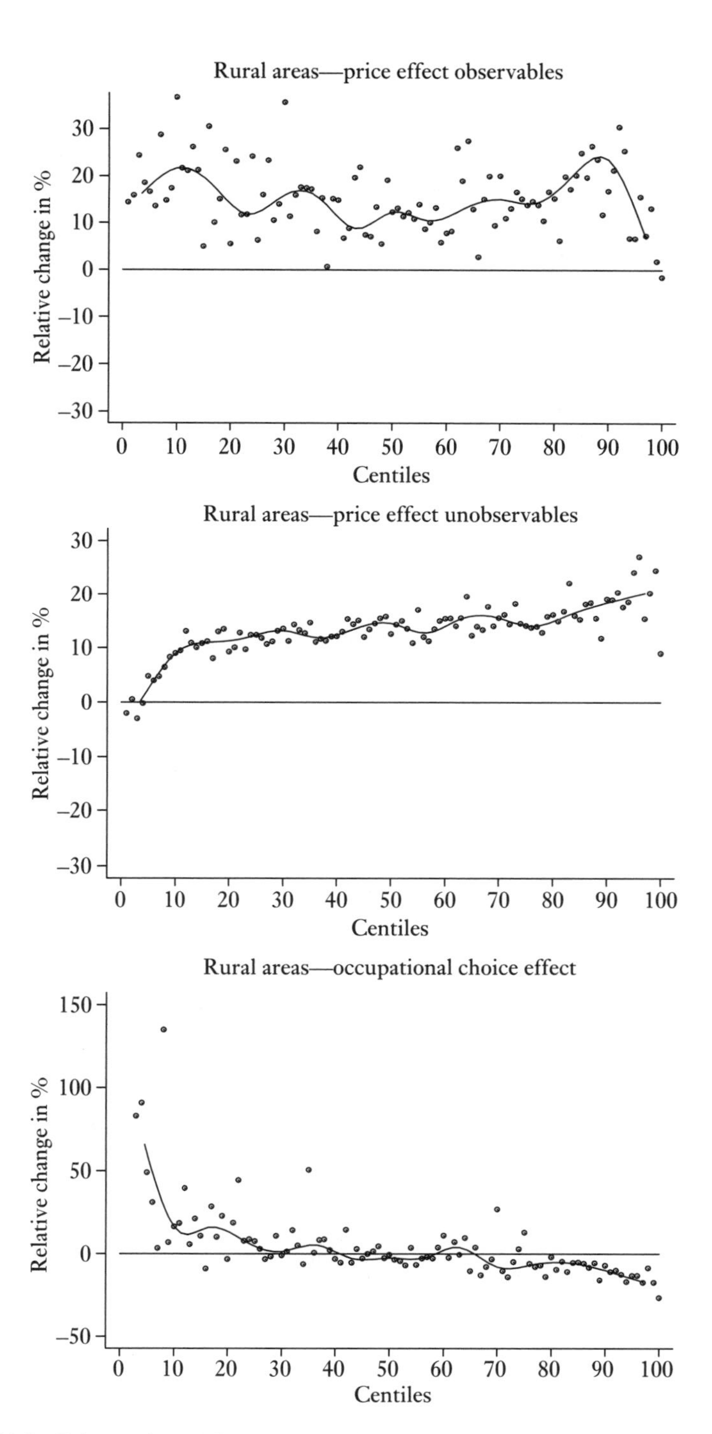

Figure 10.2. *Relative change of mean household income for each household income centile, when performing the three counterfactual simulations for rural areas using 1993 as starting point (smoothing by a cubic spline)*

In contrast, taking the population of 1998 as the initial population implies a slightly more equal income distribution (see Table 10.7). This raises, thus, the problem of 'path dependence' (see Section 3).[17] However, the distributional effects, whether equalizing or non-equalizing, are so small that we should concentrate instead on the effects of changes in returns, which seem much more important. Changes in the sociodemographic population structure, including possible changes in the distribution of land,[18] worked towards a more unequal income distribution.

In spite of the increase in inequality, poverty significantly decreased in rural areas. Decompositions not reported here show that this decline is mainly due to modifications in remuneration rates of observed and unobserved earnings determinants. Occupational choices *per se* had a poverty enhancing effect. But in connection with the price changes they allowed a large part of the rural population to rise above the poverty line.

10.4.4. *National—all Regions*

After analysing the forces behind the evolution of inequality in the three different strata 'Abidjan', 'other cities', and 'rural', it is interesting to see how these forces interacted at the national level. The decomposition of the evolution of the mean logarithmic deviation shows (Table 10.7), that within-region inequality increased, whereas between-region inequality decreased, such that overall inequality rose only slightly. The share of urban households among the poor increased from 28 to 37 per cent if the US$ 1 poverty line is retained and from 31 to 38 per cent with a US$ 2 poverty line. This result confirms the phenomenon of an urbanization of poverty in Côte d'Ivoire, which was also stated by Grimm, Guénard, and Mesplé-Somps (2002).

The simulations show that the changes in returns to observed earnings determinants had an equalizing effect on overall income distribution (−1 to −3 Gini points). Changes in returns to schooling and experience as well as regional remuneration differentials contributed mainly to this decline. Modifications in the distribution of the unobserved earnings determinants had a non-equalizing effect (+0.4 to 2.6 Gini points). Possible explanations have been given above. Changes in the employment structure had only a weak and rather ambiguous distributional effect. In contrast, changes in the sociodemographic population structure had a non-equalizing effect in all three strata and, thus, also on the national level.

[17] The problem of 'path dependence' arises frequently in this type of decomposition. For instance, in the Indonesian study of Alatas and Bourguignon (2000), this problem appears when trying to distinguish the respective contribution of changes in occupational preferences and changes in the sociodemographic population structure. The authors assume that unobserved determinants of migration decisions, which should only be taken into account by changes in the sociodemographic population structure, introduce a bias in the occupational choice functions.

[18] It is evident that the treatment of the input 'land' as an exogenous by given 'endowment' is not satisfactory. Investment in land, and decisions about its use, are without doubt crucial factors even in the short and medium term.

10.5. CONCLUSION

The purpose of this study was to analyse Ivorian income distribution between 1992/3 and 1998, to identify the various forces behind its evolution, and to connect them with the profound economic and sociodemographic changes which occurred in the 1990s, including the devaluation of the CFA Franc in 1994 and the accompanying structural adjustment policy. The microsimulations show that in Abidjan changes in the employment structure, that is, a decline in unemployment, a higher activity rate and a boost in employment in the private (formal) wage sector, in connection with changes in the returns to observed earnings determinants on the labour market led to less inequality and poverty. However, these effects were offset on the one hand by more heterogeneity in unobserved earnings determinants, probably due to the very distinct impact of macroeconomic shocks on the different economic sectors, and, on the other hand, by changes in the population structure.

In contrast, rural areas experienced strong growth in household income accompanied by a significant rise in inequality but also a remarkable decline in poverty. The major factors behind the rise in inequality were changes in the sociodemographic population structure and changes in returns on the labour market. Changes in the employment structure *per se* had only a weak and slightly ambiguous distributional effect. Furthermore, the positive evolution of the export crop sector benefited mainly the West Forest region, which also led to rising income differentials within rural Côte d'Ivoire. However, the changes in returns to the observed earnings determinants and in the distribution of unobserved earnings determinants allowed a large part of rural households to increase their incomes and to escape poverty.

Concerning the growth and inequality link, it is interesting to find that both the negative income growth in Abidjan and the positive income growth in rural Côte d'Ivoire, were connected with rising inequality. However, the devaluation of the CFA Franc, and the structural adjustment programme (including the recovery of international aid), coupled with the price boom in the coffee/cocoa sector caused a significant redistribution between rural and urban areas.[19] Within-region inequality increased and between-region inequality decreased. The share of the urban population among the poor rose. Thus the Ivorian experience between 1993 and 1998 is quite different from that of the 1980s. The 1980s were marked by a phase of structural adjustment, without devaluation of the currency, followed by a phase of destabilization. Grootaert (1995), for example, showed that during this period poverty rose in urban areas as well as in the countryside, especially among export crop farmers.

The findings in this chapter comply with most of the short and medium-term predictions of computable general equilibrium (CGE) models applied to the Ivorian case. Cogneau and Collange (1998), for instance, predict, as a result of the devaluation, a reduction in unemployment by almost two points as well as a regression of real incomes in urban areas, but an increase in real incomes in rural areas. They also

[19] ...which would have been even higher if the CAISTAB had not absorbed a part of the surplus due to the increase in coffee and cocoa prices.

find a strong redistribution between the urban and rural sector, and thus a decrease in between-inequality. Bourguignon, de Melo, and Suwa-Eisenmann (1995) underline the role of wage moderation in diminishing unemployment, and thus allowing the industry to benefit fully from the devaluation. In contrast, whereas the CGE models predicted income stability for urban (informal) self-employed workers, this study suggests that their earnings declined.

However, recent changes in the world market prices of export crops show that a large part of the Ivorian population remains vulnerable. Furthermore, the political instability evident since December 1999, and the subsequent freeze of international aid, discouraged and hindered private investment. In 2000 and 2001 Côte d'Ivoire experienced negative GDP growth (OECD 2002) suggesting that the Ivorian economy today faces a crisis comparable to that experienced at the beginning of the 1990s.

REFERENCES

Alatas, V. and Bourguignon, F. (2000). 'The Evolution of the Distribution of Income during Indonesian Fast Growth: 1980–1996'. World Bank, DELTA, Paris. Mimeo.

Banerjee, A. and Duflo, E. (2001). 'Inequality and Growth: What Can the Data Say?' Economics Department, MIT, Boston. Mimeo.

Bourguignon, F. (2000). 'Can Redistribution Accelerate Growth and Development?' Paper presented at the ABCDE/Europe, Paris 26–28 June.

—— and Berthélemy, J.-C. (1996). *Growth and Crisis in Côte d'Ivoire*. The World Bank Comparative Macroeconomic Studies. World Bank, Washington.

——, de Melo, J., and Suwa-Eisenmann, A. (1995). 'Dévaluation et compétivité en Côte d'Ivoire'. *Revue économique*, May, 739–49.

——, Ferreira, F. H. G., and Lustig, N. (1998). 'The Microeconomics of Income Distribution Dynamics in East Asia and Latin America'. The World Bank, Washington. Mimeo.

——, Fournier, M., and Gurgand, M. (1999). 'Distribution des salaires, éducation et développement: Taiwan (1979–1994)'. *Revue d'économie du développement*, 3, 3–33.

——, ——, and ——. (2001). 'Fast Development with a Stable Income Distribution: Taiwan, 1979–1994'. *Review of Income and Wealth*, 47(2), 139–64.

—— and Martinez, M. (1996). 'Decomposition of the Change in the Distribution of Primary Family Incomes: A Microsimulation Approach Applied to France, 1979–1989'. DELTA, Paris. Mimeo.

Calipel, S. and Guillaumont Jeanneney, S. (1996). 'Dévaluation, chocs externes et politique économique en Côte d'Ivoire. Analyse de leurs effets respectifs à partir d'un modèle d'équilibre général calculable'. *Revue d'économie du développement*, 3, 66–94.

Cogneau, D. and Collange, G. (1998). 'Les effets à moyen terme de la dévaluation des francs CFA: une comparaison Cameroun—Côte d'Ivoire'. *Revue d'économie du développement*, 3–4, 125–47.

—— and Mesplé-Somps, S. (2002). *La Côte d'Ivoire peut-elle devenir un pays émergent?* Karthala and OECD, Paris. Mimeo.

DIAL (2000). 'Etude de la pauvreté urbaine en Afrique de l'Ouest'. Côte d'Ivoire, Mali, Sénégal. Report prepared for the World Bank, DIAL, Paris.

Dollar, D. and Kraay, A. (2002). 'Growth is Good for the Poor'. *Journal of Economic Growth*, 7(3), 195–225, reprinted with kind permission as Chapter 2 of this volume.

Fournier, F. (1999). 'Développement et distribution des revenus. Analyse par décomposition de l'expérience taiwanaise'. PhD thesis in economics. EHESS, Paris.

Gourieroux, C., Monfort, A., Renault, E., and Trognon, A. (1987). 'Simulated residuals'. *Journal of Econometrics*, 34, 201–52.

Grimm, M. (2001). 'A Decomposition of Inequality and Poverty Changes in the Context of Macroeconomic Adjustment. A Microsimulation Study for Côte d'Ivoire'. *WIDER Discussion Papers* 2001/91. Helsinki, UNU/WIDER.

——, Guénard, C., and Mesplé-Somps, S. (2002). 'What Has Happened to the Urban Population in Côte d'Ivoire since the Eighties? An Analysis of Monetary Poverty and Deprivation over 15 Years of Household Data'. *World Development*, 30(6), 1073–95.

Grootaert, C. (1995). 'Structural Change and Poverty in Africa: A Decomposition Analysis for Côte d'Ivoire'. *Journal of Development Economics*, 47, 375–401.

—— and Kanbur, R. (1994). 'A New Regional Price Index for Côte d'Ivoire Using Data from the International Comparisons Project'. *Journal of African Economies*, 3(1), 114–41.

Heckman, J. (1979). 'Sample Selection Bias as a Specification Error'. *Econometrica*, 47(1), 153–61.

IMF (1998). 'Côte d'Ivoire: Selected Issues and Statistical Appendix'. *IMF Staff Country Reports* 98/46. IMF, Washington.

—— (2000). 'Côte d'Ivoire: Selected Issues and Statistical Appendix'. *IMF Staff Country Reports* 00/107. IMF, Washington.

Jones, C. and Ye, X. (1997). 'Issues in Comparing Poverty Trends Over Time in Côte d'Ivoire'. *Policy Research Working Papers* 1711. The World Bank, Washington.

Lee, L.-F. (1983). 'Generalized Econometric Models with Selectivity'. *Econometrica*, 51(2), 507–12.

McFadden, D. (1973). 'Conditional Logit Analysis of Qualitative Choice Behaviour'. In P. Zarembka (ed.) *Frontiers in Econometrics*. Academic Press, New York.

—— (1984). 'Econometric Analysis of Qualitative Response Models'. In Z. Griliches and M. Intriligator (eds) *Handbook of Econometrics*, vol. 2. North Holland, Amsterdam.

Mincer, J. (1974). *Schooling, Experience and Earnings*. Columbia University Press, New York.

OECD (2002). *African Economic Outlook*. OECD, Paris.

Ravallion, M. (2001). 'Growth, Inequality and Poverty: Looking Beyond Averages'. The World Bank, Washington. Mimeo.

World Bank (1997). *Poverty in Côte d'Ivoire. A Framework for Action*. Report No. 15640–IVC. The World Bank, Washington.

—— (2000). *World Development Indicators*. CD-Rom. The World Bank, Washington.

11

Educational Expansion and Income Distribution: A Microsimulation for Ceará

FRANCISCO H. G. FERREIRA AND
PHILLIPPE GEORGE LEITE

11.1. INTRODUCTION

Ever since the introduction of the human capital model by Becker and Mincer, economists have thought of earnings and income distributions as being fundamentally determined by the interaction between educational endowments and their market rates of return. In the specific case of Brazil, the seminal analysis of the country's income distribution by Langoni (1973) very much confirmed that view, and made education into the principal suspect in the search for culprits for the country's extreme levels of inequality. More recently, Barros, Henriques, and Mendonça (2000) found that about 40 per cent of overall inequality in the country's personal distribution of income could be ascribed to education.

In consequence, it has been widely assumed that if a government wishes to reduce poverty and inequality in a country like Brazil, the first policy it ought to adopt should be a general expansion of education.[1] Nevertheless, the historical evidence causes one to be less sanguine: in the United States, where 93 per cent of the population reports nine or more years of schooling, income inequality has not been falling recently. The literature speaks of a changing structure of returns to education, whereby skill-biased technical progress (and in some contexts, possibly international trade) might be increasing demand for highly educated workers, and offsetting (or more than offsetting) some of the equalizing results of expanding education. See Tinbergen (1975) for the classic reference, and Katz and Murphy (1992) for evidence on the United States.

How might a substantial increase in the stock of education affect the income distribution in Brazil? In this chapter, we simulate the impacts of a substantial expansion

The authors are grateful, without implication, to Alex Araújo, François Bourguignon, Mike Walton, and an anonymous referee for guidance and comments.

[1] Although, to be fair, a number of studies have pointed out that the convexity of the relationship between returns and years of schooling implies that increases in education might actually lead to temporary increases in earnings inequality. See, for instance, Langoni (1973), Knight and Sabot (1983), Reis and Barros (1991), and Lam (1999).

of education for the North-eastern Brazilian state of Ceará. This state was chosen precisely because of its very low educational endowments: mean years of schooling in the population (aged 15 or older) was 4.5 in 1999. In the same year, 46 per cent of that population had fewer than 4 years of schooling. At the same time, Ceará's economy was not made up exclusively of subsistence agriculture. Forty-six per cent of those employed worked in services or commerce, and another 14 per cent in industry. Under these conditions, it seemed to us that if an educational expansion would matter anywhere, it would matter here.[2]

The simulation is carried out at the household level, using the complete Ceará subsample of the IBGE's 1999 Pesquisa Nacional por Amostra de Domicílios (PNAD). In addition to simulating the effects on earnings of people having more education to

Table 11.1. *Some basic statistics, Ceará, 1999*

	Number of people	%
Population	6,979,143	
Area		
Metropolitan area	2,710,515	38.8
Urban non-metropolitan	2,024,916	29.0
Rural non-metropolitan	2,243,712	32.1
Education		
0	2,659,053	38.1
1–3	1,556,349	22.3
4	711,873	10.2
5	369,895	5.3
6	251,249	3.6
7	244,270	3.5
8	314,061	4.5
9–12	725,831	10.4
13 or more	146,562	2.1
Age		
0–15	2,554,366	36.6
16–19	621,144	8.9
20–24	593,227	8.5
25–29	509,477	7.3
30–34	488,540	7.0
35–39	439,686	6.3
40–44	355,936	5.1
45–49	300,103	4.3
50–54	258,228	3.7
55–59	237,291	3.4
60–64	202,395	2.9
65+	418,749	6.0

[2] Additional demographic and occupational information for Ceará is contained in Table 11.1.

Table 11.1. *Continued*

	Number of people	%
Gender		
Male	3,397,997	48.7
Female	3,581,146	51.3
Employed	3,213,202	93.7
Unemployed	215,424	6.3
Employed with positive income	2,376,618	—
Occupational status		
Wage sector	2,189,963	68.2
Self-employment sector	1,023,239	31.8
Sector of activity		
Agriculture	1,277,371	39.8
Industry	459,853	14.3
Services/commerce/other	1,475,978	46.0

Source: PNAD/IBGE 1999.

trade in the labour market, under different sets of assumptions about the evolution of returns, we also consider the likely effects of additional education on labour force participation, occupational choice, and fertility behaviour at the household level, and find that these matter a great deal to the overall picture.

As expected, the effects of a substantial educational expansion on poverty incidence are very substantial. The impact on inequality, however, is much more modest. Because of the changes in fertility and labour supply, we find that a very large part of the distributional changes arising from greater education depend on the behaviour of women. And location would matter marginally more, rather than less: while we do not simulate the effects on migration, our simulated poverty profile indicates that of the (fewer overall) poor people, (proportionately) more would be in rural areas.

The chapter is structured as follows. Section 2 describes the reduced-form model of the income distribution which was estimated. Section 3 describes the specific simulation exercises which were undertaken. Section 4 highlights the main results, both for earnings and for household incomes, and suggests some interpretations. Section 5 concludes.

11.2. THE MODEL

In order to understand the impacts of different policies aimed at increasing educational endowments in the population of Ceará, we estimated a simple model of household income determination. The model builds on Ferreira and Barros (1999), which was in turn heavily influenced by Bourguignon, Ferreira, and Leite (1998) and Bourguignon,

Fournier, and Gurgand (2001).[3] This model—which is estimated on 1999 PNAD data for the state of Ceará—is recursive, and consists of five blocks, as follows:

11.2.1. *Block I: Household Income Aggregation*

$$Y_h = \sum_{i \in h} w_i L_i^w + \sum_{i \in h} \pi_i L_i^{se} + Y_{0h}. \tag{11.1}$$

This equation simply adds up labour incomes for all household members, across the two sectors into which we assume the labour market is segmented: a wage sector (denoted by the superscript w) and a self-employment sector (denoted by the superscript se). L might have denoted hours, but given the nature of the information on labour supply in the PNAD data, it is actually a 0–1 participation dummy. Hence, w_i denotes the labour earnings of individual i in sector w, and π_i denotes the profits of individual i in the self-employment sector. The final term comprises all reported non-labour incomes accruing to the household.

11.2.2. *Block II: Earnings Equation*

$$\log w_i = X_i \beta^w + \varepsilon_i^w, \tag{11.2}$$

$$\log \pi_i = X_i \beta^{se} + \varepsilon_i^{se}. \tag{11.3}$$

Equations (11.2) and (11.3) are standard Mincerian earnings equations, estimated separately for the two labour market sectors. Both formal ('com carteira') and informal ('sem carteira') workers were treated as wage sector workers. Own account ('conta própria') workers were treated as self-employed. Employers were grouped alongside wage workers. Workers were assigned to the sectors of their principal occupation. The vector X, as is customary, contained characteristics both of the worker and of the job. In this case, X included years of schooling (year dummies), age, age squared, age $*$ schooling, gender dummy, race (white, non-white), spatial (metropolitan, other urban, rural), and sector (agriculture, services, industry). The estimation results for both equations are reported in Table 11.2.

11.2.3. *Block III: Occupational Choice*

$$P_i^s = \frac{e^{Z_i \gamma_s}}{e^{Z_i \gamma_s} + \sum_{j \neq s} e^{Z_i \gamma_j}}, \quad \text{where } s, j = (0, w, se). \tag{11.4}$$

This block models the choice of occupation (into wage employment, self-employment, or inactivity) by means of a discrete choice model—specifically, a multinomial logit—which estimates the probability of choice of each occupation as a function of a set of

[3] See also Juhn, Murphy, and Pierce (1993).

Table 11.2. *The estimated earnings equations for Ceará, 1999*

	Earnings				Self-employed			
	R^2	Coef	Std	p-value	R^2	Coef	Std	p-value
	0.60				0.49			
Intercept		3.74468	0.13845	0.000		4.08840	0.36039	0.000
Education								
0		−0.64439	0.12721	0.000		−2.06720	0.34671	0.000
1–3		−0.64560	0.12758	0.000		−1.80917	0.34941	0.000
4		−0.58645	0.13453	0.000		−1.60963	0.36074	0.000
5		−0.61238	0.15325	0.000		−1.69725	0.40503	0.000
6		−0.37910	0.17295	0.028		−1.22831	0.45498	0.007
7		−0.58931	0.15252	0.000		−1.15326	0.44791	0.010
8		−0.30600	0.14263	0.032		−1.03733	0.39813	0.009
9–12		−0.44252	0.12347	0.000		−0.92092	0.36618	0.012
13 or more		—	—	—		—	—	—
Age		0.09121	0.00502	0.000		0.08813	0.01042	0.000
Age^2		−0.00066	0.00005	0.000		−0.00082	0.00008	0.000
*Age * education*								
0		−0.03277	0.00318	0.000		−0.00619	0.00795	0.436
1–3		−0.03043	0.00333	0.000		−0.00924	0.00808	0.253
4		−0.02815	0.00347	0.000		−0.00888	0.00835	0.288
5		−0.02538	0.00446	0.000		−0.00127	0.01013	0.900
6		−0.03499	0.00509	0.000		−0.01196	0.01166	0.305
7		−0.02586	0.00441	0.000		−0.01572	0.01154	0.173
8		−0.03079	0.00392	0.000		−0.01169	0.00943	0.215
9–12		−0.01643	0.00328	0.000		−0.00409	0.00876	0.640
13 or more		—	—	—		—	—	—
Race—white		0.10523	0.01721	0.000		0.14007	0.03522	0.000
Gender—male		0.46123	0.01666	0.000		0.94254	0.03865	0.000
Metropolitan area		0.44765	0.03182	0.000		0.30244	0.05620	0.000
Urban non-metropolitan		0.11562	0.03477	0.001		0.10798	0.05443	0.047
Rural non-metropolitan		0.00000	0.00000	0.000		0.00000	0.00000	0.000
Sector of activity								
Agriculture		−0.17467	0.03842	0.000		−0.67360	0.05685	0.000
Industry		0.07316	0.01912	0.000		−0.10259	0.05074	0.043
Services/commerce/other		0.00000	0.00000	0.000		0.00000	0.00000	0.000

Source: PNAD/IBGE 1999.

family and personal variables, namely: age, age squared, education, age * education, gender, race, spatial location, family composition, average age in the family (excluding the individual), average education in the family (excluding the individual), dummy if head of household, dummy if the head is inactive, dummy if spouse.

Note that this occupational choice model is written in reduced form, as it does not include the wage rate (or earnings) of the individual (or of its family members) as explanatory variables. Instead, his or her productive characteristics (and the averages for the household) are included to proxy for earning potential. This approach is adopted to maintain the econometrics of joint estimation (with Block II) tractable.[4] Inactivity was used as the reference occupational category. The estimated coefficients of the model and the marginal effects they imply are reported in Table 11.3.

Table 11.3. *The estimated occupational choice multilogit model*

	Wage sector			Self-employment/ employer sector		
	Coef	*p*-value	dP_w/dx	Coef	*p*-value	dP_{se}/dx
Gender—male	1.120	0.000	0.083	1.928	0.000	0.231
Age	0.181	0.000	*	0.263	0.000	*
Age^2	−0.002	0.000	*	−0.003	0.000	*
Education						
1–3	0.794	0.000	*	0.776	0.004	*
4	0.512	0.030	*	0.954	0.001	*
5	0.840	0.011	*	0.828	0.064	*
6	−0.356	0.329	*	0.340	0.526	*
7	0.268	0.408	*	1.007	0.043	*
8	0.444	0.094	*	−0.331	0.433	*
9–12	0.985	0.000	*	0.956	0.002	*
13 or more	2.536	0.000	*	2.541	0.000	*
*Age * education*						
1–3	−0.015	0.002	*	−0.012	0.033	*
4	−0.008	0.139	*	−0.015	0.020	*
5	−0.019	0.070	*	−0.006	0.625	*
6	0.017	0.142	*	0.004	0.813	*
7	0.005	0.596	*	−0.017	0.234	*
8	−0.004	0.553	*	0.015	0.161	*
9–12	−0.008	0.134	*	−0.014	0.049	*
13 or more	−0.023	0.017	*	−0.044	0.003	*
Metropolitan area	−1.361	0.000	−0.147	−1.882	0.000	−0.199
Urban non-metropolitan	−1.055	0.000	−0.151	−1.086	0.000	−0.088
Average endowments of age	−0.004	0.123	0.000	−0.004	0.113	0.000
Education among adults in his/her household						
0	−0.517	0.005	−0.123	−0.039	0.864	0.044
1–3	−0.340	0.077	−0.108	0.244	0.298	0.077

[4] See Bourguignon, Ferreira, and Lustig (1998) for a discussion.

Table 11.3. *Continued*

	Wage sector			Self-employment/ employer sector		
	Coef	p-value	dP_w/dx	Coef	p-value	dP_{se}/dx
4	−0.444	0.036	−0.126	0.176	0.493	0.075
5	−0.252	0.287	−0.072	0.105	0.729	0.044
6	−0.422	0.099	−0.122	0.182	0.566	0.074
7	−0.338	0.168	−0.081	−0.014	0.965	0.031
8	−0.495	0.025	−0.137	0.154	0.591	0.076
9–12	−0.763	0.000	−0.192	0.047	0.843	0.084
13 or more	−1.011	0.000	−0.231	−0.174	0.626	0.069
Number of adults in the household	0.008	0.669	0.005	−0.029	0.250	−0.006
Number of children in the household	0.021	0.217	−0.002	0.073	0.000	0.011
The individual is the head in the household	0.606	0.000	0.018	1.319	0.000	0.174
The individual is not the head in the household	0.143	0.168	0.067	−0.326	0.035	−0.072
The individual is the spouse in the household	0.136	0.110	−0.017	0.510	0.000	0.077
If not the head, is the head active?	−0.101	0.420	−0.032	0.073	0.705	0.023
Intercept	−2.217	0.000	—	−6.103	0.000	—

Note:
* Marginal effects were not computed for the interaction variables.

Source: PNAD 1999/IBGE.

11.2.4. *Block IV: Demographic Choices*

$$\mathrm{ML}\ (n_c|a, e, r, s, n_a). \tag{11.5}$$

This block uses a similar model to eqn (11.4), which we now write in short form—ML stands for multinomial logit. This estimates the probability of choosing a certain number of children (0, 1, 2, 3, 4, 5+), as a function of the woman's age, education, race, spatial location, and the number of adults in the household. The variable used for the number of children in the estimation refers to the number of sons and daughters of the mother, which were alive and living in the household at the time of the survey. Five or more children was used as the reference category. The estimated coefficients of the model and the marginal effects they imply are reported in Table 11.4.

Table 11.4. *The estimated demographic choice multilogit model*

	Ceará (1999) number of children														
	0			1			2			3			4		
	Coef	*p*-value	dP_0/dx	Coef	*p*-value	dP_1/dx	Coef	*p*-value	dP_2/dx	Coef	*p*-value	dP_3/dx	Coef	*p*-value	dP_4/dx
Race—white	0.281	0.115	0.023	0.271	0.127	0.017	0.245	0.170	0.009	0.152	0.420	−0.006	−0.357	0.122	−0.032
Number of adults in the household	−0.669	0.000	−0.078	−0.408	0.000	0.001	−0.281	0.000	0.028	−0.288	0.000	0.015	−0.201	0.003	0.012
Age	0.093	0.000	0.013	0.045	0.000	−0.001	0.028	0.000	−0.004	0.021	0.000	−0.003	0.014	0.028	−0.002
Education															
1–3	0.163	0.392	−0.011	0.219	0.247	0.005	0.292	0.130	0.020	0.158	0.450	−0.005	0.239	0.309	0.002
4	0.889	0.000	0.031	0.683	0.006	−0.026	0.981	0.000	0.042	0.915	0.001	0.016	0.403	0.190	−0.022
5	1.689	0.001	0.020	1.602	0.001	−0.005	1.972	0.000	0.075	1.778	0.000	0.020	1.178	0.027	−0.025
6	1.886	0.001	0.043	1.886	0.001	0.036	2.034	0.000	0.063	1.752	0.002	0.001	0.829	0.204	−0.052
7	24.163	0.000	0.426	24.105	0.000	0.341	24.334	0.000	0.342	23.832	0.000	0.136	21.949	—	−0.045
8	2.411	0.000	0.106	2.212	0.000	0.039	2.320	0.000	0.056	1.811	0.001	−0.031	0.968	0.117	−0.062
9–12	2.834	0.000	0.164	2.490	0.000	0.051	2.453	0.000	0.036	1.830	0.000	−0.057	1.007	0.072	−0.072
13 or more	23.886	0.000	0.508	23.503	0.000	0.327	23.500	0.000	0.281	23.075	0.000	0.110	21.236	—	−0.054
Metropolitan area	0.761	0.000	0.101	0.469	0.008	0.011	0.291	0.105	−0.029	0.106	0.572	−0.040	0.040	0.852	−0.022
Urban non-metropolitan	0.301	0.146	0.076	−0.011	0.957	−0.015	−0.037	0.857	−0.018	−0.204	0.351	−0.031	−0.118	0.638	−0.009
Intercept	−1.777	0.000	—	−0.032	0.905	—	0.164	0.521	—	0.258	0.359	—	−0.066	0.841	—

Note: 5+ is the reference category.

Source: PNAD 1999/IBGE.

11.2.5. *Block V: Educational Choice*

$$\text{OPM}(e|a, r, g, s) : P(e_i|\mathbf{M}) = \Phi[c(e_i) - \mathbf{M}\delta] - \Phi[c(e_{i-1}) - \mathbf{M}\delta]. \tag{11.6}$$

This block models an individual's choice of final education attainment (in terms of years of schooling), as a function of his or her age (a), race (r), gender (g) and spatial characteristics (s), which are grouped in the matrix **M**. Unlike Blocks III and IV, educational choice follows a specific ordering by years, and is, therefore, more appropriately represented by an ordered probit model (OPM). This approach models the probability (conditional on **M**) that an individual chooses education level e_i as the difference between the cumulative normal distribution (Φ) evaluated at cut-off points estimated for levels e_i and e_{i-1}. The estimation results for eqn (11.6), containing both the estimated values for δ and the seventeen estimated cut-off points, are given in Table 11.5.

Note that we do not place any emphasis on the possible interpretations of eqns (11.2)–(11.6) as reduced forms of utility-maximizing behavioural models. Instead, we interpret them as parametric approximations to the relevant conditional

Table 11.5. *The estimated ordered probit model for education*

	Ceará (1999)		
	Coef	**Std**	***p*-value**
Age	−0.025	0.000	0.000
Gender—male	−0.206	0.001	0.000
Race—white	0.426	0.001	0.000
Metropolitan area	1.085	0.001	0.000
Urban non-metropolitan	0.597	0.001	0.000
Cut-off points			
1	−1.002	0.002	
2	−0.840	0.002	
3	−0.611	0.002	
4	−0.360	0.002	
5	0.027	0.001	
6	0.231	0.001	
7	0.385	0.001	
8	0.555	0.001	
9	0.821	0.001	
10	0.939	0.001	
11	1.059	0.001	
12	1.811	0.002	
13	1.890	0.002	
14	1.956	0.002	
15	2.011	0.002	
16	2.435	0.002	
17	3.099	0.004	

Source: PNAD 1999/IBGE.

distributions; that is to say, as descriptions of the statistical associations present in the data, under some maintained assumptions about the form of the relevant joint multivariate distributions. See Bourguignon, Ferreira, and Leite (2002) for a more detailed statistical discussion of this kind of counterfactual analysis.

11.3. SIMULATING EDUCATIONAL EXPANSIONS

Educational expansions are not, of course, all alike. One would expect to obtain very different distributional results, say, from two policies, one of which aimed to triple the number of university graduates in the state, and another which aimed to halve the number of illiterate people. How exactly the histogram of the distribution of years of schooling changes matters as much as how the overall mean evolves. In addition, and as alluded to above, the same expansion in education will have different impacts depending on how demand for skills changes in the labour market. To allow for both of these concerns to the extent possible, six simulations were undertaken, corresponding to two different 'policy choices',[5] with different aims in terms of the distribution of education; and to three sets of assumptions about returns in the labour market.

The first 'policy' was one of indiscriminate expansion. We simulate this as a rise in the mean of the distribution of years of schooling, from 4.5 (the observed level in 1999), to 7 years. Of course, one might raise the mean of a distribution in very different ways. Since we observe how educational attainment is distributed jointly with age, gender, race, and spatial location in the state, through our estimation of eqn (11.6) above, we simulate the expansion in a manner consistent with that pattern. Specifically, we implemented a computer algorithm whereby the vector of cut-off points $c(e_i)$ in the ordered probit model was translated leftwards by a constant vector $\boldsymbol{\theta} > 0$; such that $c'(e_i) = c(e_i) - \theta$. For each individual i, with observed schooling level e_i and other characteristics $\mathbf{M}_i$, the model had been estimated so that $c(e_{i-1}) < \mathbf{M}_i\delta + \zeta_i < c(e_i)$.[6] In the simulation, we simply re-compute the schooling level of individual i such that: $c'(e_{i-1}) < \mathbf{M}_i\delta + \zeta_i < c'(e_i)$. $c' < c$ for all e_i has the desired effect of increasing the frequency of educational choices at levels higher than those actually observed. The program iterated on successively higher values of $\boldsymbol{\theta}$, until the mean of the simulated distribution of years of schooling converged to seven. By shifting the distribution in this manner, without altering the estimated values for δ, we preserve the observed conditionality of educational choices on other characteristics.

The second 'policy' we investigate is a focused effort to reduce illiteracy. We change the distribution of education by moving *50 per cent* of those individuals between the ages of 15 and 40, and with 4 years of schooling or less, to 5 years (exactly), by selecting those

[5] The term 'policy' is used loosely here. The two scenarios are actually defined in terms of outcomes, rather than of policy decisions about inputs. We do not discuss which variables within the control of policy-makers might be changed—or how they might be changed—in order to persuade individuals to alter their educational choices so as to generate these desired outcomes. Such a discussion lies beyond the scope of this study.

[6] The variable ζ is an individual residual, the distribution of which is, by construction, a truncated normal $N(0, 1)$.

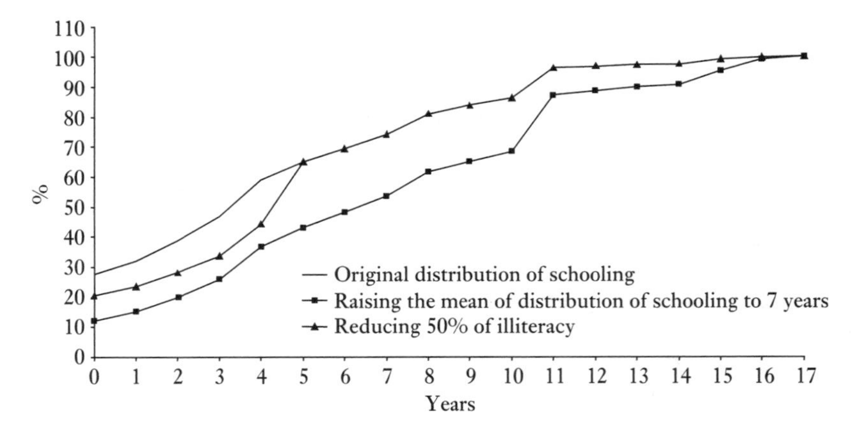

Figure 11.1. *CDFs of years of schooling in Ceará: Actual and simulated*

with the highest probability of moving from amongst all possible candidates. As before, this is implemented by translating the estimated cut-off points in the ordered probit model. This time, only the five first cut-off points are translated leftwards (by a constant value κ), such that the ensuing simulated cumulative distribution of years of schooling for 15–40-year-olds (F') is, when evaluated at $e = 4$, equal to half of its observed value: $F'(e = 4) = 0.5 * F(e = 4)$. The original cumulative distribution function of years of schooling in Ceará in 1999 (for the population aged 15 or older), as well as the two simulated distributions, are shown in Fig. 11.1.

The results of each of these two educational 'policies' are simulated under three alternative returns scenarios, namely

1. β_{99}: Keep all β values as estimated for the 1999 regressions.
2. β_{convex}: with respect to category 13+ (omitted), lower β for 0–4 years of schooling by 20 per cent; for 5–8 by 15 per cent; and for 9–12 by 10 per cent. To ensure the growth neutrality of these changes, the constant term α was adjusted to maintain mean earnings (for that category of worker and for the original observed **X** matrix) constant at its observed 1999 level.
3. β_{concave}: with respect to category 13+ (omitted), raise β for 0–4 years of schooling by 30 per cent, for 5–8 by 20 per cent and 9–12 by 10 per cent. The constant term was adjusted in a manner analogous to that in point (2) above.

So the six simulations are given by the following schematic 2×3 matrix:

Simulation	β (1999)	β_{concave}	β_{convex}
Policy One			
Policy Two			

11.4. RESULTS

The main simulation results are presented in Tables 11.6 and 11.7. Table 11.6 reports mean earnings and five different inequality measures, for each of the six simulations, for the distribution of labour earnings among earners with positive labour incomes.[7] Table 11.7 presents the corresponding results for the distribution of household incomes by individuals and includes, in addition to the same inequality measures as Table 11.6, three poverty measures—$P(\alpha)$, for $\alpha = 0, 1$, and 2.[8] The poverty line was set at R$ 68, which is the line officially suggested by the Planning Institute of the State Government of Ceará, (IPLANCE). In each of the above tables, the measures presented in the row 'Ceará' *of the panel* β_{99} are those for the actual observed distribution in 1999. The measures presented in the row 'Ceará' in the other two panels arise from imposing the simulated structure of returns (more concave or more convex) on the existing 1999 population—with its actual distributions of education and other characteristics.

For each of the six combinations of educational outcomes and returns, poverty, and inequality statistics are presented for three different simulations, denoted by sets of Greek letters. The first of these, denoted by α, β, and σ^2, consists of running the required simulation—of the first or of the second 'policy'—and feeding the simulated distribution of education through the earnings models (2) and (3), either unadjusted (β_{99}), or adjusted (β_{convex} or β_{concave}). Original residuals are used, and this generates a counterfactual (i.e. simulated) distribution of earnings, under the required assumption about returns, which corresponds to the new distribution of education. This educational distribution was, in turn, obtained from simulating an increase in schooling according to the ordered probit model in (6). In this simulation, each individual preserves his or her initial (1999) occupation and family composition. The only possible change is the amount of education they sell in the labour market and, for the convex and concave scenarios, the rate at which they do so. We call the result of this simulation the 'pure market' effect.

We know, however, that labour force participation and occupational choice are also heavily dependent on education. It is natural to suppose that changes in schooling endowments such as the ones being simulated here for Ceará are likely to have some impact on who is working, and on where they are working. This is investigated by allowing the simulated distributions of education to feed through the occupational choice model (4), the parameters of which are denoted by γ's. The second row in each panel, thus, summarizes the inequality and poverty statistics pertaining to the distributions which are simulated when, in addition to the educational endowment being transacted and to the structure of returns, we allow for occupational choices and

[7] The inequality measures used were the Gini coefficient, the Generalized Entropy indices for parameter values 0, 1, and 2; and the variance of logarithms. Simulated populations are also included, to show the simulated changes in participation.

[8] These are the poverty measures defined in Foster, Greer, and Thorbecke (1984). Simulated populations included in Table 11.7 reflect counterfactual changes in fertility behaviour.

Table 11.6. *Counterfactual distributions of individual earnings: Descriptive statistics*

	Mean earnings	Inequality					Population
		Gini	E(0)	E(1)	E(2)	V(log)	
β_{99}							
Ceará	286.7	0.590	0.650	0.784	2.223	1.116	2,275,534
First policy—raising mean schooling to 7 years							
$\alpha, \beta, e, \sigma^2$	401.6	0.616	0.722	0.796	1.923	1.306	2,275,534
$\gamma, \alpha, \beta, e, \sigma^2$	382.5	0.592	0.650	0.719	1.663	1.169	2,425,989
$\psi, \gamma, \alpha, \beta, e, \sigma^2$	379.9	0.588	0.642	0.710	1.646	1.159	2,422,323
Second policy—reducing illiteracy by 50%							
$\alpha, \beta, e, \sigma^2$	292.8	0.584	0.634	0.763	2.132	1.093	2,275,534
$\gamma, \alpha, \beta, e, \sigma^2$	270.4	0.552	0.555	0.652	1.659	0.975	2,297,828
$\psi, \gamma, \alpha, \beta, e, \sigma^2$	270.8	0.551	0.554	0.653	1.685	0.971	2,295,578
$\beta_{concave}$							
Ceará	286.7	0.556	0.569	0.683	1.821	0.998	2,275,534
First policy—raising mean schooling to 7 years							
$\alpha, \beta, e, \sigma^2$	374.8	0.584	0.638	0.709	1.623	1.164	2,275,534
$\gamma, \alpha, \beta, e, \sigma^2$	356.6	0.556	0.563	0.620	1.291	1.025	2,425,989
$\psi, \gamma, \alpha, \beta, e, \sigma^2$	358.1	0.557	0.564	0.621	1.292	1.024	2,421,087
Second policy—reducing illiteracy by 50%							
$\alpha, \beta, e, \sigma^2$	290.3	0.553	0.562	0.673	1.778	0.989	2,275,534
$\gamma, \alpha, \beta, e, \sigma^2$	266.9	0.515	0.478	0.547	1.214	0.865	2,297,828
$\psi, \gamma, \alpha, \beta, e, \sigma^2$	268.5	0.518	0.483	0.555	1.238	0.867	2,295,065
β_{convex}							
Ceará	286.7	0.616	0.717	0.864	2.593	1.218	2,275,534
First policy—raising mean schooling to 7 years							
$\alpha, \beta, e, \sigma^2$	419.9	0.639	0.791	0.866	2.207	1.428	2,275,534
$\gamma, \alpha, \beta, e, \sigma^2$	399.7	0.616	0.719	0.794	1.987	1.290	2,425,989
$\psi, \gamma, \alpha, \beta, e, \sigma^2$	396.6	0.613	0.710	0.783	1.963	1.279	2,422,323
Second policy—reducing illiteracy by 50%							
$\alpha, \beta, e, \sigma^2$	293.6	0.607	0.693	0.836	2.470	1.183	2,275,534
$\gamma, \alpha, \beta, e, \sigma^2$	271.5	0.578	0.617	0.734	2.062	1.068	2,297,828
$\psi, \gamma, \alpha, \beta, e, \sigma^2$	271.9	0.578	0.616	0.736	2.107	1.064	2,295,578

Source: PNAD/IBGE 1999.

Table 11.7. *Counterfactual distributions of household per capita incomes: Poverty and inequality*

	Mean per capita income	Inequality					Population	Poverty, poverty line equal R$ 68,00		
		Gini	E(0)	E(1)	E(2)	*V*(log)		P(0)	P(1)	P(2)
β_{99}										
Ceará	135.3	0.613	0.733	0.846	2.421	1.378	6,978,331	51.8	24.4	15.3
First policy—raising mean schooling to 7 years										
$\alpha, \beta, e, \sigma^2$	172.4	0.630	0.786	0.846	2.093	1.534	6,978,331	45.1	21.1	13.2
$\gamma, \alpha, \beta, e, \sigma^2$	174.6	0.618	0.751	0.794	1.856	1.490	6,978,331	43.4	19.9	12.3
$\psi, \gamma, \alpha, \beta, e, \sigma^2$	181.6	0.610	0.728	0.765	1.739	1.461	6,669,583	40.9	18.3	11.1
Second policy—reducing illiteracy by 50%										
$\alpha, \beta, e, \sigma^2$	137.2	0.607	0.716	0.827	2.349	1.353	6,978,331	50.1	23.4	14.5
$\gamma, \alpha, \beta, e, \sigma^2$	130.9	0.587	0.665	0.760	2.059	1.283	6,978,331	50.1	22.9	14.0
$\psi, \gamma, \alpha, \beta, e, \sigma^2$	133.0	0.582	0.651	0.747	2.010	1.252	6,868,846	48.9	21.8	13.2
$\beta_{concave}$										
Ceará	135.3	0.587	0.664	0.766	2.106	1.275	6,978,330	48.6	21.8	13.3
First policy—raising mean schooling to 7 years										
$\alpha, \beta, e, \sigma^2$	163.7	0.606	0.716	0.776	1.866	1.414	6,978,330	43.4	19.7	12.0
$\gamma, \alpha, \beta, e, \sigma^2$	165.7	0.592	0.680	0.720	1.618	1.374	6,978,330	41.4	18.5	11.1
$\psi, \gamma, \alpha, \beta, e, \sigma^2$	173.3	0.585	0.657	0.697	1.522	1.321	6,682,688	38.9	16.7	9.9
Second policy—reducing illiteracy by 50%										
$\alpha, \beta, e, \sigma^2$	136.4	0.583	0.656	0.756	2.069	1.263	6,978,330	47.4	21.3	12.9
$\gamma, \alpha, \beta, e, \sigma^2$	129.7	0.561	0.601	0.681	1.750	1.186	6,978,330	47.1	20.7	12.4
$\psi, \gamma, \alpha, \beta, e, \sigma^2$	132.4	0.558	0.592	0.678	1.752	1.155	6,860,223	45.9	19.8	11.7
β_{convex}										
Ceará	135.3	0.631	0.785	0.905	2.683	1.459	6,978,331	54.2	26.3	16.8
First policy—raising mean schooling to 7 years										
$\alpha, \beta, e, \sigma^2$	178.3	0.648	0.841	0.901	2.300	1.629	6,978,331	46.1	22.3	14.1
$\gamma, \alpha, \beta, e, \sigma^2$	180.6	0.636	0.807	0.851	2.069	1.587	6,978,331	44.5	21.1	13.3
$\psi, \gamma, \alpha, \beta, e, \sigma^2$	187.6	0.628	0.782	0.820	1.936	1.556	6,669,583	42.0	19.5	12.0
Second policy—reducing illiteracy by 50%										
$\alpha, \beta, e, \sigma^2$	137.5	0.624	0.763	0.882	2.593	1.424	6,978,331	52.3	25.0	15.8
$\gamma, \alpha, \beta, e, \sigma^2$	131.2	0.606	0.713	0.818	2.314	1.357	6,978,331	52.3	24.6	15.4
$\psi, \gamma, \alpha, \beta, e, \sigma^2$	133.4	0.601	0.698	0.806	2.262	1.323	6,868,846	51.1	23.5	14.5

Source: PNAD/IBGE 1999.

labour force participation to change.[9] These counterfactual distributions, denoted by 'γ, α, β, and σ^2', incorporate two effects: the 'pure market' effect and the 'occupational' effect.

Finally, the third row allows for family size—driven by the number of children 'demanded' by each family—to change also. This is achieved by allowing the simulated distributions of education to feed through the demographic choice model (5), the parameters of which are denoted by ψ's. This has two second-round effects on household incomes: first, as the number of children in a family changes, the income per capita denominator changes, and it is recalculated accordingly. Second, the number of children in the household is, as it must be, an independent variable in the occupational choice multilogit model (4). In this row of simulations results the γ's and ψ's interact, since changes in occupational choice reflect not only chances in the educational levels of the individuals (and of others in their families) but also changes in the number of under-16's living in the household. The resulting counterfactual distributions, denoted by '$\psi, \gamma, \alpha, \beta$, and σ^2', incorporate three effects: 'pure market', 'occupational', and 'demographic'.

While the aggregated information presented in Tables 11.6 and 11.7 tell the basic story, additional insights can be gained from looking at the entire distribution. Figures 11.2–11.13 plot the differences in the logarithms of mean incomes for each percentile, between the simulated distribution and the real 1999 distribution: Figures 11.2–11.7 refer to the earnings distribution, while Figs 11.8–11.13 correspond to the distributions of household per capita income. Each distribution is ranked by its own distributed variable. The lines for α, β, and σ^2 correspond to the 'pure market' effect: simulations where each earner had his or her level of education changed to a level drawn for it in the new distribution of education, as described above. To simulate the concave and convex cases, the β's were changed as appropriate.

As indicated above, in these simulations, people are selling more education on the labour market, but are still working in the same occupation as before, and have exactly the same family composition. The lines that include a γ simulate the additional effect of those changes in years of schooling on people's labour force participation and/or occupational choices. Those that include a ψ as well, also incorporate the effect of those extra years of schooling on the number of children each family is likely to have, and any subsequent additional impact which that may have on occupational choice.

11.4.1. *Effects on Earnings*

The overall simulated effect of Policy One—which consisted of raising mean years of schooling in Ceará from 4.5 to 7, in a manner which was consistent with individual propensities to acquire education—turns out to be both (i) income-increasing

[9] In order to simulate the earnings of new entrants into the labour force, each needs to be allocated to a sector of activity (agriculture, industry or services). We did not model those choices explicitly, and thus simply allocate each entrant randomly, using the observed 1999 sector frequencies as probabilities.

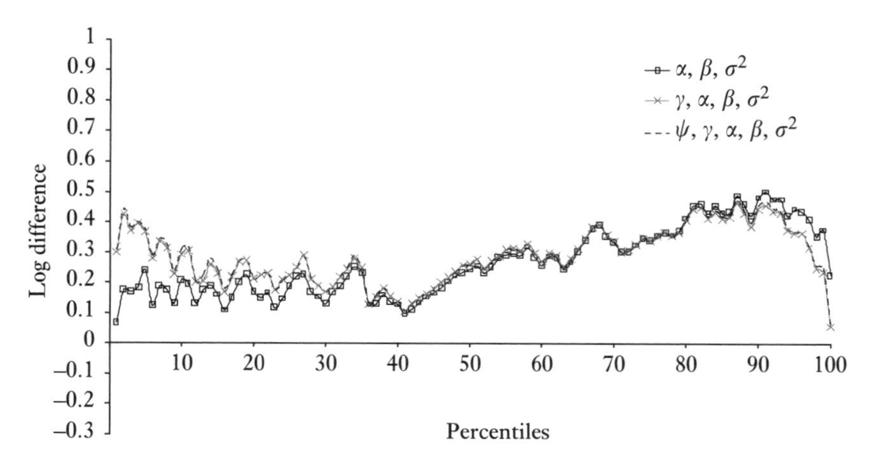

Figure 11.2. *Earnings: Raising mean schooling to 7 years,* β_{99}

and (ii) generally equalizing. This overall effect is, however, rather sensitive to the assumptions about the behaviour of the returns structure. It also reflects the aggregation of pure market effects, occupational effects and demographic effects, which are heterogeneous and interesting in their own rights.

The rise in mean earnings can be seen from a comparison of the simulated means under Policy One, with the 'Ceará' mean, in Table 11.6. In fact, mean incomes are higher than the actual 1999 mean (R$ 286.70) for all simulations, in all three returns scenarios. They are highest, in fact, for the pure market effect. As labour market participation and occupational choice effects are incorporated, mean earnings fall under all three returns scenarios. This is largely due to the fact that most entrants have earnings below the mean, thus contributing to its reduction. Despite these similarities in aggregate terms, the differences in the distribution of income gains across the returns scenarios are quite marked. This is particularly evident from inspection of Figs 11.2–11.4: whereas the educational expansion would result in large gains (between 30 and 50 per cent) for the very poor if returns to the low skilled rose (see Fig. 11.3), the increases would stay in the 0–30 per cent range if returns became more convex (Fig. 11.4).

Naturally, the effects on inequality also vary with respect to returns. When compared to the observed earnings Gini (of 0.590) in 1999, the pure market effects of an educational expansion would lower inequality if returns became flatter (Fig. 11.3), but raise it in the other two cases. Another way of seeing this is that the pure market effect when the effect of changes in the structure of returns is netted out[10]—is generally

[10] To see this, compare inequality measures in each α, β, σ^2 row with those in 'Ceará' row in the same panel.

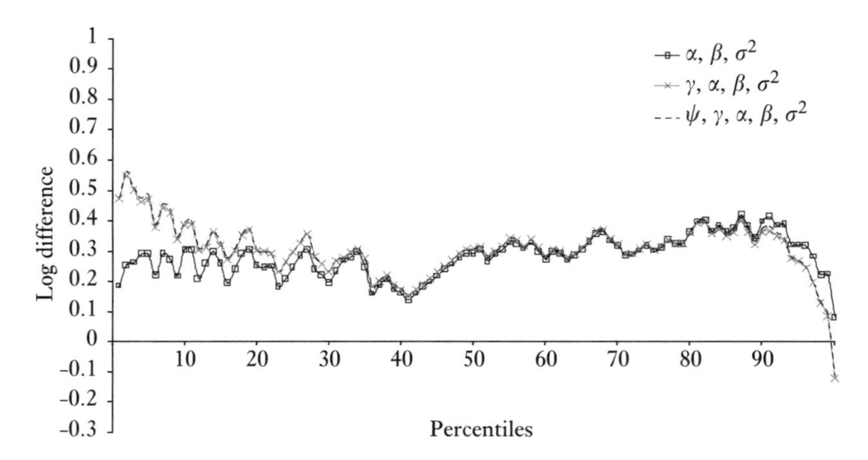

Figure 11.3. *Earnings: Raising mean schooling to 7 years, β_{concave}*

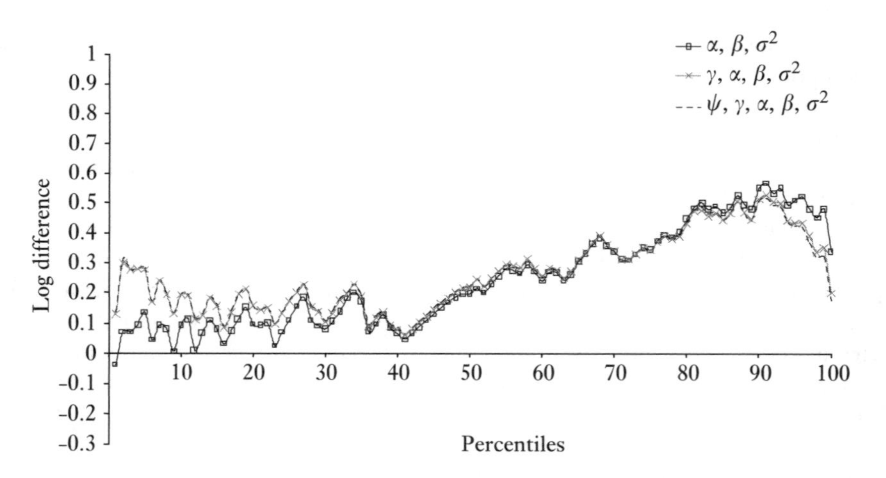

Figure 11.4. *Earnings: Raising mean schooling to 7 years, β_{convex}*

inequality-increasing. This is the case for the Gini, E(0), E(1), and the variance of logarithms in all cases.[11] This confirms the results found by Langoni (1973), Knight and Sabot (1983), and Reis and Barros (1991), that educational expansions in the presence of convex returns may lead to increases, rather than declines, in inequality.

[11] E(2), which is driven largely by the upper tail of the distribution, goes the other way.

This picture changes, however, when we allow for the impact of the educational expansion on participation and demographic behaviour. The Gini for the counterfactual earnings distributions that incorporate the occupational choice (γ), and demographic effects (ψ) of greater education is almost three points below that for the pure market effect in all three returns scenarios. In Figs 11.2–11.4 it can be clearly seen that the occupational and demographic effects make a difference at the tails of the distribution, raising incomes for the poor and lowering them somewhat for the rich. As a result of the participation effects arising from more education and from fewer children, the labour force expanded by approximately 150,000 people each time the educational effect on occupational choice was taken into account. It turns out that the composition of the net entrants into the labour force is such that it lowers overall earnings inequality.

Note that the demographic effects are muted for earnings distributions, as shown in Figs 11.2–11.7. The line for the all-effects simulation lies very close to the line for joint occupation and pure market effect simulation. This is because the only effect of reductions in fertility rates on earnings is through induced changes in participation and occupational choice. For households, the demographic effect also includes changes in the denominator of household income per capita and, as Figs 11.8–11.13 show, this makes them considerably larger.

Figures 11.14 and 11.15, which present the frequency of entrants (net of exits) per percentile of the distribution of household incomes, shows that the progressiveness of higher participation draws predominantly on the self-employment sector. The profile of net entrance into the wage sector is somewhat more regressive. Many of those entering into the higher ranges of the wage sector do, however, come themselves from self-employment.[12] Higher levels of education tend, in this sense, to upgrade

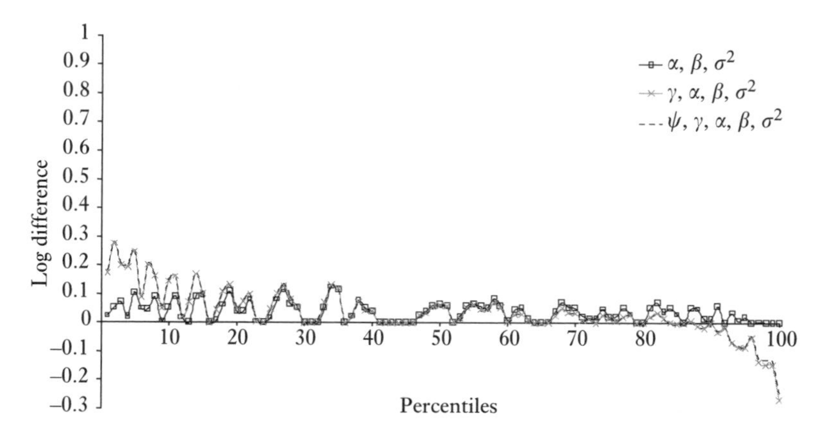

Figure 11.5. *Earnings: Reducing illiteracy by 50%, β_{99}*

[12] Recall that the simulations which include the γ parameters change the pattern of occupational structure across these two sectors, as well as changes in participation status.

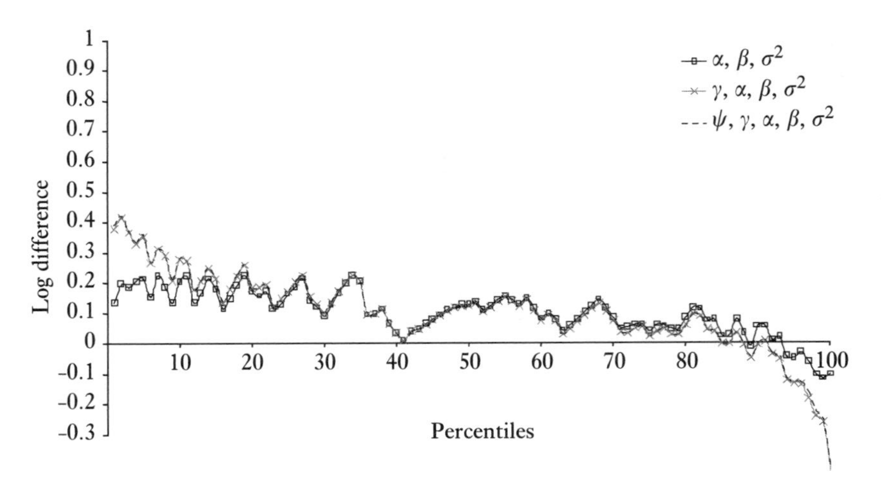

Figure 11.6. *Earnings: Reducing illiteracy by 50%, β_{concave}*

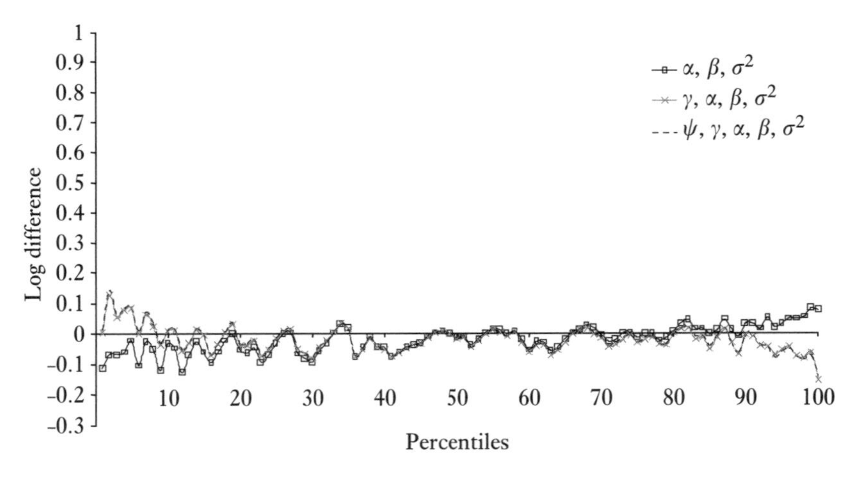

Figure 11.7. *Earnings: Reducing illiteracy by 50%, β_{convex}*

the occupational profile, as non-participants enter (largely) into self-employment, and many previously in that sector move into wage jobs.

The effects of Policy Two—which consisted of a targeted effort at reducing illiteracy, by halving the proportion of persons with 4 years of schooling or less—were rather different. The rows for simulations under Policy Two in Table 11.6 reveal much smaller increases in mean earnings for the pure market effect, and actual declines for the complete simulation. Inequality reductions, however, were considerably larger

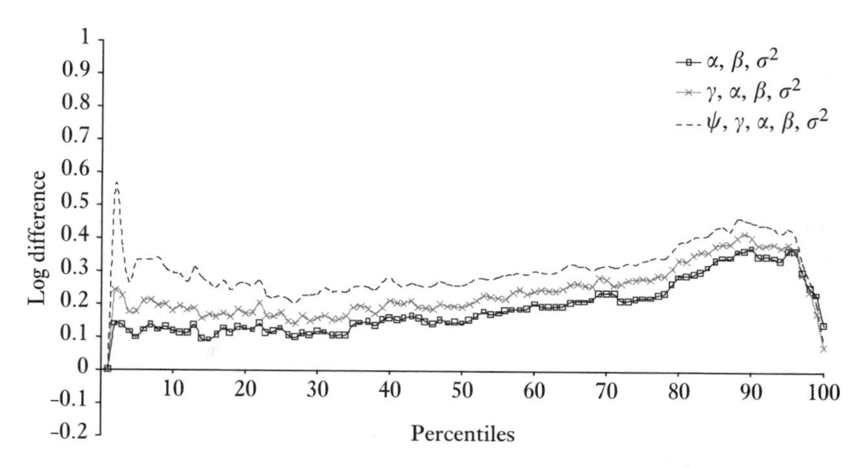

Figure 11.8. *Households: Raising mean schooling to 7 years,* β_{99}

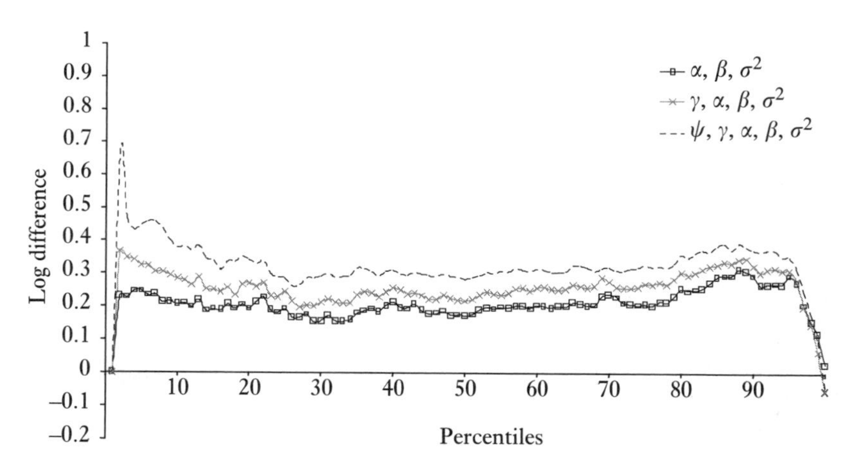

Figure 11.9. *Households: Raising mean schooling to 7 years,* β_{concave}

for Policy Two than for Policy One. This is particularly true if returns stay constant or become more concave: if the β vector remained as in 1999, the overall effect of Policy Two on the Gini would be a fall of between three and four points. If the returns became more concave, the Gini would fall seven points, to approximately 0.52. This is a fairly serious change, and leads to an inequality level which is not high by Brazilian standards.

Figures 11.6 and 11.7 confirm that, for this particular policy, the configuration of returns is crucial: if returns to the unskilled rise, then the impact of having a little more

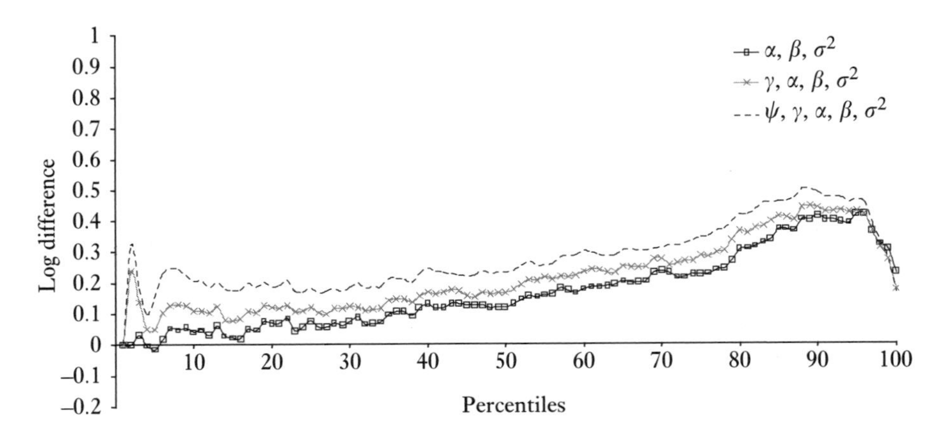

Figure 11.10. *Households: Raising mean schooling to 7 years,* β_{convex}

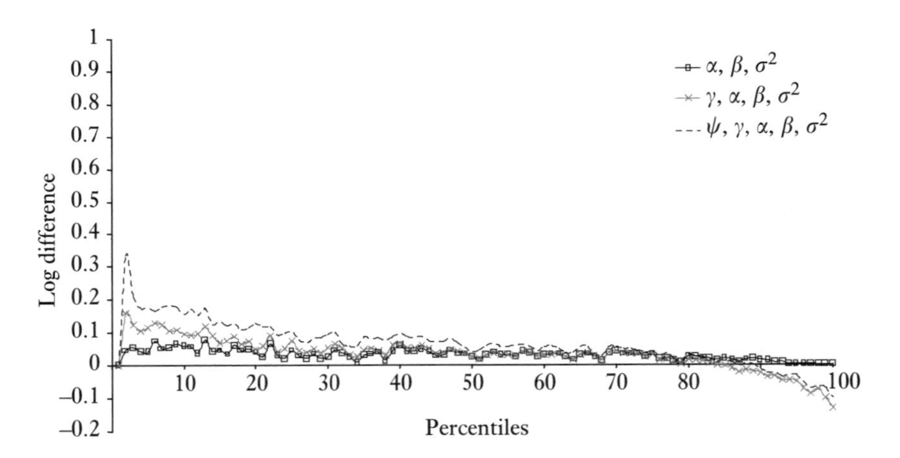

Figure 11.11. *Households: Reducing illiteracy by 50%,* β_{99}

education on the welfare of those who are at the bottom of the distribution will be positive and substantial. Most people in the bottom quintile of the distribution would have between 10 and 40 per cent higher earnings. If, on the other hand, Policy Two were combined with a decline in the returns to lower levels of schooling, as in Fig. 11.7, then educational gains would just about exactly offset the impoverishing effect of the change in returns.

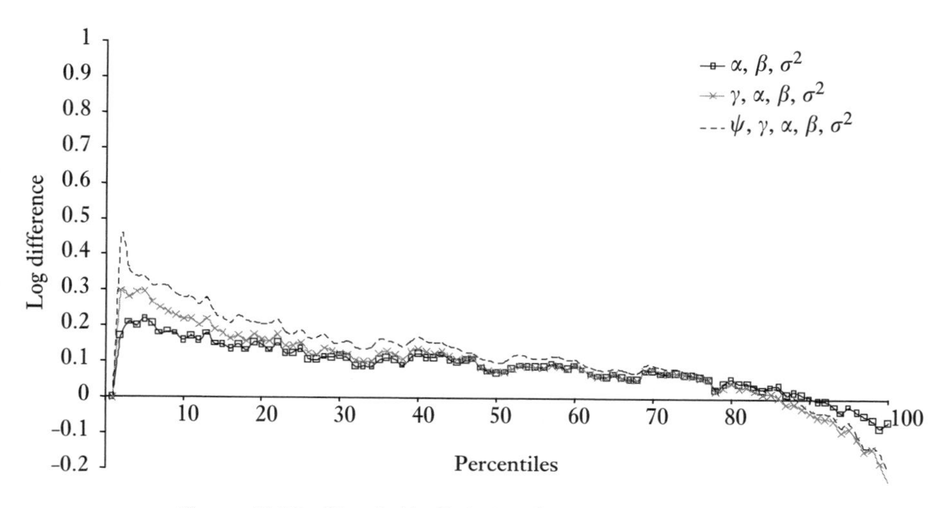

Figure 11.12. *Households: Reducing illiteracy by 50%,* β_{concave}

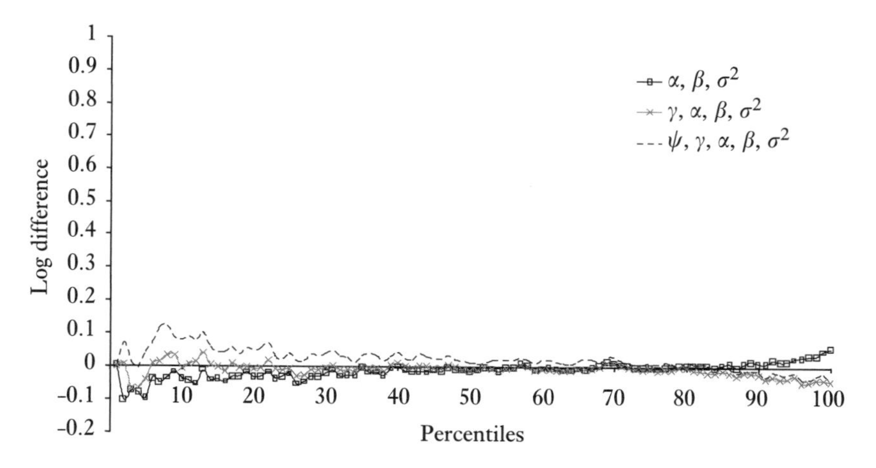

Figure 11.13. *Households: Reducing illiteracy by 50%,* β_{convex}

11.4.2. *Effects on Household Incomes*

When compared to the changes in earnings distributions, the simulations for household income distributions reveal both similarities and differences. Qualitatively, the market, occupational, and demographic effects of both 'policies' on the income distributions are rather similar to those observed for earnings. Policy One—raising the mean education level to 7 years—increases mean incomes for all return scenarios, and does so by more than Policy Two in all cases (see Table 11.7). Policy Two only raises mean income in

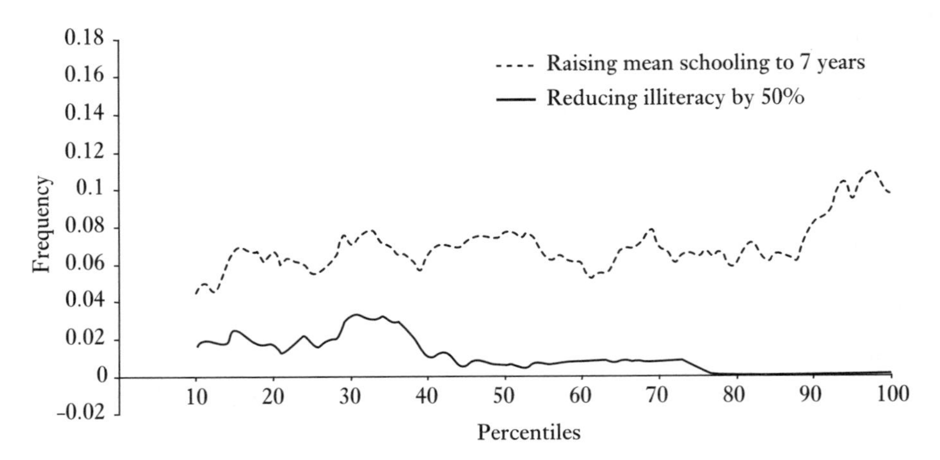

Figure 11.14. *Net entrance into the wage sector per percentile*

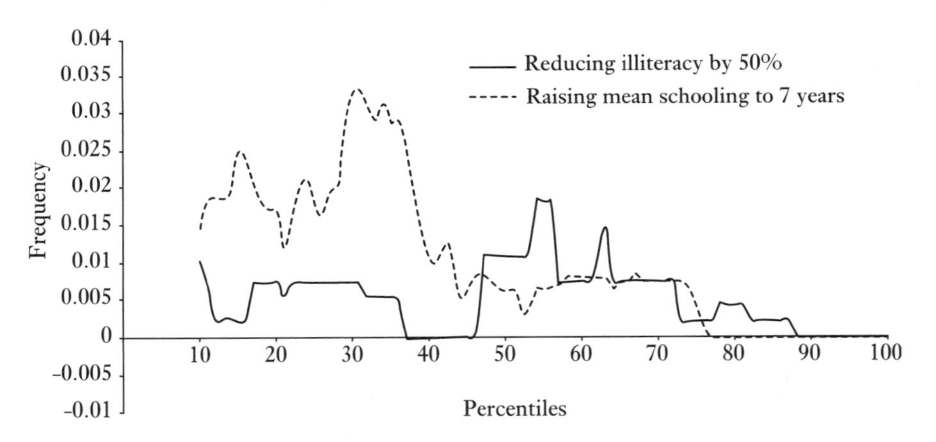

Figure 11.15. *Net entrance into self-employment per percentile*

the pure market effect simulation, and leaves it basically unchanged after all effects are taken into account. In terms of inequality reduction, the rank of the two 'policies' is reversed—as in the case of the earnings distributions. Policy Two leads to lower inequality than Policy One in every simulation, according to most (though not all) inequality measures.

Perhaps the most marked difference between the per capita income results and those for earnings are that occupational choice and demographic effects seem to matter more for the former than for the latter. One explanation is that the demographic effect is considered fully in the household simulations: the reduction in the denominator of household per capita incomes, as a result of lower fertility, is explicitly taken into account here. Another part of the explanation comes from the fact that the individuals who are considered alone in the earnings distribution are not organized into families in a random manner. Hence, many of the entrants into the labour force turn out to reside in poor families and their new labour supply becomes highly equalizing in the distribution of household incomes. It is also chiefly among the poor that the effect of more schooling on fertility—to reduce the number of children in the household, thus raising per capita incomes—is particularly pronounced.

It is, thus, that Figs 11.8–11.10 have the curves with γ indicating larger income increases for the poor than the pure market effect simulation, and those with both γ and ψ, higher still. The sharp downward turn in these log-income difference curves for the top 5 per cent of the population also contribute to an equalizing effect. This is confirmed by inspecting the inequality measures in Table 11.7: from an observed 1999 level of 0.613, the Gini could fall by almost three points under Policy One (and around 5.5 points under Policy Two) if returns became more concave.

Assumptions about the return structure continue to matter a great deal. If returns convexified—which we saw was a powerful unequalizing force on the distribution of earnings—the Gini would rise by 1.5 points under Policy One, once all effects have been taken into account. If returns were identical to those of 1999, the Gini would stay roughly constant. The different returns scenarios are clearly still very important, generating only slightly less variation in outcomes in terms of household income inequality than was the case for earnings. This is because households pool resources, and provide insurance to individual members: even if assortative mating is very pronounced in Brazil[13] (and we suspect, in Ceará), education levels still differ across individuals in the same household, so that changes in returns hurt or benefit the pooled family less than it might hurt or benefit each member.

The combination of rising mean incomes and falling inequality should spell good news for poverty reduction, as a result of the educational expansion simulated in Policy One. Indeed, with respect to the state's poverty line of R$ 68 per capita per month, we observe declines in poverty headcount (or incidence) as large as 12.9 percentage points (or about a quarter), when returns become more concave. Poverty simulation results also depend on the structure of returns, but somewhat less than inequality. If returns became more convex, Policy One would still lower $P(0)$ by 9.8 percentage points, from the 1999 level of 51.8 to 42 per cent. Each of these results takes into account all simulated effects of the greater endowment of education and, in particular, its labour supply, occupational, and demographic impacts. Their importance is once again highlighted by the fact that, in their absence, the poverty reduction effect of the educational expansion would be considerably smaller. Specifically, with constant returns, the fall excluding these effects would be of approximately 7 percentage points, rather than 11.

[13] The simple correlation coefficient between the years of schooling reported by household heads and their spouses in the 1999 PNAD (for all of Brazil) is 0.73, which compares with 0.63 in the United States, for instance.

Policy Two represents, as we have seen in the earnings simulation, a different choice along the mean-inequality trade-off. Targeted at the lower tail of the education distribution, this policy leads to smaller (or no) increases in mean income, for each stage of the simulation, and for each assumption about returns. On the other hand, it also leads to greater reductions in inequality than Policy One for most (although not all) inequality measures, in all simulations in Table 11.7. In terms of the poverty results presented on that same table, the gains in inequality reduction from choosing Policy Two over Policy One fail to compensate for the smaller increases in absolute incomes that would ensue. In fact, poverty would be higher under Policy Two than under Policy One, for all return scenarios, all simulation stages and, somewhat surprisingly, for all three poverty indices considered.

More important than the absolute number of poor people is an understanding of who they are and where they live. Table 11.8 shows the effects of the 'policies' considered above on the composition of the poor, rather than just on their level. The profile is constructed by location, gender of the household head and schooling of the household head. The first column gives the composition of the total (actual) population in 1999, broken down by those categories. The next two columns give poverty incidence in the subgroup ($P(0)$), and the share of the poor population which belongs to the subgroup (composition). The next six columns present counterfactual analogues to columns 2 and 3 for Policy One, under each alternative returns scenario. The last 6 columns do the same for Policy Two.

The poverty profile is much more robust across 'policies' and returns scenarios than absolute poverty levels were. Composition of the poor by gender is basically unchanged across all of the simulations. In contrast, some differences can be discerned across policies, for the educational and geographical dimensions of the profile. But these are not large. The profile by years of schooling hardly changes at all between the observed 1999 profile and that simulated for Policy Two. Under Policy One, however, it becomes slightly steeper, with a greater proportion of the poor having no education, and a smaller proportion among the most educated. One should always remember, of course, that this refers only to the composition of the poor. The $P(0)$ columns serve to remind us that under these simulated policies, the overall numbers of the poor would be smaller.

Finally, although neither 'policy' was designed in a spatially sensitive manner, Policy One appears to marginally reinforce the prevalence of rural poverty. This is largely because living in rural areas is currently associated with having lower educational attainment and, as a result, the ordered probit that assigns the distribution of extra years of schooling among individuals, allocates them more often to urban residents, ceteris paribus. Hence, whereas 45 per cent of Ceará's poor today live in rural areas, this might rise to just over fifty per cent if special care is not taken to encourage faster enrolment and good school supply in rural areas.[14]

[14] Notice that the more targeted Policy Two does not seem to increase the rural composition of poverty in the same way. This is presumably because, being targeted to the least educated, it is effectively (if unintentionally) targeted to rural areas.

Table 11.8. *Actual and simulated poverty profiles for Ceará*

	Frequency	Observed values		Raising mean schooling to 7 years						Reducing illiteracy by 50%					
				β_{99}		β_{convex}		$\beta_{concave}$		β_{99}		β_{convex}		$\beta_{concave}$	
		$P(0)$	Composition	$P(0)$	Composition	$P(0)$	Composition	$P(0)$	Composition	$P(0)$	Composition	$P(0)$	Composition	$P(0)$	Composition
Ceará		51.79		40.88		42.01		38.85		48.89		51.12		45.90	
Metropolitan	38.80	35.61	26.68	21.13	20.06	21.71	20.05	21.32	21.29	32.57	25.85	34.15	25.92	31.32	26.48
Urban	29.00	49.86	27.92	39.60	28.10	41.16	28.41	36.94	27.57	46.23	27.42	48.52	27.53	42.84	27.07
Rural	32.10	73.08	45.30	65.90	51.75	67.31	51.43	62.12	51.32	71.30	46.81	74.26	46.63	66.55	46.55
Men	48.70	52.84	49.69	42.09	50.15	43.18	50.05	39.97	50.10	50.02	49.82	52.32	49.85	46.79	49.65
Women	51.30	50.80	50.31	39.72	49.85	40.90	49.95	37.80	49.91	47.82	50.18	49.97	50.15	45.05	50.35
Years of schooling															
0	38.10	63.54	46.74	53.53	49.89	55.44	50.28	50.54	49.56	60.32	47.01	63.13	47.05	56.11	46.58
1	6.50	68.23	8.56	57.37	9.12	58.97	9.12	55.34	9.26	63.68	8.47	66.78	8.49	61.29	8.68
2	8.00	62.86	9.71	51.71	10.12	53.60	10.21	49.16	10.12	59.02	9.66	61.26	9.59	54.62	9.52
3	7.80	58.72	8.84	47.34	9.03	48.12	8.93	44.74	8.98	54.68	8.72	57.66	8.80	51.33	8.72
4	10.20	50.11	9.87	38.31	9.56	38.66	9.39	37.10	9.74	46.86	9.78	49.33	9.84	44.57	9.90
5	5.30	49.20	5.03	33.87	4.39	34.46	4.35	32.54	4.44	47.37	5.14	50.35	5.22	44.59	5.15
6	3.60	45.64	3.17	26.86	2.37	27.05	2.32	26.28	2.44	43.94	3.24	45.35	3.19	41.96	3.29
7	3.50	39.70	2.68	23.61	2.02	23.79	1.98	23.61	2.13	38.96	2.79	40.78	2.79	36.15	2.76
8	4.50	26.19	2.28	15.38	1.69	15.57	1.67	14.63	1.69	25.07	2.31	25.35	2.23	23.82	2.34
9	1.80	27.60	0.96	21.07	0.93	22.05	0.94	19.92	0.92	26.52	0.98	27.27	0.96	26.49	1.04
10	1.60	22.02	0.68	18.36	0.72	17.91	0.68	17.01	0.70	22.31	0.73	22.22	0.70	21.93	0.76
11	6.50	10.31	1.29	4.08	0.65	4.08	0.63	3.32	0.55	9.91	1.32	9.79	1.25	9.69	1.37
12	0.40	1.53	0.01	0.00	0.00	0.00	0.00	0.00	0.00	2.30	0.02	2.30	0.02	1.53	0.01
13	0.30	2.05	0.01	1.03	0.01	1.03	0.01	1.03	0.01	2.05	0.01	2.05	0.01	2.05	0.01
14	0.20	1.44	0.01	1.44	0.01	1.44	0.01	1.46	0.01	1.44	0.01	5.05	0.02	1.44	0.01
15	1.00	0.29	0.01	0.29	0.01	0.29	0.01	0.29	0.01	0.29	0.01	0.29	0.01	0.29	0.01
16	0.50	0.00	0.00	0.00	0.00	0.00	0.00	0.00	0.00	0.00	0.00	0.00	0.00	0.00	0.00
17	0.10	0.00	0.00	0.00	0.00	0.00	0.00	0.00	0.00	0.00	0.00	0.00	0.00	0.00	0.00

Source: PNAD/IBGE 1999.

11.5. CONCLUSIONS

As with most uses of econometric estimates to make out-of-sample predictions, the results of our microsimulation exercise should be treated with considerable circumspection: probably even more than usual. Household data is measured with substantial error. Educational data based on years of schooling, in particular, is famously a very poor measure for quality-adjusted human capital stocks. Our models of fertility and occupational choices are acceptable only as very reduced forms. And their parameters, as indeed all others, may very well change over time or as a response to policy reforms. Having said all this, the following four conclusions appear to receive broad support from our analysis, and might be of some use to those concerned with the impact of educational expansions on the distribution of economic welfare in developing societies.

First, a broad-based expansion of enrolment and a reduction in evasion rates which raised average endowments of education (from 4.5 to 7 years, in this case), would be very likely to make a substantial contribution to poverty reduction. Just how substantial seems to depend somewhat on how the structure of returns to education evolves. In this exercise, the simulated decline in $P(0)$ ranged from some ten points (or 20 per cent) when returns became more convex, to thirteen points (or about a quarter) when they became more concave. These policies would not, however, have the same impact on inequality. While the simulated educational expansion (under Policy One) would be moderately equalizing if returns became more concave, it would be neutral if returns did not change. And inequality would actually rise if returns became more convex at the same time as the expansion took place.

Second, a combination of policies which succeeded in expanding education in a more targeted way (by halving the share of 15–40-year-olds with 0–4 years of schooling, in this case) would contribute to making educational expansions more progressive. As noted above, in the presence of convex returns to schooling, educational expansions can be inequality-increasing. At best, an increase in the mean of schooling may lead to a reasonably small reduction in inequality, as just reported for Policy One. A more targeted effort, focusing on reducing illiteracy and keeping in school those most likely to leave, while not as likely to lead to large income gains across the population, can play an important role in reducing income inequality. Naturally, such a targeted exercise should not be seen as a substitute, but rather as a complement, to a broader expansion of educational opportunities across the board.

Third, as has already been noted, all results depend heavily on what happens to returns to education, which are determined by the interaction between the relative supply of, and demand for, different skills. In this chapter, we did not model the demand side of the labour market. While we provided estimates for three possible scenarios, effectively considering a range for the variation in returns, there is no guarantee that actual changes must remain within that range. Given that gains in labour earnings to the poor are very sensitive to these changes, a stagnation of demand for unskilled labour should cause particular cause for concern. The interaction between supply and demand for skills in the labour market has been an area of growing interest for researchers.[15] These advances hold out the promise of improvements in our understanding of the interaction between educational outcomes and the distribution of income.

Fourth, if our analysis shed any light on the impact of an educational expansion on the distribution of income in Ceará, it was on the crucial role played by household dynamics in the process. We saw that the State appears to have something of a 'reserve army', awaiting conditions to enter paid or self-employment. As in other places where educational levels rose rapidly, this is to a large extent composed of women.[16] As they acquire education and enter the labour force, their fertility behaviour also changes, reducing the number of children in the family.

In income terms, each of these tendencies is positive for the families to which they belong. In fact, the participation and demographic changes arising from educational expansion account for a substantial share of the overall poverty reduction impact. Figures 11.8–11.10 illustrate the great importance of these gender-sensitive effects on the overall welfare of poor families. In the labour market, however, a large inflow of women into relatively underprivileged segments may generate downward wage pressure or enhance job competition. The extent to which Ceará will be able to capitalize on a more educated labour force depends, in large measure, on how effectively it ensures a level playing field for its women.

In closing, it should be noted that a number of important choices, or dimensions of household and worker behaviour, remained outside the scope of our analysis. Key amongst these is the possible decision to migrate. Greater endowments of education might affect the flows of migrants within the state—say, from rural areas to metropolitan Fortaleza—or outwards from the state. These decisions are likely to be determined by the relative conditions of labour demand, and thus wages, in these areas, and in other states. This falls outside the scope of this simple model, but this does not make it any less important a concern for policy-makers.

REFERENCES

Barros, R., Henriques, R., and Mendonça, R. (2000). 'Pelo Fim das Décadas Perdidas: Educação e Desenvolvimento Sustentado no Brasil'. In R. Henriques (ed.) *Desigualdade e Pobreza no Brasil*. IPEA, Rio de Janeiro.

Bourguignon, F., Ferreira, F. H. G., and Lustig, N. (1998). 'The Microeconomics of Income Distribution Dynamics in East Asia and Latin America'. The World Bank DECRA, Washington. Mimeo.

[15] Katz and Murphy (1992) and Juhn, Murphy, and Pierce (1993) have suggested methods to estimate changes in the demand for different labour skill categories, based on sectoral changes in the composition of economic activity. Robillard, Bourguignon, and Robinson (2001) combine a computable general equilibrium model and micro-simulations to consider demand and supply changes in the labour market simultaneously, and in general equilibrium.

[16] See Bourguignon, Fournier, and Gurgand (2001) on the key role played by changes in female participation in the Taiwanese development process.

Bourguignon, F., Ferreira, F. H. G., and Leite, P. G. (2002). 'Beyond Oaxaca-Blinder: Accounting for Differences in Household Income Distributions across Countries'. *World Bank Policy Research Working Paper* 2828. The World Bank, Washington.

——, Fournier, M., and Gurgand, M. (2001). 'Fast Development with a Stable Income Distribution: Taiwan, 1979–1994'. *Review of Income and Wealth*, 47(2), 139–64.

Ferreira, F. H. G. and Barros, R. (1999). 'The Slippery Slope: Explaining the Increase in Extreme Poverty in Urban Brazil, 1976–96'. *Revista de Econometria*, 19(2), 211–96.

Foster, J. E., Greer, J., and Thorbecke, E. (1984). 'A Class of Decomposable Poverty Indices'. *Econometrica*, 52, 761–6.

Langoni, C. (1973). *Distribuição de Renda e Desenvolvimento Econômico do Brasil*. Expresso e Cultura, Rio de Janeiro.

Juhn, C., Murphy, K., and Pierce, B. (1993). 'Wage Inequality and the Rise in Returns to Skill'. *Journal of Political Economy*, 101(3), 410–42.

Katz, L. and Murphy, K. (1992). 'Changes in the Wage Structure 1963–87: Supply and Demand Factors'. *Quarterly Journal of Economics*, 107, 35–78.

Knight, F. and Sabot, R. (1983). 'Educational Expansion and the Kuznets Effect'. *American Economic Review*, 73(5), 1132–6.

Lam, D. (1999). 'Generating Extreme Inequality: Schooling, Earnings, and Intergenerational Transmission of Human Capital in South Africa and Brazil', *Research Reports* 99/439. University of Michigan, Population Studies Center.

Reis, J. A. and Barros, R. (1991). 'Wage Inequality and the Distribution of Education: A Study of the Evolution of Regional Differences in Inequality in Metropolitan Brazil'. *Journal of Development Economics*, 36, 117–43.

Robillard, A.-S., Bourguignon, F., and Robinson, S. (2001). 'Crisis and Income Distribution: A Micro-Macro Model for Indonesia'. IFPRI, Washington. Mimeo.

Tinbergen, J. (1975). *Income Differences: Recent Research*. North Holland Publishing, Amsterdam.

12

Growth, Income Distribution, and Poverty: A Review

ARNE BIGSTEN AND JÖRGEN LEVIN

12.1. INTRODUCTION

The most important goal for development efforts is to reduce poverty, and this can be accomplished by economic growth and/or by income redistribution. This chapter provides a selective review of recent literature dealing with the relationships between economic growth, income distribution, and poverty. It also discusses the effect of economic policies on these three factors.

The concept of development has been debated for a long time, and has major philosophical implications, which will not be considered here (for a discussion, see Sen 1989). Instead, our concern is with changes in the economic welfare of people, as captured by three dimensions of economic welfare: per capita income, income distribution, and poverty.[1] With regard to poverty, the main dividing line is between income–consumption poverty measures, and the rest. It has been argued that an exclusive focus on income and expenditure misses important aspects of well-being, which are considered important by the poor. While all researchers agree that poverty should be seen as a multidimensional concept, the defence of income poverty-measures is that income is a means by which other needs are satisfied. On the other hand, one could argue that poverty should be measured with output indicators, such as infant mortality, literacy, and enrolment rates, rather than with an input indicator such as income. Against this viewpoint, one could argue that many social indicators have a distributional element, and may improve without necessarily indicating an improvement of the well-being of the poorest.

While proponents of the different methods were for some time each arguing their own case, there has been a shift towards more of a consensus, and even attempts to combine the methods in assessing poverty. Comparative analyses using the different concepts show that some indicators may be correlated, while others are not.

Thanks for comments are due to Karin Kronlid, Tony Addison, Wlodek Bursztyn, Ola Olsson, Matz Dahlberg, and an anonymous referee.

[1] To measure poverty one may use income or consumption data or various non-monetary measures (see Dercon 2000; or White 1999).

When quantitative analyses are compared with participatory studies, inconsistencies in poverty patterns have sometimes been found (Narayan *et al.* 2000). Although, at the aggregate level, a broader definition of poverty may not change the number of poor, it expands the set of policies that are considered for poverty-alleviation (Kanbur and Squire 1999). Income or consumption is bound to be an important part of any discussion of the consequences of economic policies and reforms on the poor. Economic reforms will be judged *inter alia* on their effect on gross domestic product, and since both GDP and household income (consumption) are measured in monetary terms, income (consumption) poverty-measures will provide a useful starting point for poverty analysis.

12.2. AGGREGATE TRENDS IN POVERTY AND INEQUALITY

In an attempt to estimate the number of people living in poverty, the World Bank has used currently available national data on per capita income and income distribution. These estimates are, of course, wrought with problems and should only be taken as orders of magnitude. According to Chen and Ravallion (2000) both the global share of population (Table 12.1) and the absolute number of people living on less than 1 (or 2) dollars a day (Table 12.2) declined substantially in the mid 1990s, after increasing earlier in the decade. The declines in the numbers are almost exclusively due to a reduction in the number of poor people in East Asia, most notably in China. But progress was partly reversed by the Asian financial crisis, or was at least stalled, as in China. In South Asia, the incidence of poverty (the share of the population living in poverty) declined moderately through the 1990s, but not sufficiently to reduce the absolute number of poor, which rose steadily between 1987 and 1996. In Africa also the share declined (at least after 1993), while the numbers increased. The estimates indicate that Africa is the region with the largest share of people living below $1/day.

Table 12.1. *Headcount index, selected years, 1987–98*

Regions	**Percentage of population living on less than $ 1 a day**				
	1987	**1990**	**1993**	**1996**	**1998(est.)**
East Asia and the Pacific	26.6	27.6	25.2	14.9	15.3
(Excluding China)	23.9	18.5	15.9	10.0	11.3
Eastern Europe and Central Asia	0.2	1.6	4.0	5.1	5.1
Latin America and the Caribbean	15.3	16.8	15.3	15.6	15.6
Middle East and North Africa	4.3	2.4	1.9	1.8	1.9
South Asia	44.9	44.0	42.4	42.3	40.0
Sub-Saharan Africa	46.6	47.7	49.7	48.5	46.3
Total	28.3	29.0	28.1	24.5	24.0
(Excluding China)	28.5	28.1	27.7	27.0	26.2

Source: Chen and Ravallion (2000).

Table 12.2. *Population (millions) living on less than $ 1 per day, selected years 1987–98*

Region	1987	1990	1993	1996	1998(est.)
East Asia and the Pacific	417.5	452.4	431.9	265.1	278.3
(Excluding China)	114.1	92.0	83.5	55.1	65.1
Eastern Europe and Central Asia	1.1	7.1	18.3	23.8	24.0
Latin America and the Caribbean	63.7	73.8	70.8	76.0	78.2
Middle East and North Africa	9.3	5.7	5.0	5.0	5.5
South Asia	474.4	495.1	505.1	531.7	522.0
Sub-Saharan Africa	217.2	242.3	273.3	289.0	290.9
Total	1183.2	1276.4	1304.4	1190.6	1198.9
(Excluding China)	879.8	916.0	956.0	980.6	985.7

Source: Chen and Ravallion (2000).

In Latin America, the share of poor people remained roughly constant over the period, while the numbers generally increased. In the countries of the former Soviet bloc, poverty rose markedly, both as a share, and in terms of numbers.

Income distribution data are often fragile, and one must, therefore, be cautious when interpreting them.[2] Still, we may note that Dikhanov and Ward (2002), who use an alternative approach to estimate what has happened to world inequality between 1970 and 1999, conclude that the number in severe poverty declined from 1.4 to 1.2 billion over this period. Their end of the period estimate is, thus, close to the one obtained by Chen and Ravallion.

World inequality is mainly driven by differences between countries. When measuring inequality in terms of per capita GDP converted to dollars at official exchange rates and neglecting intra-country inequality, inequality has risen over the long haul. According to UNDP (1999) the ratio of income per capita in the richest country over that in the poorest country has increased from eleven in 1913, to thirty-five in 1950, then to forty-four by 1973; and seventy-two by 1992. It is, thus, obvious that some countries were left behind, as the now developed countries took off. However, this is not the most appropriate way to measure the gaps. Melchior, Telle, and Wiig (2000) have attempted to check more thoroughly what has happened to international inequality since 1960. In contrast to the UNDP they use PPP weighted estimates of per capita incomes of 115 countries, and they also weight the countries by population size. This means that development in China weighs heavily in the results. Their estimates of the Gini coefficients for differences in average per capita incomes suggest that international inequality has been falling more or less continuously since 1968. Their results are consistent with those of Sprout and Weaver (1992), Schultz (1998), Firebaugh (1999), and Boltho and Toniolo (1999) up to 1990. Also the study by Melchior, Telle, and Wiig show increasing international inequality until 1994, when official exchange rates

[2] The problems of interpreting Indian survey data are discussed in Srinivasan (2000), who also points out the difficulties of making valid cross-country comparisons.

are used, but for the period 1994–97 even that measure shows a declining trend. They then use the Lorenz curve to investigate what has happened to various percentiles. It is then shown that the share of the bottom 10 per cent did decline, but for the bottom 20 per cent, or any higher share, it increased. The increasing gap between 1982 and 1997 between the top and the bottom deciles mainly reflects the decline in poor countries in Africa.

These estimates neglect intra-country inequality, and Milanovic (2002) has incorporated this effect as well for the period of 1988–93. For this short period he found that world inequality did increase. Dikhanov and Ward (2002) also take intra-country inequality into account, and adjust the Chinese growth rate in per capita income downwards, citing evidence that the Chinese growth has been exaggerated. Their estimate of inequality between persons across the world increased slightly between 1970 and 1999. The Gini coefficient is estimated to have increased from 0.668 to 0.683. Looking at changes in income inequality in seventy-three countries Cornia and Court (2001) found that inequality rose in forty-eight countries, remained constant in sixteen countries and fell in nine of the seventy-three countries. Among those countries, which saw an increase in inequality, thirty-three countries are either classified as developed or transitional countries. In the group of developing countries approximately half are located in Latin America.

The results on inequality changes are thus somewhat mixed, but there does not seem to be any dramatic change in overall inequality. Even so, inter-country gaps in per capita incomes are enormous, and a major explanation of world inequality. It is also serious that the very poorest countries (mainly African ones)[3] are falling further and further behind.

12.3. DETERMINANTS OF GROWTH

While linkages between growth, income distribution, and poverty will be discussed later, we will elaborate a little on the determinants of growth. We should keep in mind, though, that there are many factors that influence economic growth, not all easily quantifiable. Early analyses of economic growth were usually done within the framework of the neoclassical growth model, as developed by Solow (1956) and others. Driven by diminishing returns to capital, this model implies convergence, meaning that the lower the starting level of per capita income, the higher the rate of growth, with the economy converging to a steady state level. This presupposes that countries are alike except for the initial capital–labour ratio, but in reality they may, of course, differ in many other dimensions.

In the neoclassical model, the steady-state per capita income level depends on the propensity to save and the position of the production function—these factors may vary across countries. If there is technical progress, the steady-state income level will gradually increase. Barro (1997) notes that the steady state also depends on government policies, for example, with regard to public consumption, protection of property

[3] See discussion in Bigsten (2002).

rights, and distortions of domestic and international markets. The concept of capital in the standard model may also be extended to include human capital in the form of education, experience, and health. The endogenous growth literature, starting with Romer (1986) and Lucas (1988), suggests that growth may go on indefinitely, since returns to investment in human capital, for example, need not be diminishing: external effects of human capital and spillovers between producers help economies avoid diminishing returns to capital.

A well-known result in the empirical literature indicates no direct correlation between the initial level of per capita income and the rate of growth, which means that there is no unconditional convergence. However, when other relevant variables are added to the model, there is an effect. There is convergence, but conditional on these other variables, which vary across countries. Barro's (1997) cross-country study shows that variables that matter for growth are, for example, the initial level of per capita income, the initial level of human capital, the fertility rate, government consumption, the rule of law,[4] terms of trade, and the investment ratio. Thus, it is far from self-evident that a country will grow fast just because it starts out poor. It could be that, because of poor policies or other conditions, it grows only slowly, or even converges to a low-level steady state. Sub-Saharan Africa might be a case in point.

It is clear that per capita incomes in the long term are determined by the levels of human capital and physical capital, and the underlying level of productivity as shown in a standard aggregate production function. But this type of formulation leads on to further questions: what determines the levels of investment in human and physical capital, and what determines productivity growth? A recent attempt to discuss these issues is due to Hall and Jones (1999), who present a cross-country analysis of per capita income levels with the very simple basic hypothesis that per capita income levels are indirectly determined by the amount of 'social infrastructure'. By social infrastructure they mean the institutions and government policies that determine the economic environment, within which individuals accumulate skills and firms accumulate capital and produce output (see below for the proxies used to try to capture this). The environment should, thus, support productive activities and encourage capital accumulation, skill acquisition, and technology transfer. Such an infrastructure must limit diversion and get prices right, so that individuals can capture the returns to their actions as private economic agents. Social control of diversion, which is a major component of 'social infrastructure', has two benefits: producers are allowed to reap the full rewards of their production, and they do not need to invest resources in avoiding diversion. The government should, therefore, try to prevent private diversion, and should refrain from diverting itself. Rent-seeking can have a very negative effect on growth (Bigsten and Moene 1996).

This analysis, thus, says that social infrastructure determines the underlying level of productivity, which then influences output per worker, and suggests that one should

[4] Barro uses an indicator from the International Country Risk Guide reflecting the quality of the bureaucracy, political corruption, likelihood of government repudiation of contracts, risk of government expropriation, and overall maintenance of the rule of law.

distinguish between the proximate causes of growth, such as human and physical capital accumulation, and the more fundamental determinants of productivity. Hall and Jones note that social infrastructure is an endogenous variable, and they, therefore, use instrumental variables to control for this, specifically geographic and linguistic variables that show how much the countries have been influenced by Western Europe. Even controlling for this, they find that social infrastructure explains most of the differences in per capita incomes. They conclude that differences in physical capital and educational attainment explain only a modest amount of the difference in output per worker across countries. Instead, it is differences in the underlying production functions that explain the vast differences in per capita incomes.

As proxies for social infrastructure, Hall and Jones used an index of government anti-diversion policies,[5] plus an index of the extent to which a country is open to international trade. Openness gives scope for specialization, but it also facilitates the adoption of new ideas and technologies. Growth problems have been most pronounced in countries that have pursued an inward-oriented policy. Opening up to international markets is, therefore, essential.

Countries with a good social infrastructure, then, have high capital intensities, high human capital per worker, and high productivity. These differences, interpreted through an aggregate production function, are able to account for the variation in output per worker. Thus, the results of Hall and Jones suggest that success in investment and productivity growth is driven by social infrastructure, as reflected in institutions and government policies. However, it should be noted that the results are not based on properly estimated production functions. The capital coefficient, for example is just assumed to be one third, which is too low for Africa. The returns to education in Africa, taken from Psacharopoulos (1994) at 13 per cent for primary education, seem much too high. The empirical estimates in the paper are, thus, debatable, but the general drift of their arguments seems very relevant.

One may conclude that the accumulation of physical and human capital, efficiency in resource allocation, and acquisition and application of modern technology are necessary for growth. The key question is how the policy environment should be organized in order for it to facilitate the accumulation of production factors and their efficient allocation, as well as the introduction of enhanced technologies. Economic policies at the micro level should clearly aim to develop and sustain efficient markets, while macro policy should be geared towards guaranteeing macroeconomic stability, and towards openness. It has also become increasingly clear that a supportive environment of efficient institutions is crucial for the functioning of the economy. Such institutions can lower transaction costs, while raising the supply of information and services to economic actors. In the African economies, for example, uncertainty is high, thus hindering the expansion of economic transactions, and reducing the scope for specialization. The general uncertainty of property rights dissuades economic actors from

[5] Hall and Jones devise a proxy for anti-diversion policies using indicators from surveys on law and order, bureaucratic quality, corruption, risk of expropriation, and government repudiation of contracts.

entering into long-term contracts, and thus constrains large investments in fixed capital: given incomplete markets for capital goods, fixed investments might be irreversible, and actors want to guard themselves against this eventuality.

What then is required for growth-supporting institutions to develop? It is not enough to instil the relevant skills in civil servants, only to put them into institutions where outsiders determine outcomes. A government primarily concerned with its own survival will not necessarily set up the institutions and establish codes of conduct necessary for economic growth. With special interest politics at centre stage, there is bound to be inefficiency, which will make investors cautious, while elsewhere in the economy resources are wasted on rent-seeking activities.

The debate on the determinants of growth has increasingly come to focus on the political economy of policy making. To be able to systematize the experiences of different countries, one needs to have a classification scheme. In their large cross-country project, Lal and Myint (1996) used a fivefold classification of countries by political environments and a threefold classification by economic structure, the latter based on their factor proportions. Countries are classified as labour abundant, land abundant, or intermediate, relative to the world endowments of labour, land, and capital. This classification makes it possible to use the three-factor trade model developed by Krueger (1977) and Leamer (1987) to discuss a whole range of different development paths. The paths depend on the accumulation of capital and labour, and imply different patterns of change in functional income distribution.

The fivefold political classification distinguishes between the objectives of the government and the constraints it faces. With regard to constraints, Lal and Myint distinguished between the autonomous and the factional state. In the former, the state works for its own ends. One might have a Platonic Guardian State, benevolently trying to maximize some social welfare function, but alternatively, one might have a predatory state, which seeks to maximize the net revenue for the ruler's use, or the bureaucratic state maximizing public employment. The factional state, on the other hand, has no objectives of its own, but tries to realize those of anyone who is able to capture the state. Here, Lal and Myint distinguish between the oligarchic state and the majoritarian democracy.

Lal and Myint found that initial resource endowment was more important in determining the policy outcome than the type of political system. Labour abundant countries, such as Korea and Taiwan, had an easy policy-making task and could follow the prescriptions from the standard Heckscher–Ohlin model, initially concentrating on labour-intensive production and then moving up the ladder of comparative advantage as capital was accumulated. A major reason why this development path is relatively smooth is that it leads to politically desirable factor price changes, that is, increasing real wages as more capital is accumulated. The bulk of the population will gain, and will, thus, not resist the policy in a factional state. Also, the various types of autonomous states will find it in their interest to pursue a development strategy that uses its abundant resource intensively.

The comparative advantage of natural resource abundant countries is also relatively straightforward, but may be more difficult to realize. Lal (2000) gives several reasons: First, with a higher supply-price of labour than in the labour abundant countries, comparative advantage lies in more capital intensive types of production. Public intervention may be required to realize bulky investments, develop specific skills, and absorb advanced technology. This opens up the field for bureaucratic failures, which may then undermine growth potential. The second point is that, if capital accumulation is not fast enough, and with a rapidly growing labour force, the optimal development path may imply falling real wages. In the case of factional government, this may lead to political pressure to avoid this by turning inward; there may be swings between populist periods and liberalization phases. Third, to avoid the falling wages, many countries have attempted to undertake big push development programmes, which have often been financed by foreign borrowing leading to high indebtedness. Fourth, given the rents available from the natural resources, there has been extensive politicization of the distribution of these rents, which has a severe effect on the rent generating sector, particularly when terms of trade decline. It may be that the wealth of natural resources leads to a policy that destroys the sector that generated the rents.[6] The intermediate resource endowment countries face a more complex task. It is not as clear what their incremental comparative advantage is; mistakes are not as easily observed. The political system may also be at odds with the pursuit of their comparative advantage (see Lal 1995 on India and China).

Generally, Lal and Myint (1996) did not find any relationship between the form of government and economic performance. Instead, they found that it was the availability, or lack, of natural resources that was the major determinant of policies, which affected the efficiency and volume of investment, and thus the rate of growth.

12.4. ECONOMIC GROWTH, INCOME DISTRIBUTION, AND POVERTY

A pro-poor growth strategy does not have to focus only on economic growth, but could also be combined with an active policy of income redistribution. However, there may be a trade-off. If more rapid reduction in poverty can be achieved through reductions in inequalities, then distributional policy takes on a greater priority; but on the other hand, if greater levels of inequality appear to secure rapid growth leading to faster poverty reduction, then there may well be greater tolerance of inequalities. Thus, the relationship between growth and inequality are important from a policy perspective.

In his famous 1955 article, Simon Kuznets investigated the relationship between per capita incomes and inequality in a cross section of countries. He found that there was an inverted-U pattern—that is, inequality first increased, and then decreased—as per capita income increased. The driving force was assumed to be structural change in a dual economy setting, in which labour was shifted from a poor and relatively undifferentiated traditional sector, to a more productive and more differentiated, modern sector.

[6] See discussion of the case of Zambia in Bigsten and Kayizzi-Mugerwa (2000) and Bigsten (2001).

Kuznets' inverted-U has been exposed to a large number of tests over the years. Deininger and Squire (1998) provide the most comprehensive attempt so far to test the Kuznets' hypothesis. They used a data set of better quality than previous researchers had, and for individual countries they had fairly comparable data for several points in time. They were also able to examine the income changes in the bottom quintiles, that is, among the poor. The result for their sample, was that there was no evidence of an inverted-U pattern for individual countries. In the majority of cases, in fact, it was impossible to find any significant change in income distribution during recent decades. They then went on to investigate whether there was a link from fast growth to increasing inequality, and again they did not find any systematic evidence in favour of such a relationship. Rapid growth was associated with growing inequality as often as it was associated with falling inequality, or with no changes at all. The results are consistent with those of an earlier study by Ravallion and Chen (1997), who did not find any systematic relationship between the rate of growth and inequality either.

The impact of growth on the poor obviously depends on how the benefits are distributed across the population. By looking at the growth and income shares of different groups, Deininger and Squire (1998) investigated how initial inequality and contemporaneous changes in inequality influence poverty. The poor (bottom 20 per cent) were found to suffer from growth reducing effects of inequality, and also to benefit from measures that stimulate growth. Ravallion and Chen (1997) also found a very strong relation from growth to reduced poverty. They distributed their observations into four quadrants, according to the direction of changes in mean consumption and in the poverty rate. Virtually all observations fell either in the quadrants with rising poverty and falling mean income or in the quadrant with falling poverty and rising mean incomes. Empirically, there is thus, on average, a strong relationship from per capita income growth to poverty reduction.[7] At least it is shown that policies that promote growth do not, in general, lead to an increase in inequality that will undo the poverty-reducing effect of growth. Of course, this is a general cross-country result that may not apply to an individual country.

Even if there is a strong relationship from GDP growth to poverty reduction it might be the case that countries with initially severe inequality may be less successful at reducing poverty. While earlier models, such as the Harrod–Domar model, predicted that greater inequality would lead to higher growth rates, there was, during the 1990s, a shift in focus towards the opposite effect: can greater inequality lead to a lower level of overall growth? Some empirical evidence from both industrialized and less-developed countries has tended to confirm the negative impact of inequality on growth. Such a relationship was found (with somewhat shaky cross-country data) by Persson and Tabellini (1994), and also by Alesina and Rodrik (1994). These authors interpreted the results in a political economy context, their argument being that when inequality is high, the median voter will push for high (distortionary) taxes on the better-off,

[7] Other studies supporting positive average effects of growth on poverty are Anand and Ravallion (1993), Ravallion and Datt (1994), Bell and Rich (1994), and Dollar and Kraay (2002). See Ravallion (2001) on looking beyond averages.

which will have disincentive effects on efforts and savings, which would then reduce growth. Further tests of this proposition have cast some doubt on its validity, however, and the evidence for disincentive effects of taxation is so far fairly weak. Another possible channel from inequality to growth is via social conflicts. Alesina and Perotti (1996) argued that inequality leads to increased political instability, which tends to reduce efficiency and investment levels, and then growth. It has also been argued that instability reduces the ability of governments to respond to external shocks (Rodrik 1997).

Deininger and Squire tested the link from inequality to growth, but found no stable relationship between the level of initial income inequality and growth. They found, though, that high inequality in the distribution of land, proxying for asset distribution, had a significantly negative effect on future growth.[8] The main factor identified as a possible explanation was credit rationing, in situations where investments are indivisible.[9] It might be impossible for the poor to finance schooling or other investments, even if they would be profitable, since they lack collateral for loans. Lack of assets might also reduce possibilities for participation in the political process, and thus also reduce access to resources. Once countries become sufficiently rich, this link between high inequality and low growth seems to disappear. Low initial inequality is thus doubly beneficial for the poor, since it not only increases overall growth, but it also specifically increases their own income generating opportunities. Other policy variables, however, affect poverty mainly through their effect on investment, and investment in new assets seems more effective than redistribution of existing ones. There may be problems with the use of a land reform policy to fight poverty if it leads to reduced investments. Birdsall, Ross, and Sabot (1995) found that the low inequality of income in East Asia contributed to its fast growth. In addition, policies that reduced poverty and income inequality, such as basic education and measures augmenting labour demand, also stimulated growth.

The debate about the empirical link between growth and inequality is not finished, however. Forbes (2000) uses a method that makes it possible to allow for fixed country effects to estimate how inequality in a given country effects its growth. She then finds, contrary to earlier studies, a robust and significant positive relation between income inequality and growth. Obviously there is need for further research on this issue before we are sure about how the relationship looks.

Still, there are some indications that there may be a negative effect from high inequality to low growth, particularly if we consider unequal asset distribution. Countries with initially severe inequality of consumption and land, may then be less successful at reducing poverty, because a given growth rate leads to slower poverty reduction, at the same time as the uneven distribution of land leads to slower growth. However, it is not easy to generalize about the impact of a change in the pattern of distribution upon

[8] Birdsall and Londoño (1997) and Deininger and Olinto (2000) found a negative relationship between initial distribution of assets and growth.

[9] On credit market failures and lack of investment in human and physical capital see Aghion, Caroli, and Garcia-Penalosa (1999) and Benabou (1996).

growth. The impact will depend on the political and social context, and the method by which the distribution of assets is adjusted.

12.5. THE POVERTY IMPACT OF ECONOMIC POLICIES

So far, we have looked at the interlinkages between growth, income distribution, and poverty. An important question that follows is whether there are any particular development strategies, or specific policies, that would simultaneously lead to high and sustained growth rates, equitable distribution, and a rapid reduction of poverty. While at least some of the evidence suggests that countries with more equal distribution grow more quickly, it is also true that economic policy can compensate for unequal initial income distribution. A major challenge is, therefore, to find combinations of policy instruments that will deliver both growth and equity.

While there are few studies analysing these issues, Lundberg and Squire (1999) argue that financial depth, openness, and land redistribution emerge as policies that consistently spur growth. With the possible exception of openness, these policies also benefit equality. Lal and Myint (1996), studying growth, inequality, and poverty, found that experiences vary a lot across countries, and that differences in performance are largely due to different policy choices. However, it seems to be rather difficult to find any systematic evidence regarding effects of macroeconomic polices on poverty (Cashin *et al.* 2001; Agenor 2002).[10] The same holds for indicators of growth promoting polices for which significant correlations between growth and inequality across countries have rarely been found (Ravallion 2001). Still, understanding policies and development strategies that have succeeded in reducing poverty can provide some guidance for other countries. The remaining part of this chapter reviews, selectively, some policy-oriented areas.

12.5.1. *Sectoral Growth Pattern*

Even if economic growth is necessary to reduce poverty, the orientation of the growth process is also important. A central question is what sectors should be given priority in a poverty oriented growth strategy. The dual economy models of Lewis (1954) and Fei and Ranis (1964) provided a first attempt to understand the role of inter-sectoral linkages, which have been considered important when formulating

[10] There have been extensive debates about the impact of structural adjustment programmes on poverty. Demery and Squire (1996) argue that countries where policy reforms were implemented saw a decline in poverty, while those where adjustment was delayed or reversed, the situation improved only marginally or deteriorated without adjustment. Dorosh and Sahn (2000) argue that availability of donor funds has been crucial for good results. Ali (1996, 1998) argues that the results of adjustment efforts on poverty are very mixed. For a synthesis of country case studies evaluating adjustment policies and the impact on income distribution, see Bourguignon and Morrison (1992). See also Kayizzi-Mugerwa and Levin (1994) and Levin (1998) for a review of the experience of sub-Saharan Africa.

development strategies.[11] In the 1960s and 1970s, those strategies were focused on the expansion of industrial activities, in order to increase demand for agricultural products. Most developing countries increased trade barriers to support the development of the domestic industry. Some countries, primarily in Asia, managed to develop a competitive industry and were able to reduce protection. One important explanation to this success was that they had undertaken land reforms and that the agricultural sector was relatively well developed. The results in Africa were poor. The import substitution policy did not lead to the creation of an internationally competitive industry and it turned out to have a devastating effect on agricultural production. Agricultural production was taxed via high trade barriers and direct export taxes. Farmers were forced to sell their goods at artificially low prices and agricultural production stagnated. This not only affected export revenues, but also employment and poverty, in both urban and rural areas. Since incomes in agriculture deteriorated, people moved to town in search of jobs, but the majority ended up in the informal sector or in open unemployment. This meant that poverty increased both in town and in the countryside.

However, a shift in emphasis took place in the 1980s, when economic reform programmes were introduced. It was now argued that incentives supporting the agricultural sector were necessary to increase agricultural production and to reduce poverty in the rural areas. It was necessary to increase producer prices, but further reforms of the rural environment have turned out to be necessary to increase growth in agriculture in a sustainable way. Increased agricultural production would in turn support domestic industry. Thus, while earlier periods focused on backward linkages, the focus today is as also on forward linkages (Bigsten and Collier 1995).

Although those earlier models took a too simplistic view of various aspects of dualism, renewed interest in the area has provided some interesting developments.[12] For example, Thorbecke and Stiefel (1999) expand the standard dualistic framework into a dual–dual framework, which distinguishes modern (formal) and informal sector activities in both urban and rural areas. With this framework, they show that population shifts between socio-economic groups are an important factor in explaining changes in poverty.

In an extended dualistic framework, Bourguignon and Morrison (1998) found that the extent of economic dualism is a major factor explaining differences in income distribution across developing countries: increased agricultural growth is the most efficient way of reducing inequality and poverty. Results from India, obtained by following the evolution of poverty through thirty-five household surveys undertaken between 1951 and 1991, also show that agricultural growth mattered more than manufacturing growth for poverty reduction (Ravallion and Datt 1996). Mellor (1999)

[11] Traditionally, intersectoral linkages are thought of as increased demand for intermediate goods when production of the final good increases (backward linkages), or with cheapening of production when events in a sector cheapen another's input (forward linkages) (Hirschman 1958).

[12] The traditional models of dualism focused on the difference between modern (formal) industry and traditional (informal) agriculture.

also argues that, even if manufacturing growth is more important for overall growth, agricultural growth is more important for employment growth and poverty reduction.

Analyses of linkages have generally focused on the production side of the economy. However, studies of rural economies suggest that the primary inter-sectoral linkages are to be found on the consumption side. They will, thus, depend on how poor rural people spend increments in income (Delgado *et al.* 1998; Haggblade, Hazell, and Brown 1989). Still, more attention needs to be paid to inter-sectoral dynamics, especially in sub-Saharan African economies (Blunch and Verner 1999).

12.5.2. *The Role of the Public Sector*

A policy of redistribution is politically complicated. Asset redistribution may have costs in terms of lost growth, so that there is an equity/growth trade-off. This could arise from efficiency and output losses from one-off redistribution, or through the impact on investment incentives. Redistribution, therefore, inevitably raises complex questions of political, social, and economic importance. As a result, governments may prefer a less *dirigiste* approach and instead use changes in tax policies and public expenditures. They must then try to achieve a balance between measures having immediate effects on poverty and measures supporting processes that bring continuing and sustainable poverty alleviation in the longer term.

Although many countries have had the intention of allocating expenditures towards activities, which would reduce inequalities and poverty, they have often failed. One reason for the disappointing results is the failure to link policy, planning, and budgeting. In many countries, policy-making, planning, and budgeting take place independently of each other. Planning is often confined to investment activities, which in many less developed countries refers to a series of donor-funded projects. Capital expenditures, are, thus, already largely accounted for through the planning process, and large portions of recurrent expenditures are simply committed to the wage bill. For this reason, annual budgeting is reduced to allocating resources thinly across donor and domestically funded 'investment' projects, and to the non-wage portion of the recurrent budget.

In the absence of effective decision-making processes, policy-making, and planning are also disconnected from each other as well as from budgeting, and they are not constrained by resource availability or by strategic priorities. Overall, this may lead to a massive mismatch, between what is promised through government policies, and what is affordable. The annual budgeting process, therefore, becomes more about scrambling to keep things afloat, rather than allocating resources on the basis of clear policy choices to achieve strategic objectives. It is, therefore, vital to reform the public sector as well as the forms of foreign aid.

A tool that is now widely used in less developed countries, and also in some industrialized countries, is the medium-term expenditure framework (MTEF) within which ministers and line ministries are provided with greater responsibility for resource allocation decisions and resource use.[13] The MTEF consists of a top-down resource

[13] See World Bank (1998) for a detailed description of the MTEF concept.

envelope, a bottom-up estimation of the current and medium-term costs of existing policy, and, ultimately, the matching of these costs with available resources. The matching of costs should normally occur in the context of the annual budget process, which should focus on the need for policy change to reflect changing macroeconomic conditions, as well as on changes in strategic priorities of the government. The MTEF provides an efficient tool for achieving a more efficient use of public resources. As the introduction of MTEFs is rather recent little comparative analysis of actual MTEFs has been undertaken. However, a recent evaluation found that MTEF reforms have not taken sufficient account of initial country conditions in basic aspects of budget management and have not paid sufficient attention to the political and institutional aspects of the reform process (Le Houerou and Taliercio 2002).

The efficiency and composition of public expenditures are critical determinants of growth and poverty. When undertaking fiscal reforms one may distinguish three types of impact from reallocation of public expenditures. First, when relative prices and factor-incomes change, income distribution and poverty will change. Second, the composition of government expenditures affects sectoral productivity, and hence labour demand and household income. Third, changes in the supply of public services, such as health care and education have an impact on household's possibilities to acquire human capital.

With regard to changes in relative prices and factor incomes following reduced government recurrent expenditures, it is mainly urban households that are hurt, due to the urban bias of government employment. Quite often rural households benefited from the resulting changes in relative prices (Dorosh 1996; Dorosh, Essama-Nssah, and Samba-Mamadou 1996; Levin 1998). However, in a number of countries, particularly in sub-Saharan Africa, political constraints induced governments to reduce capital expenditures, rather than laying off public employees. While protecting urban households from a short-term income loss, this had a long-term negative impact on the rural poor. For example, in the case of Ghana, when government investment in agriculture and rural infrastructure declined, there were negative long-term effects on production. Thus, even if the rural population benefits from a real depreciation of the exchange rate in the short run, these gains are eroded in the longer term if public investment is not kept at a reasonable level (Dorosh and Lundberg 1996).

Investment is one of the major determinants of economic growth. However, government interventions which are normally considered productive could become unproductive if there are too many of them. In particular, capital expenditures, often thought to be the key component of development, have been excessive in some developing countries, rendering them unproductive at the margin (Devarajan, Swaroop, and Zou 1996). This seems to have been the case in Tanzania. The evidence points to a negative relationship between public investment expenditure and economic growth for the period 1965–96 (Kweka and Morrissey 2000). Thus, a shake out of unproductive government investments could raise the average productivity of investment. It is also true, however, that an excessive shake-out could have the effect of lowering the productivity of private investment (Toye 2000). For example, poor infrastructure and deficient public services in Uganda significantly reduced investments of private firms

(Reinikka and Svensson 2000). In Cameroon, as public investment was squeezed, and in particular infrastructural and agricultural services, there was a negative impact on agricultural activities and the rural poor. The policy implication is that if a substantial share of the private sector's costs are due to the poorly functioning public sector, private sector response to economic reform is likely to remain limited.

A reallocation of government expenditures may also impact on the supply of health and education services, though this does not necessarily hurt the poor. Lloyd-Sherlock (2000) argues that the scale, and general allocation patterns, of public social spending in Latin America are not benefiting the poor. Despite the high level of spending, large sections of low-income groups are excluded from many areas of public welfare. The effects of entitlement restrictions are reinforced by severe problems of access and quality for supposedly universal services. Empirical results from a number of African countries also show that spending on social services, such as health care and education, is not well targeted to the poorest households (Castro-Leal *et al.* 1999; Sahn and Younger 1999). Subsidies to primary education are an exception, but they still appear inequitable when judged against the numbers of school-age children in the poorest groups. Thus, reallocation of public expenditures is not sufficient; policies must be based on a sound understanding of the factors that govern household decisions about health care and schooling, and of the means by which subsidized services can lead to better outcomes for the poor.

There are many studies showing that health improves with higher per capita incomes. For example, Kakwani (1993) investigated the relationship between income levels and welfare indicators such as life expectancy at birth, literacy, and the infant mortality rate. He found a strong relationship, particularly in the poorer countries. Higher incomes improved the indicators at a declining rate. Anand and Ravallion (1993) also found a significant relationship between national income and life expectancy and mortality indicators. Pritchett and Summers (1996) and Filmer and Pritchett (1999) found a highly significant effect from income to a range of health indicators.

However, there have been cases where structural adjustment loans led to growth without having any significant positive effect on health indicators. The relationship is, thus, complicated. While it seems that economic growth tends to improve the health of the population, the extent of the improvement depends on the character of the growth process. A process that leads to reduced poverty and to improvements in the provision of health services, will have a positive effect on health indicators. In addition, especially when considering the irreversible effects of failing to make such investments (Appleton and Teal 1999), long-term intergenerational effects of health care and education are an important reason for promoting social sector investments, despite tight current fiscal constraints.

Provision of public services in many countries is constrained by low levels of public revenue, which could, in principle, be solved by higher levels of taxation. However, in some countries, rapidly increased taxation might pose a severe constraint on private investment, and thus might impact negatively on future growth, and hence on revenue collection as well. In the case of Uganda, Chen and Reinikka (1999) suggest two reasons why increased taxes reduced investment and future growth.

First, the formal-enterprise sector typically represents a small share of output, but a high proportion of the effective tax-base. Second, limited access to bank-financing and high interest rates implies that investment is largely financed by retained earnings.

Moreover, when governments resort to distortionary taxes, the manner in which the government intervenes makes a big difference as to whether the intervention is beneficial or not (Devarajan, Xie, and Zou 1998): governments should always consider the option of subsidization before public provision, when intervening to correct an externality. Even under the extreme assumption that the public sector is as efficient as the private sector, the costs of financing public programmes through distortionary taxes may outweigh the benefits of internalizing the positive externality. Further, government spending which in one country might be growth-enhancing could be growth-impeding in another, due to the varying relative importance of both distortionary taxation and the externality being internalized.

While the allocation of expenditure matters in terms of equity and poverty, a pro-poor strategy would also entail measures targeted directly at the poor. When attempting to alleviate poverty, much of the outcome depends on the type of targeting-mechanism used.[14] The objective in targeting is to ensure that a poor household's income is increased up to the assumed poverty line. If the income of the poor was perfectly measurable and the poor could be identified it would, in principle, be possible to design a perfectly targeted policy. However, such perfect information is never available, and the costs of obtaining it would, in any case, be high. An alternative is universal targeting, where information costs are reduced to a minimum. The drawback with this type of targeting, however, is that it would also benefit those who are not considered poor. Moreover, universal subsidies, designed to benefit the whole population, have proven inefficient, distortionary, and fiscally unsustainable. However, some leakage might be crucial for the political sustainability of the programme (Gelbach and Prichett 1997; de Donder and Hindricks 1998). Both perfect and universal targeting have high costs. In order to reduce information costs, indicator targeting has been suggested as an approximation to perfect targeting. Indicator targeting relies on making the transfer contingent, not on income or consumption, but on some easily observable characteristic, such as sex, age, size of land-holding, region of residence, etc. For example, transfers can be targeted to specific socio-economic groups containing large proportions of poor households (Thorbecke and Berrian 1992).

Another approach is self-targeting, which is designed in such a way that only members of the target group find it worthwhile to participate. For example, public employment schemes use work requirements to help screen out the non-poor; subsidy programmes support items that the poor consume, but not the rich; and other controls rely on waiting time, stigma, and lower packaging quality of goods and services, to dissuade usage by the non-poor (van de Walle 1998). Self-targeted schemes also have the additional benefit of reducing incentives towards corruption and favouritism.

[14] On the principles of targeting, see Besley and Kanbur (1988), Hoddinott (1999), Thorbecke and Berrian (1992), and van de Walle (1998).

Ferreira and de Barries (1999) argue that a key to the success of a self-targeted incentive scheme is the wage rate. A relatively low wage rate can be an effective targeting device.

Other costs also need to be considered when a targeting scheme is implemented. Chia, Wahba, and Whalley (1994) argue that two effects have been largely ignored in the traditional analysis: the first relate to leakages associated with the financing scheme, and the second relate to the impact of indirect effects, through changes in relative prices. For example, in the case of Côte d'Ivoire, the amount of transfers in a universal targeting that would be thought to eliminate poverty in a partial context, would in fact reduce total poverty by only 7 percentage points, when indirect effects are considered. Thus, neglecting indirect effects can lead to the misallocation of resources directed at poverty alleviation.

Summing up the above discussion, there are at least two important issues that need to be considered: First, improved public service delivery is crucial in promoting economic growth and reducing poverty. Second, tax policies need to be redesigned, in order to satisfy an increasing demand for public services, while at the same time providing an enabling environment for private sector development.

12.5.3. *Pro-Poor Growth and Human Capital*

Human-capital accumulation has been an important factor in accounting for differences in growth rates and distribution across countries. Investing in education has been emphasized in the development literature since the early 1970s. Although an extensive literature has developed on the effects of the expansion of education on growth, relatively little is known on its effects on the distribution on income.[15] It might be the case that a sudden large increase in the supply of medium-skilled workers, say with lower secondary education, reduces the relative wage rate of that class of workers. This has, for example, happened in slow growing Kenya (Appleton, Bigsten, and Manda 1999). To avoid such an outcome, the increase in the supply of educated workers must be matched by an increase in labour demand, which in turn will depend on economic growth. If that is the case, one might see an inverted-U relationship between income equality and average years of schooling (Cornia and Court 2001). When the average educational level of the population is low, the few highly educated people are likely to obtain very high salaries. But as more educated people enter the labour market income inequality starts declining.

A change in the educational structure of a population necessarily induces changes in many dimensions of economic and social behaviour, each of which might have powerful secondary effects on growth, distribution and poverty. Labour force participation, household formation, migration, and fertility are all domains where education plays a major role, and where changes are likely to affect the development path of the economy. Thus, there is a dynamic, and intergenerational, dimension in the effects of education that must be taken into account.

[15] See, for example, Chenery *et al.* (1974) and Benabou (1996).

Bourguignon, Fournier, and Gurgand (1998) provide an innovative methodological framework that links observed changes in the distribution of individual income and earnings attributes to changes in the socio-demographic structure of the population, in particular with respect to education, to changes in labour force participation and occupational choice behaviour, and finally to changes in the structure of individual earnings as a result of changes in the labour market.

Analysis of the Taiwanese experience (Bourguignon, Fournier, and Gurgand 2001) provides a number of important insights. Several factors affected the distribution of income, but they tended to offset each other. First, increased returns to schooling occurred despite a dramatic growth in the supply of educated workers, and this contributed to increased inequality. This effect, however, was more than offset by other tendencies, such as a change in participation behaviour and the expansion of education, which equalized the distribution of schooling, and therefore of earnings. Altogether, this produced a significant drop in inequality of individual earnings.

Brazil, which has gone through substantial structural changes,[16] is another interesting case, the population grew by 47 per cent between 1976 and 1996, and became more urban. Average education rose from 3.2 to 5.3 years of schooling. The sectoral composition of the labour force changed, away from agriculture and manufacturing, towards services. The degree of formalization of the labour force declined substantially: the proportion of formal workers was almost halved, from just under 60 per cent to just over 30 per cent of all workers. And yet, despite the macroeconomic turmoil and continuing structural changes, little changed in Brazilian income distribution between 1976 and 1996.

The Brazilian experience resembles the Taiwanese case study, with distributional stability again belying a number of powerful, and often countervailing, changes: returns to education in the labour markets; the distribution of educational endowments in the population; the pattern of occupational choices; and the demographic structure resulting from household fertility choices.

Two particular puzzles in the evolution of Brazil's urban income distribution are: (1) the combination of growth in mean incomes and stable or slightly declining inequality, on the one hand, and rising extreme poverty on the other; and (2) what explains the stability in inequality and poverty, in the face of declining rates of return to schooling and experience? Results from micro-modelling analysis show that the first puzzle seems to have been caused by outcomes related to participation decisions and occupational choices, in combination with declines in the labour market returns to education and experience. The second puzzle seems to be a result of hard climbs along a slippery slope. Individuals had to gain an average of 2 years of schooling, and substantially reduce fertility, in order to counteract falling returns in both the formal labour market and self-employment. The results of these studies demonstrate clearly that the distributional outcome is a result of a complex of often countervailing forces.

[16] This discussion draws on Ferreira and de Barros (1999).

12.5.4. *Policy Measures to Reduce Risk and Income Volatility*

The *World Development Report 2000* extends the concept of poverty beyond income and consumption plus education and health, to include risk and vulnerability, as well as voicelessness and powerlessness (World Bank 2000). It is not necessarily the case that shocks affect the poor disproportionately, but it is clearly the case that they are more vulnerable, since their economic margin is slim. Vulnerability and insecurity are dynamic concepts. The poor are often exposed to highly fluctuating incomes, and, particularly in rural areas, it is common for households to move in and out of poverty (Dercon 2000; World Bank 2000). Poor households are susceptible to a wide range of risks, some which are idiosyncratic, such as illness, while others are common, such as natural disasters. As a result, poor households may adopt production plans or employment strategies to reduce their exposure to the risk, even if this entails lower average income.[17] Poor households may also try to smooth consumption by creating buffer stocks, withdrawing children from school, and developing credit and insurance arrangements. Social networks also help provide informal insurance.

The policy approach that is outlined in WDR 2000 goes somewhat beyond the approach outlined in the 1990 WDR, putting increased emphasis on empowerment and security. The concept of social capital is used to describe the ability of individuals to secure benefits as a result of membership in social networks or other social structures. The general concern is that the poor have considerable local bonding social capital and some bridging social capital, while they have little of what is called 'linking social capital', that is, linkages to society outside the local community. This makes them very vulnerable to natural disasters and economic shock, since geographically confined networks provide little protection against this type of shocks. Informal institutions are very important in helping households to manage risk and vulnerability, but the poor often lack access to the broader range of formal networks, which are needed to sustain a more complex interchange with society at large.

Given the high vulnerability of a large part of the population, Collier and Gunning (1999) argue that this provides some explanation for low growth in both rural and urban areas in Africa. Moreover, economic reforms, which could in the long-run provide more sustainable livelihoods with higher returns, may in the short-run cause households serious problems of adjustment, especially if entry into new activities is costly and is perceived as risky (Dercon 1999). Consequently, actions that reduce risk and income-volatility, or that provide insurance against risk, would help the poor to take advantage of poverty-reducing strategies. Experience suggests that a combination of public-works programmes, group-lending schemes (subsidized where necessary), and simple deposit schemes, offers some support in dealing with these issues (Kanbur and Squire 1999). Additional measures to reduce risk and vulnerability include creating opportunities for wage employment by raising agricultural productivity among small and marginal farmers, and by increasing opportunities for self-employment.

[17] For example, it has been found that households which are more vulnerable to income shocks devote a smaller share of their land to risky high-yielding varieties, compared to households with better access to coping mechanisms (Morduch 1990).

Microfinance is particularly relevant for increasing the productivity of self-employment in the informal sector of the economy. It is well documented that, for many micro-entrepreneurs, lack of access to financial services is a critical constraint to the establishment or expansion of viable micro enterprises. Microfinance may also enable small and marginal farmers to purchase the inputs they need to increase their productivity, as well as financing a range of activities adding value to agricultural output and to the rural off-farm economy. Access to savings facilities also plays a key part in enabling the poor to smooth their consumption expenditures, and in financing investments which improve productivity in agriculture and other economic activities.

Rapid and sustainable poverty reduction depends upon the interaction of a wide range of policy measures. The potential for financial development as an instrument of economic management and of poverty reduction will be unfulfilled so long as conventional financial institutions are reluctant to expand their activities beyond their traditional borrowers. Microfinance institutions can play an important role in filling this gap, and possibly also in the longer term help to reduce imperfections in the market, improving access to credit for poor households in both urban and rural areas. However, many programmes that have been successful in reaching the poor are still not financially sustainable. Whether subsidies used for administrative costs of programmes with significant poverty-focused outreach are better than subsidies in other areas is an empirical issue which needs a careful case-by-case evaluation.

12.6. CONCLUSION

We noted initially that global poverty is still extensive, but that the proportion living in poverty declined substantially over a period up to the recent Asia crisis, which again increased poverty in many countries. We also noted that the gap in incomes between the richest and the very poorest countries has increased in recent decades. We then reviewed the literature on the determinants of economic growth. This depends on the accumulation of physical and human capital, efficiency in resource allocation, and the acquisition and application of modern technology. There is, however, evidence showing that it is the social infrastructure that determines the underlying levels of productivity.

The evidence reviewed in this study show that countries that have been successful in terms of economic growth are also very likely to have been successful in reducing poverty. How strong a poverty-reducing effect growth has, depends on what happens to income distribution—there is no constant relationship between growth and changes in inequality. There are differences between countries with different development strategies, and one would certainly prefer strategies with more favourable distributional outcomes if they produced the same growth. Countries that have combined rapid growth with improved income distribution have reduced poverty the fastest. However, when policies aimed at equity have had a negative side-effect on growth, the poverty reduction impact has been limited or even negative. Thus, there may be a conflict between short-term distributional measures and immediate poverty reduction on the one hand, and long-term growth-supporting measures and long-term poverty reduction, on the other. But there may also be win-win situations, where a policy for equity has a beneficial effect on growth. Typically, those policies have built up the assets of the poor, and helped increase the demand for those assets. This has meant, for example, expansion of education (building up assets), and measures that increase the relative prices of agricultural commodities and the wages of unskilled labour (increasing demand). Along with measures to secure long-term growth of the incomes of the poor, there should also be transfer schemes that help households to cope with risk, which is high for many poor groups. One should try to create schemes that can reduce risk without having high costs in terms of reduced growth.

The main point must still be that, without growth in per capita incomes, poverty will persist in poor countries. Governments intent on poverty reduction must, therefore, create an environment that is conducive to growth. This means microeconomic policy aimed at creating well-functioning markets, macroeconomic policy aimed at stability, and openness towards the rest of the world. Government has to take responsibility for building up human capital via education, and for the creation of a growth enhancing social infrastructure. For all these efforts to be effective, the government must develop good institutions, and provide good governance. The way in which the interaction between civil society and the government is played out will have major implications for the growth outcome. Understanding the nature of domestic politics is, thus, a key to successful economic reform. Something that frequently appears in analyses of the Asian success stories is the notion of 'shared growth', which suggests that, in order to participate actively, the mass of the population must see the benefits of growth. However, it is not only the average person who must be included, but the ruling elite must also allow competing groups to progress, as well as allowing new competitors to enter the political arena. For shared growth to come about, there is need for a bureaucracy of high quality, which is sufficiently insulated from the various pressure groups. This has not as yet appeared in most of Africa.

Poverty can be reduced if there is sufficient economic growth. Growth can be substantial if the policy and institutional environment is right. The low growth rates that characterize Africa are not inevitable. But some aspects of the environment are hard to change, and some politicians may be unwilling to change them. It is, therefore, largely in the social and political arenas that poverty reduction results will be determined.

REFERENCES

Agenor, P.-R. (2002). 'Macroeconomic Adjustment and the Poor: Analytical Issues and Cross-Country Evidence'. *Policy Research Working Papers* 2788 The World Bank, Washington.

Aghion, P., Caroli, E., and Garcia-Penalosa, C. (1999). 'Inequality and Economic Growth: The Perspectives of the New Growth Theories'. *Journal of Economic Literature*, 37(4), 1615–60.

Alesina, A. and Perotti, R. (1996). 'Income Distribution, Political Instability and Investment'. *European Economic Review*, 40(6), 1203–28.

—— and Rodrik, D. (1994). 'Distributive Politics and Economic Growth'. *Quarterly Journal of Economics*, 109, 465–90.

Ali, A. A. G. (1996). 'Structural Adjustment Programmes and Poverty in Sub-Saharan Africa: 1985–1995'. CODESRIA, Dakar.

Ali, A. A. G. (1998). 'Dealing with Poverty and Income Distribution Issues in Developing Countries: Cross-Regional Experiences'. *Journal of African Economies*, AERC Supplement, 77–115.

Anand, S. and Ravallion, M. (1993). 'Human Development in Poor Countries: On the Role of Private Incomes and Public Services'. *Journal of Economic Perspectives*, 7(1), 133–50.

Appleton, S., Bigsten, A., and Manda, D. K. (1999). 'Educational Expansion and Economic Decline: Returns to Education in Kenya, 1978–1995'. *CSAE Working Papers* 99/5. Centre for the Study of African Economies, Oxford University.

—— and Teal, F. (1999). 'Human Capital and Development'. Background paper for the *African Development Report 1998*. Centre for the Study of African Economies, Oxford University.

Barro, R. J. (1997). 'Determinants of Economic Growth. A Cross-Country Empirical Study'. MIT Press, Cambridge, MA.

Bell, C. and Rich, R. (1994). 'Rural Poverty and Agricultural Performance in Post-Independence India'. *Oxford Bulletin of Economics and Statistics*, 56(2), 111–33.

Benabou, R. (1996). 'Inequality and Growth'. In B. Bernanke and R. Rotemberg (eds), *National Bureau of Economic Research Macroeconomics Annual*. MIT Press, Cambridge, MA.

Besley, T. and Kanbur, R. (1988). 'Principles of Targeting', in M. Lipton and J. van der Gaag (eds) *Including the Poor*. The World Bank, Washington.

Bigsten, A. (2001). 'Policy Making in Resource Rich Countries: Lessons from Zambia'. *World Economics*, 2(3), 139–53.

—— (2002). 'Can Africa Catch Up?' *World Economics*, 3(2), 17–33.

—— and Collier, P. (1995). 'Linkages from Agricultural Growth in Kenya', in J. W. Mellor (ed.), *Agriculture on the Road to Industrialization*. Johns Hopkins University Press, Baltimore.

—— and Moene, K.-O. (1996). 'Growth and Rent Dissipation: The Case of Kenya'. *Journal of African Economies*, 5(2), 177–98.

—— and Kayizzi-Mugerwa, S. (2000). 'The Political Economy of Policy Failures in Zambia'. *Working Paper in Economics* 23. Department of Economics, Göteborg University.

Birdsall, N. and Londoño, J. N. (1997). 'Asset Inequality Matters: An Assessment of the World Bank's Approach to Poverty Reduction'. *American Economic Review*, 87, 32–7.

——, Ross, D., and Sabot, R. (1995). 'Inequality and Growth Reconsidered: Lessons from East Asia'. *The World Bank Economics Review*, 9(3), 477–508.

Blunch, N. H. and Verner, D. (1999). 'Sector Growth and the Dual Economy Model: Evidence from Côte d'Ivoire, Ghana and Zimbabwe'. *Policy Research Working Paper*, 2175. The World Bank, Washington.

Boltho, A. and Toniolo, G. (1999). 'The Assessment: The Twentieth Century—Achievements, Failures, Lessons'. *Oxford Review of Economic Policy*, 15(4), 1–17.

Bourguignon, F. and Morrison, C. (1992). *Adjustment and Equity in Developing Countries: A New Approach*. OECD Development Centre, Paris.

—— and —— (1998). 'Inequality and Development: The Role of Dualism'. *Journal of Development Economics*, 57, 233–57.

——, Fournier, M., and Gurgand, M. (1998). 'Distribution, Development and Education: Taiwan, 1979–1994'. Mimeo.

——, ——, and —— (2001). 'Fast Development with a Stable Income Distribution: Taiwan, 1979–1994'. *Review of Income and Wealth*, 47(2), 139–63.

Cashin, P., Mauro, P., Patillo, C., and Sahay, R. (2001). 'Macroeconomic Policies and Poverty Reduction: Stylized Facts and an Overview of Research'. *IMF Working Papers* 135, IMF, Washington.

Castro-Leal, F., Dayton, J., Demery, L., and Mehra, K. (1999). 'Public Social Spending in Africa: Do the Poor Benefit?' *The World Bank Observer*, 14(1), 49–72.

Chen, D. and Ravallion, M. (2000). 'Global Poverty Measures 1987–1998 and Projections for the Future'. The World Bank, Washington.

—— and Reinikka, R. (1999). 'Business Taxation in a Low-Revenue Economy: A Study on Uganda in Comparison with Neighboring Countries'. Mimeo.

Chenery, H., Ahluwalia, M., Bell, C. L. G., Duloy, R., and Jolly, R. (1974). *Redistribution with Growth*. Oxford University Press, Oxford.

Chia N., Wahba, S., and Whalley, J. (1994). 'Poverty-Reducing Targeting Programmes: A General Equilibrium Approach'. *Journal of African Economies*, 3(2), 309–38.

Collier, P. and Gunning, J. W. (1999). 'Explaining African Economic Performance'. *Journal of Economic Literature*, 37(1), 64–111.

Cornia, G. A. and Court, J. (2001). 'Inequality, Growth and Poverty in the Era of Liberalization and Globalization'. *WIDER Policy Brief* 4. UNU/WIDER, Helsinki.

de Donder, P. and Hindricks, J. (1998). 'The Political Economy of Targeting'. *Public Choice*, 95, 177–200.

Deininger, K. and Squire, L. (1998). 'New Ways of Looking at Old Issues: Asset Inequality and Growth'. *Journal of Development Economics*, 57, 259–87.

—— and Olinto, P. (2000). 'Asset Distribution, Inequality and Growth'. *Policy Research Working Papers* 2375 The World Bank, Washington.

Delgado, C. L., Hopkins, J., Kelly, A., Hazell, P., McKenna, A. A., Gruhn, P., Hojjati, B., Sil, J., and Courbois, C. (1998). 'Agricultural Linkages in Sub-Saharan Africa'. *IFPRI Research Report* 107. International Food Policy Research Institute, Washington.

Demery, L. and Squire, L. (1996). 'Macroeconomic Adjustment and Poverty in Africa: An Emerging Picture'. *World Bank Research Observer*.

Dercon, S. (1999). 'Income Risk, Coping Strategies and Safety Nets', background note to *World Development Report* 2000/01. Centre for the Study of the African Economies, Oxford University, Oxford.

—— (2000). 'Economic Reform, Poverty Reduction and Programme Aid', paper presented for the Sida conference on Aid and Development, Stockholm, 20–21 January.

Devarajan, S., Swaroop, V., and Zou, H. (1996). 'The Composition of Public Expenditures and Economic Growth'. *Journal of Monetary Economics*, 37(2), 313–44.

——, Xie, D., and Zou, H. (1998). 'Should Public Capital be Subsidized or Provided?'. *Journal of Monetary Economics*, 41, 319–31.

Dikhanov, Y. and Ward, M. (2002). 'Evolution of the Global Distribution of Income in 1970–99'. Paper presented at the conference on 'Globalisation, Growth and Inequality' at Warwick University, 15–17 March.

Dollar, D. and Kraay, A. (2002). 'Growth is Good for the Poor'. *Journal of Economic Growth*, 7(3), 195–225. Reprinted with kind permission as Chapter 2 of this volume.

Dorosh, P. A. (1996). 'Rents and Exchange Rates: Redistribution through Trade Liberalization in Madagascar'. In D. E. Sahn (ed.), *Economic Reform and the Poor in Africa*. Clarendon Press, Oxford.

—— and Lundberg, M. K. A. (1996). 'More than just Peanuts (Groundnuts): Aid Flows and Policy Reform in The Gambia'. In D. E. Sahn (ed.), *Economic Reform and the Poor in Africa*. Clarendon Press, Oxford.

—— and Sahn, D. E. (2000). 'A General Equilibrium Analysis of the Effect of Macroeconomic Adjustment on Poverty in Africa'. *Journal of Policy Modelling*, 22(6), 753–76.

——, Essama-Nssah, B., and Samba-Mamadou, O. (1996). 'Terms-of-Trade and the Real Exchange Rate in the CFA Zone: Implications for Income Distribution in Niger'. In D. E. Sahn (ed.) *Economic Reform and the Poor in Africa*. Clarendon Press, Oxford.

Fei, J. C. H. and Ranis, G. (1964). *Development of the Labor Surplus Economy*. Homewood, IL, Irwin.

Ferreira, F. G. H. and de Barros, R. P. (1999). 'The Slippery Slope: Explaining the Increase in Extreme Poverty in Urban Brazil, 1976–1996'. Mimeo.

Filmer, D. and Pritchett, L. (1999). 'The Impact of Public Spending on Health: Does Money Matter?' *Social Science and Medicine*, 49(10), 1309–23.

Firebaugh, G. (1999). 'Empirics of World Income Inequality'. *American Journal of Sociology*, 104(6), 1597–630.

Forbes, K. J. (2000). 'A Reassessment of the Relationship Between Inequality and Growth'. *American Economic Review*, 90, 869–87.

Gelbach, J. and Pritchett, L. (1997). 'Redistribution in a Political Economy: Leakier Can be Better'. The World Bank, Washington. Mimeo.

Haggblade, S., Hazell, P., and Brown, J. (1989). 'Farm-Nonfarm Linkages in Rural Sub-Saharan Africa'. *World Development*, 17(8), 1173–201.

Hall, R. E., and Jones, C. I. (1999). 'Why Do Some Countries Produce so Much More Output per Worker Than Others'. *Quarterly Journal of Economics*, 114, 83–116.

Hirschman, A. O. (1958). *The Strategy of Economic Development*. Yale University Press, New Haven, CT.

Hoddinott, J. (1999). 'Targeting: Principles and Practice'. *IFPRI Technical Guide* 9, International Food Policy Research Institute, Washington.

Kakwani, N. (1993). 'Performance in Living Standards: An International Comparison'. *Journal of Development Economics*. 41(2), 307–36.

Kanbur, R. and Squire, L. (1999). 'The Evolution of Thinking about Poverty: Exploring the Interactions'. Mimeo prepared for the *World Development Report 2000*.

Kayizzi-Mugerwa, S. and Levin, J. (1994). 'Adjustment and Poverty: A Review of the African Experience'. *African Development Review*, 6(2), 1–39.

Krueger, A. O. (1977). 'Growth, Distortions and Patterns of Trade among Many Countries'. *Princeton Studies in International Finance* 40, Princeton University, New Jersey.

Kuznets, S. (1955). 'Economic Growth and Income Inequality'. *The American Economic Review*, 45(1), 1–28.

Kweka, J. P and Morrissey, O. (2000). 'Government Spending and Economic Growth in Tanzania, 1965–1996'. *CREDIT Research Paper* 6, University of Nottingham.

Lal, D. (1995). 'India and China: Contrasts in Economic Liberalization?' *World Development*, 23(9), 1475–94.

—— (2000). 'Political Economy of Economic Policy Making in Developing Countries. An Overview'. Paper for a conference on the diverse experiences with economic reform failure and poor economic performance, in Stockholm.

—— and Myint, H. (1996). *The Political Economy of Poverty, Equity and Growth: A Comparative Study*. Clarendon Press, Oxford.

Leamer, E. E. (1987). 'Patterns of Development in the J-factor N-good General Equilibrium Model'. *Journal of Political Economy*, 95(5), 961–99.

Le Houerou, P. and Taliercio, R. (2002). 'Medium Term Expenditure Frameworks: From Concept to Practice: Preliminary Lessons from Africa'. *Africa Region Working Paper Series* 28 The World Bank, Washington.

Levin, J. (1998). 'Structural Adjustment and Poverty: The Case of Kenya'. PhD thesis. Department of Economics, Göteborg University.

Lewis, A. (1954). *Economic Development with Unlimited Supply of Labour*. The Manchester School of Economics and Social Studies.

Lloyd-Sherlock, P. (2000). 'Failing the Needy: Public Social Spending in Latin America'. *Journal of International Development*, 12, 101–19.

Lucas, R. E. (1988). 'On the Mechanics of Economic Development'. *Journal of Monetary Economics*, 22(1), 3–42.

Lundberg, M. and Squire, L. (1999). 'Inequality and Growth: Lessons for Policy Makers'. The World Bank, Washington. Mimeo.

Melchior, A., Telle, K., and Wiig, H. (2000). *Globalization and Inequality: World Income Distribution and Living Standards, 1960–1998*. Norwegian Ministry of Foreign Affairs, Oslo.

Mellor, J. W. (1999). 'The Structure of Growth and Poverty Reduction'. The World Bank, Washington. Mimeo.

Milanovic, B. (2002). 'True World Income Distribution, 1988 and 1993: First Calculation Based on Household Surveys Alone'. *The Economic Journal*, 112, 51–92.

Morduch, J. (1990). 'Risk, Production and Saving: Theory and Evidence from Indian Households'. Department of Economics Working Paper. Harvard University, Cambridge, MA.

Narayan, D., Patel, R., Schafft, K., Rademacher, A., and Koch-Schulte, S. (2000). *Voices of the Poor: Can Anyone Hear Us?*. Oxford University Press for the World Bank, New York.

Persson, T. and Tabellini, G. (1994). 'Is Inequality Harmful for Growth?' *American Economic Review*, 84(3), 600–21.

Pritchett, L. and Summers, L. H. (1996). 'Wealthier is Healthier'. *Journal of Human Resources*, 31(4), 841–68.

Psacharopoulos, G. (1994). 'Returns to Investments in Education: A Global Update'. *World Development*, 22, 1325–43.

Ravallion, M. (2001). 'Growth, Inequality and Poverty: Looking Beyond the Averages'. *World Development*, 29(11), 1803–15.

—— and Chen, S. (1997). 'What Can New Survey Data Tell Us about Recent Changes in Distribution and Poverty?' *World Bank Research Observer*, 11, 357–82.

—— and Datt, G. (1994). *Growth and Poverty in India*. Poverty and Human Resource Division, The World Bank, Washington.

—— and Datt, G. (1996). 'How Important to India's Poor is the Sectoral Composition of Economic Growth'. *World Bank Economic Review*, 10, 1–25.

Reinikka, R. and Svensson, J. (2000). 'How Inadequate Provision of Public Infrastructure and Services Affects Private Investment'. *Policy Research Working Paper*s 2262. The World Bank, Washington.

Rodrik, D. (1997). 'Where did All the Growth Go? External Shocks, Social Conflict and Growth Collapses'. Harvard University, Kennedy School, Cambridge, MA. Mimeo.

Romer, P. M. (1986). 'Increasing Returns and Long-Run Growth'. *Journal of Political Economy*, 94(5), 1002–37.

Sahn, D. E. and Younger, S. (1999). 'Dominance Testing of Social Sector Expenditures and Taxes in Africa'. *IMF-FAD Working Paper* 172. International Monetary Fund, Fiscal Affairs Department, Washington.

Schultz, T. P. (1998). 'Inequality in the Distribution for Personal Income in the World: How it is Changing and Why'. *Journal of Population Economics*, 11, 307–44.

Sen, A. (1989). 'The Concept of Development'. In H. Chenery and T. N. Srinivasan (eds), *Handbook of Development Economics, Volume 1*. North-Holland, Amsterdam.

Solow, R. M. (1956). 'A Contribution to the Theory of Economic Growth'. *Quarterly Journal of Economics*, 70(1), 65–94.

Sprout, R. V. A. and Weaver, J. H. (1992). 'International Distribution of Income: 1960–1987'. *Kyklos*, 45, 237–58.

Srinivasan, T. N. (2000). 'Growth and Poverty Alleviation: Lessons from Development Experience'. Asian Development Bank, Manila. Mimeo.

Thorbecke, E. and Berrian, D. (1992). 'Budgetary Rules to Minimize Societal Poverty in a General Equilibrium Context'. *Journal of Development Economics*, 39(2), 189–205.

—— and Stiefel, D. (1999). 'Simulating the Effects of Trade Reform on Poverty within a Dual-Dual Framework—A CGE Model of an Archetype African Economy'. Ithaca: Cornell University. Mimeo.

Toye, J. (2000). 'Fiscal Crisis and Fiscal Reform in Developing Countries'. *Cambridge Journal of Economics*, 24, 21–44.

UNDP (1999). *Human Development Report 1999*. Oxford University Press, Oxford and New York.

van de Walle, D. (1998). 'Targeting Revisited'. *The World Bank Research Observer*, 13(2), 231–48.

White, H. (1999). 'Global Poverty Reduction: Are We Heading in the Right Direction?'. *Journal of International Development*, 11, 503–19.

World Bank (1998). *Public Expenditure Management Handbook*. The World Bank, Washington.

—— (2000). *World Development Report*. The World Bank, Washington.

Index